Delictual Liability

In Memorian
W A W

Delictual Liability

Joe Thomson LLB, FRSE, Hon FALS,
Law Commissioner, Regius Professor of Law,
University of Glasgow

Third Edition

Print on Demand Edition

Tottel
publishing

Published by
Tottel Publishing Ltd
Maxwelton House
41-43 Boltro Road
Haywards Heath
West Sussex
RH16 1BJ

Tottel Publishing Ltd
9-10 St Andrew Square
Edinburgh
EH2 2AF

ISBN 13: 978-1-84592-375-4
ISBN 10: 1-84592-375-8
© Reed Elsevier (UK) Ltd 2004
First published 1994
Second edition 1999
Third edition 2004
Formerly published by LexisNexis Butterworths

This edition reprinted by Tottel Publishing Ltd 2006

British Library Cataloguing-in-Publication Data.
A catalogue record for this book is available from the British Library.

Typeset by Phoenix Photosetting, Chatham, Kent
Printed and bound in Great Britain by
CPI Antony Rowe, Eastbourne, East Sussex

Contents

Preface   vii
Table of Statutes   ix
Table of Cases   xiii
List of abbreviations   xxxi

Introduction   1

PART I. INTENTIONAL DELICTS

1. Intentional delicts in respect of persons and property   11

2. The economic delicts and fraud   **37**

PART II. UNINTENTIONAL DELICT – GENERAL PRINCIPLES OF LIABILITY

3. The duty of care   59

4. Duty of care as a threshold device   71

5. Breach of a duty of care   115

6. Causation and related issues   135

PART III. DELICTUAL LIABILITY IN SPECIFIC AND ECONOMIC CONTEXTS

7. Professional liability   155

8. Product liability   165

9. Delictual liability for animals   177

10. Delictual liability arising from ownership or occupation of property   185

11.   Breach of statutory duty and public law issues   201

12.   Employer's liability and vicarious liability   215

13.   Delict and the family   237

14.   Delict and road traffic   251

15.   Defamation and verbal injury   259

PART IV. DAMAGES

16.   Damages   283

Index   307

Preface

Developments in the law of delict continue apace. The last five years have seen a period of judicial activity especially in the House of Lords where the search for legal principle appears increasingly to be abandoned in the interests of 'fairness' and 'distributive justice'. The European Convention on Human Rights has begun to impact on the domestic law of delict though perhaps its effects have not been as dramatic as was originally anticipated. It is therefore good to have a new edition of this book. Its purpose remains as before: to provide a clear and accurate account of this important and very interesting area of Scots Private Law.

I would like to thank my publishers for providing me with research assistance. I was extremely pleased that Tom Swan, a graduate of Glasgow University, was prepared to work as my research assistant as he did an exemplary job. Heather Ryan continues to provide excellent administrative support. My wife, Annie, not only saw me through the tribulations which inevitably attend the preparation of a new edition of a textbook but also attended the lectures and conferences where I delivered papers refining my ideas. For this and much more, I am very grateful to her.

The law is stated as at 30th April 2004 (or thereby).

Joe Thomson,
Edinburgh
1st May 2004

Table of statutes

PAGE

Administration of Justice Act
1982 243
s 8 . . . . 240, 241, 294
(1)–(3) 241
9 . . . . 242, 249, 294
(1) 241
(2), (3) 242
10 297
11(a), (b) 298
12 301
(1)(a), (b) 301
(2) 302
13 . . . . 240, 241
Age of Legal Capacity
(Scotland) Act 1991 238
s 1(1)(a) 238
(3)(c) 238
2(4) 13
(4A), (5A) 238
Animals (Scotland) Act 1987 . . 201,
206
s 1(1) 179
(b) 180, 181
(c) 181
(2)(a) 181
(b) 183
(3) 180, 181
(a) 180, 181
(b) 181
(4), (5) 182
(6) 184
(8) 179
2(1) (a), (b) 182
(c) 183, 184
(2) 183
3 179
5(1)(a), (b) 179
(2)(a)–(c) 179
s 7 181

Carriage of Goods Act 1992 . . . 108

PAGE

Children (Scotland) Act 1995
s 1(1)(d) 238
Civil Aviation Act 1982
s 76 20
Consumer Protection Act 1987 . 243
Pt I (ss 1–9) 166, 201, 206,
304
s 1(1) 166
(2) 168
(a)–(c) 169
2 305
(1) 167, 171, 173
(3) 170
(4)(f) 175
(6) 166
3(1) 171
(2) 172
(a)–(c) 172
4(1)(a), (b) 173
(c)(i), (ii) 170
(d) 173
(e) 174, 175
5(1)–(3) 167
(4) 168
6(4) 175
7 175
45(1) 167, 168
Criminal Justice (Scotland) Act
2003
s 51(1) 15
(3) 15
Criminal Procedure (Scotland)
Act 1995
s 170(1) 18

Damages Act 1996
s 1 295
Damages (Scotland) Act 1976 . 243,
250, 260
s 1 248–249
(1) 245, 246, 248
(4) 249

PAGE

Damages (Scotland) Act 1976 –
  contd
  s 1(5) 247
    (5A) 248
    (7) 250
  1A 249
  2(1) 243, 244
    (2) 243
    (3) 244
    (4) 260
  2A 243
  2A(1)(a), (b), (2) 244
  8...................... 4
  9(1), (2) 244, 295
  9A 293
    (1) 244
  10(2) 246
  Sch 1 246
Damages (Scotland) Act 1993 . 243
  s 3...................... 260
  5...................... 293
Dangerous Wild Animals Act
  1976
  s 7(4) 180
  Sch 3 180
Defamation Act 1952
  s 5 268–269
  6.................... 270
  12.................... 276
Defamation Act 1996
  s 1.................... 274
  2.................... 267
    (4) 267
  3.................... 267
    (2), (3), (5) 267
  4.................... 267
    (2), (3) 268
  13.................... 271
  14.................... 271
  15.................... 274
  Sch 1 274
Divorce (Scotland) Act 1976
  s 10.................... 17
Dogs Acts 1906–28 178
Dramatic and Musical
  Performers' Protection Act
  1958 203

Employers' Liability
  (Compulsory Insurance)
  Act 1969.............. 222

PAGE

Employers' Liability (Defective
  Equipment) Act 1969
  s 1(1) 216

Factories Act 1961 220

Guard Dogs Act 1975
  s 1 .... 183, 184

Health and Safety at Work etc
  Act 1974.............. 220
  s 47.................... 201
Hire Purchase Act 1964
  Pt III (ss 1–24) 24, 26
Human Rights Act 1998 ...... 7, 35,
                              191
  s 8(3) 7

Interest on Damages (Scotland)
  Act 1958.............. 296
Interest on Damages (Scotland)
  Act 1971.............. 296
International Transport
  Conventions Act 1983 ... 289
  s 1.................... 250

Lawburrows Acts 1429 and
  1581 5
Law Reform (Contributory
  Negligence) Act 1945 143,
                          152, 184
  s 1(1) 151
  5(a) 151
Law Reform (Husband and
  Wife) Act 1962
  s 2(1), (2) 237
Law Reform (Husband and
  Wife) (Scotland) Act 1984
  s 1(1) 16
  2(2) 17
Law Reform (Miscellaneous
  Provisions) Act 1971
  s 4.................... 247
Law Reform (Miscellaneous
  Provisions) (Scotland) Act
  1940
  s 3 .... 147, 154
Law Reform (Miscellaneous
  Provisions) (Scotland) Act
  1985
  s 10 89–90

PAGE

Law Reform (Miscellaneous
  Provisions) (Scotland) Act
  1990
  s 68   88
  69 . . . . 240, 241
Law Reform (Parent and Child)
  (Scotland) Act 1986   243
Law Reform (Personal Injuries)
  Act 1948
  s 2(1)   298

Merchant Shipping Act 1988
  s 31(1)   203

Occupiers' Liability (Scotland)
  Act 1960 . . . . 189, 195, 201,
                          206, 221
  s 1(1), (2)   195
    (3)(a)   196
  s 2(1) 196, 197, 200
    (3)   206
  3   200

Parliamentary Papers Act 1840 .   271
Prescription and Limitation
  (Scotland) Act 1973   303
  s 6   303
    (2)   304
    (4)(a), (b)   303
  7   304
    (1), (2)   304
  11(3)   304
  17(1), (2)   305
    (3)   306
  18   306
    (3)   306
  18A(1)   305
    (2)   306
  19A   306
  22A   304
  22B   305
    (4)   306
  22C   305
    (3)   306
  Sch 1, para (1)(d)   303
  Sch 1, para 2(g)–(ggg)   304
Prescription and Limitation
  (Scotland) Act 1984
  s 6(1)   304

PAGE

Prescription and Limitation
  (Scotland) Act 1984 – *contd*
  Sch 1, para 2   304
Protection from Harassment Act
  1997   243
  s 8(1)–(6) 18–19
  9   19

Regulation of Care (Scotland)
  Act 2001
  Sch 3, para 9   298
Rehabilitation of Offenders Act
  1974 . . . . 217, 264
  s 4   264
Road Traffic Act 1988 . . . . . 252, 256,
                          257
  s 1–3   252
  3(A)   252
  38(7)   251
  39   213
  143(a), (b)   254
  149   149
Road Traffic Act 1991   252

Scotland Act 1998
  s 41   272
Social Security Act 1989   298
Social Security Administration
  Act 1992
  Part IV (ss 81–104)   298
Social Security (Recovery of
  Benefits) Act 1997   298
  s 3, 6, 7   299
  Sch 1   300
  Sch 2   299
Southern Rhodesia Act 1965 . .   50

Trade Union and Labour
  Relations (Consolidation)
  Act 1992   52
  s 10(1)   260
Trespass (Scotland) Act 1865 . .   20

Unfair Contract Terms Act
  1977 . . . . 91, 92
  s 16 . . . . 88, 200
  25(5) 88, 89

Winter Herding Act 1686   178

Table of cases

A v B plc [2003] QB 195 ....31, 34
A v Essex County Council [2003] 1 FLR 615 211
A v National Blood Authority (No 1) [2001] 3 All ER 289 ...... 169, 171, 174
A v United Kingdom [1998] 2 FLR 959, (1998) Times, 1 October, ECHR   16
AB v CD (1904) 7 F 72 264
AB v Leeds Teaching Hospital NHS Trust [2004] EWHC 644 (QB) 74
AB v Tameside and Glossop Health Authority [1997] 8 Med LR 91, CA .. 159
AB v XY 1917 SC 15, 1916 2 SLT 210 263
Abouzaid v Mothercare (UK) Ltd [2001] TLR 136 .... 171, 174
Adam v Jackson [1917] AC 309 275
Admiralty Comrs v SS Susquehanna (Owners) [1926] AC 655, HL 292
Admiralty Comrs v SS Volute [1922] AC 129, HL 144
Advocate (Lord) v Scotsman Publications Ltd 1988 SLT 490, affd 1989
    SLT 705, HL 30, 31, 33
Agnew v Scott Lithgow Ltd (No 1) 2001 SC 516 305
Alcoa Minerals of Jamaica v Herbert Broderick [2002] 1 AC 371 288
Alcock v Chief Constable of South Yorkshire Police [1992] 1 AC 310,
    [1991] 4 All ER 707, HL 77, 78, 219, 220
Alexandrou v Oxford [1993] 4 All ER 328 211
Allan v Barclay (1864) 2 M 873 284
Allen v Flood [1898] AC 1, HL............................ 35, 36, 44, 47
Allied Arab Bank Ltd v Hajjar (No 2) [1988] QB 944, [1988] 3 All ER 103 . 51
Anderson v Dundee City Council 1999 GWD 1-52 191
Anderson v Marshall (1835) 13 S 1130 15
Anderson v St Andrew's Ambulance Association 1943 SC 248, 1943 SLT 258   153
Anns v Merton London Borough Council [1978] AC 728, [1977] 2 All ER
    492, HL 101–103
Ansbacher (Henry) & Co Ltd v Rinks Stern [1998] Lloyd's Rep Bank 1,
    (1997) Times 26 June, CA 55
Anthony v Brabbs 1998 SLT 1137 294
Argyll and Clyde Health Board v Strathclyde Regional Council 1988 SCLR
    120, 1988 SLT 381, OH 193
Argyllshire Weavers Ltd v A Macaulay (Tweeds) Ltd 1965 SLT 21, OH .. 277
Attorney-General v Guardian Newspapers Ltd (No 2) [1990] 1 AC 109,
    [1988] 3 All ER 545, HL 32–34
Auld v Shairp (1874) 2 R 191 260
Auld v Shairp (1875) 2 R 940 264
B v Harris 1989 SCLR 644, 1990 SLT 208 15
B (a child) v McDonald's Restaurant Ltd [2002] EWHC 490 (QB) 171
BOC v Groves 1993 SLT 360, OH 154
BP Exploration Operating Co Ltd v Chevron Transport (Scotland) 2002 SC
    (HL) 19 303

Baigent v British Broadcasting Corporation 1999 GWD 10-474 ..... 268, 275
Bank of Scotland v Fuller Peiser 2002 SLT 574 .... 89, 92, 93
Barber v Somerset County Council [2004] UKHL 13 .... 216, 218
Barnett v Chelsea and Kensington Hospital Management Committee [1969]
    1 QB 428, [1968] 1 All ER 1068 136
Barrett v Enfield London Borough Council [2001] 2 AC 550 .... 209, 210
Barrett v Ministry of Defence [1995] 3 All ER 87, CA 72, 152
Barry v Sutherland 2002 SLT 413 .... 56, 287, 290
Barrymore v News Group Newspapers Ltd [1997] FSR 600, Ch D 31
Beggs v Motherwell Bridge Fabricators Ltd 1998 SLT 1215, 1997 SCLR
    1019, OH 197, 242, 245,
                                                          247, 248
Behrens v Bertram Mills Circus Ltd [1957] 2 QB 1, [1957] 1 All ER 583 .. 178
Bell v Blackwood, Morton & Sons Ltd 1960 SC 11, 1959 SLT (Notes) 54,
    OH 231
Bennet (H & J M) (Potatoes) Ltd v Secretary of State for Scotland 1986 SLT
    665, OH 55, 56
Bennett v J Lamont & Sons 2000 SLT 17 213
Berezovsky v Forbes Inc (No 2) [2001] EMLR 48, CA 261, 263, 269
Berkoff v Burchill [1996] 4 All ER 1008, [1997] EMLR 139, CA 265
Blackhall v MacInnes 1997 SLT 649, OH 151
Blake v Lothian Health Board 1993 SLT 1248, OH 305
Bolam v Friern Hospital Management Committee [1957] 2 All ER 118,
    [1957] 1 WLR 582 158
Bolitho v City and Hackney Health Authority [1998] AC 232, [1997] 4 All
    ER 771, HL 136, 158, 159
Bolton v Stone [1951] AC 850, [1951] 1 All ER 1078, HL 124
Bonar v Trafalgar House Offshore Fabrication Ltd 1996 SLT 548 301
Bourhill v Young 1942 SC (HL) 78, 1943 SLT 105 .... 74–75, 120, 131
Bradford v Pickles [1895] AC 587, HL 21
Bradford-Smart v West Sussex County Council [2002] EWCA Civ 7 211
Brannan v Airtours (18 January 1999, unreported), CA 152
Brimelow v Casson [1924] 1 Ch 302 39
Brisco v Secretary of State for Scotland 1997 SC 14 216
Bristol and West Building Society v Aitken Nairn 1999 SLT 43, OH 160
Bristol and West Building Society v Rollo Steven and Bond 1998 SLT 9, OH
    290
British Motor Trade Association v Gray 1951 SC 586, 1951 SLT 247 .... 38, 39
British Steel Corporation v Granada Television Ltd [1981] AC 1096, [1981]
    1 All ER 417, HL 33
British Telecommunications plc v James Thomson & Sons (Engineers) Ltd
    1999 SC (HL) 9 .... 67, 98
British Transport Commission v Gourlay [1956] AC 185, [1955] 3 All ER
    796, HL 294
Brooks v Lind 1997 Rep LR 83, 1997 GWD 13-570 264
Broom v Ritchie & Co (1905) 6 F 942 278
Brown v Lee Constructions Ltd 1977 SLT (Notes) 61, OH 20
Brown v Rolls Royce Ltd 1960 SC (HL) 22, 1960 SLT 119 130
Brownlie v Thomson (1859) 21 D 480 268
Bryan v Maloney (1995) 11 Const LJ 274, HC (Aus) 103
Buckley v Farrow [1997] PIQR Q78, CA 240
Burke v Burke 1983 SLT 331, OH 16
Burns v Diamond (1896) 23 R 507, (1896) 3 SLT 274 277

C v M 1923 SC 1, 1922 SLT 634 276
Caledonian Rly Co v Greenock Corpn 1917 SC (HL) 56, 1917 2 SLT 67 . 193
Cambridge Water Co v Eastern Counties Leather plc [1994] 2 AC 264,
   [1994] 1 All ER 53, HL 186
Cameron v Hamilton's Auction Marts Ltd 1955 SLT (Sh Ct) 74, 71 Sh Ct
   Rep 285 177
Campbell v Cochrane (1905) 8 F 205 272
Campbell v F and F Moffat (Transport) Ltd 1992 SCLR 551, 1992 SLT
   962, OH 286
Campbell v Gillespie 1996 SLT 503, OH 247
Campbell v Mirror Group Newspapers Ltd [2003] QB 633 33
Campbell v Muir 1908 SC 387, 15 SLT 737 21
Campbell v North Lanarkshire Council 2000 SCLR 373 .... 74, 219
Candlewood Navigation Corpn Ltd v Mitsui OSK Lines Ltd, The Mineral
   Transporter [1986] AC 1, [1985] 2 All ER 935, PC 107, 110
Canterbury v Spence (1972) 464 F 2d 772 13
Cantwell v Criminal Injuries Compensation Board 2002 SC (HL) 1 287,
                                                          296, 297
Caparo Industries plc v Dickman [1990] 2 AC 605, [1990] 1 All ER 568,
   HL 66, 67, 85– 87, 93, 157, 208, 210
Capital and Counties plc v Hampshire County Council [1997] QB 1004,
   [1997] 2 All ER 865, CA 212
Carrick Jewellery Ltd v Ortak 1989 GWD 35-1624, OH 27
Carroll v British Broadcasting Corporation 1997 SLT (Sh Ct) 23 .... 262, 263,
                                                          269, 272
Carroll v Fearon [1998] PIQR P416, CA 165
Carson v Howard Doris Ltd 1981 SC 278, 1981 SLT 273 306
Cavanagh v Ulster Weaving Co Ltd [1960] AC 145, [1959] 2 All ER 745,
   HL 130
Cavin v Kinnaird 1993 SCLR 618, 1994 SLT 111 252
Century Insurance Co Ltd v Northern Ireland Road Transport Board [1942]
   AC 509, [1942] 1 All ER 491, HL 230
Chadwick v British Transport Commission [1967] 2 All ER 945, [1967] 1
   WLR 912 74
Charleston v News Group Newspapers Ltd [1995] 2 AC 65, [1995] 2 All ER
   313, HL 262
Charlton v Forrest Printing Ink Co Ltd [1980] IRLR 331, CA 129
Christie v Robertson (1899) 1 F 1115 269
Clark v McLean 1994 SCLR 564, 1995 SLT 235 306
Clark v Scottish Power plc 1994 SCLR 202, 1994 SLT 924 293
Clarke v Kato [1998] 4 All ER 417, [1998] 1 WLR 1697, HL 257
Clay v A J Crump & Sons Ltd [1964] 1 QB 533, [1963] 3 All ER 687, CA: 62
Cleland v Campbell 1998 SLT 642, OH 303
Clelland v Morton Fraser Milligan 1997 SLT (Sh Ct) 57 89
Clippens Oil Co Ltd v Edinburgh and District Water Trustees 1907 SC
   (HL) 9, 15 SLT 92 294
Cloy v Adams & Sons 1999 GWD 19-908 190
Cohen v Shaw 1992 SCLR (Notes) 182, 1992 SLT 1022, OH 239, 246
Colborne v Wallace 1993 GWD 17-1121 252
Coleridge v Miller Construction Ltd 1997 SLT 485, OH 67, 106
Comex Houlder Diving Ltd v Colne Fishing Co Ltd (No 2) 1992 SLT 89,
   OH 96

Commission of the European Communities v United Kingdom (C300/95)
    [1997] All ER (EC) 481, ECJ (Fifth Chamber) 175
Cooper v Firth Brown [1963] 2 All ER 31, [1963] 1 WLR 148 294
Cowie v Atlantic Drilling Co Ltd 1995 SC 288, 1995 SCLR 335, 1995 SLT
    1151 303
Cowie v Tudhope 1987 GWD 12-395 15
Craig v Inveresk Paper Merchant Ltd 1970 SLT (Notes) 50, OH 277
Credit Lyonnais Bank Nederland NV v Export Credits Guarantee
    Department [2000] 1 AC 486 224
Crofter Hand Woven Harris Tweed Co Ltd v Veitch 1942 SC (HL) 1, 1943
    SLT 2 .... 47–49, 50
Crombie v McDermott Scotland Ltd 1996 SLT 1238, 1996 Rep LR 122, OH   220
Cross v Highland and Islands Enterprise 2001 SLT 1060 218
Cullen v North Lanarkshire Council 1998 SC 451, 1998 SLT 897 221
Cullin v London Fire and Civil Defence Authority (31 March 1999, unre-
    ported), QB 74
Cunningham v Scotsman Publications Ltd 1987 SC 107, 1987 SCLR 314, OH   274
Cuthbert v Linklater 1935 SLT 94 .... 263, 265
Cutler v Wandsworth Stadium Ltd (in liquidation) [1949] AC 398, [1949] 1
    All ER 544, HL 203–204

D & F Estates Ltd v Church Commissioners for England [1989] AC 177,
    [1988] 2 All ER 992, HL 97, 99, 101
Daborn v Bath Tramways Motor Co Ltd and Smithey [1946] 2 All ER 333,
    CA 126
Dahl v Chief Constable, Central Scotland Police 1983 SLT 420, OH 18
Davidson v City of Glasgow District Council 1993 SLT 479, OH 146, 147
Davidson v Kerr 1997 Hous LR 11, 1996 GWD 40-2296, Sh Ct 191
Davidson v Lothian and Borders Fire Board 2003 SLT 939 221
Davie v New Merton Board Mills Ltd [1959] AC 604 216
Dawson v Bingley Urban District Council [1941] 2 KB 149, CA 202
Defreitas v O'Brien [1995] 6 Med LR 108 159
De Maudsley v Palumbo [1996] FSR 447, (1995) Times, 19 December, Ch
    D 32
Denheen v British Railways Board 1988 SLT (Notes) 320, 1986 SLT 249,
    OH... 241
Dennis v Ministry of Defence [2003] EWHC 793 191
Derbyshire County Council v Times Newspapers Ltd [1993] AC 534,
    [1993] 1 All ER 1011, HL 260
Derry v Peek (1889) 14 App Cas 337, HL 55
Devlin v Strathclyde Regional Council 1993 SLT 699, OH 149, 198, 200
Dimond v Lovell [2002] 1 AC 384 253
Dingley v Chief Constable of Strathclyde Police (No 1) 1998 SC 548, OH . 136
Donaghy v National Coal Board 1957 SLT (Notes) 35 146
Donald v Rutherford 1983 SLT 253, 1984 SLT 70 306
Donlon v Colonial Mutual Group (UK Holdings) Ltd 1998 SC 244, 1997
    SCLR 1088 92
Donachie v Chief Constable of Greater Manchester Police [2004] EWCA
    Civ 405 73
Donoghue v Stevenson 1932 SC (HL) 31, 1932 SLT 317 ...... 60–64, 68, 82,
                                    83, 91, 94, 95, 98, 100, 103–104,
                                    111, 157, 165, 166, 177, 185, 214,
                                    215–216, 239, 262

Dooley v Cammell Laird & Co Ltd [1951] 1 Lloyd's Rep 271 74
Dorset Yacht Co Ltd v Home Office [1970] AC 1004, [1970] 2 All ER 294,
    HL 68, 72, 122, 148
Doughty v Turner Manufacturing Co Ltd [1964] 1 QB 518, [1964] 1 All ER
    98, CA 121
Douglas v Hello Ltd (No 6) [2003] 3 All ER 996 . . . . 31, 34
Downie v Chief Constable of Strathclyde Police 1997 SCLR 603 12
Dubai Aluminium Co Ltd v Salaam [2003] 2 AC 366, [2003] 1 All ER 97 . 228,
                                                                    234
Duff v East Dunbartonshire Council 2002 Rep LR 98 198
Duff v Highland and Islands Fire Board 1995 SLT 1362 212
Duffy v Lanarkshire Health Board 1998 SCLR 1142, 1998 Rep LR 119, OH . 241
Duke of Argyll v Duchess of Argyll [1967] Ch 302, [1965] 1 All ER 611 . . 30, 31
Dulieu v White & Sons [1901] 2 KB 669 73
Dumbreck v Robert Addie & Sons (Colleries) Ltd 1928 SC 547, 1928 SLT
    341 19
Dumbreck v Robert Addie & Sons 1929 SC (HL) 51, 1929 SLT 242 195
Duncan v Associated Scottish Newspapers Ltd 1929 SC 14 266
Duncan v Glacier Metal Co Ltd 1988 SCLR 320, 1988 SLT 479, OH . . . 298
Duncan v Ross Harper & Murphy 1993 SLT 105, OH 153
Dundee (City of) District Council v Cook 1995 SCLR 559 194
Dunlop v McGowans 1979 SC 22, 1979 SLT 34 301
Dunlop v McGowans 1980 SC (HL) 73, 1980 SLT 129 304
Dunlop Pneumatic Tyre Co v Dunlop Motor Co 1907 SC (HL) 15, 15 SLT
    362 28
Dynamco Ltd v Holland and Hannen and Cubitts (Scotland) Ltd 1971 SC
    257, 1972 SLT 38 . . . . 106, 107

E v United Kingdom [2003] 1 FLR 348 209
Eastern Marine Services (and Supplies) Ltd v Dickson Motors Ltd 1981 SC
    355, OH 86
Edgar v Lord Advocate 1965 SC 67, 1965 SLT 158 240
Edwards v Butlins Ltd 1998 SLT 500, 1997 GWD 21-1052 217
Eisten v North British Railway Co (1870) 8 M 980 4
Electrical, Electronic, Telecommunication and Plumbing Union v Times
    Newspapers Ltd [1980] QB 585, [1980] 1 All ER 1097 260
Emerald Construction Co Ltd v Lowthian [1966] 1 All ER 1013, [1966] 1
    WLR 691, CA 39
Empress Car Co (Abertillery) Ltd v National Rivers Authority [1998] 1 All
    ER 481, HL 148
English v North Lanarkshire Council 1999 SCLR 310 221
Erven Warnink BV v J Townend & Sons (Hull) Ltd [1979] AC 731, [1979]
    2 All ER 927 . . . . 28, 30
Evans v Motor Insurers' Bureau [1999] Lloyd's Rep JR 30 257
Evans v Triplex Safety Glass Co Ltd [1936] 1 All ER 283 . . . . 165, 168
Exchange Telegraph Co Ltd v Giulianotti 1959 SC 19, 1959 SLT 293, OH . 32

FC Finance Ltd v Brown & Son 1969 SLT (Sh Ct) 41 . . . . 5, 23–26
FC Finance v Langtry Investment Co Ltd 1973 SLT (Sh Ct) 11 24
Faccenda Chicken Ltd v Fowler [1987] Ch 117, [1986] 1 All ER 617, CA . 30
Fairbairn v Scottish National Party 1979 SC 393, 1980 SLT 149 268
Fairchild v Glenhaven Funeral Services Ltd [2003] 1 AC 32, [2002] 3 All
    ER 305 140–141

Fairlie v Carruthers 1996 SLT (Sh Ct) 56   180
Farquhar v Neish (1890) 17 R 716   272
Faulds v Townsend (1861) 23 D 437, 33 SJ 224 ....23, 25
Feely v Co-operative Wholesale Society 1990 SCLR 356, 1990 SLT 547,
     OH...   196
Ferrelly v Yarrow Shipbuilders Ltd 1994 SCLR 407, 1994 SLT 1349   242
Fleming v McGillivray 1946 SC 1, 1945 SLT 301   153
Fletcher v Wilsons (1885) 12 R 683   268
Forbes v City of Dundee District Council 1997 SLT 1330, 1997 SCLR 682,
     OH...   209
Ford Motor Co Ltd v HLM Design Ltd 1997 SLT 837, OH   287
Forsyth's Curator Bonis v Govan Shipbuilders 1989 SCLR 78, 1989 SLT 91 .   241
Foskett v McClymont 1998 SC 96, 1998 SLT 892, OH 180, 181
Foster v Biosil (2001) 59 BMLR 178 ....   171, 173
Fraser v D M Hall & Son 1997 SLT 808, OH   293
Fraser v Mirza 1993 SC (HL) 27, 1993 SLT 527 ....   272, 274–275
Fraser v State Hospitals Board for Scotland 2001 SLT 1051   218
Frost v Chief Constable of the South Yorkshire Police [1999] 2 AC 455,
     [1999] 1 All ER 1 ....   73, 74, 78
Fry's Metals Ltd v Durastic Ltd 1991 SLT 689n, OH   188

GA Estates Ltd v Caviapen Trustees Ltd (No 1) 1993 SLT 1037, OH ..   186, 193
GKR Karate v Yorkshire Post Newspapers Ltd (No 2) [2000] EMLR 410 .   273
Galbraith's Curator ad Litem v Stewart (No 2) 1998 SLT 1305 ......   121, 238
Gallacher v Kleinwort Benson (Trustee) Ltd 2003 SCLR 384   196
Galli-Atkinson v Seghal [2003] EWCA 697   78
Galoo Ltd (in liquidation) v Bright Grahame Murray [1994] 1 WLR 1360,
     [1995] 1 All ER 16, CA................................   86, 144
Garrard & Co Ltd v Christie & Co [2001] EWCA Civ 699   42
Gaughan v Bedfordshire Health Authority [1997] 8 Med LR 182, QBD ...   160
Gibson v British Rail Maintenance 1995 SC 7, 1995 SLT 953   217
Gibson v National Cash Register Co Ltd 1925 SC 500, 1925 SLT 377 ...   54
Gibson v Orr 1999 SC 420, OH 67, 68, 211
Gilbert v Yorston 1996 SCLR 1122, 1997 SLT 879, OH 263, 275
Gilfillan v Barbour 2003 SL 1127 ....   152, 160
Gillies v Lynch 2003 SCLR 467   248
Gillon v Chief Constable of Strathclyde Police 1997 SLT 1218, (1996)
     Times, 22 November, OH   125
Girvan v Inverness Farmers Dairy (No 2) 1998 SC (HL) 1, 1998 SCLR 72,
     1998 SLT 21   296
Glove (Aberdeen) v North of Scotland Water 2000 SLT 674   194
Godfrey v Demon Internet Ltd [2001] QB 210   274
Gold v Haringey Health Authority [1987] QB 481, [1987] 2 All ER 888,
     CA 81, 159
Goldsmith v Bhoyrul [1998] QB 459, [1997] 4 All ER 268, QBD   260
Goodwill v British Pregnancy Advisory Service [1996] 2 All ER 161, CA ..   81
Gordon v Wilson 1992 SLT 849, [1992] 3 Med LR 401, OH   159
Gorrie v Marist Brothers 2002 SCLR 436 ....   227, 306
Gorringe v Calderdale MBC [2004] UKHL 15 ....   71, 208, 213
Gorris v Scott (1874) LR 9 Exch 125   206
Graham v East of Scotland Water Authority 2002 SCLR 340   199
Graham (Thomas) & Co Ltd v Church of Scotland General Trustees 1982
     SLT (Sh Ct) 26   187

Grant v Allan 1987 JC 71, 1988 SLT 11 30
Grant v Australian Knitting Mills Ltd [1936] AC 85, PC 62
Grant v Sun Shipping Co Ltd 1948 SC (HL) 73, 1949 SLT 25 146–147
Grant (William) & Sons Ltd v William Cadenhead Ltd 1985 SC 121, 1985
   SLT 291 27
Gray v Dunlop 1954 SLT (Sh Ct) 75, 70 Sh Ct Rep 270 189
Gray v Scottish Society for the Prevention of Cruelty to Animals (1890) 17
   R 1185 269
Greatorex v Greatorex [2000] 4 All ER 769 78
Green v Argyll & Bute Council 2002 GWD-295 218
Gregg v Scott [2002] EWCA Civ 1471 159
Gregg v Scott [2003] Lloyd's Rep Med 105 137
Griffiths v British Coal Corpn [2001] 1 WLR 1493 298
Grobbelaar v News Group Newspapers Ltd [2001] 2 All ER 437, CA 273
Groves v Lord Wimborne [1898] 2 QB 402, CA 202
Grunwald v Hughes 1964 SLT 94, 1965 SLT 209, OH 62
Guy v Strathkelvin District Council 1997 SCLR 405, OH 200

Haggart's Trustees v Lord President Hope (1824) 2 Sh App 125 271
Hague v Deputy Governor of Parkhurst Prison [1992] 1 AC 58, [1991] 3 All
   ER 733, HL 203
Haig (John) & Co Ltd v Forth Blending Co Ltd 1954 SC 35, 1954 SLT 2,
   OH 27, 29
Hall (Arthur J S) & Co v Simons [2002] 1 AC 615 162
Hambrook v Stokes Bros [1925] 1 KB 141, CA 76
Hamilton v Al Fayed [2001] 1 AC 395 271
Hamilton v Allied Domecq plc 2001 SC 829 89–90
Hamilton v Allied Domecq plc 2004 SLT 191, OH 290
Hamilton v Fife Health Board 1992 SCLR 288, 1992 SLT 1026, OH 245
Hamilton v Fife Health Board 1993 SC 369, 1993 SLT 624 .... 239, 245
Hamilton Jones v David and Snape [2004] 1 All ER 657 17
Hanlon v Cuthbertson 1981 SLT (Notes) 57, OH 152
Hardie v Sneddon 1917 SC 1, 1916 2 SLT 197 238
Harris v Abbey National plc 1997 SCLR 359 5
Harrison v Michelin Tyre Co Ltd [1985] 1 All ER 918, [1985] ICR 696 .. 231
Harrods Ltd v Harrodian School [1996] RPC 697, (1996) Times 3 April,
   CA 28
Harvie v Robertson (1903) 5 F 338, 10 SLT 581 194
Hatton v Sutherland [2002] 2 All ER 1 .... 216, 218
Hatton v UK [2003] All ER (D) 122 191
Hedley Byrne & Co Ltd v Heller & Partners Ltd [1964] AC 465, [1963] 2
   All ER 575, HL 83–89
Heenan v Dillon 1999 Fam LR 62 19
Henderson v Chief Constable, Fife Police 1988 SLT 361, OH 18
Henderson v John Stuart (Farms) Ltd 1963 SC 245, 1963 SLT 22, OH .. 177,
                                                               178
Henderson v Merrett Syndicates Ltd [1995] 2 AC 145, [1994] 3 All ER 506,
   HL 90–93, 97, 101, 104, 108,
                                           157, 160, 161, 162
Henderson v Merrett Syndicates Ltd (No 2) [1997] LRLR 265, QBD
   (Comm Ct) 160
Henderson v Moodie 1988 SCLR 77, sub nom Henderson v Chief
   Constable, Fife Police 1988 SLT 361, OH 18

Hicks v Chief Constable of South Yorkshire Police [1992] 2 All ER 65, HL .   243, 293

Hill v Chief Constable of West Yorkshire [1989] AC 53, [1988] 2 All ER 238, HL 208

Hill v Lovett 1992 SLT 994, OH 177, 178, 197, 210, 221

Hill v Wilson 1998 SC 81, 1998 SLT 69, OH 295, 297

Hislop v Durham (1842) 4 D 1168 215

Hodgson v Trapp [1989] AC 807, [1988] 3 All ER 870, HL 298, 300

Holmes v Bank of Scotland 2002 SLT 544 . . . . 162, 290

Horrocks v Lowe [1975] AC 135, [1974] 1 All ER 662, HL 275

Hotson v East Berkshire Area Health Authority [1987] 2 All ER 909, HL .   137, 159

Hudson v Ridge Manufacturing Co Ltd [1957] 2 QB 348, [1957] 2 All ER 348 217

Hughes v Lord Advocate 1963 SC (HL) 31, 1963 SLT 150 . . . . 120, 121, 131, 285

Hunter v British Coal Corpn [1999] QB 140, [1998] 2 All ER 97, CA 73, 219

Hunter v Canary Wharf Ltd [1997] AC 655, [1997] 2 All ER 426, HL . . .   190, 194

Hunter v Hanley 1955 SC 200, 1955 SLT 213 158

Hunter v National Specialist Steeplejacks 2004 GWD 49 287

Hutcheson v Ascosmit Co 1992 SLT 1115 303

Hutton (E) & Co v Jones [1910] AC 20 266

ICI v Shatwell [1965] AC 656, [1964] 2 All ER 999 . . . . 149, 152

Incorporation of Fleshers of Dumfries v Rankine Dec 10 1816 FC 260

Ingham v John G Russell (Transport) Ltd 1991 SC 201, 1991 SLT 739, 1991 SCLR 596 . . . . 242, 249

Initial Services Ltd v Putterill [1968] 1 QB 396, [1967] 3 All ER 145, CA .   33

Inshore Services (International) v NFFO Services [2001] EWCA Civ 1722 . .   39

Invercargill City Council v Hamlin [1996] AC 624, [1996] 1 All ER 756, PC .   103

Irving v Hiddleston 1998 SCLR 350, 1998 SLT 912, OH   292

Island Records Ltd, ex parte [1978] Ch 122, [1978] 3 All ER 824, CA . . .   203

JP v East Berkshire Community NHS Trust [2003] EWCA Civ 1151   210

Jobling v Associated Dairies Ltd [1982] AC 794, [1981] 2 All ER 752, HL . .   138

Jolley v Sutton London Borough Council [2000] 3 All ER 409 . . . . . . 121, 127, 129

Junior Books Ltd v Veitchi Co Ltd 1982 SC (HL) 244, 1982 SLT 492 . . .   94, 95–99, 101, 104, 107–109, 111, 157

K v Gilmartin's Executrix 2002 SC 602   304

Kay's Tutor v Ayrshire and Arran Health Board 1987 SC (HL) 145, 1987 SLT 577, HL, affirming 1986 SLT 435 . . . . 136, 142

Keane v Walker Contracts (Scotland) Ltd 1999 GWD 9-410   198

Keen v Tayside Contracts 2003 SLT 500 . . . . 78, 219, 220

Keicher v National Coal Board 1988 SLT 318   297

Kelvin Shipping Co, The Baron Vernon v Canadian Pacific Railway Co, The Metagama 1928 SC (HL) 21, 1928 SLT 117   285

Kemp v Secretary of State for Scotland 2000 SLT 471 . . . . 118, 152, 213

Kennedy v Glenbelle Ltd 1996 SC 95   192

Kennedy v Lees of Scotland 1997 SLT 510 241
Kent v Griffiths [2001] QB 36 . . . . 207, 209, 213
Kenyon v Bell 1953 SC 125, 1952 SLT (Notes) 79, OH 137, 159
Kenway (John) Ltd v Orcantic Ltd 1979 SC 422, 1980 SLT 46, OH 86
Kerr v Earl of Orkney (1857) 20 D 298, 30 SJ 158 . . . . 6, 185, 186
Kerr v Kennedy [1942] 1 KB 409, [1942] 1 All ER 412 263
Kirby v National Coal Board 1958 SC 514, 1959 SLT 7 . . . . 224, 230
Kirk Care Housing Association Ltd v Crerar and Partners 1996 SLT 150,
    OH 305
Knowles v Liverpool City Council [1993] 4 All ER 321, [1993] 1 WLR
    1428, HL 217
Kozikowska v Kozikowski 1996 SLT 386 241
Kubach v Hollands [1937] 3 All ER 907, KB 165
Kyle v P & J Stormonth Darling WS 1993 SC 57, 1994 SLT 191, affirming
    1992 SLT 264, OH 162

Lagden v O'Connor [2004] 1 All ER 277 . . . . 253, 288
Landcatch Ltd v The Braer Corpn; Landcatch Ltd v International Oil
    Pollution Compensation Fund 1999 SLT 1208, 1999 GWD 20-962 . 107
Lang Bros Ltd v Goldwell Ltd 1980 SC 237, 1982 SLT 309 . . . . 28, 29
Lappin v Britannia Airways Ltd 1989 SLT 181, OH 302
Larmer v Solihull MBC [2001] RTR 32 208
Latimer v AEC Ltd [1953] AC 643, [1953] 2 All ER 449, HL 128, 216
Lawson v Scotdem Ltd 1999 GWD 8-393 293
Leeds & Holbeck Building Society v Alex Morison & Co (No 2) 2001 SCLR
    41 . . . . 138, 160
Lees v Tod (1882) 9 R 807 55
Lego System A/S v Lego M Lemelstrich Ltd [1983] FSR 155 28
Leigh and Sillavan Ltd v Aliakmon Shipping Co Ltd, The Aliakmon [1986]
    AC 785, [1986] 2 All ER 145, HL, affirming [1985] 2 All ER 44,
    CA 108–110, 112
Leitch v Leydon 1931 SC (HL) 1 . . . . 22, 23
Lewicki v Brown & Root Wimpey Highland Fabricators Ltd 1996 SC 200,
    1996 SCLR 680, 1996 SLT 1283 297
Lewis v Buckpool Golf Club 1993 SLT (Sh Ct) 43 . . . . 14, 150
Liddle v Morton 1996 SLT 1143 5
Lim Poh Choo v Camden and Islington Area Health Authority [1980] AC
    174, [1979] 2 All ER 910, HL 292, 293
Lister v Hesley Hall [2002] 1 AC 215, [2001] 1 AC 315 . . . . 226, 227, 231
Lister v Romford Ice and Cold Storage Co Ltd [1957] AC 555, [1957] 1 All
    ER 125, HL 222
Littlejohn v Wood & Davidson Ltd 1997 SLT 1353, OH 203
Lomond Assured Properties v McGrigor Donald 2000 SLT 797 290
Lonrho Ltd v Shell Petroleum Co Ltd (No 2) [1982] AC 173, HL, [1981] 2
    All ER 456 . . . . 47, 50–52, 203, 205
Lonrho plc v Fayed [1990] 2 QB 479, [1989] 2 All ER 65, CA 44
Lonrho plc v Fayed [1992] 1 AC 448, [1991] 3 All ER 303, HL 51, 52
Lonrho plc v Fayed (No 5) [1994] 1 All ER 188, [1993] 1 WLR 1489, CA 49
Loutchansky v Times Newspapers Ltd (No 1) [2002] QB 321 273
Loutchansky v Times Newspapers Ltd (No 2) [2002] QB 783 273

McAllister v Imperial Chemical Industries plc 1997 SLT 351, 1996 Rep LR
    136, OH 246

McCabe v News Group Newspapers Ltd 1992 SLT 707, OH 263
McCann v Scottish Media Newspapers Ltd 1999 GWD 10-473 262
McCluskey v Wallace 1998 SC 711 238
MacColl v Hoo 1983 SLT (Sh Ct) 23 .... 185, 189
McColl v Barns 1992 SCLR 907, 1992 SLT 1188, OH 302
McCortan Turkington Breen (a firm) v Times Newspapers Ltd [2000] 2 All
    ER 913 274
McCullagh v Lane Fox and Partners [1996] 1 EGLR 35, (1995) Times, 22
    December, CA 89
McCullough v Norwest Socea Ltd 1981 SLT 201, OH 306
Macdonald v Fédération International des Football Associations 1999
    SCLR 59, OH 82
MacDougall v MacDougall's Executors 1994 SLT 1178, OH 161
McDougall v Strathclyde Regional Council 1999 SLT 1124 118
McDyer v Celtic Football and Athletic Co Ltd 2000 SLT 736 .... 189, 196
McErlean v J & B Scotland Ltd 1997 SLT 1326, 1997 GWD 6-253, OH . . 216
McFarlane v EE Caledonia Ltd [1994] 2 All ER 1 ....74, 77
McFarlane v Tayside Health Board 1997 SLT 211, OH, 2000 SC (HL) 1 . 80,
                                                                81, 288–289
McGhee v National Coal Board 1973 SC (HL) 37, 1973 SLT 14 139–142
McGlone v British Railways Board 1966 SC (HL) 1, 1966 SLT 2 198
McGregor v AAH Pharmaceuticals Ltd 1996 SLT 1161, OH 215–216
McGuffie v Forth Valley Health Board 1991 SLT 231 196
MacIver v J & A Gardner Ltd 2001 SLT 585 215
Mackay v Borthwick 1982 SLT 265, OH 151
McKay v Essex Area Health Authority [1982] QB 1166, [1982] 2 All ER
    771, CA 79
McKeen v Chief Constable, Lothian and Borders Police 1994 SLT 93, OH . . 17
McKendrick v Sinclair 1972 SC (HL) 25, 1972 SLT 110 4
Mackenzie v Cluny Hill Hydropathic Co 1908 SC 200, 15 SLT 518 17
McKew v Holland and Hannen and Cubitts (Scotland) Ltd 1970 SC (HL)
    20, 1970 SLT 68 145
McKillen v Barclay Curle & Co Ltd 1967 SLT 41 287
McKinnell v White 1971 SLT (Notes) 61, OH..................... 138
McKnight v Clydesdale Buses Ltd 1999 SLT 1167 213
McLaughlan v Craig 1948 SC 599, 1948 SLT 483 185
McLaughlan v Orr Pollock & Co (1894) 22 R 38 264
Maclean v Lothian and Borders Fire Brigade 1998 SCLR 1004, OH 293
McLelland v Greater Glasgow Health Board 2002 SLT 446 ..... 80, 289, 293
McLeod v Aberdeen City Council 1999 GWD 23-1115 216
MacLeod v Kerr 1965 SC 253, 1965 SLT 358 53
McLoughlin v Jones [2002] 2 WLR 1279 74
McLoughlin v O'Brian [1983] 1 AC 410, [1982] 2 All ER 298, HL 75
McManus' Executrix v Babcock Energy Ltd 1999 SC 569 ...... 241–242, 244,
                                                          247–248, 249, 295
McMillan v McDowall 1993 SLT 311, OH 292
McNulty v Marshalls Food Group Ltd 1999 SC 195 295
McPhee v Macfarlane's Executor 1933 SC 163, 1933 SLT 148 18
Macrae v Reed & Mallik Ltd 1961 SC 68, 1961 SLT 96 297
McRostie v Ironside (1849) 12 D 74 264
McWilliams v Lord Advocate 1992 SCLR 954, 1992 SLT 1045, OH 245
McWilliams v Sir William Arrol & Co and Lithgows Ltd 1962 SC (HL) 70,
    1962 SLT 121 137

MTM Construction Ltd v William Reid Engineering Ltd 1998 SLT 778,
  1997 SCLR 778, OH 234
Malcolm v Dickson 1951 SC 542, 1951 SLT 357 118
Malcolm v Fair 1993 SLT 342, OH 152
Maloco v Littlewoods Organisation Ltd 1987 SC (HL) 37, 1987 SCLR 489,
  1987 SLT 425 .... 122, 186, 187
Manners v Whitehead (1898) 1 F 171 ....89, 90
Marcic v Thames Water [2004] 1 All ER 135 191
Marshall v William Sharp & Sons Ltd 1991 SCLR 104, 1991 SLT 114 ... 233
Martin v Bell-Ingram 1986 SC 208, 1986 SLT 575 ....87, 88
Martin v McGuiness 2003 SCLR 548 .... 35, 278
Massey v Crown Life Insurance Co [1978] ICR 590, [1978] 2 All ER 576,
  CA 223
Mather v British Telecommunications plc 2001 SLT 325 305
Mattis v Pollock (t/a Flamingo's Nightclub) [2003] 1 WLR 2158, CA 231
Maynard v West Midlands Regional Health Authority [1985] 1 All ER 635,
  [1984] 1 WLR 634, HL 159
Mazure v Stubbs Ltd 1919 SC (HL) 112, 1919 2 SLT 160 264
Meek v Burton's Gold Medal Biscuits Ltd 1989 SLT 338, OH 301, 302
Melrose v Davidson and Robertson 1993 SC 288, 1993 SLT 611 88
Merivale v Carson (1887) 20 QBD 275, CA 270
Merkur Island Shipping Corpn v Laughton [1983] 2 AC 570, [1983] ICR
  490, HL 41, 42
Mersey Docks and Harbour Board v Coggins and Griffith (Liverpool) Ltd
  [1947] AC 1, [1946] 2 All ER 345, HL 232
Metall und Rohstoff AG v Donaldson Lufkin and Jenrette Inc [1990] 1 QB
  391, [1989] 3 All ER 14, CA 51
Middlebrook Mushrooms Ltd v Transport and General Workers' Union
  [1993] ICR 612, (1993) Times, 18 January, CA 39
Millar v Bassey [1994] EMLR 44 39
Milne v Express Newspapers [2003] 1 All ER 482 268
Mitchell v Glenrothes Development Corpn 1991 SLT 284, OH 295
Mitchell v Laing 1998 SC 342, 1998 SCLR 266, 1998 SLT 203 299
Modbury Triangle v Anzil (2000) 205 CLR 254 .... 123, 148, 197
Mogul Steamship Co Ltd v McGregor, Gow & Co (1889) 23 QBD 598, CA .. 47, 49
Monson v Tussauds Ltd [1894] 1 QB 671, CA 261, 265
Monteith v Cape Insulation Ltd 1998 SC 903 247
More v Boyle 1967 SLT (Sh Ct) 38 21
Morgans v Launchbury [1973] AC 127, [1972] 2 All ER 606, HL 234
Morrison v Ritchie & Co (1902) 4 F 645 .... 265–267, 276
Morrisson v Robertson 1908 SC 332, 15 SLT 697 53
Morrow v Neil 1975 SLT (Sh Ct) 65 5
Mortgage Corpn Ltd v Mitchells Roberton 1997 SLT 1305, OH 160
Morton v Wm Dixon Ltd 1909 SC 807, 1909 1 SLT 346 129–130
Moyes v Lothian Health Board 1990 SLT 444 14
Muir v Glasgow Corporation 1943 SC (HL) 3, 1944 SLT 60 ..... 116–118, 123
Mullin v Richards [1998] 1 All ER 920, CA 118
Murdoch v Glacier Metal Co Ltd [1998] Env LR 732, [1998] EHLR 198,
  CA 191
Murphy v Brentwood District Council [1991] 1 AC 398, [1990] 2 All ER
  908, HL 95, 102–103, 104
Murray v Fraser 1916 SC 623 16
Murray v Reilly 1963 SLT (Notes) 49, OH 163

Murray's Executrix v Greenock Dockyard Co Ltd 2004 SLT 346 . . . . . 241–242, 244, 248
Mustad (O) & Son v S Allcock & Co Ltd and Dosen [1963] 3 All ER 416, [1964] 1 WLR 109, HL   32
Mutch v Robertson 1981 SLT 217   264

Nacap Ltd v Moffat Plant Ltd 1987 SLT 221, rev 1986 SLT 326 . . . .   107, 110–112
Neill v Docherty and Akram (23 May 1996, unreported), HC   152
Neilson v Rodger (1853) 16 D 325   260
Neville v C & A Modes Ltd 1945 SC 175, 1945 SLT 189   225
Newcastle Building Society v Paterson Robertson and Graham 2001 SC 734 .   160, 290
Nolan v Iceland Frozen Foods (3 December 1997, unreported)   122
Nordic Oil Services Ltd v Berman 1993 SLT 1164, OH 86, 103
Norman v Future Publishing Ltd [1999] EMLR 325   262
North of Scotland Banking Co v Duncan (1857) 19 D 881   278

OLL v Secretary of State for the Home Dept [1997] 3 All ER 897   212
O'Brien's Curator Bonis v British Steel plc 1991 SC 315, 1991 SCLR 831, 1991 SLT 477 . . . . 287, 295
O'Connor v Matthews 1996 SLT 408, OH   296
Omega Trust Co Ltd v Wright Son & Pepper (No 1) [1997] 1 EGLR 120, CA   89
Onifade v Secretary of State for Social Security 1999 GWD 17-819   209
O'Rourke v Camden London Borough Council [1998] AC 188, [1997] 3 All ER 23, HL   205
Osborne & Hunter Ltd v Hardie Caldwell 1999 SLT 153   304
Osman v United Kingdom [1999] 1 FLR 193 . . . . 209, 210
Outram v Reid (1852) 14 D 577 . . . . 264, 266, 267
Overseas Tankship (UK) Ltd v Morts Dock and Engineering Co, The Wagon Mound [1961] AC 388, [1961] 1 All ER 404, PC   285

Pace v Culley 1992 SLT 1073, OH   151
Page v Smith [1996] AC 155, [1995] 2 All ER 736, HL 73, 120, 121, 287
Palmer v Beck 1993 SLT 485, OH   89
Palmer v Tees Health Authority (2000) 2 LGLR 69   210
Paris v Stepney Borough Council [1951] AC 367, [1951] 1 All ER 42, HL . . .   125, 218
Park v Tractor Shovels Ltd 1980 SLT 94, OH   232
Parker-Knoll Ltd v Knoll International [1962] RPC 265, HL   29
Parkinson v St James and Seacroft University Hospital Trust [2002] QB 266 .   289
Patel v Hooper & Jackson [1999] 1 All ER 992, CA   290
Paterson v Costain Mining Ltd 1988 SCLR 71, 1988 SLT 413, OH   302
Paterson v Welch (1893) 20 R 744   276
Paton v Loffland Bros North Sea 1994 SLT 784   306
Patterson v H Landsberg & Son (1905) 7 F 675, 13 SLT 62   54
Paul v Jackson (1884) 11 R 460   276
Paul v Ogilvy 2002 SLT 171   290
Pearce v United Bristol NHS Trust [1999] PIQR 53   14
Pearson v Educational Institute of Scotland 1997 SC 245, 1998 SLT 189 .   272
Peck v United Kingdom (2003) EHRR 41   35
Perrett v Collins [1998] 2 Lloyd's Rep 255, (1998) Times, 23 June, CA . . .   66

Phelps v Hillingdon London Borough Council [2001] 2 AC 619 211
Phestos Shipping Co Ltd v Kurmiawan 1983 SC 165, 1983 SLT 388 22
Phillips v Grampian Health Board 1991 SCLR 817, 1992 SLT 659, OH .. 247
Philp v Morton (1816) Hume 865 277
Pickergill v Riley (2004) Times, 2 March 160
Pickford v ICI plc [1996] ICR 566, [1996] IRLR 622, CA 216
Pickford v ICI plc [1998] ICR 673, [1998] 3 All ER 462, HL 136
Platform Home Loans Ltd v Oyston Shipways Ltd [2002] 2 AC 190, [1999]
    1 All ER 833, HL 152, 291
Platt v Liverpool City Council CCRTF 97/0072/C, CA 198
Polemis and Furness, Withy & Co Ltd, Re [1921] 3 KB 560, CA 284–286
Porter v Strathclyde Regional Council 1991 SLT 446 .... 135, 196
Potter v McCulloch 1987 SLT 308, OH 301
Powell v Boladz [1998] Lloyd's Rep Med 116, CA 53
Prentice v William Thyne Ltd 1989 SLT 336, OH 301, 302
Preston v Grampian Health Board 1988 SLT 435 297
Primrose v Waterston (1902) 4 F 783, 10 SLT 37 271
Pringle v Bremner and Stirling (1867) 5 M (HL) 55 18
Prophit v British Broadcasting Corporation 1997 SLT 745, OH 263, 269
Pullar v Window Clean Ltd 1956 SC 13, 1956 SLT 17 204

Quilty v Windsor 1999 SLT 346 .... 30, 263, 272
Quinn v Cameron and Roberton Ltd 1956 SC 224, 1957 SLT 2 127
Quinn v Leathem [1901] AC 495, HL 47
Quinn v McGinty 1999 SLT (Sh Ct) 27 222

RCA Corporation v Pollard [1983] Ch 135, [1982] 3 All ER 771, CA 50,
                                                                      203
RHM Bakeries (Scotland) Ltd v Strathclyde Regional Council 1985 SC
    (HL) 17, 1985 SLT 214, HL 186, 192–193
RSP Architects Planners and Engineers v Ocean Front Pte Ltd (1998) 14
    Const LJ 139, CA (Sing) 99
Rae v Strathclyde Joint Police Board 1999 GWD 12-571 220
Ramsay v Mackay (1890) 18 R 130 261
Ready Mixed Concrete (South East) Ltd v Minister of Pensions and
    National Insurance [1968] 2 QB 497, [1968] 1 All ER 433 223
Reavis v Clan Line Steamers Ltd 1925 SC 725, 1925 SLT 386, OH 105,
                                                               109, 131
Reckitt and Colman Products Ltd v Borden Inc [1990] 1 All ER 873, HL . 27
Reeman v Department of Transport [1997] 2 Lloyd's Rep 648, CA 86
Rees v Darlington Memorial Hospital NHS Trust [2004] 1 AC 309, [2003]
    4 All ER 987 .... 81, 288, 289
Reeves v Metropolitan Commissioner of Police [2000] 1 AC 360 ..... 72, 123,
                                                               150, 151
Reid v Edinburgh Acoustics Ltd (No 2) 1995 SCLR (Notes) 791, 1995 SLT
    982, OH 163
Reid v Mitchell (1885) 12 R 1129 12
Renfrew Golf Club v Ravenstone Securities Ltd 1984 SLT 170, OH 304
Revill v Newberry [1996] QB 567, [1996] 1 All ER 291 20
Reynolds v Times Newspapers [2001] 2 AC 127 273
Rich (Marc) & Co AG v Bishop Rock Marine Co Ltd, The Nicholas H
    [1994] 3 All ER 686, [1994] 1 WLR 1071, CA 87
Rich (Marc) & Co AG v Bishop Rock Marine Co Ltd, The Nicholas H

[1996] AC 211, [1995] 3 All ER 307, HL 66, 67
Richardson v LRC Products [2000] PIQR 164 .... 171, 173–174
Richardson v Pitt-Stanley [1995] QB 123, [1995] 1 All ER 460, CA 222
Richardson v Wilson (1879) 7 R 237, 17 SLR 122 274
Robbie v Graham and Sibbald 1989 SCLR 578, 1989 SLT 870, OH 88
Robertson v British Bakeries Ltd 1991 SLT 434, 1991 SCLR 450 302
Robertson v Fleming (1861) 23 D (HL) 8, (1861) 4 Macq 167 161
Robertson v Forth Road Bridge Joint Board 1995 SC 364, 1996 SLT 263 . 74, 77, 219
Robertson v J Sidney Smith 1999 GWD 4-214 252
Robertson v Turnbull 1982 SC (HL) 1, 1982 SLT 96 240
Robertson v Watt & Co (4 July 1995, unreported) 162
Roe v Minister of Health [1954] 2 QB 66, [1954] 2 All ER 131, CA ... 119, 174
Rome v Watson (1898) 25 R 733, 5 SLT 377 271
Rondel v Worsley [1969] 1 AC 191, [1967] 3 All ER 993, HL 162
Rookes v Barnard [1964] AC 1129, [1964] 1 All ER 367, HL 45–46, 50
Rorrison v West Lothian College 2000 SCLR 245 218
Rose v Plenty [1975] ICR 430, [1976] 1 All ER 97, CA 228–229
Ross v Bryce 1972 SLT (Sh Ct) 76 15
Rossleigh Ltd v Leader Cars Ltd 1987 SLT 355, OH 39
Roxburgh v Seven Seas Engineering Ltd 1980 SLT (Notes) 49, OH 31
Royal Bank of Scotland v Bannerman Johnstone Maclay 2003 SC 125 .... 86, 92–93, 224, 228, 232
Rubins v Walker 1946 SC 215 294
Rylands v Fletcher (1868) LR 3 HL 330 186

S v Gloucester County Council [2000] 3 All ER 346 210
Sabri-Tabrizi v Lothian Health Board 1998 SC 373, 1998 SLT 607 ...... 145, 148
Saeed v Waheed 1996 SLT (Sh Ct) 39, 1995 SCLR 504 .... 21, 82
Saif Ali v Sydney Mitchell & Co [1980] AC 198 163
Salter v U B Frozen & Chilled Foods Ltd 2003 SLT 1011 .... 74, 219
Sayers v Harlow Urban District Council [1958] 2 All ER 342, [1958] 1 WLR 623, CA 144
Scala Ballroom (Wolverhampton) Ltd v Ratcliffe [1958] 3 All ER 220, [1958] 1 WLR 1057, CA 49
Scott v Glasgow City Council 1997 Hous LR 107, Sh Ct 200
Scott v Lothian Regional Council 1999 Rep LR 15 160
Scott Lithgow Ltd v GEC Electrical Products Ltd 1989 SC 412, 1992 SLT 244, OH 96
Scottish Milk Marketing Board v Dryborough & Co Ltd 1985 SLT 253, OH .. 28
Seager v Copydex Ltd [1967] 2 All ER 415, [1967] 1 WLR 923, CA 33
Shaher v British Aerospace Flying College Ltd 2003 SLT 791 249
Shell UK Ltd v McGillivray 1991 SLT 667 22
Shogun Finance Ltd v Hudson [2004] 1 All ER 215 53
Short v J & W Henderson Ltd 1946 SC (HL) 24, 1946 SLT 230 224
Sidaway v Board of Governors of the Bethlem Royal Hospital [1985] AC 871, [1985] 1 All ER 643, HL 13, 14, 159
Sim v Stretch [1936] 2 All ER 1237, HL 262
Simaan General Contracting Co v Pilkington Glass Ltd (No 2) [1988] QB 758, [1988] 1 All ER 791, CA 99
Simmers v Morton (1900) 8 SLT 285, OH 264
Simmons v British Steel plc 2003 SLT 62 144

Simmons v British Steel plc [2004] UKHL 20 .... 73, 284
Sion v Hampstead Health Authority [1994] 5 Med LR, CA 79
Skerries Salmon Ltd v The Braer Corpn 1999 SLT 1196 107
Smart v HM Advocate 1975 JC 30, 1975 SLT 65 12
Smith v Carter 1994 SCLR 539, 1995 SLT 295, OH 87
Smith v Crossley Bros Ltd (1971) 95 So Jo 655, CA 231
Smith v Duncan Stewart & Co Ltd (No 2) 1961 SC 91, 1961 SLT 67 260
Smith v Eric S Bush; Harris v Wyre Forest District Council [1990] 1 AC
    831, [1989] 2 WLR 790, [1989] 2 All ER 514, HL 87–89, 92
Smith v Middleton 1972 SC 30 296
Smith v P & O Bulk Shipping Ltd [1998] 2 Lloyd's Rep 81, QBD 127
Smith New Court Securities Ltd v Scrimgeour Vickers (Asset Management)
    Ltd [1997] AC 254, [1996] 4 All ER 769, HL 56, 287, 290
Smoldon v Whitworth [1997] PIQR P133, (1996) Times, 18 December, CA . 150
Sneesby v Goldings [1995] 2 EGLR 102, CA 160
Solomon v A Solomon & Co Ltd [1897] AC 22, HL 91
South Australia Asset Management Corporation v York Montague Ltd
    [1997] AC 191, [1996] 3 All ER 365, HL 290
Spence v Crawford 1939 SC (HL) 52, 1939 SLT 305 53
Spring v Guardian Assurance plc [1995] 2 AC 296, [1994] 3 All ER 129,
    HL 92, 93, 272
Squires v Perth and Kinross District Council 1986 SLT 30 188
St George's Healthcare NHS Trust v S; R v Collins, ex parte S [1998] 3
    WLR 936, [1998] 3 All ER 673, CA 13
Standard Chartered Bank v Pakistan National Shipping Corporation [1995]
    2 Lloyd's Rep 365 .... 271, 291
Standard Chartered Bank v Pakistan Shipping Corporation (No 2) [2003] 1
    All ER 173 .... 91, 153
Steel v Glasgow Iron and Steel Co Ltd 1944 SC 237, 1945 SLT 70 119
Steele v Scottish Daily Record and Sunday Mail Ltd 1970 SLT 53 277
Stein v Beaverbrook Newspapers Ltd 1968 SC 272, 1968 SLT 401 ... 263, 275
Stephens v Avery [1988] Ch 449, [1988] 2 All ER 477 31
Stevenson v British Coal Corpn 1989 SLT 136 296
Stevenson v Corpn of Glasgow 1908 SC 1034 199
Stevenson v Pontifex and Wood (1887) 15 R 125 300
Stevenson v East Dunbartonshire Council 2003 SLT 97 218
Stevenson, Jordan and Harrison Ltd v MacDonald and Evans (1952) 69
    RPC 10, [1952] 1 TLR 101, CA 223
Stewart v Thain 1981 JC 13, 1981 SLT (Notes) 2 15
Stovin v Wise and Norfolk County Council [1996] AC 923, [1996] 3 All ER
    801, HL 212–213
Stratford (JT) & Sons Ltd v Lindley [1965] AC 269, [1964] 3 All ER 102,
    HL 40
Strathford East Kilbride Ltd v HLM Design Ltd 1999 SLT 121 ...... 96, 97,
                                                          101, 104
Strathclyde Regional Council v Border Engineering Contractors Ltd 1997
    SCLR 100, 1998 SLT 175, OH 304
Sturgeon v Gallacher 2003 SLT 67 241
Surrey County Council v M (A child) [2001] EWCA Civ 691 210
Sutherland v British Telecommunications plc 1989 SLT 531 263
Sutherland v North British Steel Group Ltd 1986 SLT (Sh Ct) 29 137
Sutherland v Stopes [1925] AC 47, HL 268
Swan v Andrew Minto & Son 1998 Rep LR 42 178

TP and KM v United Kingdom [2001] 2 FLR 549 209
Tait v Brown & McRae 1997 SLT (Sh Ct) 63 160
Tartan American Machinery Corp v Swan & Co 2003 SLT 1246 67
Taylor v Glasgow Corpn 1922 SC (HL) 1, 1921 2 SLT 254 197
Taylor v Glasgow City Council 2002 SLT 689 221
Taylor v Glasgow District Council 1997 SC 183, 1997 SLT 537 ..... 225, 234
Taylor v Leslie 1998 SLT 1248, 1998 Rep LR 110, OH 153
Telnikoff v Matusevitch [1992] 2 AC 343, [1991] 4 All ER 817, HL 270
Thake v Maurice [1986] QB 644, [1984] 2 All ER 513 81
Thames Trains Ltd v Health and Safety Executive [2003] EWCA Civ 720 . 205
Theakston v MGN Ltd [2002] EWHC 137 31
Thomson v British Steel Corpn 1977 SLT 26, OH 231
Thomson v Kvaerner Govan Ltd 2004 SLT 24, HL 220
Thomson v Ross 2002 SLT 807 .... 271, 274
Titchener v British Railways Board 1984 SC (HL) 34, 1984 SLT 192 149,
198, 200
Tomlinson v Congleton Borough Council [2004] 1 AC 46 ...... 127 129, 199
Torquay Hotel Co Ltd v Cousins [1969] 2 Ch 106, [1969] 1 All ER 522,
CA 41–43
Trevor Rush McCafferty Wright v Paton Farrell 2002 SCLR 1039 162
Trotman v North Yorkshire County Council [1999] LGR 584, CA 226
Turner v Metro-Goldwyn-Mayer Pictures Ltd [1950] 1 All ER 449, [1950]
WN 83, HL 270
Twomax Ltd v Dickson, McFarlane and Robinson 1982 SC 113, 1983 SLT
98, OH 86

Uddin v Associated Portland Cement Manufacturers Ltd [1965] 2 QB 582,
[1965] 2 All ER 213, CA 152
Ultramares Corpn v Touche (1931) 255 NY 170 .... 59, 85
United Wholesale Grocers Ltd v Sher 1993 SLT 284, OH 224

Vasey v Surrey Free Inns plc [1996] PIQR P373, CA 231
Veedfald v Arhus Amtskommune [2003] 1 CMLR 41 .... 170, 173
Vernon v Bosley (No 1) [1997] 1 All ER 577 78
Videan v British Transport Commission [1963] 2 QB 650, [1963] 3 WLR
374, CA 119

W v Essex CC [2001] 2 AC 592 74
Waddell v British Broadcasting Corpn 1973 SLT 246 263
Wainwright v Home Office [2003] All ER (D) 279 .... 2, 12, 15, 18,
34, 53
Walker v Northumberland County Council [1995] 1 All ER 737, [1995]
IRLR 35, CA 218–219
Walker (John) & Sons Ltd v Douglas Laing & Co 1993 SLT 156, OH 29
Walker (John) & Sons Ltd v Douglas McGibbon & Co Ltd 1972 SLT 128,
OH 29
Walker (John) & Sons Ltd v Henry Ost & Co Ltd [1970] 2 All ER 106,
[1971] 1 WLR 917 29
Wallace v City of Glasgow District Council 1985 SLT 23 196
Walters v North Glamorgan NHS Trust [2002] EWHC 321 79
Ward v Scotrail Railways Ltd 1999 SC 255 .... 19, 217
Wardlaw v Bonnington Castings Ltd 1956 SC (HL) 266, 1956 SLT 135 .138–140,
141–142

Waste Systems International Inc v Eurocare Environmental Services Ltd
  1999 SLT 198, OH 34
Waters v Commissioner of Police of the Metropolis [2000] 4 All ER 934 .. 217
Watson v Duncan (1890) 17 R 404 263
Watson v Fram Reinforced Concrete Co (Scotland) Ltd and Winget Ltd
  1960 SC (HL) 92, 1960 SLT 321 132
Watson v McEwan (1905) 7 F (HL) 109 271
Watt v Hertfordshire County Council [1954] 2 All ER 368, [1954] 1 WLR
  208, CA 126
Watt v Jamieson 1954 SC 56 190
Watt v Thomson (1870) 8 M (HL) 77 271
Waugh v James K Allan Ltd 1964 SC (HL) 102, 1964 SLT 269 116
Webster v Lord Advocate 1985 SC 173, 1985 SLT 361 191
Weir v J M Hodge & Son 1990 SLT 266 161
Weir v National Westminster Bank plc 1993 SC 515, 1994 SLT 1251 .... 93, 157
Weir v Wyper 1992 SCLR 483, 1992 SLT 579, OH 153
Wells v Wells [1998] 3 All ER 481, [1998] 3 WLR 329, HL 295
Wells v Wells [1999] 1 AC 345 295
Western Bank of Scotland v Addie (1867) 5 M (HL) 80 54
Wheeler v J J Saunders Ltd [1995] 2 All ER 697, [1995] 3 WLR 466, CA . 191
Wheeler v New Merton Board Mills Ltd [1933] 2 KB 669, CA 206
White v Chief Constable of South Yorkshire Police [1999] AC 455 220
White v Inveresk Paper Co Ltd 1987 SC 143, 1988 SLT 2, OH 301
White v Jones [1995] 2 AC 207, [1995] 1 All ER 691, HL 161–162, 290
Whitefield v Barton 1987 SCLR 259, Sh Ct 124
Whitehouse v Jordan [1981] 1 All ER 267, [1981] 1 WLR 246, HL 159
Whyte v Walker 1983 SLT 441, OH 306
Wilkinson v Downtown [1897] 2 QB 57 53
Will v Sneddon, Campbell and Munro 1931 SC 164, 1931 SLT 125 261
Williams v Hemphill (A & W) Ltd 1966 SC (HL) 31, 1966 SLT 33 229
Williams v Natural Life Health Foods Ltd [1998] 2 All ER 577, HL 91
Williamson v Umphray and Robertson (1890) 17 R 905, 27 SLR 742 274
Wilsher v Essex Area Health Authority [1988] AC 1074, [1988] All ER 871,
  HL 142
Wilson v National Coal Board 1981 SC (HL) 9, 1981 SLT 67 298
Winans v Macrae (1885) 12 R 1051 20
Winnick v Dick 1984 SC 48, 1984 SLT 185 148
Winter v News Scotland Ltd 1991 SLT 828 264
Wooldridge v Sumner [1963] 2 QB 43, [1962] 2 All ER 978, CA 150
Wormald v Walker 2004 GWD 55 178
Worsley v Tambrands Ltd [2000] PIQR 95 172
Wotherspoon v Strathclyde Regional Council 1992 SCLR 806, 1992 SLT
  1090 247
Wragg v D C Thomson & Co Ltd 1909 2 SLT 315 .... 265, 267
Wright v British Railways Board [1983] 2 AC 733, [1983] 2 All ER 698,
  HL 292

X (minors) v Bedfordshire County Council [1995] 2 AC 633, [1995] 3 All
  ER 353, HL 204, 207–209, 210
X v Schering Health Care Ltd [2002] EWHC 1420 172
X v Y [1988] 2 All ER 648, [1988] RPC 379 33

Yale v Forbes 2004 SLT (Sh Ct) 13 241

Yewans v Nokes (1880) 6 QBD 530 222
Young v Charles Church (Southern) Ltd 2000 SCLR 373 219
Young v Rankin 1934 SC 499, 1934 SLT 445 239
Youssoupoff v Metro-Goldwyn-Mayer Pictures Ltd (1934) 50 TLR 581, CA .. 263
Yukong Line Ltd of Korea v Rendsburg Investments Corpn of Liberia (No
    2) [1998] 1 WLR 294, [1998] 4 All ER 82, QBD (Comm Ct) 52

Z v United Kingdom [2001] 2 FLR 612 209

List of abbreviations

AC	Law Reports, Appeal Cases (House of Lords and Privy Council) 1890–
All ER	All England Law Reports 1936–
App Cas	Law Reports, Appeal Cases (House of Lords) 1875–90
CA	Court of Appeal
Ch	Law Reports, Chancery Division 1890–
D	Dunlop's Session Cases 1838–62
ECHR	European Court of Human Rights
ECJ	European Court of Justice
Exch	Exchequer Reports 1847–56
F	Fraser's Session Cases 1898–1906
FC	Faculty Collection (Court of Session) 1752–1825
FSR	Fleet Street Reports 1963–
GWD	Green's Weekly Digest 1986–
HL	House of Lords
Hous LR	Housing Law Reports
Hume	Hume's Decisions (Court of Session) 1871–1822
ICR	Industrial Cases Reports 1972–
IRLR	Industrial Relations Law Reports 1972–
JC	Justiciary Cases 1917–
KB	Law Reports, King's Bench Division 1901–52
LR	Law Reports
M	Macpherson's Session Cases 1862–73
M & W	Meeson & Welsby 1836–47
Macq	Macqueen's House of Lords Reports 1851–65
Med LR	Medical Law Reports
NY	Nw York Court of Appeals Reports 1847–1955
OH	Outer House
PC	Judicial Committee of the Privy Council
QB	Law Reports, Queen's Bench Division 1891–1901, 1952–
QBD	Law Reports, Queen's Bench Division 1875–90
R	Rettie's Session Cases 1873–98
RPC	Reports of Patents, Designs and Trade Marks Cases 1884–

S	P Shaw's Session Cases 1821–38
SC	Session Cases 1907–
SC (HL)	House of Lords Cases in Session Cases 1907–
SCLR	Scottish Civil Law Reports 1987–
Sh	P Shaw's Scotch Appeals (House of Lords) 1821–26
Sh Ct Rep	Sheriff Court Reports in Scottish Law Review
SJ	Scottish Jurist 1829–73
SLR	Scottish Law Reporter 1865–1925
SLT	Scots Law Times 1893–1908, 1909–
SLT (Notes)	Notes of Recent Decisions in Scots Law Times 1946–81
SLT (Sh Ct)	Sheriff Court Reports in Scots Law Times 1893–
So Jo	Solicitor's Journal 1856–
TLR	Times Law Reports 1884–
WLR	Weekly Law Reports 1953–
WN	Law Reports, Weekly Notes 1866–1952

Introduction

The essence of the modern Scots law of delict is the obligation of a person to compensate another who has suffered harm as a result of the wrongful actions of that person. This obligation to pay compensation is called reparation. The obligation to make reparation when loss has been suffered as a result of a person's wrongful actions is obediential; it arises *ex lege* regardless of the will of the wrongdoer. In this respect, delictual obligations differ from contractual obligations which arise as a result of the agreement of the parties to a contract. However, a delictual obligation is similar to the obligation to reverse an unjustified enrichment, since the latter obligation also arises *ex lege*. But unlike unjustified enrichment the delictual obligation to make reparation arises only when the loss has arisen as a result of the wrongful act of the person who caused the harm. It is only when a person has been at fault that the obligation to make reparation arises. In Scots law we use the term '*culpa*' to describe fault. *Culpa* covers both intentional and unintentional conduct which causes loss to another but before there is liability the law must regard the conduct as wrongous. This is encapsulated in the brocard *damnum injuria datum*, ie harm caused by wrongous conduct.

Some examples will make the point clearer. If A intentionally assaults B, causing him harm, A is under a delictual obligation to compensate B for his injuries: A is guilty of *culpa* because he deliberately intended to harm B by assaulting him, which the law regards as a wrongous act. If A drives his car carelessly on a public highway and as a result injures B, a pedestrian, then A is under a delictual obligation to compensate B for his injuries: A is guilty of *culpa* because of his careless driving which the law regards as a wrongous act. Thus we can say that modern Scots law begins from the premise that there is an obediential obligation on a person to make reparation to another who has sustained harm as a result of the *culpa* or fault of the wrongdoer, ie the wrongdoer's intentional or unintentional, but careless, conduct, which caused the harm. Its function is corrective justice – to put the victim, so far as an award of damages can, into the position he would have been if the wrong had never taken place.

It is not the case that a person who suffers loss as a result of another's intentional or unintentional, but careless, conduct will always be entitled to reparation. The act which causes the harm must be regarded by the law as wrongful (*injuria*). For policy reasons, certain acts are not regarded as wrongful in this sense. So for example, as we shall see,[1] A is free to undercut the prices of his competitor, B, even if B suffers economically; nor does it matter if A deliberately undercuts B's prices with the intention of putting B out of business. The reason for this is that in our society competition is to be encouraged even if persons suffer economically as a result. This is an example of *damnum absque injuria*, ie harm without wrongful conduct.

Before there is an obligation to make reparation, the victim must suffer harm. But, in addition, this harm must arise from an intrusion by the wrongdoer upon a right or interest of the victim which is recognised by the law as reparable. One of the fascinating aspects of the law of delict is to see when the courts are prepared to recognise interests as reparable and when they are not.

For example, the law has long recognised as reparable a person's right to physical integrity so that if there is an intrusion on that right as a result of culpable conduct, the wrongdoer must make compensation for pain and suffering (solatium) and any economic loss arising from the injuries sustained, such as loss of earning capacity. But the Scots law of delict has, hitherto, not recognised as a reparable interest a person's privacy per se[2] although it has, for example, protected a person's confidential information.[3]

An area which has caused controversy is whether the law should recognise as a reparable interest economic loss sustained by a person where the economic loss does not derive from injury to that person's body or damage to his property.[4] So, for example, if A carelessly damages an electric cable owned by B with the result that there is a loss of power to C's factory, should C be able to obtain compensation for his loss of production (pure economic loss) if the power cut did not cause any physical damage to the machinery in his factory? B, of course, can seek reparation from A in respect of the physical damage to B's cable.

Scottish lawyers maintain that Scots law is based on principle rather than remedies. It is probably true to argue that the modern

---

1 Page 35 below.
2 *Wainwright v Home Office* [2003] All ER (D) 279, discussed beyond p 34.
3 Breach of confidence is discussed beyond pp 30 ff.
4 This matter is discussed at length in Chapter 4.

Scots law of delict is based on the general principle of an obediential, *ex lege* obligation to make reparation for loss sustained as a
result of conduct which constitutes *culpa*. This was not always the
case and is, indeed, a comparatively recent development. In
medieval times, before there was a centralised system for the prosecution of criminal offences, there was a close relationship between
what would now be considered delictual actions and the enforcement of the criminal law. What we discover is that there were
specific remedies to deal with particular situations which were
common in those turbulent times. Stair lists the following:[1]

'besides those of a special name and nature, which are chiefly these, assythment, extortion, circumvention, spuilzie, intrusion, ejection, molestation,
breach of arrestment, deforcement, contravention, forgery, which comes in
more properly in the process of improbation'.

Three of these deserve further consideration to illustrate the close
relationship which existed at that time between delictual or quasi-
delictual liability and the enforcement of the criminal law.

Assythment was concerned with the regulation of acts which
caused death and was an attempt to avoid blood feuds. The remedy
of assythment was an action for a sum of money

'to be payit be the commirtaris of slaughter, to the kin, bairnis and friends
of any person that is slane ... gevin to thame in contentatioun of the hurt,
damnage and skeith sustenit be thane throw the wanting of the person who
is slane, and for the skaith incurrit be thame thairthrow, and for the paci-
fying of their rancor'.[2]

Several features of the action should be noted. There had to be a
crime which caused death or physical injury to the victim. The
action could be brought by any person, however remote, who was a
relative of the deceased or injured person. The damages depended
on the wrongdoer's means, ie they were not simply compensatory,
and, finally, no assythment was due if the wrongdoer was executed.
Assythment arose either if the wrongdoer was convicted and
because of his position received a lesser penalty than was due or if
there was no conviction and the family of the deceased issued a
document known as a letter of slains acknowledging receipt of
assythment and petitioning the Crown not to proceed with a prosecution. The latter situation was more important because it short
circuited the need for a criminal trial. With the establishment of a
centralised system of public prosecution it became contrary to pub-

1 *Institutions* IX, 5, 6.
2 Balfour *Practicks* p 516.

lic policy that the victim or his family should be able to circumvent the normal prosecution process by issuing letters of slains. In practice, actions for assythment died out though they were still theoretically possible if the wrongdoer had been prosecuted but had not suffered the due pains of the law. At the same time, the common law developed an action under which the spouse and ascendants and descendants of a person who had been killed as a result of the defender's *culpa* could obtain reparation in respect of the death, ie they could bring an action in delict.

An attempt to revive an action of assythment was made in *McKendrick v Sinclair*.[1] A workman was killed by an electric shock allegedly due to the negligence of his employer. He had financially supported his sister and two brothers. They could not bring an action in delict because at common law brothers and sisters of the deceased had no title to sue.[2] However, the Lord Advocate was not prepared to prosecute the defender or to concur if the relatives had sought a private prosecution. The old practice of letters of slains was inappropriate as the employer denied liability for culpable homicide. Accordingly, assythment would only have been available on the old authorities if there had been a conviction. As this was not the case, the action failed since it did not fall within the recognised parameters of the remedy.[3] Lord Simon of Glaisdale was prepared to dismiss the action on a more radical ground: that in spite of being a common law remedy assythment had fallen into desuetude, ie had become obsolescent:

'This Brunnhilde [assythment] would awake in our uncongenial modern Niebelheim. This Rip van Winkle would find *Eisten's* case firmly embodied in the law, that private prosecutions are extinct, that capital punishment for homicide has been abolished, and that damages are related to loss to the pursuer and not to the means of the defender. Even if this Sleeping Beauty were so attractive as to tempt your Lordships to favour her with your kisses she could not live happily ever after'.[4]

Assythment was finally laid to rest when it was abolished by section 8 of the Damages (Scotland) Act 1976 which extended title to sue in respect of the death of a relative to include the deceased's brothers and sisters[5] thus closing the lacuna revealed in the *McKendrick* case.

1 1972 SC (HL) 25, 1972 SLT 110.
2 *Eisten v North British Railway Co* (1870) 8 M 980.
3 *McKendrick v Sinclair* 1972 SLT 110 at 113 per Lord Reid and at 120 per Lord Kilbrandon, 1972 SC (HL) 25.
4 1972 SLT 110 at 117.
5 For discussion of the right to sue in respect of the death of a relative, see Chapter 13.

The second old remedy we should consider is contravention of lawburrows. This was a method of primitive law enforcement in the absence of an effective police force and system of public prosecution of criminal offences. If a person had reasonable grounds to believe that he or his family or their property was in danger from another person, he could apply to a court to have that person find caution (ie to lodge a sum of money in court) not to harm him or his family or their property. This was known as lawburrows. In other words, the defender was ordered not to molest the pursuer or the family or their property on pain of losing caution, ie the money lodged in court. If the defender contravened the non-molestation order, he could be sued in an action of contravention of lawburrows for forfeiture of the caution.[1] With the advent of effective law enforcement agencies, the use of lawburrows declined, though there is no doubt that the action is still technically competent.[2]

Finally there was the action of spuilzie. This action arose when the defender interfered with the possession of another's moveable property, for example, stole cattle or sheep. The pursuer was the owner of the property.[3] The action was to have the property returned, or its value. But the quasi-criminal nature of the action is illustrated by the fact that the pursuer was entitled to violent profits, ie all the profits which the pursuer might have made from the property while in possession of the defender. In many situations, spuilzie has been overtaken by the general principle of liability for *culpa*.[4]

We have seen, then, how these specific remedies had important quasi-criminal aspects. While it is clear that lawburrows and spuilzie remain, theoretically at least, part of Scots law, in practice they have largely been overtaken by the development of effective law enforcement agencies and the general principle of liability to make reparation for loss caused as a result of the defender's *culpa*. Stair laid the basis for the general principle of delictual liability when he recognised that to cause damage by delinquence gave rise to an obediential obligation to make reparation for the damage caused: *damnum injuria datum*. This was a general innominate remedy based on the defender's *culpa* which included deliberate as well

---

1 Lawburrows Acts 1429 and 1581.
2 On lawburrows generally, see 13 *Stair Memorial Encyclopaedia* paras 901–926; *Morrow v Neil* 1975 SLT (Sh Ct) 65; *Liddle v Morton* 1996 SLT 1143.
3 Though there is a dictum of the sheriff in *FC Finance Ltd v Brown & Son* 1969 SLT (Sh Ct) 41 that lawful *possession* of property was sufficient.
4 See, for example, *Harris v Abbey National plc* 1997 SCLR 359 (liability based on gratuitous deposit of property rather than spuilzie).

as careless conduct. Stair treated the nominate Scottish remedies as simply aspects of the general obligation to make reparation for loss caused by *culpa*.[1] This general obligation was accepted by the later institutional writers.[2] In attempting this synthesis, reliance was, of course, placed on Roman law and in particular liability under the Lex Aquilia which included liability for unintentional, but careless, conduct.

Although the modern Scots law of delict can be traced back to the institutional writers, their treatment is not extensive. Instead, the principles of the law of delict are largely the creation of the courts. The judges have had to develop the law to take account of the increase of potential injury to persons and damage to property created by industrialisation, mass production and distribution of goods, easier access to information, and the motor car. At the same time, they have also appreciated that there must be limits on a person's liability, particularly for unintentional conduct, if that person is to continue to engage in conduct which is socially and economically desirable, even if it is potentially harmful. The traditional Scots law solution has been to restrict liability by insisting that it is only triggered by the defender's fault and by refusing to recognise certain kinds of harm as reparable interests. This book is largely concerned with the rules of common law and statute which have developed to achieve this balance. However, in some areas it has been considered socially and economically desirable that persons should recover compensation for physical injury or damage to property without the need to establish fault on the part of the defender. While the concept of *culpa* has proved flexible enough to create liability where the degree of moral blame on the part of the defender is small,[3] nevertheless, some degree of fault is required.[4] Accordingly, legislation has been necessary to introduce into Scots law what is known as strict liability, ie where a person can be liable in delict for breach of duties imposed by a statute without the need for the person who suffers the injury or damage to establish fault. In a modem context, it is therefore important to discuss the princi-

---

1 *Stair* I, 9, 2.
2 See, for example, Erskine *Institute* III, 1.
3 Particularly as the criterion for fault in the context of unintentional conduct is the failure to reach the standards of the reasonable person, as opposed to the standards which the particular defender could morally be expected to reach: see Chapter 5 below.
4 But, for example, where a person has used his property in a potentially very dangerous way, the degree of fault is small: *Kerr v Earl of Orkney* (1857) 20 D 298, 30 SJ 158: see pp 185 ff below.

ples of strict liability in relation to the breach of statutory duties imposed by some, at least, of the most important statutes.

The Human Rights Act 1998 makes the European Convention on Human Rights directly effective in Scots – and English – domestic law. As a consequence, the Convention is having a profound effect on how the law is being developed by the courts in such areas as protection of confidential information[1] and the delictual liability of state agencies.[2] Moreover, where a public authority has infringed a Convention right, the victim may be entitled to damages under the 1998 Act,[3] whether or not the violation of the Convention right amounts to a delict. It should be noted that damages are only available against a public authority, not a private individual. Detailed discussion of damages for breach of Convention rights is outwith the scope of this book.[4]

It is the author's primary intention to concentrate on the common law principles which underlie delictual liability for *culpa*, ie intentional and unintentional wrongdoing. These are becoming more difficult to explain in a coherent way. While it has always been accepted that the imposition of a duty of care in novel situations involves the courts making decisions on grounds of legal policy,[5] once that decision was made the rules of the law of delictual liability could be applied more or less mechanically to determine whether or not the defender was liable and the extent of that liability. However, it is now clear – particularly in the House of Lords – that the courts are prepared to abandon the logical application of these rules or make exceptions to these rules when their application would produce a result which is not conducive to the judges' conception of what is a 'fair' or 'just' result or what is in accordance with 'practical' or 'distributive' justice. Such instances of judicial creativity are highlighted in the text.[6]

The book begins with a study of delictual liability for intentionally harmful conduct; the second part contains an analysis of the general principles of liability for unintentional, but careless, conduct; the third part considers delictual liability in the context of some important social and economic relationships. Included in this part is a chapter on defamation and verbal injury where different principles apply. The book ends with a short chapter on damages.

---

1 For discussion, see beyond pp 30 ff.
2 For discussion, see beyond pp 206 ff.
3 Human Rights Act 1998, s 8(3).
4 See, generally, *Damages under the Human Rights Act 1998* (Law Com No 266; Scot Law Com No 180).
5 See generally beyond Chapter 4.
6 See Joe Thomson 'Principle as Policy' (2003) 56 CLP 123.

Part I

INTENTIONAL DELICTS

Chapter 1. Intentional delicts in respect of persons and property 11

Chapter 2. The economic delicts and fraud 35

CHAPTER 1

Intentional delicts in respect of persons and property

INTRODUCTION

As we have seen,[1] *culpa* includes (a) deliberate conduct intended to harm the victim or the victim's property and (b) unintentional, but careless, conduct which has harmed the victim or the victim's property. In the case of unintentional conduct, the range of victims is prima facie indeterminate, ie it could potentially include any person who has been harmed by the conduct. Because of this, the law has had to invent devices for limiting the number of persons who are entitled to sue in delict if they suffer harm as a result of another's careless conduct. The most important of these devices is the concept of a duty of care:[2] it is only a person to whom the defender owes a duty of care who can sue in delict for harm arising from the defender's careless conduct.[3]

Where an act is done deliberately to harm a particular person, there is not the same degree of difficulty since the potential pursuer is normally determinate:[4] the pursuer is the person whom the defender *intended* to harm by his conduct and there is no need to invoke the concept of a duty of care. Intentional delicts in relation to persons and property are discussed in this chapter.

---

1 Page 1 above.
2 There are other devices such as remoteness of injury and causation: see pp 131 ff and Chapter 6 below.
3 The duty of care is discussed at Chapter 3 below.
4 There can be cases where this might not be so: A may intend to harm B by blowing up B's house but injure C instead; while it is thought that A will be liable to C, such cases are rare in practice.

B. INTENTIONAL DELICTS RELATING TO PERSONS

(1) Assault

'Everyone who lives under the protection of the law has an absolute right to the safety of his person; and wherever this right is invaded there is in Civil law a provision for redress of injury, as well as in penal law a punishment for the crime.'[1] A physical assault is a common law crime provided there is the necessary evil intent on the part of the perpetrator *(dolus)*. Assault also constitutes a delict. But even though an assault is not criminal because of the absence of *evil* intent, it is still an actionable delict provided the defender intended to invade the physical integrity of the pursuer. So where A playfully attacked B in order to make B engage in sport, it nevertheless constituted an actionable wrong even although it was done 'for a lark'.[2] If the assault does not result in serious physical harm, the damages awarded will not be substantial in spite of the insult caused to the victim.[3]

In *Wainwright v Home Office*[4] the House of Lords refused to extend the concept of assault to include the infliction of humiliation and distress without more. The plaintiffs claimed that they had suffered mental harm as a consequence of being asked to undress for the purpose of a strip search when visiting a relative in prison. Their Lordships maintained that there was no liability at common law for invasion of privacy. Where the only mental harm was distress as opposed to a recognised psychiatric disorder, there was no liability unless it could be shown that the defendant had known his conduct was unjustifiable and intended to cause mental harm. The strip searches were attempts to inhibit drug smuggling and there was no evidence that the defendants intended to cause distress. This was an English case but it is thought that a similar approach would be taken by the Scottish courts.

Where the 'victim' consents to the act, it does not amount to an assault for the purposes of delict[5] since the essence of the delict is *non-consensual* invasion of bodily integrity. Where this principle is

---

1 Bell *Principles* para 2028.
2 *Reid v Mitchell* (1885) 12 R 1129.
3 See, for example, *Downie v Chief Constable of Strathclyde Police* 1997 SCLR 603 (the pursuer was awarded £1,500 in respect of an assault by two policemen; the victim had recovered without the need of medical treatment).
4 [2003] All ER (D) 279.
5 In criminal law, if there is evil intent on the part of the accused, the consent of the 'victim' is irrelevant: a person cannot consent to a crime: *Smart v HM Advocate* 1975 JC 30, 1975 SLT 65.

important is in respect of medical procedures. If a doctor or dentist carries out a medical procedure on an adult[1] without the patient's consent, then the doctor or dentist is liable to make reparation.[2] Although this will usually not be a crime because of the absence of evil intent on the part of the doctor or dentist, it is still a delict. The patient can obtain reparation not only for any resulting patrimonial loss but also for *contumelia,* ie the insult suffered as a result of the non-consensual invasion of bodily integrity. The fact that the procedure was carried out for the patient's benefit is irrelevant.[3]

The question then arises as to when the patient's consent is valid in order that the doctor or dentist concerned can avoid potential delictual liability. It is clear that a patient must be given sufficient information upon which to give consent. All medical and dental procedures involve a risk to the patient even if *properly* carried out, for example, side effects of a drug or an operation or other medical procedure. In the United States,[4] there has evolved a doctrine known as 'informed consent'. Under this doctrine, if the patient is not informed of all the risks inherent in the proposed medical procedure which a reasonable *patient* should know, then the patient's apparent consent is vitiated and the doctor or dentist can be sued for assault.

An attempt to introduce this doctrine into English law was rejected by a majority of the House of Lords in *Sidaway v Board of Governors of the Bethlem Royal Hospital.*[5] Instead, it was held that a doctor need only disclose to a patient the risks inherent in a medical procedure which are regarded by *a responsible body of medical opinion* as proper to disclose. Two important points follow. First, provided the doctor or dentist has disclosed those risks which a responsible body of medical or dental opinion would disclose, the patient's consent is valid and the patient cannot sue in assault

1 A person under the age of 16 will have legal capacity to consent if the doctor or dentist is of the view that the young person is capable of understanding the nature and probable consequences of the medical treatment or procedure: Age of Legal Capacity (Scotland) Act 1991, s 2(4).

2 In an emergency, if the patient is, for example, unconscious, a doctor may proceed without the patient's consent if it is *necessary* for the patient's wellbeing to do so.

3 'Even when his or her own life depends on receiving medical treatment, an adult of sound mind is entitled to refuse it': *St George's Healthcare NHS Trust v S; R v Collins, ex parte S* [1998] 3 WLR 936, [1998] 3 All ER 673, CA at 685 per Judge LJ.

4 *Canterbury v Spence* (1972) 464 F 2d 772.

5 [1985] AC 871, [1985] 1 All ER 643, HL (Lord Scarman dissenting).

where she sustains harm, the risk of which it was *not* necessary to disclose. The harm must, of course, be inherent in the medical procedure when properly carried out; if the harm arose as a result of careless treatment, the patient can sue the doctor or dentist for breach of a duty of care since the patient has *not* consented to the risk of harm as a result of professional incompetence.[1] Second, if the doctor or dentist has not disclosed those risks which a responsible body of medical or dental opinion would disclose, then if the patient sustains *any* harm which is inherent in the medical procedure when properly carried out, the patient can sue the doctor or dentist; but it would appear from *Sidaway* that the patient sues for a breach by the doctor or dentist of the duty of care which they owe to their patients to disclose those risks inherent in the medical procedure which a responsible body of medical or dental opinion would disclose, ie for an unintentional wrong and not assault. In other words, the general principles of liability for *culpa* rather than assault apply to this particular issue. While *Sidaway* is an English case, it has been followed in Scotland.[2]

In practice, most patients simply sign a general consent form in respect of risks inherent in treatment. Nor is it clear when a reasonably prudent doctor should inform a patient of a particular risk inherent in a medical procedure. In *Sidaway* the risk of harm was slight, less than 1 per cent, but if it materialised the injury could have been severe. Yet the House of Lords took the view that since a majority of responsible medical practitioners would not have informed the patient of such a risk, no delictual liability was incurred.[3]

As we have seen, consent of the victim prevents delictual liability for assault from arising. This explains why there is no liability for assault in sports involving physical contact: boxing, rugby, soccer etc.[4] But the players give consent only to the physical contact inher-

---

1 On professional delictual liability, see Chapter 7 below.
2 *Moyes v Lothian Health Board* 1990 SLT 444. There it was observed by the Lord Ordinary (Caplan) at 447 that provided there was a failure to warn of risks, which amounted to a breach of a duty of care (ie that a responsible body of medical opinion would have disclosed some risks) it did not matter that the harm sustained by the pursuer was one the risk of which it was not necessary to disclose. The patient must show that he would not have agreed to the operation if the risks which should have been disclosed, had been disclosed.
3 It has been held that a significant risk of the order of 10 per cent should be disclosed while a risk of 0.2 per cent need not be disclosed: *Pearce v United Bristol NHS Trust* [1999] PIQR 53.
4 Cf non-physical sports, for example, golf: *Lewis v Buckpool Golf Club* 1993 SLT (Sh Ct) 43.

ent in the sport, so that there will be liability if injury is sustained as a result of conduct outwith the rules of the sport, if, for example, a rugby player punches, as opposed to tackles, an opponent. While an assault usually takes the form of physical contact this is not strictly necessary; thus to spit at a person or shake a fist in a threatening manner is an assault.[1]

There is a complete defence to an action of assault if it was the result of an unavoidable accident or carried out in self-defence. If the assault took place as a result of the pursuer's provocation, the damages can be reduced. 'No verbal provocation whatever can justify a blow ... But ... verbal provocation is a good ground for mitigating damages ... '.[2] The rationale is that since reparation for intentional wrong is based on *culpa*, the pursuer must come to the court with clean hands; if the pursuer's hands are not clean, the pursuer's damages can be reduced.[3]

Assaults on children by parents may be justified as an exercise of a parental right physically to chastise a child. The force used by a parent when physically chastising a child must be reasonable but it is irrelevant that a parent loses his or her temper at the time.[4] Parents can delegate the right physically to chastise their children to persons who have de facto care of the child.[5] In determining whether the assault is justifiable, the court must have regard to (a) the nature of what was done, the reason for it and the circumstances in which it took place; (b) its duration and frequency; (c) any effects – physical or mental – which it has been shown to have had on the child; (d) the child's age and (e) the child's personal characteristics (including sex and state of health) at the time of the parent's conduct.[6] If the assault on the child included or consisted of a blow to the head, shaking or the use of an implement, the court must hold that the assault was unjustifiable.[7] When the assault cannot be justified, the child will be able to sue the parent in delict. In

1 But not all conduct which causes humiliation and distress will be treated as an assault, for example requesting a person to undress for the purpose of a strip search: *Wainwright v Home Office* [2003] All ER (D) 279.
2 *Anderson v Marshall* (1835) 13 S 1130 at 1131 per the Lord President (Hope).
3 *Ross v Bryce* 1972 SLT (Sh Ct) 76.
4 *B v Harris* 1989 SCLR 644, 1990 SLT 208 (mother strapped her 7-year-old child who had called the mother 'a fucking bastard'). Cf *Cowie v Tudhope* 1987 GWD 12-395 (father hit 15-year-old son with the leg of a table).
5 *Stewart v Thain* 1981 JC 13, 1981 SLT (Notes) 2.
6 Criminal Justice (Scotland) Act 2003, s 51(1).
7 CJ(S)A 2003, s 51(3).

A v United Kingdom,[1] the European Court of Human Rights held
that the parent's 'reasonable chastisement' defence was a breach of
the child's right under article 3 to be protected from 'inhuman or
degrading treatment or punishment': in this case a caning. Such an
assault would not be justifiable in Scots law because it involves the
use of an implement.

Where an assault constitutes a crime, the victim may receive
compensation under the Criminal Injuries Compensation Scheme.

(2) Seduction and entrapment

Closely related to assault is the delict of seduction. In a case of
assault the essence of the delict is the invasion of a person's bodily
integrity without consent. Thus, for example, rape is actionable as
an assault because sexual intercourse was obtained without the
woman's consent. Conversely, if a woman consents to sexual intercourse, no assault is committed as she has consented. In the case of
seduction, the woman gives consent to sexual intercourse but her
consent is vitiated because it was obtained by the man as a result of
deception or abuse of position. In *Murray v Fraser*,[2] a young girl
who was naive in sexual matters allowed a trusted member of the
family to have sexual intercourse with her on his assurance that
nothing would happen to her; in fact she became pregnant. The
defender was held liable in seduction because he had abused a position of trust and had taken advantage of the girl's innocence. A
common example of deception was where a girl allowed a man to
have sexual intercourse with her because he promised to marry her
but had no intention to do so.[3]

Entrapment arises when a person has been fraudulently induced
to enter into a marriage which is void. The most common example
is when the defender purports to marry the pursuer, knowing that
he is already married to another and has therefore fraudulently mis-
represented that he was in a position validly to marry the pursuer.[4]

---

1 [1998] 2 FLR 959.
2 1916 SC 623.
3 It is thought that an action in seduction would continue to arise in these circumstances in spite of s 1(1) of the Law Reform (Husband and Wife) (Scotland) Act
   1984 which declares inter alia that a promise to marry does not create any rights
   or obligations; this is because the delict of seduction does not arise solely from the
   breach of promise.
4 See, for example, *Burke v Burke* 1983 SLT 331, OH.

(3) Enticement

It is a delict for A to entice B to leave B's family without justification. The most obvious reason why A would wish to entice B away from B's family is for sexual purposes but it could, for example, arise if A wished B to join A's religious sect. The pursuers are B's family.[1] There is no longer delictual liability if A induces B to leave his or her spouse.[2] A *husband* no longer has the right to sue his wife's paramour in damages;[3] these damages were awarded as solatium to the husband in respect of the unlawful sexual intercourse, ie his wife's adultery with the defender. It is arguable that a husband can still sue a man for solatium if he raped the husband's wife; the wife, of course, would sue the rapist in assault.

(4) Injuries to liberty

'Next to life is liberty; and the delinquence against it are restraint and constraint. And though liberty itself be inestimable, yet the damages sustained through these delinquencies are reparable.'[4] A slight infringement of liberty is prima facie actionable: so, for example, where a lady was alleged to have been detained against her will for a quarter of an hour by the manager of a hydropathic establishment, her action in delict was held to be relevant.[5] As a general principle, no one can be detained against his or her will; if this occurs, there is liability in delict. The loss suffered is both the loss of liberty and the affront caused to the pursuer. However, detention can be justified at common law if, for example, a store

---

1 It has been held that parents cannot sue for the loss of society of a child where the child has been removed from the parents as a result of intervention by the police in the interests of the child: *McKeen v Chief Constable, Lothian and Borders Police* 1994 SLT 93, OH. If the removal is not justified, the *child* may have the right to sue for infringement of liberty. In England, it was held in *Hamilton Jones v David and Snape* [2004] 1 All ER 657, that the loss of the company of a child is not actionable at common law.
2 Law Reform (Husband and Wife) (Scotland) Act 1984, s 2(2).
3 Divorce (Scotland) Act 1976, s 10.
4 *Stair* I, 9, 4.
5 *Mackenzie v Cluny Hill Hydropathic Co* 1908 SC 200, 15 SLT 518. In the course of his judgment, Lord Low said: 'It is averred that the manager detained this lady for fifteen minutes ... and refused to let her go until she made an apology. If that be true it was an outrage ... ': 1908 SC 200 at 206.

detective arrests a person suspected of shoplifting and detains that person for a reasonable time until the police arrive.[1]

In practice, cases of wrongful detention by ordinary members of the public are rare; instead, they arise when the person has been held under what purports to be lawful legal process. Even so, an action in delict may still arise, but the onus rests on the pursuer to show that the exercise by the authorities of their powers was neither reasonable or necessary and accordingly unjustified.[2]

Where a person is wrongfully imprisoned by a court, superior court judges are immune from liability. Inferior judges, such as justices of the peace or magistrates, can be liable if the sentence is imposed maliciously and without probable cause.[3] If, for example, a magistrate lacks jurisdiction, he will be acting ultra vires but there is no liability for a bona fide error in relation to the statutory interpretation of his jurisdiction. Before he can succeed, the pursuer must also prove that the magistrate was acting maliciously.[4] Where there has been a miscarriage of justice by the superior courts, the Secretary of State may make an *ex gratia* award of compensation to the victim.

(5) Harassment

Every individual has a right to be free from harassment.[5] Where a person pursues a course of conduct which amounts to harassment,

---

1 Where, as in the example, the arrest is made without a warrant, the defender must establish that the suspicions were justified: *Pringle v Bremner and Stirling* (1867) 5 M (HL) 55; *Dahl v Chief Constable, Central Scotland Police* 1983 SLT 420, OH. If an arrest is made under authority of a warrant, it is presumed that the detention was lawful and the onus rests on the pursuer to show that the detention was not justified.

2 See, for example, *Henderson v Chief Constable, Fife Police* 1988 SLT 361, OH. (Staff staged a 'work-in'. They were arrested. When they were put in police cells, a man was handcuffed and a woman told to remove her brassiere. The use of handcuffs was conceded to be unjustified. While it was normal practice to ask women to remove underwear to prevent suicide attempts, this was not justified in this case as the woman had co-operated, made no attempt to escape and was not a danger to herself or others.)

3 Criminal Procedure (Scotland) Act 1995, s 170(1).

4 *McPhee v Macfarlane's Exor* 1933 SC 163, 1933 SLT 148.

5 Protection from Harassment Act 1997, s 8(1). It is arguable that conduct which deliberately caused fear and alarm, even in the absence of physical harm, was delictual at common law: *Ward v Scotrail Railways Ltd* 1999 SC 255. Such conduct could certainly be controlled by an interdict (molestation) and, in theory, should have been sufficient cause for a claim in damages. It has been held in England that the infliction of humiliation and distress by conduct calculated to humiliate and distress, without more, does not give rise to liability at common law: *Wainwright v Home Office* [2003] All ER (D) 279.

the victim can bring a civil claim against him: this is known as an action of harassment.[1] Before the pursuer will succeed it must be established that the defender intended his behaviour to amount to harassment, or his behaviour occurred in such circumstances that a reasonable person would conclude that it amounted to harassment.[2] The course of conduct can include speech and must have occurred on at least two occasions.[3] If the action is successful, the court can award damages:[4] these can include compensation for anxiety and financial loss caused by the harassment.[5] The court can also grant interdict or a non-harassment order.[6] Breach of a non-harassment order is a criminal offence.[7] It is a defence to an action of harassment that the course of conduct was authorised by law or was pursued for the purpose of preventing or detecting crime or was reasonable in the particular circumstances of the case.[8] Harassment is *not* defined in the legislation but 'includes causing the person alarm or distress'.[9]

C. INTENTIONAL DELICTS RELATING TO PROPERTY

(1) Heritable property

(a) Trespass

It is often wrongly assumed that Scots law does not recognise the delict of trespass. Indeed, it has been judicially opined that the word 'trespasser' means nothing more in Scots law than 'a person who intrudes on the lands of another without that other's permission'.[10] However, as we shall see, a person who deliberately enters another's land may be interdicted from doing so again and is liable to pay damages if he has caused any harm to the property. Trespass is a *temporary* intrusion into property owned by another without

---

1 Protection from Harassment Act 1997, s 8(2).
2 PHA 1997, s 8(1)(a), (b).
3 PHA 1997, s 8(3).
4 PHA 1997, s 8(5)(a).
5 PHA 1997, s 8(6).
6 PHA 1997, s 8(5)(b). Although an interim interdict is competent, an interim non-harassment order is not: *Heenan v Dillon* 1999 Fam LR 62.
7 PHA 1997, s 9.
8 PHA 1997, s 8(4).
9 PHA 1997, s 8(3).
10 *Dumbreck v Robert Addie & Sons (Colleries) Ltd* 1928 SC 547 at 554 per the Lord President (Clyde), 1928 SLT 341.

the permission of the owner: for example, playing football in the owner's field or taking a short cut through his garden. Because heritable property is owned *a coelo usque ad centrum* (from the heavens to the centre of the earth) trespass protects an owner's air space as well as his land and the ground below his property. Thus, for example, the owner of a house successfully obtained an interdict preventing the respondent's crane from sweeping over his property when the respondent was building on adjacent land.[1] Because of this, statute provides that aircraft may fly over a person's land without liability for trespass.[2]

The primary remedy for trespass is interdict. No compensation is available unless there has been actual damage to the property as a result of the intrusion. There is therefore no liability for damages in Scots law merely for entering another's property. But the proprietor is entitled to use self-help to remove a trespasser provided it is reasonable in the circumstances; for example, the owner could ask a trespasser playing football in his field to leave but not threaten him with violence if the trespasser refuses to do so.[3] Interdict is an equitable remedy and is not granted automatically merely on proof of an unauthorised entry onto land. Before an interdict will be granted, further intrusions must be likely and the intention of the trespasser is important. Any potential damage to the land as a result of the trespass will also be a relevant consideration. In *Winans v Macrae*,[4] for example, a shooting tenant of a lease of 200,000 acres was, perhaps understandably, refused an interdict to prevent a cottar's pet lamb from entering the property.

In summary, apart from specific statutory offences, in Scots law trespass is not per se criminal, does not give rise to an action in damages unless actual damage has been done to the property and will only result in an interdict if likely to recur again and any potential damage is not *de minimis*. However, the landowner is allowed a reasonable degree of self-help to remove the trespasser.

In this section, trespass has been defined as *a temporary* intrusion onto land. If a person enters onto another's property with the intention of occupying it for an indefinite period, for example a squatter, he does commit a criminal offence under the Trespass (Scotland) Act 1865. If the owner is not in possession at the time,

---

1 *Brown v Lee Constructions Ltd* 1977 SLT (Notes) 61, OH.
2 Civil Aviation Act 1982, s 76.
3 If the self-help is excessive and results in physical harm to the trespasser, the owner can be liable for assault or negligence: *Revill v Newberry* [1996] QB 567, [1996] 1 All ER 291 (owner shot the trespasser!).
4 (1885) 12 R 1051.

the squatter is liable for the delict of intrusion; if the owner is in possession and has been wrongfully removed by the squatter, the squatter is liable for the delict of ejection. The rightful owner can seek summary ejection, violent profits[1] and compensation for actual losses incurred.

(b) Aemulatio vicini

When A owns land (X) which adjoins B's land (Y), A will be liable to B if he uses his land (X) in a way that is detrimental to B's enjoyment of his land (Y). Before A is liable for using his land *in aemulationem vicini*, A must use his land with the predominant motive of harming B and not to further A's legitimate interests. If A's predominant motive is not to harm B, then A cannot be liable for this delict but A's conduct may amount to nuisance.[2]

An example of use of land *in aemulationem vicini* would be where A intercepted water flowing below his land with the predominant purpose of preventing the water percolating onto his neighbour, B's, land.[3] However, when these facts were litigated in the English case of *Bradford v Pickles*,[4] the House of Lords held that *aemulatio vicini* was not part of English law. The case is important because Lord Watson, the Scottish Lord of Appeal in Ordinary, stated obiter that *aemulatio vicini* was also not part of Scots law.[5] This obiter dictum was contrary to institutional authority. In *Campbell v Muir*[6] where the defender spitefully exercised his right to fish from a boat in a river in such a way that it prevented anglers on the opposite bank from being able to cast their rods, the Lord President (Dunedin) held that the pursuer would have been entitled to interdict because 'the defender was on the particular occasion acting *in aemulationem vicini* against his neighbour's right, and that that was a just ground for complaint'.[7] In *More v Boyle*[8] it was accepted by the sheriff that the doctrine of *aemulatio vicini* is still part of Scots law.

---

1 Violent profits are the greatest profits the owner could have made if he was in actual possession of the land. It is thought that this should have been the remedy awarded in *Saeed v Waheed* 1996 SLT (Sh Ct) 39, 1995 SCLR 504, rather than damages for negligence.
2 On nuisance, see pp 190 ff below.
3 See Kames *Principles of Equity* (4th edn, 1800) p 42.
4 [1895] AC 587, HL.
5 [1895] AC 587 at 597–598.
6 1908 SC 387, 15 SLT 737.
7 1908 SC 387 at 393.
8 1967 SLT (Sh Ct) 38.

Liability arises only if it can be shown that the defender acted with the predominant motive of harming the pursuer. It is, of course, difficult to establish malice, so an objective assessment must be made of the defender's conduct in order to infer malice. But unlike nuisance, which is usually concerned with a continuing wrong,[1] liability for use of land *in aemulationem vicini* can arise from a single act of the defender provided the predominant motive of harm to the pursuer can be established.

(2) Moveable property

(a) Trespass

In *Leitch v Leydon*[2] the complainers sold soda water to their customers. Since the bottles were more expensive than the contents, it was a term of the contract with their customers that the complainers retained the ownership of the siphons which should be returned to them when the contents were finished. Instead, some customers went to the respondent to have the bottles filled with his soda water. The House of Lords held that the complainers were not entitled to an interdict preventing the respondent from filling their bottles with soda water. While the complainers might have an action for breach of contract against their customers, the respondent had not incurred any delictual liability in filling the bottles with soda water at the request of the complainers' customers who had lawful possession of the siphons. In the course of his speech, Viscount Dunedin said that the concept of trespass to moveables[3] 'in a Scottish lawyer's mouth is a perfectly unmeaning phrase'.[4]

Nevertheless, where there have been 'sit-ins' on board a ship[5] or offshore oil installations,[6] it has been held that the delict of trespass was committed even although neither the ship nor off-shore oil installations constitute heritable property. The Lord Ordinary (Dunpark) maintained that 'Scots law offers remedies for the unlawful *occupation* of property, be it heritable or moveable'.[7] It

---

1 See pp 190 ff below.
2 1931 SC (HL) 1.
3 Delictual liability would arise if the respondent had intended to 'pass off' the soda water as that of the complainer. On passing off, see p 27 below.
4 1931 SC (HL) 1 at 12.
5 *Phestos Shipping Co Ltd v Kurmiawan* 1983 SC 165, 1983 SLT 388.
6 *Shell UK Ltd v McGillivray* 1991 SLT 667.
7 *Phestos Shipping Co Ltd v Kurmiawan* 1983 SLT 388 at 391.

would appear, therefore, that where the trespass consists of the unlawful occupation of moveable property, for example, a car or caravan, a ship or an oil installation, there is delictual liability even though the property concerned is technically moveable rather than heritable. Where the moveable property cannot be occupied, like the soda siphons in *Leitch v Leydon*,[1] merely to handle the property does not per se constitute the delict of trespass.

(b) Wrongful interference with moveable property

Unless moveable property is actually occupied, in Scots law the delict of trespass is not available to the owner. This does not mean that the owner of a moveable is without legal redress if a person wrongfully interferes with the property. But the owner's remedy may lie in areas of the law other than the law of delict. Consider the following examples:

(1) A owns a horse. B steals the horse. Under the law of property, A is entitled to sue B for the return of the horse, ie A can vindicate (claim ownership of) the horse. If B had sold the horse to C, a bona fide purchaser for value, A can still vindicate against C because a *vitium reale* attaches to the horse.

(2) A owns a horse. B steals the horse and sells it to C. C slaughters the horse and boils it down to make glue. Under the law of property, the glue belongs to C. A can no longer vindicate since the horse, ie A's property, no longer exists. What remedies are available to A? First, if the delict still exists, A could sue B for spuilzie.[2] Second, he may have a delictual action against C on the general principles of *culpa*. If C knew the horse belonged to A, then A can sue C for intentionally destroying the horse. But even if C did not know that the horse belonged to A, A may be able to sue C if, in the circumstances, C was at fault in going ahead in boiling down the horse without inquiring whether or not B was the animal's true owner. Thus, in *Faulds v Townsend*,[3] a thief stole a horse which he sold in the middle of the night to the defender who turned the unfortunate animal into chemicals. Because of the circumstances of the sale and the fact that the horse was in good condition, the

---

1 1931 SC (HL) 1.
2 See p 5 above. For an attempt to revive the delict see *FC Finance Ltd v Brown & Son* 1969 SLT (Sh Ct) 41.
3 (1861) 23 D 437, 33 SJ 224.

court held that the defender was under a duty to inquire as to the ownership of the horse; he had not done so and was therefore at fault and the owner could sue for damages under the general principles of *culpa*.[1] Finally, even if fault could not be established, on principles of unjustified enrichment, A may seek recompense from C in respect of his use of the horse and, indeed, could obtain any profits which C made from the sale of the glue.

(3) The modern equivalent of the horse is, of course, the motor car. As a general rule, the same principles would apply if A's car was stolen. Difficulties can arise where A is technically the owner of a car, for example a finance company, the car being purchased by B, a hirer, on a contract of hire purchase; what is A's remedy if B sells the car in breach of the hire contract to C, a third party? These difficulties are illustrated by *FC Finance v Langtry Investment Co Ltd*[2] FC Finance owned a motor car which was hired to Allan under a contract of hire purchase. In breach of the contract, Allan sold the car to McKay who traded as Medwin Motors. McKay sold the car on hire purchase to Kennedy. The hire purchase was financed by Langtry Investment Co and Kennedy paid the instalments. Part III of the Hire Purchase Act 1964 provides an exception to the *nemo dat quod non habet* principle and Kennedy as an innocent private purchaser acquired a good title to the car.[3] Therefore FC Finance could not vindicate against Kennedy. McKay was a man of straw. FC Finance had registered the car with HP Information Ltd; any finance company could telephone HP Information Ltd and discover, before buying the car, whether it was subject to an existing hire purchase agreement. These complex facts are summarised in the diagram on page 26 below.

FC Finance's primary remedy was to sue Allan for breach of contract. However, Allan had emigrated to Canada. In these circumstances, FC Finance sought redress against Langtry Investment. It was held that there was no duty on Langtry Investment to check with HP Information Ltd before financing

---

1 Ie because of his careless conduct in not satisfying himself as to the true ownership of the horse.
2 1973 SLT (Sh Ct) 11.
3 Before Part III of the 1964 Act applies, there must be a valid contract of hire between the finance company and the person who sells the car to the bona fide private purchaser: if the contract of hire is void the 1964 Act does not apply and the bona fide private purchaser does not acquire title to the property: *Shogun Finance Ltd v Hudson (FC)* [2004] 1 All ER 215.

Kennedy's hire purchase of the motor car. But because Medwin Motors had offered them cars subject to subsisting hire purchase agreements on previous occasions, Langtry Investment should have been on their guard and were therefore at fault – like the defender in *Faulds v Townsend*[1] – for not making inquiries. Therefore they were liable on general principles of *culpa*. The parties agreed that if the defenders were liable, the measure of damages would be the balance of the outstanding hire purchase payments owed by Allan to FC Finance.

This decision is controversial. The pursuer's loss was purely economic – there was no physical damage to the car. As we shall see below, in cases of unintentional wrongs the courts have been reluctant to allow recovery for pure economic loss. It is therefore doubtful whether there was sufficient proximity between the parties to impose a duty of care on the defender to prevent the pursuer suffering pure economic loss as a result of the defender's careless conduct. This might have been a case where spuilzie should have been resurrected, since the defender had wrongfully interfered with the possession of the pursuer's moveable property. Another solution might have been for the pursuer to have sued in unjustified enrichment for the amount that the defender was *lucratus* as a result of the mistaken dealings with the car. Whatever the answer, the case is an important example of how the law of delict cannot be treated in isolation from other areas of law when considering the difficult issues that can arise in modern commercial dealings.

1 (1861) 23 D 437, discussed at p 23 above.

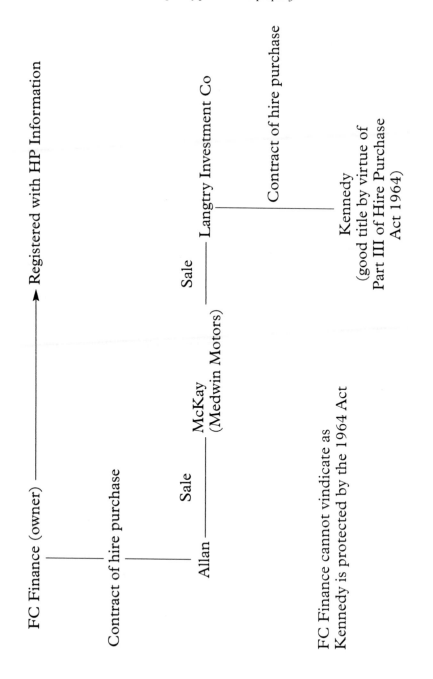

FC Finance (owner) ──────────▶ Registered with HP Information

Contract of hire purchase

Allan ────── Sale ────── McKay (Medwin Motors) ────── Sale ────── Langtry Investment Co

Contract of hire purchase

Contract of hire purchase

Kennedy
(good title by virtue of
Part III of Hire Purchase
Act 1964)

FC Finance cannot vindicate as
Kennedy is protected by the 1964 Act

(c) Goodwill – passing off

The goodwill and reputation of a business can be a very valuable asset. Important elements of goodwill are the marketing devices used to enable customers to recognise the product and distinguish it from the products of competitors. These devices include trade names, personal and geographical names associated with a product, for example Rennie Mackintosh jewellery[1] or Glenfiddich whisky,[2] and the 'get up' of the product, for example a distinctive container.[3] If a competitor markets a product using a similar name or get up, this may cause confusion among actual or potential customers resulting in damage to the goodwill of the original trader through loss of custom or loss of reputation if the rival product is inferior. In order to protect a trader's goodwill, the delict of 'passing off' has been developed.

Goodwill consists of the features of a business which attract customers to trade with that business. Before there is an action for passing off it must be established that there is a close association between the trader and the particular device which identifies the product or services for existing or potential customers, ie that the device is part of the goodwill of the trader. It may be very difficult, particularly in relation to ordinary words, as opposed to invented words, to show that the word is a marketing device peculiar to the goodwill of a particular trader. Some words, such as 'hoover', may become part of ordinary usage and lose their distinctive quality of being associated with a particular manufacturer. On the other hand, other words, such as 'Scotch', while describing a geographical situation, may, as in relation to whisky, acquire a secondary meaning peculiar to a particular product. Similar difficulties can arise if a trader claims that the shape of a product is sufficiently distinctive to constitute a protectable device; but a lemon-shaped container of lemon juice has been held to have a secondary meaning associated with a particular product.[4] Once it is established that the device is part of his goodwill, the law will protect the goodwill of the trader from being undermined by a competitor passing off his own product by using a similar name or get up.

---

1 *Carrick Jewellery Ltd v Ortak* 1989 GWD 35-1624, OH.
2 *William Grant & Sons Ltd v William Cadenhead Ltd* 1985 SC 121, 1985 SLT 291.
3 *John Haig & Co Ltd v Forth Blending Co Ltd* 1954 SC 35, 1954 SLT 2, OH (Dimple bottle); *Reckitt and Colman Products Ltd v Borden Inc* [1990] 1 All ER 873, HL (Jif plastic lemon).
4 *Reckitt and Colman Products Ltd v Borden Inc* [1990] 1 All ER 873, HL.

The criteria of the delict were articulated by Lord Diplock in the leading case of *Erven Warnink BV v J Townend & Sons (Hull) Ltd*[1] Passing off consists of:

'(1) a misrepresentation (2) made by a trader in the course of trade, (3) to prospective customers of his or ultimate consumers of goods or services supplied by him, (4) which is calculated to injure the business or goodwill of another (in the sense that this is a reasonably foreseeable consequence) and (5) which caused actual damage to a business or goodwill of the trader by whom the action is brought or (in a *quia timet* action) will probably do so'.[2]

The essence of the delict is that by using the same or similar device which forms part of the goodwill of the pursuer, the defender misrepresents his product as that of the pursuer, thus causing actual or potential damage to the pursuer's business. There is little difficulty if the exact device is used: but an action of passing off will lie even where there are differences provided there is likelihood of confusion among a substantial number of the pursuer's customers or potential customers. If there is no likelihood of confusion, then there is no passing off even if, for example, the same name is used.[3] Thus, in *Dunlop Pneumatic Tyre Co v Dunlop Motor Co*[4] it was held that the pursuers, a large manufacturer of tyres, would not be confused with a small family-owned garage of a similar name in Kilmarnock. There is less likelihood of confusion where the products do not belong to a 'common field of activity'. In *Scottish Milk Marketing Board v Dryborough & Co Ltd*,[5] for example, the pursuer, who marketed 'Scottish Pride' butter, failed to interdict the defender from selling 'Scottish Pride' lager since it was unlikely that the products – being so different – would be confused. Although confusion is more likely to be established where there is a common field of activity, a common field of activity is not essential where the device to be protected is, for example, a household name.[6] If there is sufficient

---

1 [1979] AC 731 at 742, [1979] 2 All ER 927, HL. This approach was applied by the Second Division of the Inner House of the Court of Session in *Lang Bros Ltd v Goldwell Ltd* 1980 SC 237, 1982 SLT 309.

2 For a slightly different formulation, see also the speech of Lord Fraser of Tullybelton in *Erven Warnink BV v J Townend & Sons (Hull) Ltd* [1979] AC 731 at 755 and 756, [1979] 2 All ER 927, HL.

3 *Harrods Ltd v Harrodian School* [1996] RPC 697, (1996) Times, 3 April, CA.

4 1907 SC (HL) 15, 15 SLT 362.

5 1985 SLT 253, OH.

6 In *Lego System A/S v Lego M Lemelstrich Ltd* [1983] FSR 155, a toy manufacturer successfully obtained an injunction preventing the manufacturers of irrigation equipment from using the name 'Lego' on the basis that their goodwill might be affected if they entered the same type of business as the defendant sometime in the future.

likelihood of confusion, it may not be permissible for the defender to use his own name.[1]

In *John Haig & Co Ltd v Forth Blending Co Ltd*[2] the pursuers established that a particular type of bottle (Dimple) was distinctive to their product's get up and successfully interdicted a rival from using a similarly shaped bottle in spite of its having a different label and stopper. The court was satisfied that when in use in a bar, there was a sufficient degree of likelihood of confusion to constitute passing off.

It has been held that manufacturers of Scotch whisky may interdict persons from exporting Scotch whisky which they know will be mixed with local spirit abroad and passed off in the foreign country as the genuine article.[3] Similarly, passing off actions will lie where a spirit not distilled in Scotland is marketed as Scotch.[4] In *Lang Bros Ltd v Goldwell Ltd*[5] the defender manufactured 'Wee McGlen', a whisky Mac, a blend of Scotch whisky and ginger wine which was made in England. This get up consisted of various words and phrases as well as a caricature of a betartaned Scotsman. The Lord Ordinary (Wheatley), a well-known teetotaller, held that the action was relevant. The get up could mislead the public into thinking that the whole product, ie the ginger wine as well as the whisky, was made in Scotland. This misrepresentation as to the origin of the ginger wine could endanger the reputation and goodwill which attaches to Scotch whisky because of its origins. This decision seems to push the delict to its limits since the defender was not misrepresenting his product as Scotch whisky nor was the get up proved to be part of the exclusive goodwill of the pursuer.[6]

At one time it was thought that passing off was simply a particular aspect of the delict of fraud. This is no longer thought to be sound – at least if the only remedy sought is interdict as opposed to damages. Although the misrepresentation which constitutes passing off must be 'calculated to injure' the pursuer's business or goodwill, it is enough if this is a reasonably foreseeable

---

1 *Parker-Knoll Ltd v Knoll International* [1962] RPC 265, HL.
2 1954 SC 35, 1954 SLT 2, OH.
3 *John Walker & Sons Ltd v Douglas Laing & Co* 1993 SLT 156, OH.
4 *John Walker & Sons Ltd v Douglas McGibbon & Co Ltd* 1972 SLT 128, OH; *John Walker & Sons Ltd v Henry Ost & Co Ltd* [1970] 2 All ER 106, [1971] 1 WLR 917. Nevertheless, the author has noted that 'House of Lords' whisky, sold in the Crush Bar at Covent Garden, is manufactured in England!
5 1980 SC 237, 1982 SLT 309.
6 See, further, H L MacQueen 'Wee McGlen and the Action of Passing Off' 1982 SLT (News) 225.

consequence of the misrepresentation.[1] In other words, the 'calculated to injure' element is objectively ascertained.

The primary remedy is interdict. Damages may be restricted to cases of actual fraud. It is extremely difficult to assess and quantify damages in respect of loss of custom, potential custom and goodwill.[2]

(d) Confidential information

Information can be very valuable. However, the law has not yet been prepared to regard information per se as a form of property.[3] Nevertheless, it is now clear that Scots law recognises a general obligation arising *ex lege* not to divulge information given in confidence.[4] But what is not clear is whether this obligation is delictual *stricto sensu* or whether, given the influence of equitable principles on the development of the obligation in English law,[5] it is better treated as an obligation *sui generis*. In these circumstances, only a basic outline of the law will be discussed in this section.[6]

The essence of the obligation is the duty not to disclose information given in confidence. There is generally no limit on the type of information which is protected; it is the fact that it is given in confidence which is important.[7] Information which has been protected includes sensitive government intelligence, trade secrets and personal information as to a person's sexual activities.

At first the obligation not to disclose information given in confidence arose from a contractual relationship between the parties. The classic example is, of course, employer and employee. In *Duke of Argyll v Duchess of Argyll*[8] the Duke of Argyll obtained an

1 *Erven Warnink BV v J Townend & Sons (Hull) Ltd* [1979] AC 731 at 742 per Lord Diplock.
2 On passing off generally, see 18 *Stair Memorial Encyclopaedia* paras 1451–1500.
3 *Grant v Allan* 1987 JC 71, 1988 SLT 11.
4 *Lord Advocate v Scotsman Publications Ltd* 1988 SLT 490 at 502–503 per Lord Justice Clerk (Ross), at 508–509 per Lord Dunpark and at 514 per Lord McDonald; 1989 SLT 705, HL at 708 per Lord Keith of Kinkel.
5 The view has been taken that the *substance* of the law is the same in both Scotland and England: *Lord Advocate v Scotsman Publications Ltd* 1989 SLT 705, HL at 708 per Lord Keith. It has been observed that this is a developing area of Scots law and could evolve differently from the law in England: *Quilty v Windsor* 1999 SLT 346 at 356 per the Lord Ordinary (Kingarth).
6 For a full account, see 18 *Stair Memorial Encyclopaedia* paras 1451–1500.
7 An employee may use information given in confidence by a former employer provided it is not a trade secret and there is no valid restrictive covenant: *Faccenda Chicken Ltd v Fowler* [1987] Ch 117, [1986] 1 All ER 617, CA.
8 [1967] Ch 302, [1965] 1 All ER 611.

injunction [interdict] to prevent the Duchess divulging information as to his private life which he had given to her when they were married. While there is, of course, a contractual nexus between husband and wife, the obligation is also recognised where there is no contract between the parties but the relationship is clearly one of confidence, for example, doctor and patient, priest and parishioner, co-habitees whether heterosexual or homosexual, or even friends.[1] Confidentiality does not, however, attach to all acts of physical, ie sexual, intimacy: the degree of intimacy, the nature of the relationship of the parties and the effect of disclosure on third parties, for example children, are all relevant factors.[2] The transitory relationship between a prostitute and a customer in a brothel was not confidential and the fact that sexual activity has taken place does not per se create a relationship of confidentiality.[3]

It is therefore clear that if A gives information to B, where there is a confidential relationship between the parties, then even if there is no contract between A and B, B is under an obligation not to divulge the information. If B divulges the information to C, the question then arises whether C owes an obligation to A not to disclose the information. At first, the Scottish courts were reluctant to impose an obligation on C unless there was an agreement between A and C that the information was given in confidence.[4] It is now settled that C does owe an obligation to A if C knows or ought to have known that the information was confidential.[5] The test would appear to be that an obligation arises if a reasonable person would have realised in all the circumstances that he/she was bound to treat the information as confidential.

---

1 *Stephens v Avery* [1988] Ch 449, [1988] 2 All ER 477; *Barrymore v News Group Newspapers Ltd* [1997] FSR 600, Ch D.
2 *A v B plc* [2003] QB 195 (married professional footballer's adulterous affairs with two women not confidential).
3 *Theakston v MGN Ltd* [2002] EWHC 137.
4 *Roxburgh v Seven Seas Engineering Ltd* 1980 SLT (Notes) 49, OH.
5 *Lord Advocate v Scotsman Publications Ltd* 1988 SLT 490, affd 1989 SLT 705, HL. In *Douglas v Hello Ltd (No 6)* [2003] 3 All ER 996, the defendant knew that the plaintiffs had agreed that another magazine had an exclusive right to publish the plaintiffs' wedding photographs. A paparazzo managed to evade the security at the wedding and took unauthorised photographs which the defendant published. The photographic representation of the wedding was held to have the necessary quality of confidence and could be protected as a trade secret. Given that the defendant knew about the arrangements for the exclusive right to publish the wedding photographs, as a reasonable person he must have known that the paparazzo's photographs constituted a breach of confidence, so that the defendant's publication of those photographs was in turn a breach of confidence.

The 'reasonable person' test explains not only why, in the example above, C owes an obligation to A not to disclose the information but also why B owes a similar obligation to A. For where there is an agreement between A and B not to disclose the information, or where there is a confidential relationship with or without a contractual nexus, a reasonable person in B's position would realise that the information is given in confidence. It is therefore submitted that there should only be one test for determining whether a person owes an obligation not to disclose information, ie whether in all the circumstances a reasonable person in that position would have realised that the information was confidential. Factors to be considered would include the nature of the information itself, for example love letters or government information; the relationship between the parties, for example employer and employee or lovers; whether or not there is an express statement as to confidentiality[1] or an implied term as to confidentiality between the parties; whether or not the information was obtained by illegal or improper means, for example industrial espionage or computer 'hacking'.[2] If the 'reasonable person' test is satisfied, then the obligation not to divulge the information arises.

The obligation not to disclose information only continues if the information remains confidential. But merely because the information is known to some other people, for example specialists in a scientific field, does not prevent the information being confidential. In *Exchange Telegraph Co Ltd v Giulianotti*,[3] the pursuer transmitted the results of races to subscribers. It was held that the information was still confidential even though the spectators at the event knew the result. But if the information is clearly in the public domain, it is no longer confidential and the obligation ceases to exist.[4] Thus, if A gives confidential information to B, and A later divulges the information to the world, B's obligation not to disclose the information comes to an end.[5] This principle has also been extended to the following situation: A gives information in confidence to B and B gives the information to C in circumstances where C as a

---

1   The fact that the parties considered themselves to be under an obligation of confidence is important but not decisive. The test is ultimately objective: *De Maudsley v Palumbo* [1996] FSR 447, (1995) Times, 19 December, Ch D.

2   See further 'Breach of Confidence' (SLC no 90; Cmnd 9385 (1984)) p 64.

3   1959 SC 19, 1959 SLT 293, OH.

4   *Attorney-General v Guardian Newspapers Ltd (No 2)* [1990] 1 AC 109, [1988] 3 All ER 545, HL.

5   *O Mustad & Son v S Allcock & Co Ltd and Dosen* [1963] 3 All ER 416, [1964] 1 WLR 109, HL.

reasonable person would realise it is confidential; if B divulges the information to the world, then C's obligation comes to an end. A will, of course, have a remedy in damages against B for breach of confidence.[1]

Although it has been held in England that there can be liability for unintentional breach of confidence,[2] it is thought that a pursuer would be unlikely to obtain damages in Scots law unless the defender intended to breach the confidence.[3]

The obligation not to disclose information given in confidence is not absolute. A defence is available if disclosure was in the public interest. Thus disclosure is justifiable if the information concerned the commission of a crime or a civil wrong.[4] Information disclosed to a public official or agency which could take appropriate action, for example the police, is more likely to provide justification than simple disclosure to the media.[5] The courts must engage in a balancing exercise between the public interest in protecting confidential information and the public interest in access to information which should be known. In *X v Y*[6] a newspaper disclosed the identity of two doctors suffering from AIDS. The newspaper argued that it was in the public interest that patients should know the HIV status of their medical practitioners. In rejecting this defence, the court took the view that the public interest in maintaining confidentiality prevailed because it encouraged persons suffering from AIDS, including doctors, to seek treatment. In the case of government information, the Crown cannot obtain an interdict merely because the information is confidential: the public interest in open government will justify disclosure.[7] However, the

---

1 *Attorney-General v Guardian Newspapers Ltd (No 2)* [1990] 1 AC 109, [1988] 3 All ER 545, HL. A could not obtain an interdict against B to prevent further disclosure since the information was no longer confidential.

2 *Seager v Copydex Ltd* [1967] 2 All ER 415, [1967] 1 WLR 923, CA.

3 Since the test of confidentiality is that of the reasonable person, ie an objective test, it is theoretically possible that a person could breach the obligation when he or she did not subjectively know that the information was confidential, ie because the person had not in fact reached the standard of the reasonable person.

4 *Initial Services Ltd v Putterill* [1968] 1 QB 396, [1967] 3 All ER 145, CA.

5 *British Steel Corpn v Granada Television Ltd* [1981] AC 1096, [1981] 1 All ER 417, HL. The publication by a newspaper of confidential information relating to a celebrity model's drug addiction has been held to be in the public interest: *Campbell v Mirror Group Newspapers Ltd* [2003] QB 633.

6 [1988] 2 All ER 648, [1988] RPC 379.

7 *Lord Advocate v Scotsman Publications Ltd* 1988 SLT 490, affd 1989 SLT 705, HL.

public interest in disclosure will be 'trumped' if the disclosure of the information would be damaging to national security.[1]

The primary remedy for breach of confidence is interdict.[2] Damages are possible though difficult to assess. The person divulging the information may be required to account for any profits made from doing so.[3]

This is an area where the European Convention on Human Rights is now playing a particularly significant role. Article 8(1) provides that everyone has the right to respect for his private and family life, his home and correspondence. On the other hand, article 10(1) gives everyone the right to freedom of expression. It is, however, expressly provided by article 10(2) that the right to freedom of expression must be exercised responsibly, taking into account inter alia restrictions which are necessary in a democratic society for the reputation or the rights of others. The potential conflict between these rights is readily apparent.

In *Wainwright v Home Office*[4] the House of Lords held that English law did not have to accept some high-level legal principle of privacy in order to comply with article 8: it is thought that this would also be the position in Scots law. But the protection of confidential information will often have the effect of protecting the privacy of a person's private life[5]. In *A v B plc*[6] the Court of Appeal held that in a conflict between an individual's right to respect for his private life under article 8 and freedom of expression under article 10, any interference with the freedom of the press had to be justified irrespective of whether the publication of the information was in the public interest. This is because the victim of a breach of confidence is, of course, entitled to damages if the press cannot establish that the disclosure was justified. Where the material published is untrue a person's article 8 right will be protected by the

---

1   *Attorney-General v Guardian Newspapers Ltd (No 2)* [1990] 1 AC 109, [1988] 3 All ER 545, HL. Although the information in that case was prima facie damaging to national security, by the time the case reached the House of Lords knowledge of the material was so widespread that an injunction on further serialisation of the information was refused; in other words, the information was no longer confidential.

2   The general criteria for granting interdict must, of course, be present: see, for example, *Waste Systems International Inc v Eurocare Environmental Services Ltd* 1999 SLT 198, OH.

3   *Attorney-General v Guardian Newspapers Ltd (No 2)* [1990] 1 AC 109, [1988] 3 All ER 545, HL.

4   [2003] All ER (D) 279.

5   *Douglas v Hello* [2003] 3 All ER 996.

6   [2003] QB 195.

law of defamation[1]. The restrictions of the law of defamation on the right of expression are recognised by article 10(2).

In *Peck v United Kingdom*[2] the applicant had been filmed on CCTV walking around his home town carrying a knife; he intended to kill himself. The police were alerted and he was saved. The local council allowed the footage to be used by the media to promote the utility of CCTV. The material was not defamatory and its publication did not constitute a breach of confidential information. Nevertheless the European Court of Human Rights held that there had been a breach of article 8(1) as the disclosure of the footage could not be justified as being in the public interest since the applicant had not been engaged in the commission of a crime. The applicant was awarded damages against the government.

This case illustrates how an action for damages may lie when there is a breach of the Convention even though the defender's conduct which constituted the breach would not be regarded as delictual under Scots law. This issue arose again in *Martin v McGuiness*.[3] The pursuer claimed that the conduct of the defender's private investigator in pretending to be a former army colleague when questioning his wife in their home, causing her distress, constituted a breach of his rights under article 8(1). The court held that while the investigator's conduct could amount to an infringement of the pursuer's article 8(1) right, nevertheless it was open to the defender to argue that it was a reasonable and proportionate step to take to preserve his rights in accordance with article 8(2) (no unlawful interference with a person's article 8(1) right if the infringement is for the protection of the rights of others). In these circumstances the court did not have to answer the difficult question of the nature of the pursuer's remedy if there had been a breach. As we have seen,[4] damages under the Human Rights Act 1998 can only be awarded against a public authority and there was no existing delictual remedy apt to provide redress in relation to the infringement of privacy which Martin had suffered.

---

1 On the law of defamation see beyond Chapter 15.
2 (2003) EHRR 41.
3 2003 SCLR 548.
4 See p 7 above.

CHAPTER 2

The economic delicts and fraud

A. THE ECONOMIC DELICTS

(1) Introduction – the general principle

In a free market, competition is regarded as essential and in the public interest. This can result in one business being successful while another goes to the wall. The common law therefore took the view that A was entitled to harm B economically provided A used lawful means, for example undercutting the price of his product, in order to do so. Towards the end of the nineteenth century and during the twentieth century, the courts developed a range of delicts which set parameters beyond which parties could not wield their economic and social power. These are known as the economic delicts. Since then, important statutory provisions and principles of EU law have been introduced directly to regulate competition, for example the Office of Fair Trading. Competition law is outwith the scope of this book. The economic delicts remain important and will be treated in this chapter.

The basic principle was laid down by the House of Lords in *Allen v Flood*.[1] In this case boilermakers objected to the practice of employing shipwrights to repair ironwork on board ships. The plaintiffs were shipwrights who were employed to repair woodwork on certain ships. Members of the boilermakers' union discovered that they had previously been employed by another employer to repair ironwork on ships. Incensed, a trade union representative approached the current employer of the shipwrights and informed him that unless he dismissed the plaintiffs, his other employees would strike. This was done maliciously, to punish the plaintiffs. The employer dismissed the plaintiffs who brought the action against the trade union representative.

Three points should be noticed. First, the case proceeded on the basis that there was no conspiracy, ie no agreement among the

1 [1898] AC 1, HL.

boilermakers that they would strike; it was simply the individual trade unionist who said that there would be a strike. Second, if there had been a strike, the employees would have terminated their contracts of employment lawfully. Third, when the employer dismissed the plaintiffs he did so by lawfully terminating their contracts. In other words, the individual trade unionist used lawful means (the threat of a lawful strike) to compel the employer to use lawful means (the lawful dismissal) to harm the plaintiffs economically (the loss of their employment). In these circumstances, the House of Lords held that no delict was committed even though the defendant had acted maliciously.

Accordingly, *Allen v Flood* is authority that an individual, A, can wield economic pressure to force B to act to his own or another's economic harm provided the means used by A are lawful. If, as in this case, the means used are lawful, no delict is committed even if A acts maliciously to harm B or another person rather than to further A's economic interests. This result, while harsh, is an inevitable consequence of a free market economy. But if the means used are *not* lawful, delictual liability may arise. It is to these circumstances that we shall now turn.

(2) Inducing breach of contract – procuring breach of contract

If A induces B to break his contract with C, C can sue B for breach of contract. Alternatively, C can sue A in *delict* for inducing B to break his contract with C. This delict was recognised as part of Scots law in *British Motor Trade Association v Gray*.[1] There Lord Russell approved counsel's concession that

'by the law of Scotland an actionable wrong is committed by one who intentionally and without lawful justification induces or procures someone to break a contract made by him with another, if damage has resulted to that other, provided the contract creates contractual relations recognised by law'.[2]

The delict can be represented by the diagram on page 39 below.

Thus if A, with the intention of harming C, induces B to break his contract with C, C can sue A in *delict* for inducing the breach, as an alternative to suing B for breach of contract.

Before A is liable, A must know of the existence of the contract between B and C. It is not enough in Scots law that A was reckless

1   1951 SC 586, 1951 SLT 247.
2   1951 SC 586 at 603.

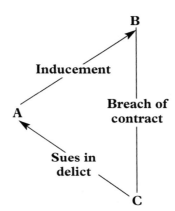

or turned a blind eye to whether or not a contract existed between B and C.[1] But A does not need to know the specific terms of the contract between B and C. The court will readily infer that A knew of the existence of the contract if a reasonable person in A's position would know that a contract existed between B and C. A must intend that B should break his contract with C in order to harm C.[2] A must in fact induce B to break the contract.[3] It is not necessary that A's inducement takes the form of unlawful means, for example threatening to assault B: A will still be liable to C if the means used are lawful and, indeed, beneficial to B, for example giving B a gift to break his contract with C. C must suffer loss as a result of the inducement but proof of specific damage is not required and once inducement of the breach is established, some damage will readily be inferred by the court.[4] Finally, A will have a defence if the inducement of the breach is justified, for example inducing female artistes to break their contracts of employment to obtain better wages so that they do not have to resort to prostitution.[5]

1 *Rossleigh Ltd v Leader Cars Ltd* 1987 SLT 355, OH. Cf the position in England where constructive knowledge is sufficient, ie turning a blind eye: *Emerald Construction Co Ltd v Lowthian* [1966] 1 All ER 1013, [1966] 1 WLR 691, CA; *Inshore Services (International) v NFFO Services* [2001] EWCA Civ 1722.
2 While the point is controversial, the Court of Appeal has held that A does not have to intend to harm C. It is enough that A knows that her deliberate conduct vis-à-vis B will have as its probable consequence a breach by B of his contract with C: *Millar v Bassey* [1994] EMLR 44. Given that Scots law has rejected the notion of A's constructive knowledge of the contract between B and C, it is doubtful whether *Millar* would be followed in Scotland.
3 The inducement must be directed at B, the person in the contractual relationship with the victim, C: *Middlebrook Mushrooms Ltd v Transport and General Workers' Union* [1993] ICR 612, CA.
4 *British Motor Trade Association v Gray* 1951 SC 586, 1951 SLT 247.
5 *Brimelow v Casson* [1924] 1 Ch 302.

We have been considering the situation where A induces or persuades B to break his contract with C. However, if B is unwilling to break his contract with C, A may nevertheless be able to procure the breach of contract by B. Before there is liability in this situation, A must use *unlawful* means to procure the breach. Procurement can arise directly if, for example, A steals B's tools with the result that B cannot fulfil his contract and breaks his contract with C: the theft constitutes the unlawful means. But it is much more likely that procurement will be done indirectly, ie if A with the intention of harming C induces D to break his contract with B so that B cannot perform his contract with C. The delict can be represented as follows:

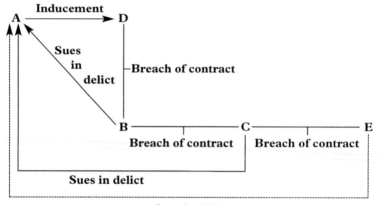

Here B could sue A in delict for directly inducing a breach of his contract with D. But C can also sue A for procuring a breach of C's contract with B: A's direct inducement of a breach of B's contract with D (ie a delict) constitutes the unlawful means used by A which are essential before A can be liable for procuring the breach of contract between B and C.[1] It should be emphasised that it does not matter whether the means used by A directly to induce D to breach her contract with B are lawful: direct inducement does *not* require unlawful means for delictual liability. But once A has directly induced the breach D–B, because direct inducement is a delict, it constitutes the unlawful means for the procurement of the breach B–C and so on.

Before there is liability, A must know of the existence of B's contract with C. If, as a result, C is unable to fulfil his contract with E,

1 *Stratford (J T) & Sons Ltd v Lindley* [1965] AC 269, [1964] All ER 102, HL.

E will also be able to sue A in delict provided A knows of C's contract with E and intended to harm E.[1] As we have emphasised, A must use unlawful means before there is liability for procurement. Justification can be a defence to procuring a breach of contract in the same way as in a case of direct inducement.

(3) Wrongful interference with performance of contract

Arising from the delict of inducement of breach of contract, the English courts have developed the delict of wrongful interference with performance of a contract where there has technically been no breach. Like the delict discussed above this can take two forms – direct interference where unlawful means are not required and indirect interference where unlawful means are essential.

The origin of the delict is the case of *Torquay Hotel Co Ltd v Cousins*.[2] The Transport and General Workers' Union (TGWU) attempted to organise the workforce at a Torbay hotel but another union was recognised by the hotel. The TGWU brought its members at the hotel out on strike. The manager of the Imperial Hotel at Torquay, who was the President of the Torquay Hotel Association, unwisely said that he wished to stamp out trade unions in hotels in Torquay. There were no members of the TGWU at the Imperial Hotel. The TGWU had members who were employed by Esso to deliver supplies of oil to the Imperial Hotel. The TGWU instructed those drivers not to deliver oil to the Imperial Hotel. The contract between the Imperial Hotel and Esso contained an exclusion clause under which Esso was not to be liable for failure to supply oil as a result of industrial action. The Imperial Hotel obtained a delivery of oil from Alternative Fuels. When the TGWU discovered this, the union informed Alternative Fuels not to enter any contract to supply the hotel with oil or else their drivers who were members of TGWU would boycott the hotel. In refusing to deliver oil to the hotel, the drivers were in breach of their contracts of employment with Esso and would have been in breach of their contracts of employment with Alternative Fuels. This complex factual situation can be shown by the diagram on page 43 below.

Although the TGWU had directly persuaded Esso not to perform the contract with the Imperial Hotel and had indirectly

---

1 *Merkur Island Shipping Corpn v Laughton* [1983] 2 AC 570, [1983] ICR 490, HL. A's liability could continue indefinitely; for example, if E cannot fulfil his contract with F, F can sue A provided A has knowledge of the contract between E and F.
2 [1969] 2 Ch 106, [1969] 1 All ER 522, CA.

procured the non-performance of the contract by using unlawful means (the breach of the drivers' contracts of employment in refusing to deliver the oil to the hotel), the delicts of inducement or procurement of *breach* of contract were not applicable since as a result of the exclusion clause in the contract there was no breach of contract by Esso in failing to perform. The Court of Appeal nevertheless held that it was not necessary to have a technical breach of contract before the TGWU was liable to Imperial Hotels.[1] It was enough that the TGWU had wrongfully interfered with Esso's performance of the contract with the Imperial Hotel. Thus, a new delict, wrongful interference with performance of a contract, was born. As in the case of inducement/procurement of a breach of contract, the defender must know of the existence of the contract and intend to interfere with its performance. If there is direct interference, unlawful means are not required; if there is indirect interference, unlawful means are necessary. There is also the defence of justification.

It will be noticed that a contract to supply oil existed between the Imperial Hotel and Esso. While Alternative Fuels had made one delivery of oil, no contract to supply oil subsisted between the Imperial Hotel and Alternative Fuels. At most there was a prospective contract. Nevertheless, the Court of Appeal held that the TGWU was liable to the Imperial Hotel for indirectly interfering with its prospective contract with Alternative Fuels by using unlawful means (the breach of the drivers' contracts of employment with Alternative Fuel in refusing to deliver oil to the hotel). Again a new delict, preventing a person from entering into a contract by unlawful means, was born.

(4) Wrongful interference with business

As a result of the decision in the *Torquay* case, particularly in respect of the prospective contract with Alternative Fuels, the English courts have begun to argue that inducing or procuring a breach of contract, wrongful interference with the performance of a contract and preventing by unlawful means a person from entering into a contract, are merely species of a more general delict: wrongful interference with business.[2]

1 Esso could, of course, sue the TGWU for inducing its employees to breach their contracts of employment.
2 See, in particular, *Merkur Island Shipping Corpn v Laughton* [1983] 2 AC 570, [1983] ICR 490, HL. See also *Garrard & Co Ltd v Christie & Co* [2001] EWCA Civ 699.

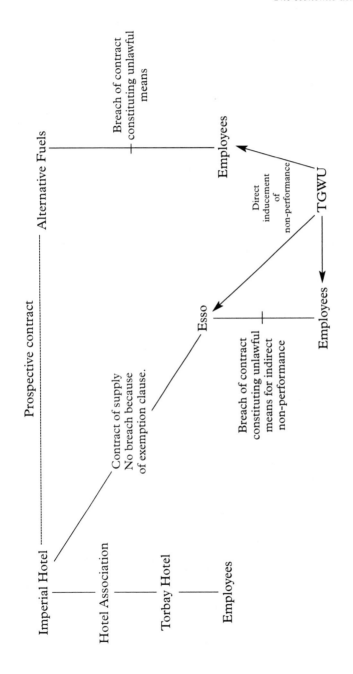

The leading case is *Lonrho plc v Fayed.*[1] Lonrho was attempting a takeover of Harrods. The Secretary of State for Trade and Industry referred the matter to the Monopolies Commission and obtained an undertaking from Lonrho that it would not purchase any more shares before the Monopolies Commission reported. Before the Commission reported, Fayed made a bid. Induced by allegedly fraudulent misrepresentations made by Fayed as to its business reputation, the Secretary of State did not refer Fayed's bid to the Commission and Fayed took over the company. Lonrho argued that as a result of its allegedly fraudulent misrepresentations to the Secretary of State – unlawful means – Fayed had wrongfully interfered with Lonrho's business. If the Secretary of State had known the true position, he would have referred Fayed's bid to the Commission and Lonrho might have been able to make a successful bid when its undertaking was no longer applicable. The Court of Appeal held that Lonrho had an arguable case of wrongful interference with business. To succeed, the following criteria have to be satisfied:

(1) the plaintiff has to establish that the defendant intended to harm the plaintiff's business; this intention does not, however, have to be the defendant's predominant intention or motive;

(2) the plaintiff has to establish that a business interest has been damaged by the defendant's conduct;

(3) the defendant's actions have to constitute unlawful means and there has to be a causal nexus between the unlawful act and the alleged loss;

(4) the loss sustained by the plaintiff has to be sufficient to sustain an action in damages.

Because of the need for *unlawful* means, the new delict can be distinguished from the general principle of non-liability for causing economic harm laid down in *Allen v Flood.*[2]

(5) Intimidation

Intimidation arises when A threatens B with an unlawful act unless B harms C economically. If B yields to the threat and harms C, C can sue A. The delict can be represented as follows:

---

1 [1990] 2 QB 479, [1989] 2 All ER 65, CA.
2 [1898] AC 1, HL discussed at p 37 above.

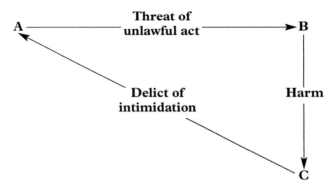

The existence of this delict was 'discovered' by the House of Lords in *Rookes v Barnard*.[1] British Overseas Airways Corporation (BOAC) and the draughtsmen's union, Association of Engineering and Shipbuilding Draughtsmen (AESD), had an informal 100 per cent union membership agreement (closed shop). Rookes was an employee of BOAC who had left the union. Two trade union officials, who were employees of BOAC, and Silverthorne, who was not an employee, told BOAC that unless Rookes was dismissed within three days, the AESD employees would withdraw their labour. As a result of a 'no strike' clause which had been incorporated from a collective agreement into the employees' contracts of employment, the threatened strike would have been a breach of the employees' contracts of employment. Under this pressure, BOAC lawfully dismissed Rookes. Rookes sued the three officials. This complex factual situation can be shown thus:

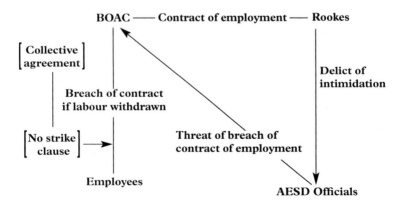

1 [1964] AC 1129, [1964] 1 All ER 367, HL.

The House of Lords held that Silverthorne and the other two employees were guilty of the delict of intimidation. By *threatening* a strike in breach of BOAC's employees' contracts of employment, they were threatening BOAC with *unlawful* means in order that BOAC should harm Rookes economically. As BOAC had yielded to the pressure and had dismissed Rookes, Rookes could sue the defendants on the basis of intimidation since the threat was made with the intention of harming Rookes.

To succeed, the following criteria have to be satisfied:

(1) there has to be a threat as opposed to a warning;
(2) it must be a threat of unlawful means.[1] The means do not necessarily have to be within the power of all the defendants: Silverthorne was not an employee of BOAC. Unlawful means include threats of violence, delicts or a breach of contract;
(3) the threat must be made with the intention that the person threatened will harm the pursuer;
(4) the person threatened must yield to the threat and harm the pursuer; if he does not comply with the threat, it is not intimidation. If the person threatened resists and the threat is carried out, depending on the nature of the unlawful act, he may have a remedy in delict or for breach of contract.

There is always the possibility of the defence of justification: if, for example, Rookes had been a dealer in drugs who upset the rest of the workforce.

Rookes was concerned with three-party intimidation, ie A threatens B with unlawful means in order that B should harm C; if B yields, C can sue A for intimidation. The question arises whether there can be two-party intimidation, ie if A threatens B with unlawful means, can B sue A for intimidation? In the present writer's view there is no delict of two-party intimidation because it is unnecessary. If A threatens B with violence that is itself an assault and B can sue in delict. If A threatens B with breach of contract by A, that is an anticipatory breach of contract and B can sue A in contract. If A threatens B with other delictual conduct, B must be robust and wait until the threat is carried out and then sue in delict; B cannot sue for an 'anticipatory' delict since he has not yet suffered any loss. If, however, the threat of unlawful means interferes with B's business, A could be liable for the delict of wrongful interference with B's business.[2]

---

1 So, for example, if A threatened B that A would inform the Inland Revenue that B had failed to disclose all her income, that would not amount to intimidation because the conduct threatened is not unlawful.
2 Discussed at p 42 above.

(5) Conspiracy

Allen v Flood[1] was concerned with the situation where A uses lawful means to harm B economically. There it was held that A was not liable in delict to B, even if his predominant motive or intention was to harm B rather than further A's legitimate business interests. Only three years later, in *Quinn v Leathem*,[2] the House of Lords held that if A and B combine together with the intention to harm C, then A and B are liable in delict for harm caused to C as a result of their combination or conspiracy against him. The rationale of the delict of conspiracy is that while a person can be expected to withstand the harmful but lawful acts of another, he cannot be expected to withstand the harm caused by a combination or conspiracy of persons to harm him.[3] This rationalisation has been doubted, for a multi-national conglomerate or oil company may exercise far greater economic power than a combination of small businesses.[4]

The essence of conspiracy is therefore a combination of persons, who come together with the intention of harming the pursuer economically. There are two types of conspiracy: (a) where the means used by the conspirators are lawful in the sense that they would not be actionable if carried out by one person alone (lawful means conspiracy); (b) where the means used by the conspirators are unlawful in the sense that *either* they would be actionable if carried out by one person alone, for example if the means constitute a delict or breach of contract, *or* they involve a crime or a breach of statute which does not provide a civil remedy for breach (unlawful means conspiracy).

(a) Lawful means conspiracy

A combination of persons will be liable in conspiracy if they come together with the predominant motive or intention of harming the pursuer rather than furthering their own legitimate interests. Thus, if A and B come together with the predominant motive or intention to harm C, A and B are liable in conspiracy even if their actions, for example undercutting C's prices, would not be actionable in delict

---

1 [1898] AC 1, HL. Discussed at p 37 above.
2 [1901] AC 495, HL.
3 *Mogul Steamship Co Ltd v McGregor, Gow & Co* (1889) 23 QBD 598, CA, at 616 per Bowen LJ.
4 *Lonrho Ltd v Shell Petroleum Co Ltd (No 2)* [1982] AC 173, [1981] 2 All ER 456, HL, at 464 per Lord Diplock; see also *Crofter Hand Woven Harris Tweed Co Ltd v Veitch* 1942 SC (HL) 1 at 8 per Viscount Simon LC.

if carried out by A or B alone. It is the *combination* of A and B together *and* their predominant motive or intention of harming C which renders their conspiracy delictual. If the predominant motive or intention of A and B is not to harm C but to further their own legitimate interests, the conspiracy is not delictual even though C suffers economic loss as a result of the actions of A and B, always provided these actions are lawful. Where lawful means are used, a conspiracy is delictual only if the predominant motive or intention of the conspirators is to harm the pursuer.

These principles were laid down in the leading case of *Crofter Hand Woven Harris Tweed Co Ltd v Veitch*.[1] Millowners on the Island of Lewis who made and sold tweed cloth from yarn spun on the island were unable to agree a 100 per cent union membership agreement (closed shop) with the TGWU because of competition from rival producers on the island (the pursuers) who obtained cheaper yarn from the mainland, wove it into cloth and sold it at a lower price than the millowners. The TGWU and the millowners came together. They instructed the members of the TGWU who were employed at the port to refuse to handle the yarn being imported by the pursuers to the island from the mainland. The case proceeded on the basis that the dockers were not in breach of their contracts of employment with the port authority in refusing to handle the imported yarn because they were never asked by their employer to do so. The question was whether the combination amounted to an actionable conspiracy. This complex factual situation can be shown thus:

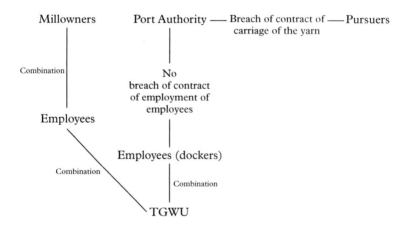

---

1   1942 SC (HL) 1, 1943 SLT 2.

The House of Lords held that since no unlawful means were used because the dockers were not in breach of their contracts of employment, ie there was no conduct which would be actionable if done by one person alone, the conspiracy would be delictual only if the pursuers could establish that the predominant motive or intention of the conspirators was to harm the pursuers. In this case, the predominant motive or intention was to further the union's legitimate interests, ie 100 per cent union membership. Harm to the pursuers was not their primary intention: it was only incidental to achieving their goal. Accordingly, the defenders were not liable.

It can, of course, be a very difficult issue of fact to establish whether the predominant purpose of the conspiracy is to harm the pursuer or whether the damage done to the pursuer is simply incidental to the furtherance of the conspirators' legitimate interests, be they commercial[1] or trade union interests as in the *Crofter* case. In *Scala Ballroom (Wolverhampton) Ltd v Ratcliffe*[2] it was held to be legitimate for trade union officials to organise a boycott among their members from playing at a dance hall which operated a colour bar; although this objective did not bring any financial benefits to the members of the union, it was genuinely thought by them to be in the interests of the union.

To summarise: when the combination uses lawful means, ie means which would not be actionable if done by one person alone, then the conspiracy is not delictual unless the predominant motive or intention of the conspirators is to injure the pursuer. The onus rests on the pursuer to prove that the predominant purpose of the conspiracy was to harm the pursuer economically. Moreover, the pursuer must prove economic loss.[3]

(b) Unlawful means conspiracy

In considering unlawful means conspiracy, two situations have to be discussed. First is the case where the means used are unlawful in the sense that they would be actionable as a breach of contract or

---

1 As in *Mogul Steamship Co Ltd v McGregor, Gow & Co* (1889) 23 QBD 598, CA.
2 [1958] 3 All ER 220, [1958] 1 WLR 1057, CA.
3 In *Lonrho plc v Fayed (No 5)* [1994] 1 All ER 188, [1993] 1 WLR 1489, CA, the Court of Appeal accepted that the defendants could be liable in conspiracy even if the statements they had made about the plaintiff were true, ie when they would have had a defence to an action of defamation. Since the means were lawful, their predominant motive would have had to have been harm to the plaintiff. Only damages for patrimonial loss would be recoverable; cf loss of reputation. On defamation, see Chapter 15 below.

delict if committed by one person alone. So, for example, if the boycotting of the imported yarn in the *Crofter* case had involved a breach of the dockers' contracts of employment (unlawful means), the union would have been liable to the pursuers for procurement of a breach of their contract with the port authority to carry the imported yarn. Where the means are delictual or amount to a breach of contract, the pursuer will usually sue on the substantive delict or breach of contract without relying on the conspiracy.[1]

Second, the means may be unlawful but not actionable as a breach of contract or a delict if committed by one person alone. This will usually arise where the means used involve a breach of a statutory provision. While breach of some statutes gives rise to an action in delict,[2] not all breaches of statute give a person who suffers harm as a result the right to sue in delict. In particular, the pursuer will not generally have title to sue in delict unless the statute was specifically designed to protect the interests of a class of persons to which the pursuer belongs.[3] In this situation, since the means used do not constitute a substantive delict, conspiracy may be the only form of redress.

The criteria for an actionable unlawful means conspiracy have been the subject of two decisions of the House of Lords concerned with Lonrho. The first is *Lonrho Ltd v Shell Petroleum Co Ltd (No 2)*.[4] Lonrho owned a pipeline running from Beira in Mozambique to a refinery in Southern Rhodesia. The pipeline was operated under an agreement between Lonrho and oil companies including Shell. When Southern Rhodesia declared unilateral independence, the British government made a sanctions order under the Southern Rhodesia Act 1965. As a result of the sanctions order, oil was no longer shipped to Beira, the pipeline ceased to be used and Lonrho lost profits. Before unilateral independence was declared, the oil companies gave assurances to the Rhodesian government that they would supply petroleum products to Rhodesia through South Africa. After independence had been declared, the defendants supplied the oil to Rhodesia in breach of the sanctions order. In an action of conspiracy against the defendants, Lonrho argued that the breach of the sanctions order enabled unilateral independence to last longer and thereby led to a loss of its revenue as a result of the prolonged non-use of its pipeline.

---

1 Similarly, in *Rookes v Barnard* [1964] AC 1129, [1964] 1 All ER 367, HL, Silverthorne was sued for the substantive delict of intimidation rather than conspiracy to break the employees' contracts. See p 45 above.
2 See Chapter 11 below.
3 *RCA Corpn v Pollard* [1983] Ch 135, [1982] 3 All ER 771, CA.
4 [1982] AC 173, [1981] 2 All ER 456, HL.

While the supply of the oil was a breach of the sanctions order, this was simply a criminal offence. In other words, the sanction order was not imposed for the benefit of persons like Lonrho who had traded with Rhodesia before independence. There was therefore no substantive delict arising from the defendants' breach of the order. The only delictual claim had to be based on conspiracy. Both the Court of Appeal and the House of Lords held that the conspiracy was not actionable because Lonrho had failed to establish that the defendants had *intended* to harm Lonrho when they breached the sanctions order. In the course of his speech in the House of Lords, Lord Diplock expressed the view that he did not wish to extend the delict of conspiracy beyond its existing limits.[1] Since the previous cases had been concerned with lawful means conspiracy where there is no liability unless the predominant motive or intention of the conspirators was to harm the pursuer, Lord Diplock's dicta were subsequently taken as authority that there was also no liability for an unlawful means conspiracy unless the primary aim of the combination was to harm the pursuer.[2]

The issue was purportedly clarified by the House of Lords in the second Lonrho case, *Lonrho plc v Fayed*.[3] In addition to the claim based on wrongful interference with business,[4] Lonrho also argued that the defendants had committed an unlawful means conspiracy against them, the alleged fraudulent misrepresentation to the Secretary of State constituting unlawful means. The House of Lords held that Lord Diplock's analysis in *Lonrho Ltd v Shell Petroleum Co Ltd (No 2)*[5] was not intended as a definitive account of the law relating to unlawful means conspiracy.[6] While accepting that a lawful means conspiracy was delictual only if the predominant motive or intention of the conspirators was to harm the pursuer, an unlawful means conspiracy was actionable if the pursuer could establish that the conspirators had *an* intention to harm the pursuer even though that was not their *predominant* motive or intention. This intention could not be proved merely by showing

---

1 [1981] 2 All ER 456 at 464.
2 *Allied Arab Bank Ltd v Hajjar (No 2)* [1988] QB 944, [1988] 3 All ER 103; *Metall und Rohstoff AG v Donaldson Lufkin and Jenrette Inc* [1990] 1 QB 391, [1989] 3 All ER 14, CA.
3 [1991] 3 All ER 303, HL. For the facts, see p 44 above.
4 Discussed at p 44 above.
5 [1982] AC 173, [1981] 2 All ER 456, HL.
6 *Lonrho plc v Fayed* [1992] 1 AC 448, [1991] 3 All ER 303 at 312 per Lord Bridge; Lord Bridge had been a member of the House of Lords in *Lonrho Ltd v Shell Petroleum Co Ltd (No 2)* [1982] AC 173, [1981] 2 All ER 456, HL.

that the defenders had used unlawful means: otherwise, Lonrho should have succeeded in the *Shell Petroleum* case. If the conspirators have an intention to harm the pursuer, an unlawful means conspiracy is delictual even if the unlawful means used would not be actionable if done by one person alone.[1]

To summarise: if the means used are lawful, a conspiracy is delictual only if the *predominant* motive or intention of the conspirators is to harm the pursuer; if the means used are unlawful, a conspiracy is actionable if *an* intention of the conspirators was to harm the pursuer even though that was not their primary purpose. Unlawful means include means which are delictual if done by one person alone or which constitute a breach of contract or amount to a breach of criminal law even though this would not give rise to a delictual action if done by one person alone.

(7) Postscript

As we have seen, many of these economic delicts were developed in the context of industrial conflict between employers and trade unions. Most forms of effective industrial action will involve the commission of one or more of the economic delicts. In order to obtain a balance between the power of capital and labour for the purpose of collective bargaining, legislation has been passed to give immunity to trade unions and trade unionists from civil liability in respect of some, at least, of these delicts. Immunity arises only if the acts which prima facie constitute an economic delict are carried out in contemplation or furtherance of a trade dispute. There are now stringent balloting requirements of the members of a trade union which must be satisfied before the statutory defences are applicable; and the defences do not apply to some forms of secondary industrial action. The law has now been consolidated in the Trade Union and Labour Relations (Consolidation) Act 1992 (as amended) and the reader seeking an account of the law relating to industrial action is referred to the textbooks on labour law.

---

1 In *Yukong Line Ltd of Korea v Rendsburg Investments Corpn of Liberia (No 2)* [1998] 1 WLR 294, [1998] 4 All ER 82, QBD (Comm Ct), Toulson J has suggested that the plaintiff in an unlawful means conspiracy must have title to sue on the unlawful means if committed by one person alone: otherwise, the conspiracy is not actionable unless the defendants' predominant motive was harm to the plaintiff. With respect, it is thought that this decision runs counter to the thrust of the decision of the House of Lords in *Lonrho plc v Fayed* [1992] 1 AC 448, [1991] 3 All ER 303.

B. FRAUD

Fraud is the paradigm of an intentional delict in Scots law. It has been defined as 'a machination or contrivance to deceive'.[1] Fraud will usually cause pure economic loss to the pursuer. As we shall see, this provides a stark contrast to the situation where unintentional conduct results in pure economic loss; there the courts have been unwilling to allow damages in negligence for pure economic loss. But fraud is not restricted to economic loss. If A lies to B when A tells B that B's wife and children have been seriously injured, with the result that B suffers distress or a psychiatric disorder, B can recover damages from A for fraud.[2]

Much confusion has arisen in this area because the fraudulent conduct will often take the form of a misrepresentation which induces the misrepresentee to enter into a contract with the misrepresentor. In these circumstances, the misrepresentee may have two sets of remedies, ie contractual and delictual. If the fraudulent misrepresentation prevented the formation of the contract, the contract is null;[3] if, however, a contract is concluded but the misrepresentee was induced by the fraudulent misrepresentation to contract under essential error, the contract may be reduced provided *restitutio in integrum* is possible.[4] But, in addition, the misrepresentee can sue in *delict* for damages. Thus if A lies to B to induce B to enter a contract with A, B will have contractual remedies against A, for example reduction, and the right to sue A for damages in delict. If A lies to B who as a result enters into a contract with C, B will have no contractual remedies against C (unless A was acting as C's agent) but B will be able to sue A in delict.

Although the institutional writers had a flexible view of the concept of fraud, as a result of developments in the nineteenth century fraud as a delict was confined to a relatively narrow range of situations where the defender *intended* to harm the pursuer. In effect, the Scots delict of fraud was equated with the English tort of deceit.[5]

1 Erskine *Institute* III, 1, 16.
2 *Wilkinson v Downtown* [1897] 2 QB 57; *Wainwright v Home Office* [2003] All ER (D) 279. *Cf Powell v Boladz* [1998] Lloyd's Rep Med 116, CA (defendant had no intention to harm plaintiff by falsifying medical records). Similarly if A obtained sexual intercourse with B as a result of fraudulent misrepresentation.
3 *Morrisson v Robertson* 1908 SC 332, 15 SLT 697; *Shogun Finance Ltd v Hudson* [2004] 1 All ER 215.
4 *Spence v Crawford* 1939 SC (HL) 52, 1939 SLT 305; *MacLeod v Kerr* 1965 SC 253, 1965 SLT 358. See generally MacQueen and Thomson *Contract Law in Scotland* (2000) pp 154 ff.
5 On these developments see, generally, 11 *Stair Memorial Encyclopaedia* paras 701–789.

Before delictual liability arises for fraud, there must be a positive act by the defender which causes loss to the pursuer. This will often take the form of a misrepresentation by words. But positive conduct can amount to a fraudulent misrepresentation, for example supplying reconditioned as opposed to new cash registers[1] or selling reproduction furniture 'got up' to look like antiques.[2] As a general rule, non-disclosure does not amount to a misrepresentation unless there is a fiduciary relationship between the parties or the contract is a contract *uberrimae fidei*.[3]

Before there is liability for fraud, the pursuer must establish that the defender had the requisite mental element, *mens rea*. In other words, the pursuer has to show that at the time of the misrepresentation the defender's state of mind was such that he did not, or could not, believe his statement was true. It is, of course, extremely difficult to prove this mental element; as a result, the law has developed liability for negligent – as opposed to fraudulent – misrepresentation where the defender's conduct can be tested objectively.[4]

What, then, will constitute the *mens rea* of fraud? The first situation is where the defender makes a statement which he knows is false. For example, A tells B there is a gold seam in A's garden when A knows that no seam is there. In these circumstances, A is lying. The second situation is where the defender makes a statement which he does not positively *know* is false but which he positively *believes* to be false. For example, A tells B there is a gold seam in A's garden; A has not dug up his garden and therefore does not know that there is no gold seam but A believes no gold seam is there. If in fact there is no gold seam, then A can be sued by B for fraud. B will have great difficulty in proving that A believed his statement was false if A maintains he believed it was true. However, the court will infer fraud if the statement was destitute of all reasonable grounds for believing it was true or the least inquiry would immediately correct.[5]

The final situation is where the defender makes a statement which he does not positively know is false and does not positively believe is false but is recklessly indifferent to whether it is true or false. If the matter is of no importance to speaker and listener, this

1 *Gibson v National Cash Register Co Ltd* 1925 SC 500, 1925 SLT 377.
2 *Patterson v H Landsberg & Son* (1905) 7 F 675, 13 SLT 62.
3 For example, a contract of insurance.
4 On these developments, see pp 81 ff below.
5 *Western Bank of Scotland v Addie* (1867) 5 M (HL) 80.

is not dishonesty. But if it is a matter of importance between them, it is fraud since the speaker has attempted to induce a belief in the listener, ie that the statement is true, which the speaker does not actually entertain.[1] For example, A tells B there is a gold seam in A's garden. A has done tests which establish that the strata are not inconsistent with a gold seam but A, nevertheless, has serious doubts whether a gold seam is actually there. Assuming B has an interest in the statement, although A does not positively know that the statement is false and does not positively believe that it is false, if he does not care whether it is true or false, he is liable in fraud to B if in fact there is no gold seam in the garden.[2] Proof of the requisite *mens rea* in this situation will be difficult but again will be inferred if the statement was destitute of all reasonable grounds for believing it was true or the least inquiry would immediately correct.

To summarise,[3] *mens rea* for the purposes of fraud arises if the misrepresentor:

(1) positively knows the statement is false;[4] or
(2) positively believes the statement is false even though he does not positively know it is false: liability if in fact untrue;
(3) does not positively believe the statement is true even though he does not positively know or believe it is false: liability if in fact untrue, provided both parties have an interest in what has been said.

There can, therefore, be no liability in fraud if the defender positively believes that the statement is true. In these circumstances, if he did not take reasonable care in making the statement, there may be liability for negligent misrepresentation.

Because fraud is an intentional delict, the pursuer is entitled to recover damages for all the losses directly arising from the fraud – even if the losses are not reasonably foreseeable by the defender. Suppose, for example, A bought shares from B for £100K. A was induced by B to purchase the shares as a result of B's fraudulent misrepresentation as to the value of the shares. In fact their value is only £80K. However, unknown to A and B, at the time of the transaction the shares were in fact overvalued at £80K because of a

---

1 *Lees v Tod* (1882) 9 R 807.
2 *H & J M Bennet (Potatoes) Ltd v Secretary of State for Scotland* 1986 SLT 665, OH (revsd on another point 1988 SLT 390).
3 The *locus classicus* is to be found in *Derry v Peek* (1889) 14 App Cas 337, HL, at 374 per Lord Herschell.
4 See, for example, *Henry Ansbacher & Co Ltd v Rinks Stern* [1998] Lloyd's Rep Bank 1, (1997) Times, 26 June, CA.

fraud by C. When C's fraud is subsequently discovered, the shares fall in value to £30K. A can recover the full extent of his loss, ie £70K as opposed to £20K, from B since A has been the victim of a fraudulent misrepresentation: B is liable for all A's losses directly arising from B's fraud, even though they were unforeseeable and, indeed, the result of the actions of a third party. In other words, A is put back into the position he would have been if he had not entered the transaction.[1] It is not possible to exclude liability for fraud by an exemption clause.[2]

1 *Smith New Court Securities Ltd v Scrimgeour Vickers (Asset Management) Ltd* [1997] AC 254, [1996] 4 All ER 769, HL. The House of Lords indicated that B would not be liable for *all* A's losses if C's fraud had occurred *after* the transaction on the basis that the causative influence of B's fraud on A's losses vis-à-vis C's fraud had faded: *sed quaere?* In *Barry v Sutherland* 2002 SLT 413, the pursuers bought a pub as a result of the seller's fraudulent misrepresentation concerning the business accounts. The Lord Ordinary (Eassie) held that the pursuers were able to recover damages for trading losses they had incurred when running the business: they were not restricted to compensation for the difference in the price paid as opposed to the true price of the pub. In other words, they were entitled to recover for the losses which directly flowed from entering into the sale and running the business.
2 Hence the necessity to plead fraud in *H & J M Bennet (Potatoes) Ltd v Secretary of State for Scotland* 1986 SLT 665, OH.

Part II

UNINTENTIONAL DELICT – GENERAL PRINCIPLES OF LIABILITY

Chapter 3.   The duty of care   59

Chapter 4.   Duty of care as a threshold device   71

Chapter 5.   Breach of a duty of care   115

Chapter 6.   Causation and related issues   135

CHAPTER 3

The duty of care

A. INTRODUCTION

In the first part of this book we examined the intentional delicts. *Culpa* or fault is the basis of delictual liability and is present in those delicts because the defender intended to harm the pursuer. Moreover, and this is important, the range of potential pursuers in those delicts is automatically restricted to those persons whom the defender intended to harm. In Scots law the concept of *culpa* also covers conduct which is merely careless, ie where the defender causes harm to the pursuer *unintentionally*. Immediately, a difficulty arises. If A acts in a careless manner, ie his conduct fails to meet the standard of care demanded by society of a person in his position, then prima facie A is liable to anyone who suffers harm as a result of such conduct.[1] In order to *limit* A's potential liability in delict to an indeterminate class of persons, the law has had to develop devices which restrict the number of persons who can claim damages for harm incurred by A's unintentional, but careless, conduct.

While there are many ways to restrict A's potential liability,[2] modern Scots law has accepted as a general principle that A will be liable for careless conduct only if he owed a duty of care to the person harmed by his actions. This duty of care must pre-exist the careless conduct. Whether a duty of care is owed by A to a particular person or class of persons is ultimately a question of law to be determined by the courts. In deciding whether or not to recognise the existence of a duty of care in particular circumstances, the courts are influenced by issues of policy as well as legal principle. By recognising – or refusing to recognise – the existence of a duty of care, the courts in effect set the parameters of delictual liability for unintentional, but careless, conduct.

---

1 Cardozo J's phrase 'liability in an indeterminate amount for an indeterminate time, to an indeterminate class' elegantly summarises the point: *Ultramares Corpn v Touche* (1931) 255 NY 170 at 179.
2 For example by developing a doctrine of proximate causation before A will be liable.

B. *DONOGHUE v STEVENSON*: THE NEIGHBOURHOOD PRINCIPLE

The starting point of any discussion of the duty of care in Scots law is the famous case of *Donoghue v Stevenson*.[1] One Sunday evening Mrs Donoghue went to visit a friend in Paisley.[2] They went to Wellmeadow Café at Wellmeadow Place, Paisley. The café was owned by Mr Minchella. They decided to have 'iced drinks', ie ice cream over which was poured lemonade. Mrs Donoghue's friend bought the ice cream and a bottle of 'ginger'.[3] The case proceeded on the assumption that Mrs Donoghue's friend had in fact bought ginger beer which would have been contained in an opaque bottle. The friend poured some of the ginger beer over Mrs Donoghue's ice cream; but when, later in the evening, the friend poured the rest of the ginger beer over Mrs Donoghue's melting ice, out floated the decomposing remains of a snail. The sight of the snail and her consumption of the snail-tainted iced drink resulted in Mrs Donoghue becoming ill. Mrs Donoghue sued Stevenson, the manufacturer of the ginger beer, in delict. The question before the courts was whether the manufacturer was liable to Mrs Donoghue in delict even if she could prove the facts alleged and Stevenson had, in fact, been careless.

A most important point to notice is that there was no contractual nexus between Mrs Donoghue and Stevenson. The facts of the case can be shown thus:

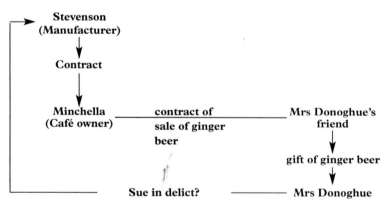

---

1 1932 SC (HL) 31, 1932 SLT 317. The literature on this case is voluminous but see in particular A F Rodger 'Mrs Donoghue and Alfenus Varus' (1998) 41 CLP 1.
2 The sex of the friend changes as the case proceeds through the courts!
3 In the parlance of the West Coast of Scotland at the time, 'ginger' was a generic term covering all kinds of aerated drinks.

Mrs Donoghue's friend could sue Minchella for breach of the contract of sale on the grounds that the ginger beer was not of merchantable (ie satisfactory) quality; however, the friend's damages would be minimal since the friend did not suffer any ill-effects.[1] Mrs Donoghue could not sue Minchella because she was not a party to the contract. Minchella could also have sued Stevenson in contract if he had suffered any loss. But Mrs Donoghue had no contractual remedy. Therefore the issue before the House of Lords was whether *in the absence* of any contractual nexus between them, Mrs Donoghue, the ultimate consumer of the product, could sue the manufacturer in delict.

It was held by a majority of the House of Lords[2] that Mrs Donoghue was entitled to sue Stevenson in delict because he owed her a duty of care: if he had *in fact* broken his duty towards her by his careless conduct and she had suffered harm, then she would succeed.[3] In other words, the relationship between the pursuer and defender was sufficiently proximate that the majority was prepared to hold that Stevenson owed Mrs Donoghue a duty of care for the purpose of liability in delict. Lord Atkin concluded:[4]

' ... a manufacturer of products, which he sells in such a form as to show that he intends them to reach the ultimate consumer in the form in which they left him, with no reasonable possibility of intermediate examination, and with the knowledge that the absence of reasonable care in the preparation or putting up of the product will result in an injury to the consumer's life or property, owes a duty to the consumer to take that reasonable care'.

Lord Macmillan had

'no hesitation in affirming that a person, who for gain engages in the business of manufacturing articles of food and drink intended for consumption by members of the public in the form which he issues them, is under a duty to take care in the manufacture of these articles. That duty, in my opinion, he owes to those whom he intends to consume his produce ... '[5]

At its most specific level *Donoghue v Stevenson* is authority that a manufacturer of food and drink which he intends to be used by the

---

1 For that reason it would have been pointless for the friend to have assigned his or her rights under the contract to Mrs Donoghue.
2 Lord Atkin, Lord Thankerton and Lord Macmillan; Lord Buckmaster and Lord Tomlin dissented.
3 After the decision of the House of Lords on the relevancy point, the case was settled and did not go to proof.
4 1932 SC (HL) 31 at 57.
5 1932 SC (HL) 31 at 71. On the genesis of Lord Macmillan's speech, see A F Rodger (1992) 168 LQR 236.

ultimate consumer without the opportunity of inspection or interference before use owes a duty of care to the ultimate consumer to
prevent him sustaining harm to his person or property as a result of
the manufacturer's carelessness when manufacturing the product.
In other words, the relationship between manufacturer and ultimate consumer was sufficiently proximate in these circumstances
that the court was prepared to impose a duty of care on the manufacturer towards the ultimate consumer. Four years later, the Privy
Council refused to interpret *Donoghue v Stevenson* in such a narrow
way and held that the manufacturer of underpants owed a duty of
care to the ultimate consumer even though the product was not for
internal consumption, the underpants had been removed by the
retailer from packets in which they had been delivered and they
could have been – but had not been – washed by the ultimate consumer before use.[1] *Donoghue v Stevenson* thus becomes authority
for the more general principle that a manufacturer of *any* product
owes a duty of care to the ultimate consumer not to cause harm to
his person or property as a result of a latent defect in a product
which could not be discovered by inspection before use and was
intended by the manufacturer to be used by the ultimate consumer
in the same condition as it left the manufacturer. If by his careless
conduct the manufacturer breaches this duty, causing harm to the
ultimate consumer's person or property, then he is liable in delict to
make reparation for the harm sustained by the consumer.

Even at this more general level, there are two important limitations on the extent of the duty of care laid down in *Donoghue*:

(1) The duty only extends to *latent* defects; the bottle of ginger
    beer was opaque and the snail could not be seen before the
    contents were used.[2] If the defect is patent, ie obvious, and the
    consumer chooses to use it, the manufacturer may escape lia-
    bility because the chain of causation is broken[3] or the damages

---

1 *Grant v Australian Knitting Mills Ltd* [1936] AC 85, PC. The plaintiff suffered
  dermatitis because free sulphites used in the manufacturing process had not been
  washed out of the garments before they were marketed. The fact that, unlike Mrs
  Donoghue, the plaintiff could have sued the retailer for breach of contract did not
  prevent recovery against the manufacturer in delict.
2 Similarly, the defect in the underpants in *Grant* was latent.
3 On causation, see Chapter 6 below. Where the defect was originally latent, the
  chain of causation is not necessarily broken if the defect later comes to the attention of the consumer or the fact that a third party had the opportunity or indeed
  an obligation to inspect the product. In the latter circumstances, the manufacturer and the third party can be jointly and severally liable: see *Grunwald v Hughes*
  1964 SLT 94, OH, 1965 SLT 209; *Clay v A J Crump & Sons Ltd* [1964] 1 QB
  533, [1963] 3 All ER 687, CA.

will be reduced by the ultimate consumer's contributory negligence.[1]

(2) The duty is to prevent harm to the ultimate consumer's person or property. If A is physically injured by a defective product, carelessly manufactured by B, A can sue B for damages for pain and suffering (solatium). A can also sue B for economic loss which derives from his injuries (derivative or parasitic economic loss), for example loss of wages when in hospital, loss of wages in the future if A is permanently incapacitated and so forth.[2] If A's property is damaged by a defective product carelessly manufactured by B, then A can recover damages from B in respect of the damage to his property: for example if A's dog dies as a result of contaminated dog food or a defective vacuum cleaner damages A's carpet. But A is not able to sue B in delict if the only property damaged is the defective product itself. A cannot sue B in delict for the cost of repairing a defective car or for replacing a defective vacuum cleaner which blew up without harming A's person or damaging any property other than the vacuum cleaner itself. In these situations, A has suffered *pure*, as opposed to derivative or parasitic, economic loss, ie the cost of repair or replacement or the difference in value between the property with and without the defect. As we shall see, the courts are reluctant to allow a person to recover damages for pure economic loss in *delict*; A's remedy lies in *contract* against the person who sold him the goods, not the manufacturer.[3] Similarly, if the defect is discovered before there has been any harm done to A's person or property, the cost of repairing the defect is pure economic loss and cannot be recovered in delict.[4]

Donoghue is therefore an important decision in relation to product liability. But what makes the case remarkable is that two of the judges attempted to lay down criteria to determine the existence of a duty of care which would be applicable whenever an action for reparation as a result of unintentional, but careless, conduct arose. Lord Macmillan sets the scene:[5]

---

1 On contributory negligence, see pp 150 ff below.
2 On damages generally, see Chapter 16 below.
3 Of course A may not have a contract; for example if the goods were a gift. But the purchaser could assign his contractual rights against the seller to A.
4 On economic loss, see further pp 81 ff below. There is no such restriction in the case of the intentional delicts.
5 *Donoghue v Stevenson* 1932 SC (HL) 31 at 70 (italics added).

'The law takes no cognisance of carelessness in the abstract. It concerns itself with carelessness only where there is a duty to take care and where failure in that duty has caused *damage*.[1] In such circumstances carelessness assumes the legal quality of negligence and entails the consequences in law of negligence. What then are the circumstances which give rise to this duty to take care? In the daily contacts of social and business life, human beings are thrown into, or place themselves in, an infinite variety of relations with their fellows; and *the law can refer only to the standards of the reasonable man in order to determine whether any particular relationship gives rise to a duty to take care as between those who stand in relation to each other.* The grounds of action may be as various and manifold as human errancy; and the conception of legal responsibility may develop in adaption to altering social conditions and the changing circumstances of life. *The categories of negligence are never closed.* The cardinal principle of liability is that the party complained of should owe to the party complaining a duty to take care, and that the party complaining should be able to prove that he has suffered damage in consequence of a breach of that duty.'

Lord Macmillan is arguing that given changes in society, the courts, using as a yardstick the values of the reasonable man, may consider that new relationships are sufficiently proximate to impose a duty of care, breach of which gives rise to delictual liability for unintentional, but careless, conduct. *Donoghue v Stevenson* thus introduces a dynamic into the law which can extend the parameters within which there is delictual liability for careless conduct; this is done by the court deciding that a duty of care exists between parties in new social or economic relationships. Conversely, the court can refuse to extend the boundaries of delictual liability for careless conduct by deciding that a duty of care does not exist between parties in the circumstances of the case. In determining whether or not to impose a duty of care, the courts will clearly be influenced by policy considerations as well as legal principle.

In *Donoghue v Stevenson* Lord Atkin attempted to provide a criterion for the existence of a duty of care which, at first sight, appears to be more objective. In a famous passage, he said:[2]

'The liability for negligence, whether you style it such or treat it as in other systems as a species of "*culpa*", is no doubt based upon a general public sentiment of moral wrongdoing for which the offender must pay. But acts

---

1 It cannot be emphasised enough that in Scots law there is no delictual liability unless a breach of a duty of care has caused harm: *damnum injuria datum*. Harm is a constituent of negligence as well as a consequence of negligence. We can owe a duty of care and be careless, but there is no liability unless our carelessness has caused harm to the pursuer.
2 1932 SC (HL) 31 at 44 (italics added).

or omissions which any moral code would censure cannot, in a practical world, be treated so as to give a right to every person injured by them to demand relief. *In this way rules of law arise which limit the range of complaints, and the extent of their remedy.* The rule that you are to love your neighbour becomes in law, you must not injure your neighbour; and the lawyer's question, Who is my neighbour? receives a *restricted* reply. You must take reasonable care to avoid acts or omissions which you can *reasonably foresee* would be likely to injure your neighbour. Who, then, in law, is my neighbour? The answer seems to be – persons who are so *closely and directly* affected by my act that I ought reasonably to have them in contemplation when I am directing my mind to the acts or omissions which are called in question.'

Thus, for Lord Atkin a duty of care arises when it is reasonably foreseeable by the defender that a person in the position of the pursuer would be affected by the defender's acts or omissions. The neighbourhood principle therefore explains why a duty of care arises in many situations. A driver owes a duty of care to other road users because it is reasonably foreseeable that if he drives carelessly he may harm other road users. The occupier of property owes a duty of care to those who enter her property because it is reasonably foreseeable that they may be injured if the occupier is careless in the way she maintains the property. An employer owes a duty of care to his employee because it is reasonably foreseeable that if he is careless in the way he runs his system of working the employee may be harmed. A manufacturer of a product owes a duty of care to the ultimate consumer because it is reasonably foreseeable that the ultimate consumer may be injured or suffer harm to his property if the product is defective.

It will be noticed that in these examples the duty of care is to prevent *physical* harm to the pursuer or physical damage to his property and will enable the pursuer only to recover economic loss which is *derivative* from the injuries or damage sustained. But in situations where the pursuer does not suffer physical harm or damage to property, for example pure economic loss, the courts tend to be reluctant to impose a duty of care even though the loss to the pursuer would have been reasonably foreseeable by a person in the position of the defender. In other words, the reasonable foreseeability criterion, while a necessary condition for the existence of a duty of care, might not be sufficient to persuade the court to impose a duty of care in areas where no precedent for such a duty exists. Initially, in relation to recovery in delict for pure economic loss,[1] the House of Lords refused to impose a duty of care simply

---

1 For full discussion, see pp 81 ff below.

because the loss was reasonably foreseeable: in *Caparo Industries plc v Dickman*,[1] their Lordships held that not only had loss to the pursuer to be reasonably foreseeable but, in addition, there had to be a close degree of proximity between the parties *and* it had to be 'fair, just and reasonable' to impose a duty of care.

This tripartite test, the *Caparo* criteria was applied to a case of *physical* damage to property by the House of Lords in *Marc Rich & Co AG v Bishop Rock Marine Co Ltd, The Nicholas H*.[2] A surveyor (the defendant) advised the owner of a damaged vessel to continue on her voyage. The vessel sank and the cargo was lost. It was held that the surveyor did not owe a duty of care to the owner of the *cargo* (the plaintiff) to avoid damage to his property.

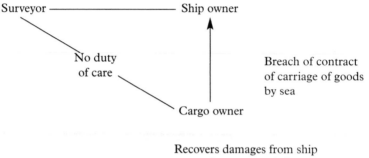

Although it was reasonably foreseeable that the surveyor's careless advice could result in *physical* harm to the plaintiff's property, nevertheless no duty of care arose since the relationship between the parties was not sufficiently proximate and it would have been unfair, unjust and unreasonable to hold otherwise. To have imposed a duty of care in this case would have disturbed 'the intricate blend' of internationally accepted rules of shipping law under which the owner of the cargo has a remedy against the owner of the ship in *contract* but the amount of compensation is limited.[3]

---

1   [1990] 2 AC 605, HL, at 616–618 per Lord Bridge, at 628 per Lord Roskill, and at 633–634 per Lord Oliver.
2   [1996] AC 211, [1995] 3 All ER 307, HL.
3   When a passenger was injured in an aircraft, it was held that a safety inspector owed him a duty of care on the basis of reasonable foreseeability of harm per se, without having to resort to the tripartite test. This was because it was not a novel situation and it concerned personal injuries: *Perrett v Collins* [1998] 2 Lloyd's Rep 255, (1998) Times, 23 June, CA.

The tripartite test has now been transplanted into Scots law to determine the existence of a duty of care in novel situations not governed by existing precedent. In *Coleridge v Miller Construction Ltd*,[1] for example, the defender cut an electric cable supplying power to the pursuer's factory. The absence of electricity caused damage to the pursuer's furnace and to the glass being manufactured. Although the pursuer had sustained physical damage to his property, the Lord Ordinary (MacLean) held that the defender did not owe the pursuer a duty of care. His reasoning was that although damage was reasonably foreseeable and there was sufficient proximity between the parties, it was not fair, just and reasonable to impose a duty of care because this would upset the well-established liabilities of the parties' insurers.[2] The tripartite test has also been adopted where the pursuer has suffered personal injuries,[3] although it is accepted that in these circumstances 'it is self-evident that a civilised system of law should hold that a duty of care has been broken'.[4]

Put shortly, where the courts are being asked to extend delictual liability into hitherto uncharted waters, under the guise of determining whether or not there is a sufficient degree of proximity for the imposition of a duty of care and whether it is fair, just and reasonable to do so, the courts are undoubtedly influenced by policy considerations. In doing so they are governed by their concept of a fair distribution of risk in contemporary society – allowing the loss to be compensated in some areas, letting the risk lie where it has fallen in others.

To summarise: Lord Atkin's neighbourhood principle, based on reasonable foreseeability of harm, undoubtedly explains why a duty of care arises in many situations where there is the risk of physical harm to the pursuer or physical damage to the pursuer's property. But at the parameters of the field of existing delictual liability, the courts, for policy reasons, may refuse to extend the frontiers even though loss to the pursuer is reasonably foreseeable. On the other

---

1 1997 SLT 485, OH. Cf *Tartan American Machinery Corp v Swan & Co* 2003 SLT 1246 (packer of goods on ship owed duty of care to the owner of the goods to prevent them being damaged during the voyage: *Caparo* criteria used).

2 See also *British Telecommunications plc v James Thomson & Sons (Engineers) Ltd* 1999 SC (HL) 9. The House of Lords, reversing the Second Division of the Court of Session, held that a domestic sub-contractor did owe a duty of care to an employer whose insurance covered only nominated sub-contractors. Lord Mackay of Clashfern accepted that the tripartite test was appropriate: 1999 SC (HL) 9 at 12.

3 *Gibson v Orr* 1999 SC 420, OH.

4 *Marc Rich & Co AG v Bishop Rock Marine Co Ltd, The Nicholas H* [1996] AC 211 at 235 per Lord Steyn.

hand, there may be other factors present – as well as reasonable foreseeability of harm – which will persuade the courts that a duty of care should be imposed in the particular circumstances.

Although *Donoghue v Stevenson*[1] was a milestone in the development of the law of negligence, Lord Atkin's neighbourhood principle based on reasonable foreseeability of harm is no longer adequate as the touchstone for the impositiion of a duty of care. The *Caparo* criteria – the three elements of reasonable foreseeability, proximity and the 'fair, just and reasonable' criterion – has overtaken it in novel situations, ie those not governed by existing precedent. In *Gibson v Orr*, in the course of his judgment, the Lord Ordinary (Hamilton) said:[2]

'Although there is no authority directly binding on me, the three element test now falls ... to be applied in Scotland in personal injury actions based on a duty of care as well as in other actions of damages so based. The more traditional approach in Scotland has been to apply the test laid down by Lord Atkin in *Donoghue v Stevenson*.[3] In *Dorset Yacht Co Ltd v Home Office* Lord Reid said that *Donoghue v Stevenson* might "be regarded as a milestone".[4] A milestone is an object encountered in the course of a journey. The relevant journey did not end in 1932 but went on, albeit not perhaps in a straight line ... to the present day. Progress on that journey does not mean that milestones passed are no longer relevant; they remain important stages in the development of the law. However, I see no logical justification in modern circumstances and as the law has developed for applying a different test for the existence of a duty of care in respect of personal injury from that applicable relative to physical damage to property or to economic loss.'

The 'fair, just and reasonable' criterion expressly recognises that ultimately the imposition of a duty of care is an issue of policy and that any extension of delictual liability will occur on an incremental basis. In certain situations the *Caparo* tripartite test has itself been overtaken by other criteria for the imposition of a duty of care. In the next chapter we shall consider some important examples of this process. The important point is that the concept of a duty of care is used as a *threshold* device, enabling the courts to extend the scope of delictual liability or to refuse to do so, depending on policy considerations. The duty of care allows the courts, if they so wish, to give an inch without fear that pursuers will take the proverbial mile.

---

1 1932 SC (HL) 32, 1932 SLT 317.
2 1999 SC 420, OH, at 431. For full discussion of this case, see pp 211 ff below.
3 1932 SC (HL) 31 at 44.
4 *Dorset Yacht Co Ltd v Home Office* [1970] AC 1004 at 1027, [1970] 2 All ER 294 at 297.

The position has been admirably summarised by the Hon Justice Michael Kirby when he said extra-judicially:[1]

'Novel cases therefore require judges with the responsibility of decision to evaluate the choices they make by reference to considerations of legal policy. Will the imposition of a duty of care for negligence impose indeterminate liability on too many people? Will it expose people unreasonably to liability to others? Will it result in intolerable economic burdens upon citizens? Will it have adverse implications for the availability of liability insurance? Will it offend legitimate freedom of action by people in the position of the defendant? Will it drive some useful participants out of a valuable economic market? Will refusing it leave a vulnerable party without recompense reasonable to the circumstances?'

---

1 'Judicial Activism' (2004) 55 Hamlyn Lectures (forthcoming at the time of press).

CHAPTER 4

Duty of care as a threshold device

We shall now consider four examples of how the existence or non-existence of a duty of care has been used to extend or limit liability in delict for careless acts or omissions.

A. PURE OMISSIONS

A, a professor of law, is standing in the quadrangle of the university. He sees B, another professor, who is very shortsighted, walking with a white stick across the quadrangle. There is a banana skin lying in B's path. Instead of warning B, A merely stands and watches. B slips on the banana skin. A walks away, giggling. Is A liable to B in delict for A's failure to warn B about the banana skin? The answer is no. Why? In spite of the fact that it is reasonably foreseeable by A that B may slip on the banana skin if A does not warn him, A does not owe B a duty of care. As a matter of policy, the law does not compel us to be good Samaritans[1]. There must be additional factors creating a closer degree of proximity between the parties before the defender is liable in delict for an omission to act. Thus, for example, a parent is under a duty to rescue his child provided it is reasonable to do so; similarly, a nurse or a doctor owes a duty of care to tend their patients. But unless, as in these examples, there is some pre-existing relationship between the parties, the law

---

1 'Reasonable forseeability of physical injury is the standard criterion for determing the duty of care owed by people who undertake an activity which carries a risk of injury to others. But it is insufficient to justify the imposition of liability upon someone who simply does nothing: who neither creates the risk not under takes to do anything to avert it': *Gorringe v Calderdale MBC* [2004] UKHL 15 at [17], per Lord Hoffman.

does not impose a duty of care on the defender to rescue the pursuer or to act in such a way that the pursuer will avoid an accident.[1]

Returning to the example, it does not follow that B is without remedy. The university, as his employer, owes B a duty to take reasonable care for his safety at work;[2] moreover, as the occupier of the premises,[3] the university owes B a duty to take reasonable care that he is not harmed as a result of the state of the premises. If, of course, A deliberately dropped the banana skin in B's path, A would be liable for assault if A intended that B should slip. If A had carelessly dropped the banana skin, he could be liable since it is reasonably foreseeable that another person in the quadrangle could slip on the skin. But that duty of care is triggered by A's positive act in dropping the banana skin; it is no longer a case of a 'pure' omission.[4]

We must be careful to distinguish the cases of 'pure' omission where there is no liability, from the situation where there is a duty of care to prevent harm to the pursuer caused by the defender's careless conduct. In the latter situation, for example in the case of the driver of a vehicle and other road users or the manufacturer of a product and the ultimate consumer, it is irrelevant for the purpose of the law of delict that the carelessness involves an omission to act, as opposed to a positive action. Overtaking without first checking in the mirror is just as careless as driving too fast: failing to check whether a product is infested by a snail is just as careless as giving the wrong instructions on how a product is to be used. Where the defender is under a duty to protect the pursuer, he will be liable if he fails to do so.[5]

B. MENTAL HARM

The law has long recognised that A can owe a duty of care to B to prevent B suffering mental harm as a result of A's unintentional,

1 In *Barrett v Ministry of Defence* [1995] 3 All ER 87, CA, the Court of Appeal held that the Royal Navy did not owe a duty of care to prevent an adult naval airman from becoming drunk off-duty. However, after the deceased had collapsed and was no longer capable of looking after himself, it was accepted that the Royal Navy had a duty to provide him with adequate medical care.
2 On employers' liability, see Chapter 12 below.
3 On occupiers' liability, see Chapter 10 below.
4 For an interesting discussion of pure omissions, see T B Smith *A Short Commentary on the Law of Scotland* (W Green, 1962) p 672.
5 *Dorset Yacht Co Ltd v Home Office* [1970] AC 1004; *Reeves v Metropolitan Commissioner of Police* [2000] 1 AC 360.

but careless, conduct.[1] In order to succeed, the mental harm must amount to a recognised psychiatric disorder, not simply a fright. Initially at least, the duty of care arose only when the pursuer was in danger of suffering potential physical harm as a result of the defender's conduct. Put another way, where it was reasonably foreseeable by the defender that the pursuer could be physically injured as a result of the defender's conduct, it was also reasonably foreseeable that the pursuer might suffer mental harm if the defender's conduct did not actually cause physical injury to the pursuer but the pursuer had been terrified that it might do so. There was therefore a duty of care not to cause a psychiatric disorder to a person who was within the area of risk of physical harm as a result of the defender's careless conduct. In the leading case of *Page v Smith*,[2] the plaintiff was involved in a road accident caused by the defendant's careless driving. The accident was not serious and the plaintiff suffered no physical harm. However, the accident brought on a recurrence of the plaintiff's ME which had been in remission. The House of Lords held[3] that because the plaintiff was within the area of potential physical harm, he was to be regarded as a primary victim of the accident. In these circumstances, the defendant owed him a duty of care to prevent him suffering physical or psychiatric harm. It was irrelevant that he had not suffered physical harm or that a psychiatric disorder was not reasonably foreseeable because a person of ordinary fortitude would not have suffered mental harm in the circumstances. Thus a duty of care to prevent mental harm arises whenever the pursuer is a primary victim, ie when it is reasonably foreseeable that she might suffer physical injury. It does not matter that she did not sustain physical harm or that a psychiatric disorder was unforeseeable.

It is therefore important to determine when a person is a primary victim. Since the decision of the House of Lords in *Frost v Chief Constable of the South Yorkshire Police*,[4] it might appear that the test is simply whether or not he has been exposed to physical danger:[5] in other words, whether or not the victim has been within the area of

---

1 See, for example, *Dulieu v White & Sons* [1901] 2 KB 669.
2 [1996] AC 155, [1995] 2 All ER 736, HL. In *Simmons v British Steel plc* [2004] UKHL 20 it was accepted by the House of Lords that *Page* was authoritative in Scotland. See also *Donachie v Chief Constable of Greater Manchester Police* [2004] EWCA Civ 405.
3 Lords Ackner, Browne-Wilkinson and Lloyd; Lords Keith and Jauncey dissented.
4 [1999] 2 AC 455, [1999] 1 All ER 1, Lords Browne-Wilkinson, Steyn and Hoffmann; Lord Goff dissented and Lord Griffiths dissented in part.
5 Or had reasonable grounds to believe that he was in danger: see, for example, *Hunter v British Coal Corpn* [1999] QB 140, [1998] 2 All ER 97, CA.

potential physical harm. Accordingly, persons who witnessed the death of fellow employees have been held not to constitute primary victims when they were not themselves in physical danger at the time of the accident.[1] Similarly, no duty of care is owed to prevent rescuers suffering mental harm unless they are also in potential physical danger.[2] But there can be exceptional cases where a pursuer will be treated as a primary victim even though he was not at risk of physical harm. These have included cases where the pursuer mistakenly thought that he had killed or injured a fellow employee[3]; parents who felt responsible for the sexual abuse of their children by a foster child introduced into their home by the defendant[4]; and parents whose dead children's organs were removed without permission.[5] An employee may recover damages for psychiatric disorder when his employer is in breach of his general duty to take reasonable care for the safety of his employees.[6]

Where a person sustains mental harm as a consequence of witnessing or learning of an accident to a third party (the primary victim), she is known as a secondary victim. For a long time, it was trite law that a defender did not owe a duty of care to a secondary victim to prevent her suffering a psychiatric disorder. The leading case in Scots law is *Bourhill v Young*.[7] Young was a motorcyclist. Driving too fast, he overtook a stationary tramcar on its near side. He then crashed into a car which was turning right into a side street some 50 feet from the tramcar. Young was killed. It was accepted that the accident was caused by Young's careless driving. At the

---

1 *Robertson v Forth Road Bridge Joint Board* 1995 SC 364, 1996 SLT 263 (pursuer saw fellow employee blown off lorry on Forth Road Bridge); *McFarlane v EE Caledonia Ltd* [1994] 2 All ER 1 (plaintiff witnessed Piper Alpha explosion from a supply ship); *Campbell v North Lanarkshire Council* 2000 SLCR 373 (proof before answer allowed to determine whether pursuer was in personal danger).

2 *Frost v Chief Constable of the South Yorkshire Police* [1999] 1 All ER 1, [1999] 2 AC 455. Cf *Chadwick v British Transport Commission* [1967] 1 WLR 912, where the plaintiff was within the area of potential physical harm and *Cullin v London Fire and Civil Defence Authority* (31 March 1999, unreported), QB.

3 *Dooley v Cammell Laird & Co Ltd* [1951] 1 Lloyd's Rep 271; *Salter v U B Frozen & Chilled Foods Ltd* 2003 SLT 1011 (pursuer actively involved in the accident which caused the death of a fellow employee for which the pursuer was blameless).

4 *W v Essex CC* [2001] 2 AC 592. See also *McLoughlin v Jones* [2002] 2 WLR 1279 (plaintiff suffered a nervous breakdown having been wrongfully imprisoned as a consequence of his solicitor's negligence in preparing his defence. Plaintiff was treated as a primary victim in his claim against the solicitor for negligence).

5 *AB v Leeds Teaching Hospital NHS Trust* [2004] EWHC 644 (QB).

6 For employers' liability for psychiatric disorder, in particular as a consequence of stress at work, see discussion beyond at pp 218 ff.

7 1942 SC (HL) 78, 1943 SLT 105. For a discussion of this case, see W W McBryde 'Bourhill v Young: the Case of the Pregnant Fishwife' in *Comparative and Historical Essays in Scots law* (Butterworths, 1992) pp 66 ff.

time of the accident the pursuer, Mrs Bourhill, a fishwife, was on the far side of the tramcar, putting her creel on her back. She therefore did not see the collision but she heard the crash and, after Young's body was removed, saw the blood on the road. She maintained that as a result of the accident she suffered a 'nervous shock' which had caused her to miscarry. She sued Young's executor in delict. The complex factual situation can be shown as follows:

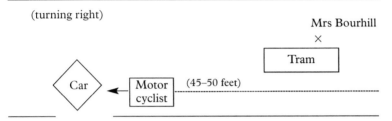

At the time of the accident Mrs Bourhill was 45–50 feet from the collision and on the far side of the tramcar. She was not within the area of risk of potential physical harm and – as we would say today – was therefore not a primary victim. In those circumstances, the House of Lords held that Young did not owe the pursuer a duty of care to prevent her suffering mental harm as a result of his careless driving. It was accepted that a driver owes a duty of care to other road users or persons in premises adjoining the highway, but only when they were 'so placed' that they could reasonably be expected to be physically harmed by the defender's failure to take care.[1] Lord Macmillan stated that:[2]

'The duty to take care is the duty to avoid doing or omitting to do anything the doing or omitting to do which may have as its reasonable and probable consequence injury to others, and the duty is owed to those to whom injury may reasonably and probably be anticipated if the duty is not observed.'

But while Young owed such a duty to the occupants of the motor car, he did not owe it to Mrs Bourhill because she was outwith the area of risk of potential physical harm. As Lord Wright observed,[3] she 'was completely outside the range of the collision. She merely heard a noise which upset her ... She saw nothing of the actual accident, or indeed any marks of blood until later'. Lord Porter expressly articulated the policy considerations involved:[4]

1 1942 SC (HL) 78 at 86 per Lord Russell of Killowen.
2 1942 SC (HL) 78 at 88.
3 1942 SC (HL) 78 at 93.
4 1942 SC (HL) 78 at 98.

'In the case of a civil action there is no such thing as negligence in the abstract. There must be neglect of the use of care towards a person towards whom the defendant owes the duty of observing care ... The driver of a car or vehicle, even though careless, is entitled to assume that the ordinary frequenter of the streets has sufficient fortitude to endure such incidents as may from time to time be expected to occur in them, including the noise of a collision and the sight of injury to others, and is not to be considered negligent towards the one who does not possess the customary phlegm.'

Thus, as a general rule, there was no duty of care to prevent secondary victims from suffering mental harm; liability only extended to primary victims, ie persons who were placed in physical danger or reasonably in fear of such danger as a result of the defender's careless conduct.

In *McLoughlin v O'Brian*[1] the House of Lords was persuaded to widen the scope of potential delictual liability for psychiatric disorder. In this case, the plaintiff's husband and three children were involved in a road accident at 4 pm. They were taken to hospital where it was discovered that one child was dead. The plaintiff was told of the accident at 6 pm and went to the hospital where she saw the victims. She later suffered a psychiatric disorder. The Court of Appeal took the view that while it was reasonably foreseeable that a wife and mother might sustain mental harm in these circumstances, the defendant did not owe the plaintiff a duty of care because she was not present at the accident. In other words, she was not a primary but a secondary victim. The House of Lords rejected this argument and held that a duty of care existed in spite of the fact that the plaintiff had not been directly involved in the accident. While it was reasonably foreseeable that the spouse and mother of persons injured in an accident might suffer mental harm this in itself was not sufficient to create a duty of care. However, there were additional factors present in the case which provided the necessary degree of proximity between the parties from which a duty of care could be inferred. First, the plaintiff was with the victims shortly after the accident; accordingly, she had witnessed the aftermath of the accident. Second, she had personally *seen* the effects of the accident on her family and had not simply learned of the accident by letter or on television or from a third party.[2] It follows from *McLoughlin* that before a duty of care is owed to a secondary victim, not only must the risk of a psychiatric disorder to the pursuer be reasonably foreseeable but other factors must be

---

1 [1983] 1 AC 410, [1982] 2 All ER 298, HL. For an earlier example of liability to a secondary victim, see *Hambrook v Stokes Bros* [1925] 1 KB 141, CA.
2 *McLoughlin v O'Brian* [1983] AC 410 at 421–423 per Lord Wilberforce.

present which show a sufficient degree of proximity between the parties. If these additional factors are *not* present, the court will not impose a duty of care.

These issues were further explored by the House of Lords in *Alcock v Chief Constable of South Yorkshire Police*.[1] Friends and relations of persons crushed to death at Hillsborough football ground brought claims for mental harm. The House of Lords held that before a duty of care arose, it had to be reasonably foreseeable that the plaintiffs would suffer a psychiatric disorder. The criterion could not be satisfied unless there was a close tie of love and affection between the plaintiff and the victim. This would be presumed if they were spouses or parent and child, but merely because they were related in some way would not per se be sufficient. Conversely, if they were not related, a plaintiff might still succeed if it could be shown that the requisite degree of love and affection *in fact* existed between the plaintiff and the victim.[2] Their Lordships then maintained that reasonable foreseeability was not sufficient and two *extra* factors for proximity had also to exist. The plaintiff had to witness the calamity or its aftermath (for example, by being at the stadium); identifying a dead relative or friend eight hours after the event was not enough. Secondly, the plaintiff must have seen or heard the accident: watching the event on television did not suffice since the defendant knew that it was the policy of the television company in such circumstances to ensure that no specific person who was injured could be identified.

To summarise: a duty of care to prevent mental harm to a secondary victim will only arise if:

(1) there is a tie of love and affection between the secondary victim and the primary victim;
(2) the secondary victim was present at the accident or at its immediate aftermath; and
(3) the psychiatric disorder was caused by direct perception of the accident or its immediate aftermath: it is not enough merely to have been informed of the accident.

---

1 [1992] 1 AC 310, [1991] 4 All ER 707, HL.
2 In *Alcock*, the House suggested that in exceptionally horrific circumstances a duty of care might arise even though the secondary victim did not fulfil the 'love and affection' criterion. This is doubtful. In *Robertson v Forth Road Bridge Joint Board* 1994 SC 364, for example, the fact that the pursuer who had witnessed his fellow employee being blown off the Forth Road Bridge had been a friend of the deceased and had socialised with him for many years was held not to be sufficient to constitute the necessary degree of 'love and affection'. The same kind of reasoning was applied in *McFarlane v EE Caledonia Ltd* [1994] 2 All ER 1 where the plaintiff had witnessed the Piper Alpha explosion. So, in this respect, *Alcock* has never been followed – what could have been more horrific than the accidents in *Robertson* and *McFarlane*?

The *Alcock* criteria for the imposition of a duty of care in relation to secondary victims were reaffirmed by the House of Lords in *Frost v Chief Constable South Yorkshire Police*.[1]

The law now appears to be settled but its application can lead to arbitrary results. In *Vernon v Bosley (No 1)*,[2] for example, two children were drowned when the car their nanny was driving crashed into a river. Their father was called to the scene and saw the unsuccessful attempts to rescue his children trapped in the car. The father's claim for damages for a psychiatric disorder was successful. The defendant owed him a duty of care because:

(1) he was the father of the primary victims; and
(2) he witnessed the aftermath; and
(3) his psychiatric illness arose from direct perception of the failed rescue attempt.

But if for example, he had not been able to be present at the rescue but was simply informed of his daughters' deaths by telephone, no duty of care would have arisen because of the absence of reasons (2) and (3). Similarly, Mrs Bourhill would still fail in her claim since there was no tie of love and affection between her and Young's primary victims.[3]

There is authority that there is no breach of a duty to prevent mental harm unless it has been induced by a nervous shock, ie the 'sudden appreciation by sight or sound of a horrifying event, which violently agitates the mind'.[4] Claims have therefore been refused

---

1 [1999] 2 AC 455 where the police constables could not establish a sufficient tie of love and affection with the primary victims they were attempting to rescue: therefore the constables' claims as secondary victims failed. They were not within the area of potential physical harm and therefore could not be regarded as primary victims. See also *Keen v Tayside Contracts* 2003 SLT 500 (employee treated as secondary victim where he sustained mental harm by witnessing an accident and not being allowed to leave the scene by his supervisor: discussed beyond pp 219 ff).

2 [1997] 1 All ER 577. See also *Galli-Atkinson v Seghal* [2003] EWCA 697 where a mother visited a hospital mortuary to see her child whom she refused to believe was dead: this was regarded by the Court of Appeal as part of the aftermath of the accident.

3 But could she have sued if she had been related to Young who was killed in the accident as a result of his own negligence? It is submitted that she could. *Cf Greatorex v Greatorex* [2000] 4 All ER 769 (father claimed damages for a psychiatric disorder sustained when he rescued his son from a car crash. The *Alcock* criteria were satisfied. However, the claim was refused on policy grounds as the son was solely responsible for his own injuries and the court could not countenance a parent suing his own child in such circumstances. *Sed quaere?*).

4 *Alcock v Chief Constable of South Yorkshire Police* [1992] 1 AC 310 per Lord Ackner at 401.

where a psychiatric disorder has been caused by a gradual process, for example nursing a dying child.[1]

The law in this area is considered to be unsatisfactory and Scottish Ministers have made a reference to the Scottish Law Commission to consider reform.[2]

C. WRONGFUL LIFE, WRONGFUL BIRTH AND WRONGFUL CONCEPTION

(1) Wrongful life

It is generally accepted that a person owes a duty of care not to harm a foetus, ie a child *in utero*. Where a foetus is injured in its mother's womb, if the child is subsequently born alive, the *child* can sue the defender in delict in respect of its physical harm even though the injuries were sustained when the child was a foetus. In *McKay v Essex Area Health Authority*[3] a mother contracted rubella (German measles) during her pregnancy. When the child was born, the baby was badly deformed as result of the mother's illness. The mother alleged that owing to the hospital's carelessness, she had not been informed that her baby might be born with deformities. Since no tests had been carried out, the mother had been denied the opportunity of a lawful termination of her pregnancy. The Court of Appeal held that the hospital may have been in breach of a duty of care towards the *mother* which would entitle her to damages for having to bring up a deformed child. But the hospital did not owe a duty of care towards the *child* to allow the child's mother the opportunity to terminate the pregnancy. A child has no right to be born whole or not at all. This denial of the existence of a duty of care towards a foetus to terminate the pregnancy if the foetus is deformed is clearly based on principles of public policy.[4] Thus the

---

1 *Sion v Hampstead Health Authority* [1994] 5 Med LR 170, CA. Damages may be awarded if there is a sudden realisation of the danger to the primary victim within a continuing process: *Walters v North Glamorgan NHS Trust* [2002] EWHC 321.

2 See SLC *Discussion Paper on Damages for Psychiatric Injury* (Discussion Paper No 120).

3 [1982] QB 1166, [1982] 2 All ER 771, CA.

4 Moreover, even if such a duty existed, the child's deformities were not caused by the careless conduct of the hospital but by the rubella; on the necessity for causation, see Chapter 6 below. Of course, if the hospital had caused the child's deformities, it *would* have been liable to the child, if born alive; see discussion beyond.

law has refused to recognise wrongful life actions by denying the existence of a duty of care: again, we see the duty of care being used as a threshold device.

(2) Wrongful birth

While there will be no duty of care towards a foetus to terminate the pregnancy because it might be born deformed, the Court of Appeal emphasised that the defendant could have been in breach of its duty towards the *mother* in not allowing her the opportunity of a termination. This is known as a wrongful birth action. In *McLelland v Greater Glasgow Health Board*[1] an Extra Division accepted that wrongful birth actions can be pursued in Scots law. Thus a hospital owes a duty of care to the parents of a child to provide the mother with an opportunity to terminate her pregnancy if her child is likely to be born physically or mentally handicapped. While both parents can recover solatium for the distress of having a handicapped child and the mother can recover solatium in respect of the pregnancy and birth, the basic economic cost of maintaining the child cannot be recovered: but any additional costs stemming from the special needs of a handicapped child can be recovered.[2]

(3) Wrongful conception

In *McFarlane v Tayside Health Board*,[3] the pursuers sought damages for the birth of a healthy child who had been born as a result of a failed sterilisation on the father. The Lord Ordinary (Gill) admitted that the defenders owed a duty of care to the pursuers who were their patients but denied the pursuers' action of damages. Lord Gill argued that the parents had not sustained any reparable loss. He refused to classify pregnancy and labour as physical injury to the mother and he did not regard the cost of rearing the child as economic loss since such loss was outweighed by the inestimable benefits of being the parents of a healthy child. This decision was reversed by the Second Division.[4] There it was held that the parents' right not to have a child had been infringed, ie that the unplanned conception constituted the harm (*damnum*). This was a

1 2002 SLT 446.
2 For full discussion, see beyond pp 288 ff.
3 1997 SLT 211, OH, 2000 SC (HL) 1.
4 2000 SC (HL) 1.

reparable interest in modern Scots law.[1] Consequently in a wrongful conception action the mother could recover damages for pain and suffering caused by the pregnancy and birth; and both parents could recover compensation for the economic costs of bringing up the child whose birth had not been planned. Moreover, their damages would not be reduced because the mother had refused to terminate the pregnancy.

This decision was in turn appealed to the House of Lords. There it was accepted that a doctor does owe a duty of care to a man or a woman who undergoes sterilisation and if as a result of medical negligence an unplanned conception occurs then there is a breach of that duty of care. The House agreed that the mother could recover solatium for pain and suffering caused by the pregnancy and birth as well as any derivative economic loss of earnings during that period. But their Lordships held that it was contrary to contemporary values of distributive justice that the parents should be able to recover for the economic cost of maintaining a healthy and normal child.[2] The principle of non-recoverability for the cost of bringing up a normal and healthy child was reaffirmed by the House of Lords in *Rees v Darlington Memorial Hospital NHS Trust*.[3] However, a majority of their Lordships felt that an award of solatium did not adequately recognise the wrongful infringement of the mother's freedom to limit the size of her family and made her a conventional non-compensatory award of £15,000 to afford some measure of recognition of the wrongful conception of her child.

D. PURE ECONOMIC LOSS

It is in the area of liability in delict for pure economic loss that the concept of a duty of care has been extensively used by the courts as

---

1 In England, wrongful conception actions had been recognised for a long time. See, for examples, *Thake v Maurice* [1986] QB 644, [1984] 2 All ER 513; *Gold v Haringey Health Authority* [1987] 2 All ER 888, CA. In *Goodwill v British Pregnancy Advisory Service* [1996] 2 All ER 161, CA, the Court of Appeal held that the duty of care did not extend to advising the future sexual partners of male patients that their vasectomy could undergo a spontaneous reversal. *Sed quaere?* Counsel for Ms Goodwill was Ms Cherie Booth QC!

2 For further discussion on the damages issues, see p 288 below. See also Joe Thomson 'Abandoning the Law of Delict' 2000 SLT (News) 43.

3 [2004] 1 AC 309, [2003] 4 All ER 987. *McFarlane* was followed even although the mother in *Rees* was blind. For further discussion, see p 288 below.

a threshold device. *Donoghue v Stevenson*[1] is authority for the principle that a duty of care arises when it is reasonably foreseeable by the defender that his careless acts or omissions would cause physical harm to the pursuer or physical damage to the pursuer's property. The pursuer can recover damages for economic loss which derives from the pursuer's injuries or the physical damage to his property, for example, loss of earnings while in hospital and loss of earnings in the future when the pursuer is unable to work.[2] This is known as *derivative* or *parasitic* economic loss, ie economic loss which derives from or is parasitic upon the pursuer's physical injuries or the physical damage to the pursuer's property. However, the law does not, as a general rule, allow recovery in *delict* where the pursuer only sustains economic loss as a result of the defender's careless conduct.[3] In the case of a defective product, for example, which has not physically harmed the pursuer or damaged other property belonging to the pursuer, the cost of repair or the difference in value between a defective and a non-defective product is not recoverable in *delict*. The pursuer has sustained pure economic loss and the courts have refused to impose a duty of care on the manufacturer in respect of such losses even though such a loss is reasonably foreseeable. Where the pursuer has bought the product, she, of course, can sue the retailer for breach of contract on the ground that the goods are not of satisfactory quality. The reluctance to allow recovery in delict for pure economic loss is to protect the defender from potentially indeterminate liability.[4]

Although reasonable foreseeability of pure economic loss is not sufficient for the imposition of a duty of care, the courts have, in

---

1   1932 SC (HL) 31, discussed at pp 60 ff above.

2   On damages generally, see Chapter 16 below. Derivative economic losses may not be recoverable if they are too remote: see pp 283 ff below.

3   Where the defender has intended to cause economic loss, for example by fraud or by wrongful occupation of property, Scots law does provide compensation: see, for example, *Saeed v Waheed* 1996 SLT (Ch Ct) 39, 1995 SCLR 504. The reasoning in *Saeed* is controversial because the Sheriff Principal (Nicholson) relied on English cases concerned with liability for pure economic loss arising from negligence. It is thought that the pursuer should have been awarded violent profits: see p 21 above.

4   So when a Scottish football team supporter claimed damages against FIFA and the SFA for economic loss incurred as a result of the delay to a World Cup match between Scotland and Estonia, it was held that the SFA and FIFA did not owe the pursuer a duty of care to ensure that the match took place as scheduled: *Macdonald v Fédération Internationale des Football Associations* 1999 SCLR 59, OH.

certain situations, been prepared to hold that a duty of care does exist. But there must be factors *in addition* to reasonable foreseeability of pure economic loss which demonstrate that there is a sufficient degree of proximity between the parties so that it is fair, just and reasonable for a duty of care to be inferred. These additional requirements are simply a rationalisation by the courts of why they are, or are not, prepared to extend the parameters of liability in delict. It is the paradigm of the duty of care being used as a threshold device.

We shall now examine these developments in detail.

(1) Careless misrepresentation

A may make a statement to B which causes B physical harm or damage to B's property: for example A tells B that it is safe to drink contaminated water. A will owe B a duty of care if it is reasonably foreseeable that B will suffer physical harm or damage to his property if A's statement is made carelessly. This is a simple application of the *Donoghue* neighbourhood principle.[1] But A may make a statement to B which causes B pure economic loss. For example, A tells B that B should enter into a contract with C. Relying on A's advice, B enters into the contract with C. As a result, B loses money. Can B sue A in delict for the pure economic loss B has sustained, if A's statement was made carelessly?[2] The answer depends on whether A owes a duty of care to B not to make careless statements which cause B pure economic loss.

The criteria for the existence of such a duty were laid down by the House of Lords in *Hedley Byrne & Co Ltd v Heller & Partners Ltd*.[3] The plaintiffs through their bankers asked E's bankers, the defendants, whether E was a respectably constituted company. E's bankers replied that E was. On reliance of this statement, the plaintiffs became E's advertising agents. E later went into liquidation. As a result, the plaintiffs suffered pure economic loss. The facts of the case can be shown as follows:

1 For full discussion, see pp 60 ff above.
2 Cf if A made the statement fraudulently, when, of course, A is liable for fraud. On fraud, see pp 53 ff above.
3 [1964] AC 465, [1963] 2 All ER 575, HL.

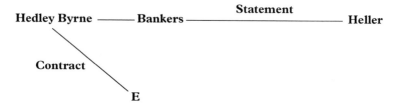

It will be clear that there was no contract between Hedley Byrne and Heller. The question was whether the plaintiffs could sue the defendants in delict. The House of Lords held that the defendants owed a duty of care to the plaintiffs if the defendants had undertaken responsibility for the accuracy of the statement and knew or ought to have known that the plaintiffs would rely on that statement. If the duty was broken as a result of the statement being made carelessly, the defendants could be liable for the plaintiffs' pure economic loss. In the course of his speech, Lord Devlin stated[1] that before there was liability, the plaintiffs had to show that the defendants owed the plaintiffs 'a special duty' to take care. The categories of relationships where this duty arose included not only contractual relationships (ie where there was a contract between the parties) or fiduciary relationships (for example, principal and agent, trustee and beneficiary) but also relationships which were the 'equivalent to contract'. One example of this would be where the defender had voluntarily assumed responsibility for the accuracy of the statement and knew or ought to have known that the pursuer would rely on the information. The paradigm situation is where the defender is a professional business man, for example a banker, solicitor or accountant, who in the absence of a contract between them, gives advice to the pursuer in the course of the defender's business, knowing that it will be relied on by the pursuer.

It is important to notice that reasonable foreseeability of loss to the pursuer is not per se sufficient to establish a duty of care. There must be additional factors present from which the courts will infer the necessary proximity of relationship between the parties. These factors include the defender's knowledge of the identity of the pursuer, either as an individual or as a member of an identifiable class; and the defender's knowledge that the information will be communicated to and used by the pursuer in connection with a particular transaction or transactions of a particular kind.

---

1   [1963] 2 All ER 575 at 610.

These limitations on *Hedley Byrne v Heller* liability were recognised by the House of Lords in *Caparo Industries plc v Dickman*.[1] The auditor of a company carelessly carried out an audit showing that the company was in a better financial position than was in fact the case. It was reasonably foreseeable (a) that potential investors in reliance on the audit would invest in the company to their loss; and (b) that existing shareholders, in reliance on the audit, would purchase more shares in the company to their loss. This, in fact, happened. Although the auditor had a contract with the company, he did not have a contract with existing and potential shareholders. Although the losses which had been incurred were reasonably foreseeable, the House of Lords held that the auditor did not owe a duty of care to the shareholders or potential shareholders to prevent them suffering pure economic loss as a result of the careless audit. The reasons were that their relationships were not sufficiently proximate and that it was not fair, just and reasonable to impose a duty of care. In other words, the factors additional to reasonable foreseeability did not exist in this case. Lord Bridge explained:[2]

'The salient feature of all these cases [ie where a *Hedley Byrne v Heller* duty of care was recognised] is that the defendant giving advice or information was fully aware of the nature of the transaction which the plaintiff had in contemplation, knew that the advice or information would be communicated to him directly or indirectly and knew that it was very likely that the plaintiff would rely on that advice or information in deciding whether or not to engage in the transaction in contemplation. In these circumstances the defendant could clearly be expected ... specifically to anticipate that the plaintiff would rely on the advice or information given by the defendant for the very purpose for which he did in the event rely on it. So also the plaintiff ... would in that situation reasonably suppose that he was entitled to rely on the advice or information communicated to him for the very purpose for which he required it. The situation is entirely different where a statement is put into more or less general circulation and may foreseeably be relied on by strangers to the maker of the statement for any one of a variety of different purposes which the speaker has no specific reason to anticipate. To hold the maker of the statement to be under a duty of care in respect of the accuracy of the statement to all and sundry for any purpose for which they may choose to rely on it is not only to subject him, in the classic words of Cardozo CJ to "liability in an indeterminate amount for an indeterminate time to an indeterminate class",[3] it is also to confer on the world at large a quite unwarranted entitlement to appropriate for their own purposes the benefit of the expert knowledge or professional expertise attributed to the maker of the statement.'

1 [1990] 2 AC 605, [1990] 1 All ER 568, HL.
2 [1990] 1 All ER 568 at 576.
3 *Ultramares Corpn v Touche* (1931) 255 NY 170 at 179.

Accordingly, the House of Lords held that an auditor did not owe a duty of care to a member of the public at large who relied on the audit to purchase shares or increase an existing shareholding in the company: such a duty would arise only if the auditor knew that his statement would be communicated to the plaintiff and relied upon by the plaintiff in a particular transaction of a particular kind.[1]

Hedley Byrne v Heller was an English case. The principle has been accepted as part of Scots law.[2] One area where it has been applied is in relation to the liability of surveyors. Consider the following example. A wishes to purchase a house from B. He approaches a bank for a loan. Before it can give the loan the bank must obtain a report on the value of the property from a surveyor. It is a term of A's contract with the bank that A will pay the surveyor's fee. Instead of obtaining an independent survey, A relies on the valuation report commissioned for the bank and goes ahead with the purchase. The house turns out to have faulty foundations which will cost £20,000 to repair. The facts of the case can be represented in the diagram on page 87 below.

Since A has not been physically harmed and the faulty foundations have not caused physical damage to any other property owned by A, A has suffered only pure economic loss. This is either the cost of repairs or the difference in value between the house with faulty foundations and the house if the foundations were sound. Although A has a contract of sale with B, the seller of heritage does not usually warrant that a house built on the land conveyed is sound. Therefore A has no *contractual* remedy against B. Moreover, although A paid for the survey, he has no contract with the sur-

---

1 In *Nordic Oil Services Ltd v Berman* 1993 SLT 1164, OH, the Lord Ordinary (Osborne) held that directors of a company did not owe a duty of care to creditors of the company to prevent them suffering economic loss as a result of the acts or omissions of the company. In *Reeman v Department of Transport* [1997] 2 Lloyd's Rep 648, CA, it was held by the Court of Appeal that before a duty of care could arise by virtue of *Caparo*, the defendant's statement had to be plaintiff-specific, purpose-specific and transaction-specific. Thus if an auditor is aware that a particular identified bidder or lender would rely on the audited accounts and the auditor intends that the bidder or lender should rely on them, he owes that party a duty of care: *Galoo Ltd (in liquidation) v Bright Grahame Murray* [1994] 1 WLR 1360, [1995] 1 All ER 16, CA; *Royal Bank of Scotland v Bannerman Johnstone Maclay* 2003 SC 125.

2 *John Kenway Ltd v Orcantic Ltd* 1979 SC 422, 1980 SLT 46, OH; *Eastern Marine Services (and Supplies) Ltd v Dickson Motors Ltd* 1981 SC 355, OH; *Twomax Ltd v Dickson, McFarlane and Robinson* 1982 SC 113, 1983 SLT 98, OH. The last decision must now be read in the light of the limitations laid down in *Caparo Industries plc v Dickman* [1990] 2 AC 605, [1990] 1 All ER 568, HL.

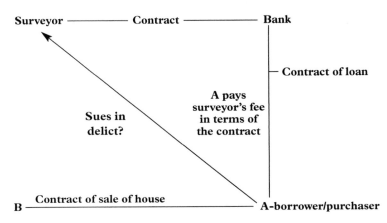

veyor: the surveyor's contract is with the bank. However, it has been held that the surveyor owes a duty of care to A, if the surveyor knows that the report will be used by A and will be relied upon by A to purchase the house.[1] As well as reasonable foreseeability of loss to A, the surveyor's knowledge of A and the particular transaction, A's reliance on the report, and the fact that A paid for the report, provide the additional factors which create a sufficient degree of proximity between A and the surveyor for a *Hedley Byrne v Heller* duty of care to arise. Accordingly, if the report was made carelessly, A can recover damages for pure economic loss from the surveyor. If, however, A later sold the house to C and C relied on the valuation report rather than commission a new survey, the surveyor would not owe a duty of care to C. For although it is reasonably foreseeable that the report would be relied on by a singular successor of A (ie a subsequent purchaser of the house), since the surveyor did not know the identity of C at the time of the survey and C did not pay the fee, the additional factors are not present and the duty of care does not arise.[2]

1 *Martin v Bell-Ingram* 1986 SC 208, 1986 SLT 575; *Smith v Eric S Bush; Harris v Wyre Forest District Council* [1990] 1 AC 831, [1989] 2 WLR 790. See also *Smith v Carter* 1994 SCLR 539, 1995 SLT 295, OH, where the survey was commissioned by A acting as the undisclosed agent of B. It was held that a duty of care was owed to B because it is not uncommon for one person to commission a report on behalf of joint purchasers.

2 This would follow from the ratio of *Caparo Industries plc v Dickman* [1990] 2 AC 605, [1990] 1 All ER 568, HL. Similarly, the absence of such additional factors prevented the surveyor owing a duty of care to the owner of the lost cargo in *Marc Rich & Co AG v Bishop Rock Marine Co Ltd, The Nicholas H* [1994] 3 All ER 686, [1994] 1 WLR 1071, CA (affd [1995] 3 All ER 307, HL), discussed at p 66 above.

Although the existence of a duty of care to prevent pure economic loss to the plaintiff was recognised in *Hedley Byrne & Co Ltd v Heller & Partners Ltd*,[1] in fact the plaintiff did not obtain damages in that case. When they provided the information, the defendants expressly stated that it was given 'without responsibility on the part of the bank'. The House of Lords held that this disclaimer was effective to protect the defendants from liability. After their potential delictual liability towards purchasers of property was established, surveyors started to insert a similar disclaimer in their valuation reports or in the bank's contract with the borrower/purchaser. Provided the disclaimer came to the notice of the purchaser before the purchaser entered into the contract of sale,[2] for a time these disclaimers were effective to protect the surveyor from liability in delict.[3] However, where the disclaimer is a term of the purchaser's contract with the bank,[4] it cannot be relied on unless it satisfies the requirement of reasonableness under the Unfair Contract Terms Act 1977.[5] Moreover, the controls in UCTA 1977 now extend to disclaimers which are not contractual terms.[6] This includes any disclaimers in the surveyor's valuation report. Consequently, a surveyor cannot escape delictual liability by relying on a disclaimer unless it satisfies the requirement of reasonableness. In *Smith v Eric S Bush; Harris v Wyre Forest District Council*,[7] the House of Lords, applying the parallel English provisions of the Unfair Contract Terms Act 1977, held that a disclaimer was not reasonable when the purchaser was of limited means and buying domestic property. If the purchaser was wealthy or the property bought was commercial, then a surveyor might be able to establish that the disclaimer was

---

1 [1964] AC 465, [1963] 2 All ER 575, HL.
2 If it did not come to the purchaser's notice before the contract of sale was agreed, the disclaimer was not effective: *Martin v Bell-Ingram* 1986 SC 208, 1986 SLT 575.
3 *Robbie v Graham and Sibbald* 1989 SCLR 578, 1989 SLT 870, OH.
4 *Melrose v Davidson and Robertson* 1993 SC 288, 1993 SLT 611.
5 Unfair Contract Terms Act 1977, ss 16 and 25(5). See *Melrose v Davidson and Robertson* 1993 SC 288, 1993 SLT 611.
6 Law Reform (Miscellaneous Provisions) (Scotland) Act 1990, s 68.
7 [1990] 1 AC 831, [1989] 2 All ER 514, HL.

reasonable.[1] A similar view has been taken by the courts in Scotland.[2]

The classic example of *Hedley Byrne v Heller* liability is where A makes a misrepresentation to B which B relies on to enter a contract with C. A owes B a duty of care which enables B to sue A in *delict* for pure economic loss. Does A owe B a *Hedley Byrne v Heller* duty of care when A makes a misrepresentation to B which induces B to enter a contract with A? For many years, as a result of the decision in *Manners v Whitehead*,[3] B was denied a remedy in delict against A unless A's misrepresentation was fraudulent.[4] The rule in *Manners v Whitehead* has been abolished.[5] Accordingly, provided the *Hedley Byrne v Heller* criteria are established,[6] A will owe B a duty of care so that B can sue A in *delict* if the misrepresentation was made carelessly and caused B pure economic loss. In addition or as an alternative, B will have contractual remedies, for example reduction, arising from the misrepresentation.[7] In *Hamilton v Allied Domecq plc*,[8] the first reported decision in Scotland where an action for negligent misrepresentation in delict was successfully brought against the other party to the contract,[9] the effect of s 10 appears to have been misunderstood. The Lord Ordinary (Carloway) suggested that s 10 equated a negligent misrepresentation with a

---

1 As happened, for example, in *Omega Trust Co Ltd v Wright Son & Pepper (No 1)* [1997] 1 EGLR 120, CA.
2 *Bank of Scotland v Fuller Peiser* 2002 SLT 574. The House of Lords in *Smith v Eric S Bush; Harris v Wyre Forest District Council* [1990] 1 AC 831, [1989] 2 All ER 514, HL, also rejected the argument that the disclaimer prevented a duty of care arising in the first place. Instead, it held that the duty of care existed in spite of the disclaimer and that the disclaimer was therefore an exemption clause purporting to exclude liability. The matter is academic: by UCTA 1977, s 25(5) any clause which purports to prevent a duty of care from arising is also subject to the requirement of reasonableness before it can be effective. Where the disclaimer satisfies the requirement of reasonableness, no duty of care arises: *McCullagh v Lane Fox and Partners* [1996] 1 EGLR 35, (1995) Times, 22 December, CA; *Bank of Scotland v Fuller Peiser* 2002 SLT 574.
3 (1898) 1 F 171.
4 On fraud, see pp 53 ff above.
5 Law Reform (Miscellaneous Provisions) (Scotland) Act 1985, s 10.
6 And it is submitted that in this situation they usually are.
7 These are the same as the contractual remedies available after a fraudulent misrepresentation, discussed at p 53 above.
8 2001 SC 829. After proof, defenders have been held liable: 2004 SLT 191.
9 An attempt failed in *Palmer v Beck* 1993 SLT 485, OH, on the ground that s 10 of the Law Reform (Miscellaneous Provisions) (Scotland) Act 1985 was not retrospective. See also *Clelland v Morton Fraser Milligan* 1997 SLT (Sh Ct) 57, where an action under s 10 failed because it was not brought against the other party to the pursuer's contract.

fraudulent misrepresentation and therefore there was no need to establish a special relationship between the parties before a duty of care arose. With respect, it is thought that this is wrong.[1] The function of s 10 was merely to abolish the rule in *Manners v Whitehead* and allow the courts to develop negligent misrepresentation untrammelled by that rule. It is submitted, therefore, that the pursuer must establish a special relationship between the defender and himself, though, as in *Hamilton* itself, this should not be too difficult given that *ex hypothesi* they are parties to the same contract.[2]

(2) *Henderson v Merrett* – A general duty of care to prevent pure economic loss?

An attempt to rationalise the law on delictual liability for pure economic loss was made by the House of Lords in *Henderson v Merrett Syndicates Ltd*.[3] Actions for damages were brought by Lloyd's 'names' against Lloyd's members' agents and managing agents of syndicates. The 'names' alleged that they had suffered losses as a result of the negligence of the agents. Under contracts with their members' agents, the names gave the agents the exclusive right to undertake risks and reinsurance on their behalf. This was done directly through the members' agents or indirectly by the members' agents delegating the tasks to managing agents through a sub-agency contract. This can be illustrated as follows:

CONTRACT

Names ———————————————— Members' agents

                                                               sub-agency
                                                                agreements

Management agents

The obvious remedy was for the names to sue the members' agents for breach of contract. Unfortunately, this action was time-barred. So an action against them and the management agents could lie only in tort/delict. The question before the House of Lords was

---

1 For full discussion see Joe Thomson 'Misrepresentation' 2001 SLT (News) 279.
2 This issue may have been overtaken by the development of a general duty of care to prevent pure economic loss discussed in the next section of this chapter.
3 [1995] 2 AC 145, [1994] 3 All ER 506, HL.

whether the management agents and the members' agents owed a duty of care to the names. Their Lordships held that they did. Why?

Lord Goff of Chieveley maintained that a duty of care arises to prevent the plaintiff sustaining pure economic loss when the defendant has voluntarily assumed responsibility for the economic interests of the plaintiff with the knowledge that the plaintiff is relying on the defendant's expertise. This assumption of responsibility covers the provision of services as well as information; careless omissions as well as careless actions. When the parties are linked directly or indirectly by contracts, the terms of the contracts may exclude liability in delict but to be effective any such exemption clauses or disclaimers will have to satisfy the requirements of reasonableness under the Unfair Contract Terms Act 1977.

Like Lord Atkin with his neighbourhood principle,[1] Lord Goff was laying down a general duty of care: if the two criteria are satisfied, ie voluntary assumption of responsibility and concomitant reliance, then a duty of care exists and it is not necessary to consider whether or not it is fair, just and reasonable to impose a duty of care ie the *Caparo* tripartite criteria are irrelevant.[2]

To summarise: a general duty of care to prevent pure economic loss will arise if:

(1) the defender has voluntarily assumed responsibility for the economic interests of the pursuer;

(2) the defender knows that the pursuer is relying on the defender's professional expertise; and

(3) the terms of any contract linking the pursuer and defender do not negative delictual liability.

Whether or not the defender has voluntarily assumed responsibility for the pursuer's economic interests is objectively ascertained from all the circumstances of the care. The absence of an exemption clause or disclaimer is thus indicative that the defender

---

1 See *Donoghue v Stevenson* 1932 SC (HL) 31, 1932, SLT 317.

2 The general nature of the duty was emphasised by the House of Lords in *Williams v Natural Life Health Foods Ltd* [1988] 2 All ER 577, HL, at 581 per Lord Steyn. A director of a company was held not to owe a duty of care to the plaintiff in this case because he had not assumed personal responsibility for the plaintiff's financial interests: the company was, of course, liable. This decision is of vital significance in company law where a creditor's limited resource to the assets of the company as opposed to the personal assets of the director/shareholder is a fundamental reason for incorporation: *Solomon v A Solomon & Co Ltd* [1897] AC 22, HL. But a managing director (as well as the company) is personally liable for a *fraudulent* misrepresentation: *Standard Chartered Bank v Pakistan Shipping Corpn (No 2)* [2003] 1 All ER 173.

undertook such responsibility.[1] Where there is such a clause, it must satisfy the requirement of reasonableness under the Unfair Contract Terms Act 1977 before it will be effective to prevent the duty of care from arising. In *Bank of Scotland v Fuller Peiser*,[2] for example, the defender provided the purchaser of a hotel with a valuation of the property. The valuation report stated that the defenders accepted 'no responsibility' for anyone other than the purchasers. The pursuers relied on the report when they lent money to the purchaser. When the purchaser defaulted, the pursuer sought damages in delict from the defender. The Lord Ordinary (Eassie) held that the disclaimer satisfied the requirement of reasonableness under the 1977 Act because both parties were of equal bargaining power and could equally bear the loss. The disclaimer was therefore effective to prevent a duty of care from arising as the defender had *not* voluntarily assumed responsibility for the pursuer's economic interests.[3] Moreover, the defender must know that the pursuer does or will rely on his expertise. The necessity for 'concomitant reliance' by the pursuer, which is known to the defender, provides an element of mutuality between the parties which restricts the defender's potential delictual liability.[4]

The *Henderson v Merrett* criteria provide a rationale for the liability for negligent misrepresentations discussed in the previous section. They also explain other situations where delictual liability for pure economic loss has been recognised. In *Spring v Guardian Assurance plc*,[5] for example, the House of Lords held that an employer owed a duty of care to a former employee when providing a reference for him. Because of the defendant's carelessness, the plaintiff had been unable to obtain a job. By agreeing to provide a reference, the employer had voluntarily assumed responsibility for Spring's financial interests, knowing that he would rely on the employer to prepare the reference carefully.[6]

---

1   *Royal Bank of Scotland v Bannerman Johnstone Maclay* 2003 SC 125.
2   2002 SLT 574. See J Thomson 'A General Duty to Prevent Pure Economic Loss' 2002 SLT (News) 225.
3   *Cf Smith v Eric S Bush; Harris v Wyre Forest District Council* [1990] 1 AC 831, [1989] 2 All ER 514, HL, discussed above.
4   It is enough that the defender knows that the pursuer will rely on his expertise; there is no need to show that the defender intended the pursuer to do so. See *Royal Bank of Scotland v Bannerman Johnstone Maclay* 2003 SC 125.
5   [1995] 2 AC 296, [1994] 3 All ER 129, HL.
6   See also *Donlon v Colonial Mutual Group (UK Holdings) Ltd* 1998 SC 244, 1997 SCLR 1088 (failure by employer to exercise reasonable care in ensuring that facts communicated to third parties were accurate).

It is the present writer's view that the concepts of voluntary assumption of responsibility and concomitant reliance do provide the basis for a general duty of care to prevent pure economic loss. As a result of the defender's carelessness, the pursuer is prevented from entering into prospective contracts[1] or induced to enter an uneconomic contract, or an existing contract becomes less profitable. We can call this interference with the pursuer's contracts 'relational economic loss'. The defender's liability arises from his assumption of responsibility *and* his knowledge of the pursuer's reliance – which provides the necessary proximity.

At the time of writing, it appears that the *Henderson v Merrett* general duty of care has been transplanted successfully into Scots law.[2]

(3) Liability arising from defective performance of a contract

A enters a contract with B. In order to fulfil his contract with A, B enters into a contract with C. C's performance of his contract with B is carried out carelessly. As a result, A suffers pure economic loss. The facts can be represented as follows:

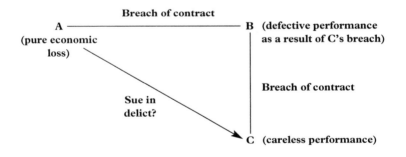

---

1 As in *Spring v Guardian Assurance plc* [1995] 2 AC 296, [1994] 3 All ER 129, HL.
2 *Bank of Scotland v Fuller Peiser* 2002 SLT 574; *Royal Bank of Scotland v Bannerman Johnstone Maclay* 2003 SC 125. But the *Caparo* tripartite test may still be used: *Weir v National Westminster Bank plc* 1994 SLT 1251 (extending bank's liability to detect and report forged signatures to include the agent of a disclosed principal who under a power of attorney was the sole signatory on the account).

A's obvious remedy is to sue B for breach of contract. But if this is not possible (for example if there is an exemption clause in A's contract with B) or not desirable (for example if B is bankrupt) can A sue C in delict?

If C's careless performance of his contract with B had caused physical harm to A or physical damage to A's property, C would owe A a duty of care provided A's injury or the damage to A's property was reasonably foreseeable: ie the *Donoghue v Stevenson* neighbourhood principle would apply.[1] Since A suffers only pure economic loss, reasonable foreseeability of such loss is not sufficient to give rise to a duty of care. But A, B and C are connected by a series of contracts. If C had broken his contract with B with the intention of harming A, A can sue C in *delict* for wrongful interference with B's performance of his contract with A and can recover for pure economic loss.[2] In this case, however, C has not broken his contract with B in order to harm A. Instead, C has by his *careless* conduct broken his contract with B with the result that B's performance of his contract with A is defective, causing A economic loss. In these circumstances, does C owe a duty of care to A not to perform his contract with B in a careless manner if it will cause A economic loss to do so?

In *Junior Books Ltd v Veitchi Co Ltd*,[3] the House of Lords held that such a duty of care could exist. The pursuers entered into a contract with Ogilvie (Builders) Ltd (the main contractor) for the construction of a factory. The pursuers' architects nominated Veitchi, a floor specialist, to lay a floor in the factory. In other words, Veitchi was a nominated sub-contractor. However, Veitchi's contract to lay the floor was with the main contractor, not Junior Books. The floor laid was seriously defective and had to be replaced by the pursuers. There was no averment that the floor laid was dangerous so as to be likely to cause physical harm to any persons in the factory or any damage to the pursuers' property. The pursuers sought damages from the defenders for the cost of replacing the floor. This complex factual situation can be illustrated as follows:

1 *Donoghue* v *Stevenson* 1932 SC (HL) 31, 1932 SLT 317. For discussion, see pp 60 ff above.
2 On the relevant delicts, see pp 38 ff above.
3 1982 SC (HL) 244, 1982 SLT 492.

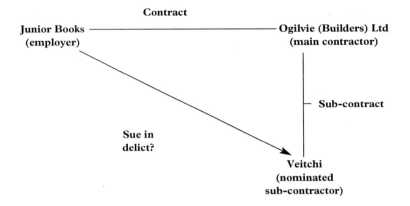

Although nominated by Junior Books' architect, Veitchi had no contractual relationship with Junior Books. Although Junior Books could have sued the main contractor for breach of contract, they chose not to do so. Their only remedy against Veitchi, therefore, lay in delict. Since there was no danger of any physical harm to persons in the factory or damage to the pursuer's property, the case fell outside the neighbourhood principle of reasonable foreseeability of harm laid down in *Donoghue v Stevenson*.[1] In other words, the case was concerned with the recovery of pure economic loss, ie the cost of replacing the defective floor. Nevertheless, the House of Lords held[2] that in the circumstances there was sufficient proximity between the parties for a duty of care to arise: the defenders were under a duty to prevent loss to the pursuers as a result of the defenders' careless performance of their contract with Ogilvie (Builders) Ltd.

Lord Roskill identified eight factors from which the requisite proximity for a duty of care could be inferred:[3]

'(1) The appellants [Veitchi] were nominated sub-contractors. (2) The appellants were specialists in flooring. (3) The appellants knew what products were required by the respondents [Junior Books] and their main contractors and specialised in the production of those products. (4) The

---

1 Lord Keith of Kinkel took the view (1982 SC (HL) 244 at 267) that if such a danger was present, the neighbourhood principle in *Donoghue* was wide enough to cover the cost of averting such a danger. This is doubtful after the decision of the House of Lords in *Murphy v Brentwood District Council* [1991] 1 AC 398, [1990] 2 All ER 908, HL, discussed at pp 102 ff below.
2 Lords Fraser of Tullybelton, Russell of Killowen, Keith of Kinkel and Roskill; Lord Brandon dissented.
3 *Junior Books Ltd v Veitchi Co Ltd* 1982 SC (HL) 244 at 277.

appellants alone were responsible for the composition and construction of the flooring. (5) The respondents relied upon the appellants' skill and experience. (6) The appellants as nominated sub-contractors must have known that the respondents relied upon their skill and experience. (7) The relationship between the parties was as close as it could be, short of actual privity of contract. (8) The appellants must be taken to have known that if they did the work negligently (as it must be assumed that they did) the resulting defects would at some time require remedying by the respondents expending money upon the remedial measures as a consequence of which the respondents would suffer financial or economic loss.'

Several points should be noted. First, the defender and the pursuer are connected by a series of contracts which are subsisting at the time of the defenders' careless acts (ie the installation of the defective floor). Second, Veitchi had been nominated by the pursuers' architect. This is important because as a nominated sub-contractor, Veitchi must have known the identity of the employer, Junior Books, who was contracting with the main contractor, Ogilvie (Builders) Ltd. Third, because Veitchi knew that Junior Books required their services, knew that Junior Books relied upon their expertise, and knew that careless performance of their contract would require the floor to be repaired by Junior Books, Veitchi must have *known* that careless performance by them of their contract with Ogilvie (Builders) Ltd would cause *economic* loss to the pursuer.

Thus, for a *Junior Books* duty of care to arise, the pursuer A and defender C must be connected by a series of contracts: A–B–C.[1] In addition to reasonable foreseeability of loss as a result of his careless acts, C must know the identity of the pursuer A, know that A has a contract with B and know that A will suffer economic loss as a result of C's careless performance of his contract with B, since this will, in turn, render defective B's performance of his contract with A. In establishing this degree of knowledge, the fact that C is a nominated sub-contractor is important but not necessary.[2] A's reliance on C's expertise etc is important. It provides *evidence* that C knows that his careless performance will cause A economic loss. The crucial point is that C must know that the careless perfor-

1 *Comex Houlder Diving Ltd v Colne Fishing Co Ltd (No 2)* 1992 SLT 89, OH; *Scott Lithgow Ltd v GEC Electrical Products Ltd* 1989 SC 412, 1992 SLT 244, OH; *Strathford East Kilbride Ltd v HLM Design Ltd* 1999 SLT 121.
2 In *Scott Lithgow Ltd v GEC Electrical Products Ltd* 1989 SC 412, 1992 SLT 244, OH, the Lord Ordinary (Clyde) thought at 250 ff that it would be enough if the defender had been approved by the pursuer.

mance of his contract with B will cause A economic loss as a result of B's consequent defective performance of his contract with A.[1]

It is the present writer's submission that *Junior Books* liability could be seen as an extension of the economic delict of wrongful interference with performance of a contract. If in the above example, C broke his contract with B with the result that B renders defective performance of his contract with A, it is long settled that A can sue C in delict for pure economic loss if C broke his contract with B *with the intention* of harming A. *Junior Books* goes a step further by providing that A can sue C in delict where C carelessly performs his contract with B with the result that B renders defective performance of his contract with A, provided C *knew* that his careless performance of his contract with B would cause economic loss to A, ie C owes a duty of care to A not to perform his contract with B in a careless manner.

Read this way, the duty of care held to exist in *Junior Books* is kept within the narrowest of limits. First, it only applies where the parties are connected by contracts which are existing at the time of the defender's careless acts. In *D & F Estates Ltd v Church Commissioners for England*,[2] for example, the Church Commissioners owned a block of flats built by the main contractors. The main contractors sub-contracted the plaster work to sub-contractors. The plaster was defective but was not a source of danger. *After* the flats were built, a flat was leased to the plaintiffs. The plaintiffs sued inter alios the main contractors in delict for the cost of repairing the plaster work. The House of Lords held that the main contractors and the sub-contractors were not under a duty of care to prevent economic loss to the plaintiffs as a result of the defective plaster.[3]

In the present writer's view, there was also no possibility of a *Junior Books* duty of care in this case because there was no contractual nexus between the plaintiffs and the main contractor or sub-contractor at the time of the careless act, as illustrated below:

1 On the other hand, if A's reliance on C's expertise is held to be necessary and given that C must know that A will suffer economic loss by C's careless performance of the contract, it could be argued that *Junior Books* liability is simply an example of the general *Henderson v Merrett* duty of care to prevent relational economic loss.

2 [1989] AC 177, [1988] 2 All ER 992, HL. See also *Strathford East Kilbride Ltd v HLM Design Ltd* 1999 SLT 121.

3 For discussion of the absence of a duty of care to prevent economic loss arising from a defective building, see pp 100 ff below.

Second, even if there is an existing contractual nexus, no *Junior Books* duty of care will arise unless the defender knows the identity of the pursuer; this will therefore prevent such a duty of care arising in most cases involving mass production. For example, if A manufactures components for B who uses them to produce products which he sells to C, a distributor, who sells them to X, Y and Z etc, A does not owe a *Junior Books* duty of care to X, Y or Z to prevent *economic loss* [1] due to A's careless performance of his contract with B in supplying B with defective components. This is because A will generally not know of the contracts between C and X, Y and Z:

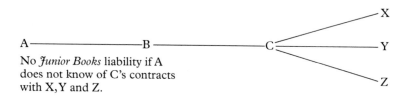

Third, even if there is an existing contractual nexus and the defender knows the identity of the pursuer, the terms of the contracts between the parties, for example exemption or indemnity clauses, may indicate that the parties intended to exclude potential liability in delict.[2] In those circumstances, the court is unlikely to

---

1 Of course, A may owe a *Donoghue v Stevenson* duty of care to X, Y and Z to prevent them suffering physical injury or damage to their property as a result of A's careless manufacture of the components.

2 Cf *British Telecommunications plc v James Thomson & Sons (Engineering) Ltd* 1999 SC (HL) 9 when the contractual relationships between the parties were taken into account to determine whether or not there was a duty of care on the defender to prevent the pursuer sustaining damage to his property.

find the existence of a *Junior Books* duty of care. Finally, the defender must anticipate loss to the particular pursuer as a result of the defender's defective performance.[1]

The limitations which are inherent in the *Junior Books* duty of care are therefore sufficient to keep potential liability for pure economic loss within relatively narrow parameters. Once again we see the duty of care operating as a threshold device.

If it is accepted that the *Junior Books* duty of care is simply an extension of the delict of wrongful interference with the performance of a contract so as to trigger liability as a result of the defender's careless conduct as well as conduct intended to harm the pursuer, then it is thought that there is a future for *Junior Books* liability. Although it has been followed in Scotland, *Junior Books Ltd v Veitchi Co Ltd* [2] has been consistently distinguished in cases south of the border. In *D & F Estates Ltd v Church Commissioners for England* [3] Lord Bridge opined[4] of *Junior Books*:

'The consensus of judicial opinion, with which I concur, seems to be that the decision of the majority is so far dependent on the unique, albeit non-contractual, relationship between the pursuer and the defender in that case and the unique scope of the duty of care owed by the defender to the pursuer arising from that relationship that the decision cannot be regarded as laying down any principle of general application in the law of tort or delict.'

The reason for this scepticism is that *Junior Books* has *not* been regarded as a case which is only concerned with wrongful interference with the pursuer's existing contracts (ie recovery of relational economic loss). Instead, it has been read as laying down potential liability for economic loss arising from the careless manufacture of a defective product which is not dangerous in the sense of causing physical harm to the pursuer or damage to her property (ie non-relational economic loss). If this were the case, then there would, indeed, be cause for concern. But if analysed as above, *Junior Books* liability does not have this potential. Within its relatively narrow sphere, *Junior Books* is both an important and principled decision.[5]

---

1 *Simaan General Contracting Co v Pilkington Glass Ltd (No 2)* [1988] QB 758, [1988] 1 All ER 791, CA.
2 1982 SC (HL) 244, 1982 SLT 492.
3 [1989] AC 177, [1988] 2 All ER 992, HL.
4 [1988] 2 All ER 992 at 1003.
5 *Junior Books* has been approved by the Court of Appeal in Singapore: see *RSP Architects Planners and Engineers v Ocean Front Pte Ltd* (1998) 14 Const LJ 139, CA (Sing).

(4) Liability arising from defective products and buildings

As we have seen, A owes a duty of care to B when it is reasonably foreseeable that B will sustain physical harm or physical damage to his property as a result of A's careless acts or omissions. In *Donoghue v Stevenson* [1] it was held that the manufacturer of a product owed a duty of care to the ultimate consumer to prevent the consumer suffering personal harm or physical damage to his property as a result of a defect in the product caused by the manufacturer's carelessness. The consumer is entitled to damages not only for pain and suffering but also for economic loss which *derives* from his personal injuries or the damage to his property, ie derivative economic loss.

There is an important limitation on the scope of *Donoghue v Stevenson* liability. The duty of care extends only to the pursuer's physical injuries or damage to his property which was caused by the defective product. The damage must be done to property other than the defective product itself. For example, if a defective vacuum cleaner explodes and burns the pursuer or burns the pursuer's carpet there is *Donoghue v Stevenson* liability. But if the defective vacuum simply does not work or it explodes and does not physically harm the pursuer or does not damage any other property of the pursuer there is no *Donoghue v Stevenson* liability. Why? In these circumstances, the pursuer has sustained only *pure* economic loss, ie the cost of repairing the vacuum cleaner or the difference in value between a defective and a non-defective cleaner. The courts have consistently refused to allow the pursuer to recover compensation in *delict* for such losses. Instead, the pursuer must resort to the law of contract to obtain compensation:

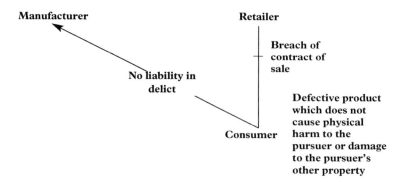

Manufacturer

Retailer

Breach of
contract of
sale

No liability in
delict

Defective product
which does not
cause physical
harm to the
pursuer or damage
to the pursuer's
other property

Consumer

---

1 1932 SC (HL) 31, 1932 SLT 317, discussed at pp 60 ff above.

The consumer cannot sue the manufacturer in delict because the consumer has suffered only pure economic loss. The consumer must sue the retailer for *breach of contract* to recover any loss suffered as a result of the product being defective. If the ultimate consumer does not have a contract with the retailer, if, for example, the defective product was a gift from a third party, the consumer has prima facie no remedy. But the third party could assign the rights under *his* contract with the retailer to the consumer, thus enabling the consumer to recover damages for breach of contract.

It should also be noticed that there will generally be no possibility of *Junior Books* liability in this situation. This is for two reasons: (1) no contractual chain or nexus exists between the manufacturer and the consumer at the time of the careless act since the consumer will only enter into a contract with the retailer *after* the product has been manufactured; and (2) the manufacturer will not know the identity of the consumer.[1] Similarly, there is no *Henderson v Merrett* general duty of care[2] to prevent relational economic loss because the defender manufacturer does not voluntarily assume responsibility for the ultimate consumer's financial interests and there is no concomitant reliance on the consumer's part.

This principle of non-liability for economic loss also applies to the provision of services. In *D & F Estates Ltd v Church Commissioners for England*[3] the plaintiffs incurred expense in repairing defective plasterwork. The defective plasterwork was not a danger to the plaintiffs' person or property. The House of Lords held that the plaintiffs could not sue the defendants who were responsible for the defective plasterwork in *delict* because they had only suffered pure economic loss, ie the cost of repair. The plaintiffs' only remedy could be in contract.

At one time there appeared to be an exception in respect of defective buildings. Local authorities are under a duty to ensure that buildings conform to building regulations and bye-laws: this is done by a local authority engineer approving the plans and the design of the proposed building. In *Anns v Merton London Borough Council*[4]

---

1 It might, of course, be different in both respects if the manufacturer were supplying a product specifically designed for the consumer.
2 See *Henderson v Merrett Syndicates Ltd* [1995] 2 AC 145, [1994] 3 All ER 506, HL, and pp 90 ff above.
3 [1989] AC 177, [1988] 2 All ER 992, HL. There was *no Junior Books* liability in this case. See p 97 above. See also *Strathford East Kilbride Ltd v HLM Design Ltd* 1999 SLT 121.
4 [1978] AC 728, [1977] 2 All ER 492, HL.

the defendants approved the design of the foundations of a building. After it was built, the foundations were discovered to be defective. The House of Lords held that the local authority owed the owner[1] of the house a duty of care in this situation and that damages could include the cost of repair. It was also decided that the builder owed a similar duty of care to the owner of the property. The fact that the plaintiff had only suffered pure economic loss appeared to be irrelevant. The concept of the duty of care was clearly being used as a threshold device significantly to extend the parameters of delictual liability for pure economic loss. In a famous passage, Lord Wilberforce explained:[2]

'The position has now been reached that in order to establish that a duty of care arises in a particular situation, it is not necessary to bring the facts of that situation within those of previous situations in which a duty of care has been held to exist. Rather the question has to be approached in two stages. First one has to ask whether, as between the alleged wrongdoer and the person who has suffered damage there is a sufficient relationship of proximity or neighbourhood such that, in the reasonable contemplation of the former, carelessness on his part may be likely to cause damage to the latter, in which case a prima facie duty of care arises. Secondly, if the first question is answered affirmatively, it is necessary to consider whether there are any considerations which ought to negative, or to reduce or limit the scope of the duty or the class of person to whom it is owed or the damages to which a breach of it may give rise.'

Applying these principles, Lord Wilberforce held that a local authority owed a duty of care to the owner of a building which was subject to latent defects in construction when the plans had been inspected and approved by the local authority. The fact that the owner may suffer only pure economic loss was not sufficient to deny the existence of the duty on policy grounds since the class of potential plaintiffs was restricted to the owners or lessees of the property.

This was to prove to be the high-water mark of the extension of the parameters of delictual liability for defective buildings. The courts thereafter refused to use Lord Wilberforce's two-stage test further to extend the scope of liability. At length, *Anns* itself came to be doubted and was ultimately overruled in *Murphy v Brentwood*

---

1 Technically, the plaintiff in this case was a lessee of the property.
2 [1978] AC 728 at 751–752.

District Council.[1] In this case, a builder laid foundations of a house in accordance with designs approved by the local authority. The foundations proved to be defective. The owner could not afford the £45,000 required for repairs; instead he sold the house for £35,000 less than its market value would have been if the foundations had been sound. The owner sued the local authority for the loss of the value of the house. The House of Lords held that *Anns* was wrongly decided. Neither a local authority nor a builder owes the owner of a house a duty of care in respect of pure economic loss arising from the defective construction of the property; and pure economic loss includes the cost of repairs or the loss of the property's value.

The House of Lords was also sceptical of what is known as the 'complex structure' doctrine. It can be argued that the foundations should be regarded as separate from the rest of the house. If they are defective and cause physical damage to another part of the house, for example by cracks in the walls, this is damage to 'other' property and falls within the *Donoghue v Stevenson* duty of care. The view was taken that this approach is unrealistic:[2]

'The reality is that the structural elements in any building form a single indivisible unit of which the different parts are essentially interdependent. To the extent that there is any defect in one part of the structure it must to a greater or lesser degree necessarily affect all other parts of the structure. Therefore any defect in the structure is a defect in the quality of the whole and it is quite artificial, in order to impose a legal liability which the law would not otherwise impose, to treat a defect in an integral structure, so far as it weakens the structure, as a dangerous defect liable to cause damage to "other property".'

But where a distinct item, such as a central heating boiler, is incorporated into the structure of a building there can be *Donoghue*

---

1 [1991] 1 AC 398, [1990] 2 All ER 908, HL. The House of Lords doubted the value of Lord Wilberforce's two-stage test for the existence of a duty of care. Instead, a duty should only be imposed by analogy with earlier precedents, ie it is an incremental process. In this respect, *Murphy* has been followed in Scotland. '[I]n determining the existence and scope of a duty of care in a context in which a claim is made for economic loss, the court must have particular regard to the traditional categorisation of situations in which duties may or may not be recognised in particular circumstances': *Nordic Oil Services Ltd v Berman.* 1993 SLT 1164 at 1171 per the Lord Ordinary (Osborne). *Murphy* has not been followed in Australia or New Zealand: see *Bryan v Maloney* (1995) 11 Const LJ 274, HC (Aus); *Invercargill City Council v Hamlin* [1996] AC 624, [1996] 1 All ER 756, PC.

2 *Murphy v Brentwood District Council* [1990] 2 All ER 908 at 928 per Lord Bridge.

v Stevenson liability if, as a result of a defect, it causes damage to the house. The owner in these circumstances could sue the manufacturer of the boiler for physical damage to his 'other' property, ie his house.

It is important to examine the implications of *Murphy* for purchasers of heritable property. Consider the following example. A, a company, enters into a contract with B to build a block of flats. After the flats are completed, A sells the flats to various purchasers including C. After a few years, cracks appear in C's flat. It is discovered that the foundations are unsound and that it will cost approximately £10,000 to have them repaired:

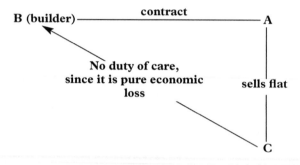

As a result of *Murphy*, C has no delictual remedy against B because C has suffered only pure economic loss; ie B does not owe C a duty of care in respect of the cost of repairs.[1] Although there is a contractual relationship between A and C, this will not help C because a seller of a flat (land) does not warrant the quality of the buildings sold. Moreover, B does not owe C a *Junior Books* duty of care.[2] This is because there is no contractual nexus between B and C at the time of the careless act since C only purchases the property *after* it is built. Even if C had an option from A to purchase a flat while it was being built, a *Junior Books* duty of care will not arise unless B knows the identity of the purchaser, C.[3] Similarly, there is no *Henderson v Merrett* general duty of care[4] to prevent relational economic loss because there is no voluntary assumption of responsibility and concomitant reliance.

---

1 If C was physically injured or any property of C's other than the house was damaged, C can sue B in delict as B owes C a duty of care under the *Donoghue v Stevenson* neighbourhood principle.
2 *Strathford East Kilbride Ltd v HLM Design Ltd* 1999 SLT 121.
3 See pp 98 ff above.
4 See pp 90 ff above.

Because of the absence of a delictual claim against B or a contractual claim against A, in order to protect his interests C should obtain an independent survey *before* purchasing the property. If, as a result of the surveyor's carelessness, the defects are not discovered, C can sue the surveyor for breach of contract. And, as we have seen,[1] even if C relied upon a survey carried out on behalf of C's bank for the purpose of obtaining a loan, C may be able to sue the surveyor in delict on the ground of careless misrepresentation, where damages for pure economic loss are recoverable.

(5) Non-liability for secondary economic loss

We have been considering the situation where the defender has directly caused pure economic loss to the pursuer. However, there is a second situation where pure economic loss can arise. This is where the defender has caused physical harm to A or A's property and as a result B suffers pure economic loss. This will most often arise where B has a contract with A and as a consequence of the defender's delictual conduct A can no longer perform the contract or the contract becomes less profitable. This is known as secondary economic loss.

In *Reavis v Clan Line Steamers Ltd*[2] Mrs Reavis and her orchestra were involved in a collision at sea which was caused inter alia by the fault of the defender, the owner of the ship in which they were sailing. Some members of the orchestra drowned while others were injured and the orchestra had to be disbanded. Mrs Reavis claimed that the services of the players had been secured by contracts of employment and she sought damages from the defender for the loss of profits she had sustained as a result of having to disband the orchestra.

The court held that she was not entitled to recover. An employer is not entitled to sue in delict in respect of secondary economic loss sustained as a result of the death or personal injury of an employee caused by the negligence of a third party. In other words, the defender did not owe Mrs Reavis a duty of care to prevent her sustaining pure economic loss as a result of her employees being no longer able to perform their contracts of employment with her. If Mrs Reavis had been physically harmed, she could, of course, recover for derivative economic loss arising from her *own* injuries – but she could not sue in respect of the death or injury of her employees. (The injured employees and the families of the

1 See pp 86 ff above.
2 1925 SC 725, 1925 SLT 386, OH.

deceased employees, would, of course, have separate claims in delict against the defender.)

Thus, where a person is physically harmed or property is damaged, prima facie it is only the injured person or the owner of the property who has title to sue. Third parties who suffer economic loss as a result of the personal injuries or damage to the property are not entitled to sue for secondary economic loss because the defender does not owe them a duty of care. Thus, for example, in *Dynamco Ltd v Holland and Hannen and Cubitts (Scotland) Ltd* [1] the defender's excavator damaged an underground electric supply cable owned by the South of Scotland Electricity Board. As a result, there was a power cut at the pursuer's factory which lasted for 15½ hours. The pursuer sued for the loss of profits while the factory was closed. The court held that although the defender owed a duty of care to the electricity board not to damage its property, ie the cable, the defender did not owe a duty to the pursuer in respect of secondary economic loss, even though such loss was reasonably foreseeable. In *Coleridge v Miller Construction Ltd*,[2] the power cut physically damaged the glass that the pursuer manufactured in his factory. The Lord Ordinary (MacLean) held that the test for the existence of a duty of care should be the same whether or not the pursuer suffered physical damage to his property or pure economic loss. In the absence of avements that the defender knew that the pursuer required a continuous supply of electricity, it was not reasonably foreseeable that the pursuer would suffer damage to his products if an electric cable were cut. Moreover, even if damage had been reasonably foreseeable it was not fair, just and reasonable to impose a duty of care in these circumstances because the pursuer should have insurance to cover any losses arising from power cuts howsoever caused. Thus secondary physical damage is irrecoverable, as well as secondary economic loss.[3]

---

1   1971 SC 257, 1972 SLT 38.
2   1997 SLT 485, OH.
3   In *Skerries Salmon Ltd v The Braer Corpn* 1999 SLT 1196, the Lord Ordinary (Gill) held that the defender did not owe the pursuers a duty of care to prevent them from having to sell their salmon at low prices. The pursuers alleged that this was caused by a loss of public confidence in the quality of Shetland salmon after the *Braer* oil tanker had run aground. In the absence of any evidence that the pursuers' fish had been contaminated with oil, this was a case of secondary economic loss and no duty was owed. In *Landcatch Ltd v The Braer Corpn; Landcatch Ltd v International Oil Pollution Compensation Fund* 1999 SLT 1208 the pursuers were unable to supply fish farmers in Shetland with salmon smolt because salmon farming had been banned in designated areas contaminated by oil from the *Braer*. There were no contracts subsisting between the fish farmers and the pursuers at the time. This was held to be secondary economic loss and no duty of care arose.

In the important case of *Nacap Ltd v Moffat Plant Ltd*,[1] the pursuers entered into a contract with British Gas to lay a pipeline owned by British Gas in the North Sea. During the work, the defenders damaged the pipeline. As a result, Nacap were unable to complete the work in the time agreed in their contract with British Gas and consequently suffered economic loss. The Inner House held that the pursuers had no title to sue because they were not the owners of the pipeline. In other words, they could not sue in delict for the secondary economic loss they had suffered as a result of the damage to property owned by a third party, ie British Gas.

This approach has been followed in England. In *Candlewood Navigation Corpn Ltd v Mitsui OSK Lines Ltd, The Mineral Transporter*[2] the plaintiffs time-chartered a vessel from the owners of a ship. The vessel was damaged by the defendants. The Privy Council held that the plaintiffs could not recover damages for the hire charges they had to continue to pay and the loss of profits they had incurred while the ship underwent repairs. The defendants did not owe a duty of care to the plaintiffs in respect of the secondary economic loss they had suffered as a result of their contract with the owners becoming less profitable:

Owner of ship ◄——————————— **Defendants damage ship**

Charterparty

Plaintiffs – contract becomes less profitable

In this and the previous cases, a *Junior Books* duty of care does not arise because there is no contractual nexus between the parties. Even if, in *Dynamco Ltd v Holland and Hannen and Cubitts (Scotland) Ltd*,[3] the defender had been engaged on a contract with the electricity board, who had, of course, a contract with its customer, Dynamco, *Junior Books* liability would still not have arisen because the defender would not have known the identity of the pursuer. Similarly, no *Henderson v Merrett* general duty of care arises because in none of these cases did the defender voluntarily assume responsibility for the financial interests of the pursuers.

---

1 1987 SLT 221, reversing 1986 SLT 326.
2 [1986] AC 1, [1985] 2 All ER 935, PC.
3 1971 SC 257, 1972 SLT 38.

Nevertheless, in other circumstances it is thought that there could be sufficient proximity between the parties for a *Junior Books* or *Henderson v Merrett* duty to arise. In *Leigh and Sillavan Ltd v Aliakmon Shipping Co Ltd, The Aliakmon*,[1] the plaintiff (the buyers) entered into a cost and freight (c & f) contract for the purchase of steel coils. Under a c & f contract the seller arranges for the shipping of the goods and obtains a bill of lading from the shipper. The bill of lading is the contract of carriage of the goods. The buyer becomes the owner of the goods when the bill of lading is indorsed by the seller and delivered to the buyer against payment by the buyer of the price. On indorsement, the buyer 'steps into the shoes' of the seller in relation to the bill of lading issued by the shipper. Accordingly, if the goods are damaged in transit, the buyer can sue the shipper for breach of contract. This did not happen in this case because the c & f contract was varied by the parties with the effect that the seller remained owner even though the risk of damage to the goods passed to the buyers. The bill of lading was not indorsed, so that the buyers did not have title to sue the shippers for breach of contract. When they eventually became the owners of the goods, the plaintiff attempted to sue the shippers in delict. The complex facts can be shown thus:

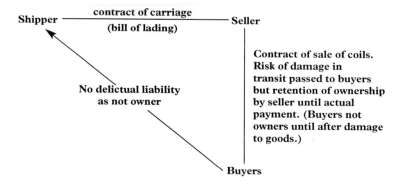

Because the buyers assumed the risk under the contract of sale, they had no right to sue the seller for breach of contract when the

---

1 [1986] AC 785, [1986] 2 All ER 145, HL, affirming [1985] 2 All ER 44, CA. The contractual position has now been overtaken by the Carriage of Goods Act 1992 which makes it easier for the buyer who undertakes the risk to sue the shipper for breach of contract.

goods were damaged. As a result of the variation, the buyers could not use the usual remedy in a c & f situation of suing the shipper for breach of contract. The House of Lords held that the buyers could not sue the shipper in delict because they were not the owners of the goods at the time the goods were damaged. *Junior Books Ltd v Veitchi & Co Ltd*[1] was distinguished on the ground that the pursuer in that case was the owner of the floor when it was carelessly laid.[2] But if *Junior Books* had been argued as a wrongful interference with contracts case, there could have been liability if the shipper had known the identity of the buyers and the existence of the c & f contract when they carelessly performed their contract with the sellers. Such an argument would probably have failed because the shipper had no knowledge of the variation of the contract between the sellers and the buyers and that consequently the buyers had not become the owners of the goods in the usual way.

In the *Aliakmon* case,[3] an attempt was made to circumvent the principle of non-recovery in delict for secondary economic loss by invoking the doctrine of 'transferred loss'. In the Court of Appeal Goff LJ formulated the doctrine thus:[4]

'Where A owes a duty of care in tort [delict] not to cause physical damage to B's property, and commits a breach of that duty in circumstances in which the loss of or physical damage to property will ordinarily fall on B but (as is reasonably foreseeable by A) such loss or damage, by reason of a contractual relationship falls on C, then C will be entitled, subject to the terms of any contract restricting A's liability to B, to bring an action in tort against A in respect of such loss or damage to the extent that it falls on him, C.'

This would have enabled the plaintiff to succeed in *Aliakmon* provided such loss was reasonably foreseeable by the defendant; it is submitted that it would have been reasonably foreseeable as in a

---

1 1982 SC (HL) 244, 1982 SLT 492.
2 For similar reasons, it would be unlikely that the shipper had voluntarily assumed responsibility for the financial interests of the buyers. But if in *Reavis v Clan Line Steamers Ltd* 1925 SC 725, 1925 SLT 386, OH, Mrs Reavis had been killed or injured with the result that her employees suffered economic loss, it is submitted that there would now be a possibility of their recovering damages for economic loss under *Junior Books* if the defender, who had a contract of carriage with Mrs Reavis, had known the identity of her employees and the existence of the contracts of employment.
3 See *Leigh and Sillavan Ltd v Aliakmon Shipping Co Ltd, The Aliakmon* [1986] AC 785, [1986] 2 All ER 145, HL, affirming [1985] 2 All ER 44, CA.
4 [1985] 2 All ER 44 at 77.

normal c & f contract the buyer would have had an action to sue on
the bill of lading if the goods were damaged in transit. Similarly, in
Nacap Ltd v Moffat Plant Ltd [1] the pursuer could have relied on this
doctrine, although it might have been more difficult to establish
that the loss suffered as a result of the contract with British Gas was
reasonably foreseeable.[2] However, the introduction of the principle
of transferred loss into English law was vigorously rejected by the
House of Lords.[3] It is thought, after *Nacap,* that the principle would
not fare any better north of the border.

Thus, it appears that the courts have set their face against recovery in delict for secondary economic loss by restricting title to sue
to the person who has been physically harmed or the owner of the
damaged property. But where a person has a possessory title to the
property, he may be able to sue. For example, if A pledges his watch
worth £500 to B in return for a loan of £300, B, the pledgee, has a
possessory title to the watch. If the watch is damaged by C, B can
sue C in delict to the extent of his interest in the watch, ie up to
£300.

Cases of possessory title apart, it is clear from *Nacap* that merely
to have lawful possession of the property is not sufficient; the pursuers in that case had lawful possession of the pipeline which they
were laying but title to sue in delict was denied. In *North Scottish
Helicopters Ltd v United Technologies Corpn Inc (No 2),*[4] however, the
pursuers were allowed to sue in respect of economic loss sustained
as a result of damage to a helicopter which they leased but did not
own. Under the lease agreement with the owner, a finance company, the second pursuer had to maintain the helicopter, indemnify
the finance company if the helicopter was damaged or destroyed
and replace or repair the helicopter at the pursuer's expense. It was
agreed with the finance company that the helicopter could be flown
by the first pursuer, a subsidiary company of the second pursuer.
The finance company had no obligation to provide a replacement if
the helicopter was not operational. Owing to a fault in the manufacturing process, the helicopter went on fire and was destroyed.

1 1987 SLT 221, discussed at p 107 above.
2 Goff LJ expressly stated ([1985] 2 All ER 44 at 77) that the doctrine would not
   have helped the plaintiff in *Candlewood Navigation Corpn Ltd v Mitsui OSK Lines
   Ltd, The Mineral Transporter* [1986] AC 1, [1985] 2 All ER 935, PC; the present
   writer would have thought that loss to a time-charterer from a collision would be
   reasonably foreseeable by a shipowner: see p 102 above.
3 [1986] 2 All ER 145 at 157 per Lord Brandon.
4 1988 SLT 778n, OH.

The pursuers sought damages for the economic loss sustained in indemnifying the finance company in terms of the lease and loss of profits sustained due to the absence of a helicopter. The complex facts can be shown thus:

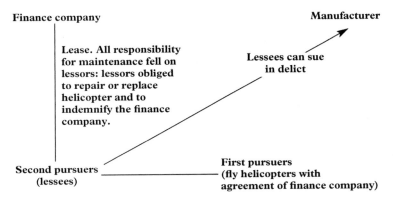

Finance company

Lease. All responsibility for maintenance fell on lessors: lessors obliged to repair or replace helicopter and to indemnify the finance company.

Manufacturer

Lessees can sue in delict

Second pursuers (lessees)

First pursuers (fly helicopters with agreement of finance company)

The Lord Ordinary (Davidson) held that because of the onerous terms of the lease and the fact that the finance company had agreed that the helicopter could be flown by the first pursuers, the second pursuers were 'owners' of the helicopter as a matter of substance even if, technically, the finance company was the owner as a matter of law. In other words, the pursuers had far more than lawful possession of the helicopter and this gave them title to sue in spite of not being the legal owner of the property. Thus it appears that there can be exceptional circumstances when a non-owner has title to sue.

It was assumed in this case that the manufacturer owed a duty of care to the pursuer. It should be noticed, however, that the destruction of the helicopter was pure economic loss: the defective product did not cause physical harm to the pursuers or damage to any other property owned by the pursuers – it only destroyed itself. The manufacturer's duty of care could therefore not have arisen by virtue of the *Donoghue v Stevenson* neighbourhood principle. Nor could there be a *Junior Books* duty of care[1] owing to the absence of a contractual nexus between the pursuer and defender at the time of the fault in the manufacturing process. The action could therefore have been defended on the ground that the defender did not owe a duty of care to prevent pure economic loss arising to the pursuers and,

1 See *Junior Books Ltd v Veitchi Co Ltd* 1982 SC (HL) 244, 1982 SLT 492.

indeed, the finance company, rather than the absence of the pursuers' title to sue for secondary economic loss.

In the cases we have been discussing, the only remedy available to a person who has suffered secondary economic loss is to obtain an assignation of the owner's rights against the defender. In Scots law, delictual rights as well as contractual rights can be assigned. For example in *Nacap Ltd v Moffat Plant Ltd*,[1] British Gas could have assigned to the pursuer its rights as owner of the pipeline to sue the defender in delict. The difficulty here is that British Gas's loss arising from damage to its pipeline is not the same as the losses incurred by Nacap in being unable to perform their contract on time. But where, as in *Aliakmon*,[2] the owner has a contractual remedy against the defender, the assignation of the contractual rights to the pursuer will provide a just solution provided, of course, the owner is prepared to assign his rights.

(6) Conclusion

The law on delictual liability for pure economic loss has been an area of extensive judicial activity where the concept of the duty of care has been used to mark the boundaries of liability. These have shifted from time to time and the current position remains controversial as well as conceptually difficult and, indeed, uncertain. Why this is so has been summarised admirably by Mummery LJ in *The Rebecca Elaine*:[3]

'The judicial line has not been drawn arbitrarily; it is explicable by rational and pragmatic considerations, some more potent than others, some more often articulated than others: the disproportionate burden of imposing indeterminate liability of the kind envisaged by Judge Cardozo in the *Ultramares* case; the evidential difficulties in establishing causation and delimiting remoteness; the relative cost and practicability of obtaining insurance cover for risks of pure financial loss suffered to an unlimited degree by an amorphous class of claimants; the apprehension of a deluge, in an already overstretched legal system, of litigation by an indefinite number of claimants with multiple claims arising out of a single incident ... the dubious and lethal colonization by the tort [delict] of negligence of the conceptual territory of contract; the perception that financial loss occupies

---

1 1987 SLT 221.
2 See *Leigh and Sillavan Ltd v Aliakmon Shipping Co Ltd, The Aliakmon* [1986] AC 785, [1986] 2 All ER 145, HL.
3 *The Rebecca Elaine* [1999] 2 Lloyd's Rep 1 at 8.

a significantly lower place than physical injury to person and property in the scale of contemporary social and ethical values; and the inevitability (and acceptability) of widespread and uncompensatable financial loss in a free market economy, in which even intentional infliction of substantial financial loss (eg by one trade competitor on another) does not normally attract legal liability.'

CHAPTER 5

Breach of a duty of care

A. INTRODUCTION

We have been considering situations where an action in delict fails at the outset because there is no duty of care owed by the defender to prevent harm to the pursuer as a result of the defender's unintentional, but careless, conduct. This is done by the courts utilising the concept of a duty of care as a threshold device and the decision whether or not to recognise the existence of a duty of care in particular circumstances ultimately involves issues of policy. The duty of care enables the courts to determine the parameters of liability in delict for unintentional, but careless, conduct.

Even where it is recognised that the defender owes the pursuer a duty of care, a pursuer is not entitled to succeed unless it can be shown that the harm sustained by the pursuer arose as a result of a *breach* by the defender of the duty of care which he owed to the pursuer. In this chapter we shall examine the criteria which must be satisfied before the defender's act or omission will constitute a *breach* of the duty of care which, *ex hypothesi*, the defender owes to the pursuer. Only when these criteria are satisfied, ie when there is a breach by the defender of the duty of care he owes to the pursuer, will the defender be liable to make reparation to the pursuer for harm sustained as a result of the defender's breach of duty. [1]

B. THE CRITERIA USED TO ESTABLISH A BREACH OF A DUTY OF CARE

(1) Voluntary act or omission of the defender

Before there is a breach by the defender of a duty of care owed to the pursuer, the relevant act or omission must be voluntary on the

---

1 In this chapter, I owe an immense debt to W A Wilson 'The Analysis of Negligence' in *Introductory Essays on Scots Law* (2nd edn, 1984) pp 126–148.

part of the defender. In *Waugh v James K Allan Ltd* [1] a lorry driver, Gemmell, suffered symptoms consistent with a gastric attack. When he felt he had recovered, he drove the lorry. In fact the symptoms were the onset of thrombosis and he shortly thereafter died at the wheel. The lorry swerved and seriously injured a pedestrian. Although the lorry driver clearly owed the pursuer a duty of care, it was held that there was no breach of duty in this case. On the medical evidence, the driver had no reason to anticipate the onset of the thrombosis and had therefore acted reasonably in driving the lorry after he felt better. Accordingly, the driver's act which injured the pursuer, ie his death, was involuntary and there was therefore no breach of the duty of care. If, however, the driver should have realised that he was seriously ill, then the act of driving while unfit to do so would have been a voluntary act which could have amounted to a breach of duty. But, in the circumstances, Lord Reid observed:[2]

'I am therefore of opinion that the appellant [the pursuer] has failed to prove that Gemmell acted rashly or negligently in driving off so soon after his illness, and no other fault can be imputed to him. One must have great sympathy with the appellant who has suffered so severely through no fault of his own, but I find it impossible to blame Gemmell. Accordingly, I would dismiss this appeal.'

(2) The defender's act or omission must have as its reasonable and probable consequence harm to the pursuer

Before there is a breach of a duty of care, harm to the pursuer must be a reasonable and probable consequence of the acts or omissions of the defender. The leading case is *Muir v Glasgow Corpn.*[3] Members of the Milton Free Church were having a Sunday school picnic in King's Park, Glasgow. Although it was a June afternoon, it began to rain. Mrs Alexander, the manageress of a tea room/sweet shop in the park, gave permission to the party to have their tea in the tea room. Access to the tea room was through a narrow passage where the sweet shop was situated. Some of the children were queuing in the passage to purchase sweets from the shop. When two members of the party carried a tea-urn full of boiling water through

---

1 1964 SC (HL) 102, 1964 SLT 269. The pursuer was suing the driver's employer as vicariously liable for the employee's delict: on vicarious liability, see pp 221 ff below.
2 1964 SC (HL) 102 at 106.
3 1943 SC (HL) 3, 1944 SLT 60.

the passage in order to gain entry to the tea room, the tea-urn dropped, scalding several children. It was never established how the urn was upset. We can illustrate the case as follows:

Clearly the persons carrying the urn owed a duty of care to the scalded children but no action in delict was brought against them either because of difficulty in establishing the cause of the accident or, more likely, because they had no assets or insurance. Instead, an action was brought against the Glasgow Corporation on the basis that, as Mrs Alexander's employer, the corporation was vicariously liable for any delicts she committed in the course of her employment.[1] It was accepted that as manageress of the tea room Mrs Alexander owed a duty of care to any persons she allowed to enter the premises. But, in order to succeed, the pursuer had to show that by allowing the urn to be carried through the passage crowded with children, Mrs Alexander was in breach of the duty of care she undoubtedly owed to them. The House of Lords took the view that Mrs Alexander could only be liable for those consequences of her actions which a reasonable person in her position would have had in contemplation in the circumstances of the case. Lord Thankerton said:[2] ' ... it has long been held in Scotland that all that a person can be held bound to foresee are the reasonable and probable consequences of the failure to take care, judged by the standard of the ordinary reasonable man [sic]'. Lord Wright considered[3] that:

'It is not, of course, a question of what she [Mrs Alexander] actually thought at the moment, but what the hypothetical reasonable person could have foreseen. That is the standard to determine the scope of her duty. This involves the question: Was the operation of carrying the tea-urn something

1 On vicarious liability, see pp 221 ff below.
2 1943 SC (HL) 3 at 8.
3 1943 SC (HL) 3 at 15.

which a reasonable person in Mrs Alexander's position should have realised would render the place in which it was performed dangerous to the children in the circumstances? This is the crucial issue of fact and the acid test of liability.'

The House of Lords held that the answer to this question was no. Mrs Alexander was entitled to assume that the tea-urn would be carried by responsible persons and that if carried with reasonable care would cause no harm to the children. A reasonable person in her position would not therefore have foreseen as a possibility, let alone a probability, that the urn would slip and the children would be scalded. Thus, because injury to the children could not have been foreseen as a *reasonable* and *probable* consequence of allowing the urn to be carried through the passage, Mrs Alexander had not broken the duty of care she owed the children.[1]

Muir v Glasgow Corpn is therefore authority that before a breach of a duty of care can arise the defender's acts or omissions must have as their *reasonable* and *probable* consequence injury to the pursuer or damage to the pursuer's property. The test is the reasonable foresight of the hypothetical reasonable person in the position of the defender as opposed to what the particular defender actually foresaw. But since the hypothetical reasonable person is in effect the court, it will be obvious that the scope of the duty of care in a particular case is, to some extent at least, determined by the judges.[2]

Thus, for example, in *Malcolm v Dickson*[3] a painter who was working on a house set the house on fire. A guest who was staying there attempted to save some of the property. As a result of his

---

1 Lord Wright thought it would have been different if, for example, Mrs Alexander had allowed lions or tigers to be taken through the passage: 1943 SC (HL) 3 at 16.
2 In *Mullin v Richards* [1998] 1 All ER 920, CA, the Court of Appeal held that a reasonable 15-year-old schoolgirl could not foresee as a probable consequence of play fighting with plastic rulers that her friend (the plaintiff) could lose her eye as a result of the plastic snapping. See too *McDougall v Strathclyde RC* 1996 SLT 1124 (PE instructor not in breach of his duty to assist a pupil when pupil chose to perform an exercise not previously performed without supervision during teacher's absence to assist another pupil: not reasonably foreseeable as a probable consequence of instructor's absence that pupil would try out the difficult exercise); *Kemp v Secretary of State for Scotland* 2000 SLT 471 (in determining whether a kerb they were obliged to maintain was a hazard to pedestrians, a local authority was not entitled to assume that all pedestrians using the footpath would behave with reasonable care at all times. While they were not bound to foresee every extremity of folly, it was foreseeable, at least in Scotland, that some pedestrians would use the road while under the influence of drink. In these circumstances it was reasonably foreseeable as a probable consequence of failing to light the raised kerb that a pedestrian who had had a drink might fall over it: pursuer held one-third contributorily negligent).
3 1951 SC 542, 1951 SLT 357.

exertions, the guest collapsed and died. The court held that the painter had not broken the duty of care he owed to the deceased because it could not have been anticipated by a reasonable person in the defender's position that an occupant of the house would die as a result of trying to salvage furniture. As Lord Patrick said:[1]

'It would not occur to the ordinary reasonable man that a reasonable and probable consequence of his being careless in burning paint from a window frame would be that some intervener would suffer a substantial injury through over-exertion, strain and excitement in carrying furniture from the house.'

It is important to note in this case that the deceased died from a heart attack. If he had died as a result of the fire, for example suffocated by smoke, it is submitted that there would have been a breach of the duty of care because it is foreseeable as a reasonable and probable consequence of carelessly setting a house on fire that an occupant might die from the smoke.

Since policy considerations are inevitably involved in determining what the hypothetical reasonable person can be deemed to have foreseen, it should occasion little surprise that, as a general rule, the courts take the view that when a person causes an accident, it is a reasonable and probable consequence of his carelessness that a rescuer may appear on the scene and be injured.[2]

In determining whether or not the injury was a reasonable and probable consequence of a careless act or omission, the scientific knowledge available to the hypothetical reasonable person at that time can be crucial. In *Roe v Minister of Health*[3] a patient was given a spinal anaesthetic. As was ordinary practice at the time, the phials containing the anaesthetic were kept in a solution of phenol. Unknown to the hospital, the phials developed invisible cracks and the anaesthetic became impregnated with phenol. As a result of the phenol in the anaesthetic, the patient was paralysed. The court held that the defendant had not broken the duty of care owed to the plaintiff: given the state of scientific knowledge at the time, a reasonable medical practitioner could not have foreseen that paralysis of a patient was a reasonable and probable consequence of storing the phials in phenol.

Before there is a breach of the duty of care, the act or omission must have as its reasonable and probable consequence injury to the

---

1 1951 SC 542 at 556.
2 See, for example, *Steel v Glasgow Iron and Steel Co Ltd* 1944 SC 237, 1945 SLT 70; *Videan v British Transport Commission* [1963] 2 QB 650, [1963] 3 WLR 374, CA.
3 [1954] 2 QB 66, [1954] 2 All ER 131, CA.

pursuer. In *Bourhill v Young*,[1] for example, even if Young had owed Mrs Bourhill a duty of care, he did not breach that duty in respect of her because a reasonable motor cyclist could not have foreseen as a reasonable and probable consequence of his careless driving that a pedestrian who was 50 feet or so away from the collision, ie outwith the area of potential physical danger, would be harmed. Mrs Bourhill was, of course, a secondary victim. In *Page v Smith*,[2] the House of Lords held that the defender was in breach of his duty of care to a primary victim even though a psychiatric disorder was not reasonably forseeable as a probable consequence of the defendant's careless driving. This can only be justified on the basis that *physical* harm was reasonably foreseeable, since otherwise the plaintiff would not have been a primary victim. However, when the pursuer is a secondary victim, a psychiatric disorder will only be treated as a reasonably foreseeable, probable consequence of the defender's carelessness if a person of ordinary phlegm would have suffered psychiatric harm in the circumstances.

It is not necessary reasonably to foresee the *extent* of the pursuer's injuries; it is enough that the injuries actually sustained by the pursuer are of a *kind* which would be foreseeable as a reasonable and probable consequence of the defender's careless conduct. Nor does every aspect of the accident have to be reasonably foreseeable. These points were settled by the House of Lords in the important decision, *Hughes v Lord Advocate*.[3] In order to work on underground cables, Post Office workers uncovered a manhole. They erected a canvas shelter over the manhole. At 5 pm, when it was dusk, they left the manhole unattended; they also left outside the shelter a ladder, a rope, and paraffin warning lamps. Two boys[4] saw the shelter and decided to explore. They carried the ladder, the rope and a paraffin lamp inside the tarpaulin. One boy tripped over the lamp which fell into the manhole. The paraffin spilled from the lamp, was vaporised by the heat and there was an explosion. There was a rush of flame and one of the lads fell into the manhole and suffered severe burns. It was agreed by expert witnesses that in the circumstances[5] an explosion was not reasonably foreseeable. But it was accepted that the workmen were careless in leaving the manhole unattended.

The House of Lords held that it was foreseeable as a reasonable and probable consequence of leaving the manhole unattended that

1 1942 SC (HL) 78, 1943 SLT 105: for full discussion see pp 74 ff above.
2 [1996] AC 155, [1995] 2 All ER 736, HL.
3 1963 SC (HL) 31, 1963 SLT 150.
4 The pursuer, aged 8, and his 10-year-old *uncle*!
5 Cf if they had been working on a gas main.

a child might enter the tent with a lamp, that the paraffin might spill and the child suffer a burn, ie that a boy might be burned by the lamp. This was sufficient to establish a breach of the duty of care which the workmen undoubtedly owed to prevent physical harm to pedestrians by leaving the manhole unattended. The fact that there had been an unforeseeable explosion and that the child's burns were therefore much worse than could have been reasonably anticipated was irrelevant. As Lord Morris of Borth-y-Gest explained:[1]

'The circumstances that an explosion as such could not have been contemplated does not alter the fact that it could reasonably have been foreseen that a boy who played in and about the canvas shelter and played with the things that were thereabouts might get hurt and might in some way burn himself. That is just what happened. The pursuer did burn himself, though his burns were more grave than would have been expected. The fact that the features and developments of an accident may not reasonably have been foreseen does not mean that the accident itself was not foreseeable. The pursuer was, in my view, injured as a result of the type or kind of accident or occurrence that could reasonably have been foreseen.'

Hughes v Lord Advocate is therefore authority that a breach of a duty of care will occur when the pursuer suffers the kind or type of injury which is a reasonable and probable consequence of the defender's careless act or omission;[2] the fact that the injuries sustained are greater than could have been reasonably foreseen and/or that some of the causes of the accident were unforeseeable is irrelevant as long as the type of injury suffered by the pursuer and the fact that an accident could occur as a result of the defender's carelessness are reasonably foreseeable.[3]

1 *Hughes v Lord Advocate* 1963 SC (HL) 31 at 43–44.
2 One of the difficulties with *Page v Smith* [1996] AC 155, [1995] 2 All ER 736, HL is that foreseeable physical harm is a different type of injury from the unforeseeable psychiatric disorder which in fact occurred.
3 In *Galbraith's Curator ad Litem v Stewart (No 2)* 1998 SLT 1305, the Lord Ordinary (Nimmo Smith) held that it was enough that it was reasonably foreseeable that children would be attracted to pipes left unsecured overnight and that they might suffer personal injuries when playing with them: the precise nature of the accident which had occurred did not have to be reasonably foreseeable. In *Jolley v Sutton London Borough Council* [2000] 3 All ER 409, the House of Lords held that an accident to a child while attempting to repair an abandoned boat left near a block of council flats was reasonably foreseeable. The council had conceded that it was reasonably foreseeable that a child might be injured by falling through rotten planking when playing *on* the boat: but that it was not reasonably foreseeable that a child might be injured by the boat falling on the child who was *underneath* the boat attempting to repair it! Their Lordships held that it was sufficient that it was reasonably foreseeable that children might sustain physical harm by meddling with the boat. See also *Doughty v Turner Manufacturing Co Ltd* [1964] 1 QB 518, [1964] 1 All ER 98, CA.

Finally, there can be difficulties if a defender has been careless but the harm to the pursuer has been caused as a result of the intervention of a third party. As a general rule, there will be no breach by the defender of his duty of care in these circumstances unless it is foreseeable as a reasonable and probable consequence of the defender's carelessness that a third party would intervene and harm the pursuer. In *Maloco v Littlewoods Organisation Ltd* [1] the defender owned an empty cinema. Vandals broke in and started a fire which damaged neighbouring property. While the defenders owed the pursuers, as neighbouring proprietors, a duty of care not to damage their property, the House of Lords held that there had been no breach of the duty in the circumstances. The defenders did not know that vandals were trespassing on their property and kindling fires there. Accordingly, it was not foreseeable that the defenders' failure to mount a 24-hour guard on the property would have as a reasonable and probable consequence the destruction by fire of neighbouring properties. As Lord Mackay of Clashfern explained: [2]

'While no doubt in this case … it was probable that children and young persons might attempt to break into the vacated cinema, this by no means establishes that it was a probable consequence of its being vacated with no steps being taken to maintain it lockfast that it would be set on fire with consequent risk of damage to neighbouring properties.' [3]

On the other hand, in *Dorset Yacht Co Ltd v Home Office* [4] borstal boys were working on the Isle of Wight under the custody and control of three borstal officers. The officers went to bed, leaving the boys to their own devices. Seven boys decided to escape. They went on board a yacht moored off the island, which collided and damaged the plaintiff's yacht. The House of Lords held that the borstal officers owed a duty of care to the plaintiff which they had broken in the circumstances. The officers were responsible for the boys. It was foreseeable as a reasonable and probable consequence of leaving the boys alone that they would try to abscond. Since the only means of escape was by sea, it was also reasonably foreseeable as a probable consequence that they would steal a yacht and, being inexperienced mariners, collide with another vessel. [1] It should be

1 1987 SC (HL) 37, 1987 SCLR 489, 1987 SLT 425: discussed in the context of delictual liability of owners of heritage at pp 186 ff below.
2 1987 SLT 425 at 431.
3 Cf *Nolan v Iceland Frozen Foods* (3 December 1997, unreported), CC (Liverpool), where a supermarket was held liable for damage caused by children misusing abandoned trolleys – not an unusual occurrence.
4 [1970] AC 1004, [1970] 2 All ER 294, HL.

noted, however, that there was a special relationship between the officers and the third party who caused the damage, ie the boys; for the officers were under a duty to guard the lads.[2] It therefore remains a general principle that a person is not liable in delict for damage caused as a result of the deliberate acts of third parties.[3]

(3) The standard of care – negligence

Before a defender is in breach of a duty of care, it must be established that the careless act or omission which caused harm to the pursuer constituted *culpa*. In modern terminology, the careless act or omission must amount to *negligence*. What the law requires is that the defender's conduct should not fall below the standard of the reasonable person in the position of the defender. If the defender's act or omission does not fall below the standard of the reasonable person, there is no breach of duty even though damage to the pursuer was foreseeable as a reasonable and probable consequence of the defender's conduct. But when the defender's conduct has not met the standards of the reasonable person in the position of the defender, the defender is negligent and the law demands reparation. The law does not expect the defender to go beyond the standards of the reasonable person. The defender is only obliged to take reasonable care: he is not expected to ensure that his acts or omissions never harm the pursuer. This point was forcibly made in *Muir v Glasgow Corpn*,[4] where the House of Lords held that the duty of the manageress was only to take reasonable care and not to prevent any accident occurring on the premises.

How then do we determine the standard of care of a reasonable person in any particular circumstance? Once again, since the standard of care is that of the hypothetical reasonable person in the position of the defender, the issue is ultimately a question for the

1 It is important to note that the duty was owed to the plaintiff only because it was reasonably foreseeable that damage might be caused to his yacht because the only method of effecting escape was by sea. If the boys had broken into a shop to steal food and drink, it is unlikely the court would have imposed a duty of care on the officers towards a member of the general public who suffered damage as a result of the acts of an absconding criminal.

2 See also, for example, *Reeves v Metropolitan Commissioner* [2000] 1 AC 360 (prison officers under a duty to prevent a prisoner from harming himself while in confinement).

3 *Modbury Triangle v Anzil* (2000) 205 CLR 254 (owner of a car park not liable for the assault on the plaintiff carried out by a third party in the unlit car park).

4 1943 SC (HL) 3, 1944 SLT 60, discussed at pp 116 ff above.

court. What the judges do is to consider a number of relevant factors and then determine what steps a reasonable person would have taken to prevent a foreseeable risk of harm to the pursuer. If the defender did not take these steps – or their equivalent – then she has been negligent and has broken the duty of care which she owed to the pursuer, always provided that harm to the pursuer is a reasonable and probable consequence of her failure to do so.

This involves a balancing process. The relevant factors to be considered include the probability of injury, the seriousness of the injury, the practicability of precautions, the cost of the precautions and the utility of the defender's activities. The practice of other persons in the same type of business or profession as the defender can also be important. The court then balances the costs of preventing harm to the pursuer against the risk of injury to the pursuer. By such a calculus of risk, there emerges the standard of the reasonable person in the position of the defender. If the defender's conduct has *in fact* not reached that standard, she has been negligent and therefore in breach of the duty of care owed to the pursuer.

Considering the factors in more detail:

(a) Probability of injury to the pursuer

Even if harm to the pursuer is foreseeable, a defender who causes such an injury is not negligent in failing to take precautions to avoid it if the risk of such an injury is so improbable that a reasonable person in the position of the defender would not have taken any precautions. Thus, for example, in *Bolton v Stone*[1] the plaintiff was injured by a cricket ball which had been hit out of a cricket ground. This had happened on six occasions in the previous thirty years and no one had been injured. The House of Lords held that the defendants had not been negligent in failing to take precautions since the risk of injury was so slight in the circumstances that a reasonable person in the position of the defendants would not have taken any precautions. Lord Reid explained:[2]

'In my judgment, the test to be applied here is whether the risk of damage to a person on the road was so small that a reasonable man in the position of the appellants [the defendants], considering the matter from the point of view of safety, would have thought it right to refrain from taking steps to

1 [1951] AC 850, [1951] 1 All ER 1078, HL.
2 [1951] 1 All ER 1078 at 1086. See in relation to golf balls 'driven' off course where the pursuer succeeded: *Whitefield v Barton* 1987 SCLR 259, Sh Ct.

prevent the damage. In considering the matter I think that it would be right to take into account, not only how remote is the chance that a person might be struck, but also how serious the consequences are likely to be if a person is struck, but I do not think that it would be right to take into account the difficulty of remedial measures. If cricket cannot be played on a ground without creating a substantial risk, then it should not be played there at all.'

In *Gillon v Chief Constable of Strathclyde Police*,[1] it was held that the risk of a police officer being injured by a player at a football match was so small that a reasonable employer – and the football club – were not required to take any precautions.

(b) Seriousness of injury to potential pursuer

As Lord Reid indicated in the passage cited above, the seriousness of the consequences for a person if he is injured is a relevant factor. In *Paris v Stepney Borough Council*,[2] a mechanic who had the use of only one eye was not supplied with goggles. When he was removing a rusty bolt from a car with a hammer, a chip of metal flew into his good eye and as a result he became totally blind. The employer had known that the plaintiff had only one eye. It was accepted that it was not the practice in the industry to supply goggles to workers engaged on the plaintiff's tasks. The question, however, was whether the employer had been negligent in failing to provide goggles for an employee whom they knew was already partially sighted. In the Court of Appeal,[3] the plaintiff's claim failed. Asquith LJ took the view that while the greater risk of injury was a relevant factor, the risk of greater injury was not. The House of Lords[4] held, however, that the seriousness of the consequences of an injury for a particular plaintiff was a relevant consideration. Since the consequences of an eye injury for an already partially sighted person could be total blindness, the court held that the employer had been negligent in failing to provide him with goggles. It was irrelevant that the defendants might not have been negligent in failing to provide goggles to two-eyed workers. Lord Normand observed:[5]

'The court's task of deciding what precautions a reasonable and prudent man would take in the circumstances of a particular case may not be easy. Nevertheless, the judgment of the reasonable and prudent man should be

1 1997 SLT 1218, (1996) Times, 22 November, OH.
2 [1951] AC 367, [1951] 1 All ER 42, HL.
3 [1949] 2 All ER 843, CA.
4 [1951] AC 367, [1951] 1 All ER 42, HL.
5 [1951] 1 All ER 42 at 49.

allowed its common every day scope, and it should not be restrained from considering the foreseeable consequences of an accident and their seriousness for the person to whom the duty of care is owed . . . the seriousness of the injury or damage risked and the likelihood of its being in fact caused may not be the only relevant factors. For example Asquith LJ in *Daborn v Bath Tramways Motor Co Ltd and Smithey* [1] pointed out that it is sometimes necessary to take account of the consequences of not assuming a risk.'

(c) Utility of the activity

Daborn v Bath Tramways Motor Co Ltd and Smithey[2] concerned an ambulance with a left-hand drive which was used during the Second World War. The plaintiff had put a sign at the back of the vehicle which said, 'Caution – Left hand drive – No signals'. When she was turning to the right, having given a hand signal, she collided with a bus which she could not see was trying to overtake her. The plaintiff was injured. The defendant argued that the plaintiff, as well as the bus driver, had been negligent and that her damages should be reduced on the grounds of her contributory negligence.[3] The Court of Appeal held that the plaintiff had not been negligent. In the course of his judgment Asquith LJ said:[4]

'I think that the plaintiff did all that in the circumstances she could reasonably be required to do if you include in those circumstances, as I think you should: (i) the necessity in time of national emergency of employing all transport resources which were available and (ii) the inherent limitations and incapacities of this particular form of transport. In considering whether reasonable care has been observed, one must balance the risk against the consequences of not assuming that risk, and in the present instance that calculation seems to me to work out in favour of the plaintiff.'

Thus the social utility of the activities which it is foreseeable may cause injury must be taken into account. In *Watt v Hertfordshire County Council*[5] a woman was trapped under a vehicle. The fire service sent a lorry with a jack. During the attempt to rescue the woman, the jack slipped and a fireman was injured. He claimed that the defendants, his employers, were negligent in not using a specially adapted lorry. The court held that given the emergency

1 [1946] 2 All ER 333, CA.
2 [1946] 2 All ER 333, CA.
3 On contributory negligence, see pp 150 ff below.
4 [1946] 2 All ER 333 at 336.
5 [1954] 2 All ER 368, [1954] 1 WLR 208, CA.

the employers were justified in using the vehicle which was available, ie a reasonable employer would have used the vehicle. They had not therefore fallen below the standard of the reasonable person in their position and therefore had not broken the duty of care which they owed to their employee.

There can also be a social value in not taking steps to prevent a foreseeable accident. In *Tomlison v Congleton Borough Council*,[1] the House of Lords held that a local authority was not under an obligation to take steps to reduce or eliminate the dangers of swimming in a lake. It was enough that they had provided warning notices. To do more would hinder the general public from enjoying the amenities of the lakeside:

'The majority of people who went to the beaches to sunbathe, paddle and play with their children were enjoying themselves in a way which gave them pleasure and caused no risk to themselves or anyone else. This must be something to be taken into account in deciding whether it was reasonable to expect the council to destroy the beaches.'[2]

Conversely, if there is no social value in the defender's failure to take reasonable steps to eliminate or reduce a risk, the defender's omission to do so will be negligent.[3]

(d) Practicality of precautions

The hypothetical reasonable person in the position of the defender will – indeed, can – only take such precautions as are practicable to avoid the risk of harm. In *Quinn v Cameron and Roberton Ltd*,[4] for example, the pursuer developed pneumoconiosis as a result of prolonged exposure to silica dust where he was working. His case against his employers failed on the basis that since the danger to employees from silica dust in iron foundries was not appreciated during the period when the pursuer was working for the employer (nine years prior to 1951), the defenders were not in breach of their

---

1 [2004] 1 AC 46.
2 [2004] 1 AC 46 per Lord Hoffmann at 84. His speech at 82–86 provides an excellent example of the calculus of risk. Lord Hoffmann also considered that as a general rule the owner or occupier of property did not owe a duty of care to prevent persons engaging in activities on their land such as swimming or mountaineering, which involved an inherent risk of personal harm: [2004] 1 AC 46 at 84.
3 *Jolley v Sutton Borough Council* [2000] 3 All ER 409 (no social value in failing to remove a rotting boat from a council estate!).
4 1956 SC 224, 1957 SLT 2. See also *Smith v P & O Bulk Shipping Ltd* [1998] 2 Lloyd's Rep 81, QBD (employer could not have known about danger from asbestos when plaintiff was employee).

duty of care by not providing precautions. Another reason why they had not been negligent was that effective dust-extraction appliances were not available to the employers until 1950. The Lord President (Clyde) explained:[1]

'The Lord Ordinary has held it proved that the provision of dust extraction appliances at plough buffs was not general practice between 1946 and 1951, and the expert evidence is really unanimously in favour of this conclusion. Indeed any apparatus to cope with the dangerous dust only seems to have come into the market in 1950, and went into general practice thereafter.'

(e) Cost of precautions

The hypothetical reasonable person in the position of the defender will take into account the cost of precautions and balance this against the probability of risk of harm and the seriousness of any injuries likely to be sustained. The defender's duty is not to be negligent; it is not to act to eliminate all risks of injury to the pursuer. Thus, for example, in *Latimer v AEC Ltd*[2] a factory floor became slippery as a result of a phenomenal rainstorm. In an attempt to avoid accidents, the employer spread three tons of sawdust on the floor. Nevertheless, an employee slipped and was injured on a part of the floor *not* covered by sawdust.[3] The plaintiff argued that the employer should have closed down the factory while the floor was properly cleaned thus eliminating the risk of employees slipping. This would, of course, have involved loss of production. The House of Lords held that the employer did all that a reasonable person would have done and was therefore not negligent. For Lord Tucker[4] the only question was:

'Has it been proved that the floor was so slippery that, remedial steps not being possible, a reasonably prudent employer would have closed down the factory rather than allow his employees to run the risks involved in continuing work? ... The absence of any evidence that anyone in the factory during the afternoon or night shift, other than the appellant, slipped, or experienced any difficulty, or that any complaint was made by or on behalf of the workers, all points to the conclusion that the danger was, in fact, not such as to impose on a reasonable employer the obligation [to close down the factory].'

1 1956 SC 224 at 233.
2 [1953] AC 643, [1953] 2 All ER 449, HL.
3 In spite of using three tons, some areas were left uncovered!
4 [1953] 2 All ER 449 at 455.

In *Charlton v Forrest Printing Ink Co Ltd*[1] it was one of the tasks of a group of employees to collect the wages for the workforce from a bank and take them to the factory. The employer had warned them of the possibility of being robbed and advised them to vary the times – and the transport used – when they went to collect the wages. Nevertheless, there was a robbery and the plaintiff was blinded by acid which had been thrown in his face. The Court of Appeal held that the employer had taken reasonable precautions and had not been negligent in failing to use the services of Securicor to uplift the wages, which could have been done at a very modest cost. On the other hand, if a risk can be eliminated or reduced at little cost, then the defender's failure to do so will be negligent.[2]

(f) Practice of other persons in the same business, trade or profession as the defender

The standard to be reached is that of the hypothetical reasonable person in the position of the defender. The practice of other persons in the same business, trade or profession as the defender will be at least an indication of the standard expected by a reasonable person in that situation. This was recognised by the Lord President (Dunedin) in *Morton v Wm Dixon Ltd*[3] There a miner sued his employer on the basis that the employer had been negligent in failing to provide a 'shielding contrivance' to prevent coal falling between a cage and the side of the mine shaft. In determining whether the employer was negligent and in breach of his duty of care, Lord Dunedin said:[4]

'I look upon this matter as one of great importance not merely for this particular case, but for cases of this sort generally. Where the negligence of an employer consists of what I may call a fault of omission, I think that it is absolutely necessary that the proof of fault of omission should be one of two kinds, either – to shew that the thing which he did not do was a thing which was commonly done by other persons in like circumstances, or – to

1 [1980] IRLR 331, CA. The case was concerned with an employer's *contractual* duty to take reasonable care for the safety of employees; but the point is also applicable in respect of the employer's *delictual* duty of care towards his employees.

2 *Jolley v Sutton Borough Council* [2000] 3 All ER 409. It should be noted that in *Tomlinson v Congleton Borough Council* [2004] 1 AC 46, Lord Hoffmann at 83 did not regard the cost of destroying the lakeside as an important factor as opposed to the loss of social utility which that would have involved.

3 1909 SC 807, 1909 1 SLT 346.

4 1909 SC 807 at 809.

shew that it was a thing which was so obviously wanted that it would be folly in anyone not to provide it.'

While the determination whether the particular defender has fallen below the requisite standard is a question of fact, the standard of care demanded is that of the hypothetical reasonable person and is ultimately the standard which the court decides is appropriate in a particular situation. If, for example, an employer does not take certain precautions, the court may still take the view that he did not reach the standard of care of the reasonable person in that situation even though he was following the usual practice in his trade or business in not taking the precautions. In *Cavanagh v Ulster Weaving Co Ltd*[1] an employee who was wearing rubber boots slipped off a roof ladder while carrying cement. No handrail was provided on the ladder. There was evidence that it was not the practice in the building trade to provide a handrail in these circumstances. The House of Lords held that evidence of the practice, while important, was not conclusive in establishing the requisite standard of care: that remained the standard of the reasonable person in the defendant's position. Given the circumstances of this case, including the fact that the employee's boots were two sizes larger than they should have been, a reasonable employer would have supplied a handrail and therefore the defendant was negligent. Lord Dunedin's formula in *Morton v Wm Dixon Ltd*,[2] while important, was not 'intended to depart from or modify the fundamental principle that an employer is bound to take reasonable care for the safety of his workmen'.[3]

Conversely, where the defender has not followed the usual practice in his trade or profession, he may nevertheless have taken reasonable care. In *Brown v Rolls Royce Ltd*[4] it was common practice in the defenders' industry to supply workers in the position of the pursuer with a barrier cream. The defenders considered that barrier cream was ineffective and instead took other precautions advised by a medical officer. The pursuer contracted dermatitis. The House of Lords held that while the defenders' failure to follow the usual practice was prima facie evidence of negligence, it was not conclusive. Because the defenders had taken other precautions against the risk of their employees suffering dermatitis, the defend-

---

1 [1960] AC 145, [1959] 2 All ER 745, HL.
2 1909 SC 807 at 809.
3 *Cavanagh v Ulster Weaving Co Ltd* [1959] 2 All ER 745 at 751 per Lord Keith of Avonholm.
4 1960 SC (HL) 22, 1960 SLT 119.

ers had not failed to take reasonable care. In relation to Lord Dunedin's formula, Lord Keith of Avonholm observed:[1]

'As has been said before in this House, Lord Dunedin was laying down no proposition of law; nor did he say that, if a practice was averred and proved which might have avoided the accident, this was necessarily conclusive of negligence on the part of an employer who had not followed the practice. The ultimate test is lack of reasonable care for the safety of the workman in all the circumstances of the case.'

The standard of care required of professional men and women, such as members of the medical and legal professions, is discussed later in the book.[2]

(4) Remoteness of injury

In some earlier Scottish cases, delictual liability has been rejected on the ground that the harm suffered by the pursuer was 'too remote'. In *Reavis v Clan Line Steamers Ltd*,[3] for example, the court denied Mrs Reavis compensation for the loss of her orchestra on the simple basis that this loss was 'too remote'. It is submitted that the better analysis is that the defender did not owe her a duty of care to prevent her suffering secondary economic loss. Similarly, in *Bourhill v Young*,[4] it was argued by some of the judges that the pursuer could not sue in delict because the mental harm she sustained was too remote. Again it is submitted that Mrs Bourhill's claim failed because Young did not owe her a duty of care in respect of inflicting mental harm because she was a secondary victim. Conversely, *Hughes v Lord Advocate*[5] has been treated as a case where the pursuer's injuries were not regarded as too remote. But it is thought that that decision is better analysed as an example of how a breach of duty occurs. In other words, since physical harm to the pursuer was foreseeable as a reasonable and probable consequence of the defender's carelessness, there was a breach of duty even though the extent of the pursuer's injuries could not have been reasonably foreseen. It is thought that the concept of remoteness of injury has no part to play in determining the existence of a

1 1960 SC (HL) 22 at 26.
2 See Chapter 7 below.
3 1925 SC 725, discussed at pp 105 ff above.
4 1942 SC (HL) 78, 1943 SLT 105, discussed at pp 74 ff above.
5 1963 SC (HL) 31, 1963 SLT 150, discussed at pp 120 ff above.

duty of care or the breach of such a duty in the modern Scots law of delict.

Remoteness of injury must not be confused with remoteness of damages. Where there has been a breach of a duty of care and the pursuer has suffered harm, the pursuer may not be able to recover for all the losses suffered as a result of the defender's negligence. Some losses may be considered by the court to be too remote. For example, if A injures B as a result of negligent driving, B is entitled to damages for pain and suffering and derivative economic loss, such as loss of wages, loss of future earnings etc. But when as a result of the accident B was unable to post his football coupon, could he recover damages from A for the fortune he would have won if the coupon had been sent? In other words, is the loss of the winnings too remote to be compensated by A? This is a question of remoteness of damages and is discussed later in the book.[1]

C. CONCLUSION

In this chapter we have been discussing when a breach of a duty of care arises. The defender's act or omission must be voluntary; harm to the pursuer must be foreseeable as a reasonable and probable consequence of the defender's act or omission, and, finally, the act or omission must constitute negligence ie the defender must have failed to reach the standard of care of the hypothetical reasonable person in the position of the defender. Where these criteria are satisfied, there is a breach of the duty of care owed to the pursuer and a delict is committed when the pursuer sustains harm as a result of the defender's breach of the duty of care. Even though there has been a breach of the duty of care, it is important to appreciate that the delict is only completed and delictual liability is only incurred when harm is sustained by the pursuer.[2] There must be a concurrence of *damnum* (loss or harm sustained) and *injuria* (breach of the duty of care) before delictual liability arises (*damnum injuria datum*).[3] If there is no harm or loss to the pursuer as a result of the

---

1 See pp 283 ff below.
2 *Watson v Fram Reinforced Concrete Co (Scotland) Ltd and Winget Ltd* 1960 SC (HL) 92, 1960 SLT 321.
3 Thus, for example, the prescriptive period will only begin to run from the date that the pursuer suffers harm, not the date of the breach of duty: for example, when Mrs Donoghue became ill, not when Stevenson manufactured the ginger beer carelessly.

defender's breach of a duty of care which he owes to the pursuer then there is no delictual liability. Harm to the pursuer is a constituent of, as well as a consequence of, negligence.

However, before the pursuer can succeed, she must prove that the harm or loss suffered was caused by the defender's breach of a duty of care owed to her. It is to the difficulties inherent in the concept of causation that we now turn.

CHAPTER 6

Causation and related issues

Before there is liability in delict, the pursuer must prove that the defender's breach of her duty of care was the cause of the loss or harm suffered by the pursuer. The concept of causation is a complex and difficult subject raising fundamental philosophical as well as legal issues. In a work of the present compass, only an outline of the relevant issues is given.[1]

A. FACTUAL CAUSATION

The first essential is that the defender's acts or omissions are a cause of the pursuer's injury or loss. This is a question of fact. If the defender's conduct is not a factual cause of the pursuer's injury or loss, there is no liability even if the defender has broken a duty of care which he owed to the pursuer. To use Latin terminology, the defender's breach of duty must be a *causa sine qua non* of the pursuer's injury or loss. In other words, 'but for' the defender's conduct, the pursuer would not have suffered harm. If the pursuer would have suffered the same injury notwithstanding the defender's breach of duty, then the defender's conduct is not a factual cause of the harm, ie it is not a *causa sine qua non*. Accordingly, to determine whether the defender's breach of duty is a factual cause of the pursuer's injury, we must ask ourselves whether 'but for' the breach of duty, the pursuer's injury would have occurred. If it would *not* have occurred, the defender's act or omission is a factual cause of the pursuer's injury:[2] if it would still have occurred,

---

1 For a superb account of the subject, see Hart and Honoré *Causation and the Law* (2nd edn, 1985). The book is an excellent example of the constructive use to which linguistic philosophy can be put in the context of law.
2 It is enough if it can be shown that 'but for' the defender's act or omission it was probable that the injury would not have occurred: *Porter v Strathclyde Regional Council* 1991 SLT 446.

the defender's act or omission is *not* a factual cause of the pursuer's injury. The onus of satisfying the 'but for' test rests on the pursuer.[1]

In *Barnett v Chelsea and Kensington Hospital Management Committee*,[2] for example, the plaintiff's husband drank a cup of tea and became violently ill because the tea had been poisoned. The hospital doctor refused to treat the husband telling him to see his own doctor. The husband died. It was held that although the defendant may have been in breach of a duty of care, the hospital was not liable because the husband would still have died of the poison even if he had been treated by the hospital doctor ie the husband did not die 'but for' the hospital's negligence. Accordingly, the breach of duty was not a *causa sine qua non* of the husband's death and the plaintiff's action failed.

In *Kay's Tutor v Ayrshire and Arran Health Board*[3] a child was brought into hospital suffering from meningitis. He was given a massive overdose of penicillin.[4] The child thereupon suffered severe convulsions but, as a result of treatment, recovered. However, the child was left deaf. In an action against the hospital, the defenders admitted that they were in breach of their duty of care in administering the overdose of penicillin but denied that this breach of duty had caused the child's deafness. The House of Lords held that the onus lay on the pursuer (the child's father) to prove that 'but for' the overdose the child would not be deaf. In the absence of evidence to show that an overdose of penicillin caused deafness in a patient and given that deafness is common in patients who suffer meningitis, the pursuer failed to establish that 'but for' the breach of duty deafness would not have occurred. The breach was therefore not a *causa sine qua non* of the child's deafness and the pursuer's action failed.

This concept was taken a stage further by the House of Lords in *Bolitho v City and Hackney Health Authority*.[5] It was accepted that a doctor had been in breach of her duty of care by failing to attend

---

1 See, for example, *Dingley v Chief Constable of Strathclyde Police (No 1)* 1998 SC 548, OH (pursuer failed to establish on the balance of probabilities that a whiplash injury sustained in a road accident had triggered the onset of symptomatic multiple sclerosis); *Pickford v ICI plc* [1998] ICR 673, [1998] 3 All ER 462, HL (onus was on plaintiff to prove that her condition had an organic cause: the employer's failure to prove that the condition was psychogenic was no more than a relevant factor in determining whether or not the plaintiff had discharged the burden of proof. In the circumstances the plaintiff had failed to do so).

2 [1969] 1 QB 428, [1968] 1 All ER 1068.

3 1987 SC (HL) 145, 1987 SLT 577, HL, affirming 1986 SLT 435.

4 30 times the prescribed amount.

5 [1998] AC 232, [1997] 4 All ER 771, HL.

her patient, a child. The child died. It was also accepted that the only way in which the child's life could have been saved was by intubation. However, evidence was led that a responsible body of medical opinion would not have intubated in the circumstances. In other words, if the doctor had attended her patient, she would not have been negligent if she had not attempted to save the child's life by intubating her. Consequently, the child would still have died even if the doctor had attended her. The logic appears strained but it is nevertheless compelling. Since the patient would still have died even if she had received reasonable care, ie no intubation, the doctor's negligence in failing to attend her was not a factual cause of her death.[1] Where the treatment of a patient would have had less than a 50 per cent chance of success, the failure to treat is not regarded as the cause of the pursuer's injuries or illness: in other words, the chances of success must be more than 50 per cent.[2]

Another striking example of the 'but for' test is *McWilliams v Sir William Arrol & Co and Lithgows Ltd.*[3] The pursuer's husband, a steel erector, was killed. It was held that the defenders were in breach of their duty of care towards McWilliams in failing to provide him with a safety belt. But it was also established that even if they had provided him with a safety belt, McWilliams would not have worn it. In these circumstances, the pursuer failed to prove that 'but for' the defenders' breach of duty the accident would not have occurred. The defenders' breach was not a *causa sine qua non* of McWilliams' death and the pursuer's action failed.

Where the pursuer suffers loss which he would have suffered anyway, but as a result of the defender's breach of duty he suffers the loss at an earlier date, the Scottish courts have held that the 'but for' test is satisfied and an action will lie in delict.[4] Conversely, where a pursuer is injured as a result of the defender's breach of duty but later suffers an accident or disease unrelated to the defender's conduct, the fact that he would have been debilitated by

---

1 It would still be very difficult to explain to the child's parents why their action failed given the doctor's admitted negligence in not attending their child.

2 See *Kenyon v Bell* 1953 SC 125, 1952 SLT (Notes) 79, OH; *Hotson v East Berkshire Area Health Authority* [1987] 2 All ER 909, HL; *Gregg v Scott* [2003] Lloyd's Rep Med 105 (defendant's negligence delayed the treatment of the plaintiff's cancer by nine months. The evidence established that the prospects of a cure were less than 50 per cent so that it was more probable than not that the plaintiff would have been in the same position even had the treatment commenced earlier).

3 1962 SC (HL) 70, 1962 SLT 121.

4 *Sutherland v North British Steel Group Ltd* 1986 SLT (Sh Ct) 29 (accelerated hernia operation).

the later accident or disease is taken into account in assessing the pursuer's loss.[1]

The 'but for' test also applies when the pursuer's claim is for pure economic loss. For example, D provides P with information about C which P uses to decide whether or not to enter into a transaction with C. P sustains economic loss as a consequence of the transaction with C. In an action to recover the loss from D, P must prove that he would not have entered into the transaction with C 'but for' D's misrepresentation in respect of C. If P would have entered into the transaction with C in the absence of D's advice, the action will fail for lack of factual causation.[2]

Difficulties arise where there is more than one potential cause of the pursuer's injuries, ie the defender's breach of a duty of care and another source of danger which is not the responsibility of the defender. The starting point of the discussion is *Wardlaw v Bonnington Castings Ltd*.[3] A workman contracted pneumoconiosis from breathing dust in the atmosphere of his workplace. Some of the dust was caused by a hammer in relation to which there were no known or available precautions which could be taken to prevent the employee breathing contaminated air. Therefore the defender was not in breach of the duty of care owed to the pursuer in respect of the dust caused by the hammer. However, there were other machines in the workshop which also produced dust for which adequate extraction plant was available and the employers were held responsible for not adequately maintaining the extracting plant.[4]

There were therefore two possible sources of the dust which had caused the pursuer's illness for only one of which the defender was delictually liable ie the dust from the other machines. The House of Lords held that the onus lay on the pursuer to show that on the balance of probabilities the dust from the machines was a *causa sine qua non* of his illness. In the situation of two potential sources of danger, the pursuer would discharge the onus if he could show that the source for which the defender was responsible had materially contributed to his injury. Lord Reid observed:[5]

'It appears to me that the source of his [the pursuer's] disease was the dust from both sources, and the real question is whether the dust from the

---

1 See *Jobling v Associated Dairies Ltd* [1982] AC 794, [1981] 2 All ER 752, HL.
2 *Leeds & Holbeck Building Society v Alex Morison & Co (No 2)* 2001 SCLR 41.
3 1956 SC (HL) 26, 1956 SLT 135.
4 This was a breach by the employer of their statutory duty under the Grinding of Metals (Miscellaneous Industries) Regulations 1925, SR & O 1925/904. On breach of statutory duty, see Chapter 11 below.
5 *Wardlaw v Bonnington Castings Ltd* 1956 SC (HL) 26 at 32.

swing grinders [the other machines] materially contributed to the disease. What is a material contribution must be a question of degree. A contribution which comes within the exception *de minimis non curat lex* is not material but I think that any contribution which does not fall within that exception must be material.'

In this case, the dust from the machines did materially contribute to the pursuer's illness and the pursuer was successful. Thus, where there are two or more sources of harm to the pursuer which operate concurrently, the source for which the defender is responsible will be regarded as a *causa sine qua non* of the pursuer's injury if it materially contributed to the injury.

The concept of factual causation was taken a considerable step further in *McGhee v National Coal Board*.[1] The pursuer worked all day in a hot and dusty kiln. He had to cycle home unwashed because the defender failed to provide on-site washing facilities. After several days, the pursuer contracted dermatitis. It was admitted that the dermatitis was attributable to the work the pursuer did in the brick kiln but the defender was not in breach of a duty of care in allowing the pursuer to work there. The breach of duty was the failure to provide on-site washing facilities. This omission only resulted in the pursuer cycling home unwashed: clearly, it did not relate to the hours he spent working in the kiln. Common sense would suggest that it was far more likely that the dermatitis was contracted when he was working in the kiln, for which the employer was not delictually liable, rather than during the short time he cycled home. But the expert evidence could not establish how dermatitis was actually contracted. *Wardlaw v Bonnington Castings Ltd*[2] could therefore not provide a solution since it could not be proven that the additional exposure to injury caused by cycling home unwashed had materially contributed to his injury. *Wardlaw v Bonnington Castings Ltd* is concerned with two sources of danger operating *concurrently*; but *McGhee v National Coal Board* is concerned with two sources of danger operating *consecutively* where the defender was responsible only for the later one. Therefore it can be argued that the pursuer in *McGhee* would have to prove – which on the evidence he could not – that the later source of danger had caused, or at least materially contributed to, his dermatitis.

However, the House of Lords was prepared to take a broader view of causation. The medical evidence suggested that the fact that

---

1 1973 SC (HL) 37, 1973 SLT 14; see Lord Hope of Craighead 'James McGhee – A Second Mrs Donoghue?' [2003] CLJ 587.
2 1956 SC (HL) 26, 1956 SLT 135.

the pursuer had to cycle home caked with grime and sweat added materially to *the risk* that the disease might develop, although it could not explain why this was so. In the view of the House, materially to increase the risk of the pursuer's injuries was to be regarded as a material contribution to the injury. Lord Reid opined:[1]

'But it has often been said that the legal concept of causation is not based on logic or philosophy. It is based on the practical way in which the ordinary man's mind works in the every-day affairs of life. From a broad and practical viewpoint I can see no substantial difference between saying that what the defender did materially increased the risk of injury to the pursuer and saying that what the defender did made a material contribution to his injury.'

Lord Salmon observed:[2]

'In the circumstances of the present case,[3] the possibility of a distinction existing between (a) having materially increased the risk of contracting the disease and (b) having materially contributed to causing the disease may no doubt be a fruitful source of interesting academic discussions between students of philosophy. Such a distinction is, however, far too unreal to be recognised by the common law'!

Thus, where there are two or more sources of danger for only one of which the defender is delictually liable, factual causation will be established if the pursuer can prove on the balance of probabilities *either* that the defender's breach of duty materially contributed to his injury *or* that the defender's breach of duty materially increased the risk of the pursuer sustaining injury. It does not matter if the sources of danger operate concurrently or consecutively.[4]

McGhee v National Coal Board was approved and extended by the House of Lords in *Fairchild v Glenhaven Funeral Services Ltd.*[5] F was employed by E1 and E2 at different times and for different

---

1 *McGhee v National Coal Board* 1973 SC (HL) 37 at 53–54.
2 1973 SC (HL) 37 at 62.
3 Given the defender's admitted breach of a duty of care.
4 The implications of *McGhee* are remarkable. For example, suppose A has smoked cigarettes for 30 years. B, her employer, allows C and D, fellow employees, to smoke in a room occupied by A. A contracts lung cancer a week later. Since A's passive smoking of C and D's cigarette smoke materially increases the risk of A contracting lung cancer, C and D's smoking (and B's allowing them to smoke) could be treated as the cause of A contracting the disease. But common sense would suggest that A contracted the disease as a result of her own smoking habit. A would, of course, be contributorily negligent: see pp 150 ff below.
5 [2003] 1 AC 32, [2002] 3 All ER 305. See Joe Thomson 'The Raising of Lazarus: The Resurrection of *McGhee v National Coal Board*' (2003) 7 Edin LR 80.

periods. Both E1 and E2 were in breach of a duty of care to P by allowing him to breathe asbestos dust. F contracted cancer. The medical evidence established that the disease was contracted by breathing asbestos dust but, because of the limits of scientific knowledge, it could not be established that the cancer was the result of inhaling asbestos dust during his employment with E1 or E2 or both employers. But it was also proven that once the disease had been contracted, F's condition would not deteriorate as a consequence of further exposure to asbestos dust. Thus causation could not be established on the basis of a material contribution to F's illness. On the other hand, it was accepted that the *risk* of contracting the cancer increased in relation to the total exposure to asbestos dust. In these circumstances, their Lordships took the view that the normal 'but for' test should be suspended. Lord Nicholls considered that the plaintiff should succeed as 'any other outcome would be deeply offensive to instinctive notions of what justice requires and fairness demands'.[1] Since both E1 and E2 were in breach of the duty of care they owed to F and these breaches had materially increased the risk of F contracting cancer, *McGhee* was applicable and the causal requirement was satisfied.[2] It should be noted that in *McGhee*, the pursuer sustained harm as a consequence of the defender's breach of duty or the defender's non-delictual conduct, both of which materially increased the risk of his contracting dermatitis: even if the illness was not contracted as a result of the defender's breach of duty, it was nevertheless caused by the defender's conduct – albeit conduct that might not have been negligent. *Fairchild* goes further in that by increasing the risk of the pursuer sustaining harm as a result of the defender's breach of duty, the defender may be held to have caused the pursuer's illness when it was in fact caused by the negligence of another person.

There are, however, important limitations. First, the principle in *McGhee* and *Fairchild* only applies when it is impossible to establish scientifically the cause of the pursuer's injury. Second, while the *sources* of danger may be different, it must be established that each source could have in fact been the cause of the pursuer's injuries. In *Wardlaw*, *McGhee* and *Fairchild* it was clear that dust caused the pursuers' diseases: the only question was whether the defenders'

---

1 [2002] 3 All ER 305 at 336. See also Lord Bingham at 312 and Lord Hoffmann at 341.
2 If *in fact* F had contracted cancer while in the employment of E1, it is difficult to see how the exposure to asbestos dust while in the employment of E2 materially increased the risk of F contracting cancer!

breach of duty had materially contributed to, or increased the risk of, the pursuers' illnesses. By way of contrast, in *Kay's Tutor v Ayrshire and Arran Health Board*,[1] there was no evidence that the defender's breach of duty in giving the overdose of penicillin could in fact have caused the child's deafness. In these circumstances, *Wardlaw*, *McGhee* and *Fairchild* are irrelevant. As Lord Griffiths explained:[2]

'The principle in *McGhee* would only fall for consideration if it was first proved that it was an accepted medical fact that penicillin in some cases caused or aggravated deafness. The question would then arise whether when there are two competing causes of deafness, namely meningitis and penicillin, the law should presume in favour of the plaintiff [sic] that the tortious [sic] [delictual] cause was responsible for the damage.'

Moreover, the departure from the ordinary 'but for' rule only applies when there are two or more sources of the *same* noxious agent which caused the pursuer's illness or injuries: if there is more than one noxious agent which could have caused the pursuer's injuries or illness, the threshold 'but for' test of causal connection will not be relaxed. In *Wilsher v Essex Area Health Authority*,[3] a baby's medical condition could have been caused by a noxious agent (a) which arose as a consequence of the defendant's breach of duty: but there were another four different noxious agents – for which the defendant was not responsible – each of which could equally have harmed the child. The fact that the defendant's negligence materially increased the risk of the child from being harmed by noxious agent (a) was held not to be a sufficient causative link when the child's condition could have been caused by noxious agents (b), (c), (d) or (e).

B. LEGAL CAUSATION

For the purpose of liability in delict, it is not enough that the defender's breach of duty is a factual cause or *causa sine qua non* of the pursuer's harm or loss. While factual causation is a necessary condition of delictual liability, it is not sufficient. In addition, the defender's breach of duty must be the legal cause of the pursuer's injury. To use Latin terminology, it must be the *causa causans*.

---

1 1987 SC (HL) 145, 1987 SLT 577. Discussed at p 136 above.
2 1987 SLT 577 at 581.
3 [1988] All ER 871, HL, approved by the House of Lords in *Fairchild*.

Various terms are used to describe legal causation: these include the direct, decisive, proximate, real, dominant, efficient, effective and substantial cause of the pursuer's loss or harm.

For example, A drops a brick on B's foot, breaking his toe. B is taken to hospital in an ambulance. The ambulance is driven carelessly and B is killed in a road accident. A's breach of duty is a *causa sine qua non* of B's death since 'but for' A's dropping the brick on his toe, B would not have been in the ambulance in which he died. But should A be delictually liable for B's death which was caused by the ambulance driver's careless driving? The answer is no. A's breach of duty, although a *causa sine qua non* of B's death, is not treated as the legal cause, ie it is not the *causa causans*. The *causa causans* is the ambulance driver's careless driving. We can say that the chain of causation between A's breach of duty and B's death has been broken as a result of the careless act of the ambulance driver, which prevents A's breach of duty from being the legal cause of B's death. To use legal terminology, the ambulance driver's conduct is a *novus actus interveniens* which breaks the chain of causation so that A is not delictually liable for B's death, although A remains liable for B's broken toe.

In this example, the *novus actus interveniens* was the conduct of a third party: the ambulance driver. But the conduct of the victim may also break the chain of causation. So, for example, if A drops a brick on B's foot, breaking his toe, whereupon B cuts his own throat to put himself out of pain, A will not be delictually liable for B's death. B's action has broken the chain of causation and, as a result, A's breach of duty is not regarded as the legal cause, the *causa causans*, of B's death.

When, then, will an act of a third party or the act of the victim constitute *a novus actus interveniens*, breaking the chain of causation? Since we are concerned with determining legal causation, this is ultimately a question for the courts: the judges will *evaluate* whether or not in the circumstances it is fair to relieve the defender of his delictual liability. At one time, this was a crucial decision where the victim had contributed to his own injuries: for if the court decided that the pursuer's conduct was a *novus actus interveniens* so that the defender's breach of duty was not the *causa causans*, the pursuer was denied any compensation. However, as a result of the Law Reform (Contributory Negligence) Act 1945, the court now has the power to reduce the damages awarded to the pursuer in proportion to the pursuer's responsibility for her own injuries.[1] Although the 1945 Act has, in so far as the pursuer's con-

---

1 On contributory negligence, see pp 150 ff below.

duct is concerned, reduced the importance of determining a single cause or *causa causans*, the court still retains the power of limiting a defender's delictual liability for breach of a duty of care. It does this by deciding that the breach is not the legal cause of the pursuer's injuries, for example because of the intervention of a third party. Therefore, the determination of legal causation remains important.

The decision as to whether or not a breach of duty constitutes the *causa causans* of the pursuer's injuries 'must be dealt with broadly and upon common sense principles as a jury would probably deal with it'[1] Two factors are important, as we shall now see.

(1) Foreseeability

Where there has been a breach of duty by the defender, the act of a third party or the victim will not generally break the chain of causation if it was reasonably foreseeable that the subsequent act would take place. Thus, for example, in *Sayers v Harlow Urban District Council*[2] the plaintiff entered a cubicle in a public lavatory maintained by the defendant. Owing to a fault in the lock, she could not reopen the door. She banged on the door and put her hand out of the window in unsuccessful attempts to attract attention. After 15 minutes, she tried to escape through the space between the top of the door and the roof. She put her left foot on the lavatory seat, her right foot on the toilet roll holder, one hand on the lavatory cistern and the other hand on the top of the door. When she found it impossible to squeeze through the space, she proceeded to come down but, because of her weight, the toilet roll holder rotated, she lost her balance and fell. The court held that it was reasonably foreseeable that a person in Mrs Sayers' position would try to escape and that this was not a hazardous enterprise. Accordingly, her attempted escape was not a *novus actus interveniens* and the defendant's breach of duty was the *causa causans* of the accident. However, when she found she could not escape, she was careless in putting so much weight on the toilet roll holder: although this did not break the chain of causation, it did constitute

---

1 *Admiralty Comrs v SS Volute* [1922] AC 129, HL, at 144 per Birkenhead LC; *Galoo Ltd (in liquidation) v Bright Grahame Murray* [1995] 1 All ER 16, CA at 29 per Glidewell LJ, quoting an Australian decision: 'The answer in the end is "By the application of the court's common sense"'; *Simmons v British Steel plc* 2003 SLT 62 per the Lord Justice-Clerk (Gill) at 65: 'This is a case where the question of causation can be decided straightforwardly on a common sense view of the whole evidence.'
2 [1958] 2 All ER 342, [1958] 1 WLR 623, CA.

contributory negligence and her damages were reduced by 25 per cent.[1]

Even if the subsequent act of a third party or the pursuer is reasonably foreseeable, it may break the chain of causation if it was hazardous for the third party or the pursuer to act in such a way. In *McKew v Holland and Hannen and Cubitts (Scotland) Ltd,*[2] the pursuer injured his ankle as a result of the defender's breach of duty. Because of the fracture, his leg was liable to 'give way' from time to time. After the accident, the pursuer went to see a flat. The stairway leading to the flat had no handrail. Although he knew that his leg was likely to give way at any time, after visiting the flat the pursuer went down the stairs in a normal manner ie he did not go down slowly so that he could sit on a step if his leg 'gave way'. His leg gave way and in panic the pursuer jumped down 10 steps and was injured.

The court held that the defender was not liable for the second injury. Although it was reasonably foreseeable that the pursuer might climb stairs which had no handrail, he had acted in a hazardous manner in walking down the stairs in the normal way without assistance. The defender's breach of duty which had caused the injury to the pursuer's ankle was not the *causa causans* of the pursuer's second injury. Instead, the pursuer's carelessness in walking down the stairs without assistance constituted hazardous conduct on the pursuer's part which broke the chain of causation between the defender's breach of duty and the pursuer's second injuries.

In *Sabri-Tabrizi v Lothian Health Board,*[3] the pursuer became pregnant as a result of a failed sterilisation. She had a termination. Knowing that she was fertile, she had sexual intercourse with her husband on several occasions. She fell pregnant again. Although the defenders admitted liability for the first pregnancy, they denied liability for the second. The Lord Ordinary (Nimmo Smith) agreed:[4]

'The alleged negligence resulted in the pursuer's being still fertile, just as she would have been had the failed sterilisation operation never been carried out. The pursuer knew this, and consequently knew that there was a risk of her becoming pregnant if she had sexual intercourse with her husband ... She avers that she took precautions, but in so far as there remained a residual risk, in a question between her and the defenders I

1 On contributory negligence, see pp 150 ff below.
2 1970 SC (HL) 20, 1970 SLT 68.
3 1998 SC 373, 1998 SLT 607.
4 1998 SC 373, at 378.

think that it is unreasonable of her to expose herself to that risk. Accordingly I regard her decision to have sexual intercourse in the knowledge that she was not sterile as constituting a *novus actus interveniens,* breaking the chain of causation, with the result that the defenders cannot be held liable for the second pregnancy and the consequences thereof.'

(2) The order of events

The order of events may be important in determining whether or not the defender's breach of duty is the *causa causans* of the pursuer's injuries. In *Donaghy v National Coal Board,*[1] the defender broke the duty of care which was owed to the pursuer by leaving a detonator lying around the workplace. The pursuer took the detonator home and hit it with a hammer. As a result, he was injured. The court held that the pursuer's conduct amounted to a *novus actus interveniens:* it was unforeseeable, unreasonable, ie hazardous, and was the last act which had led to the accident. On the other hand, in *Davidson v City of Glasgow District Council,*[2] the second defender supplied the pursuer's employer, the first defender, with planks which were too short for a particular task. The employer rejected the planks but owing to the employer's alleged carelessness one of the short planks was not rejected. As a result of the plank being too short, there was an accident and the pursuer was injured. The pursuer sued the employer (first defender) and the supplier (the second defender). The second defender argued that the employer's failure to reject all the planks constituted a *novus actus interveniens.* The court held that merely because the employer's conduct was the 'last act' that led to the accident, this did not necessarily mean that it amounted to a *novus actus interveniens:*

'Even although there was in effect an intermediate inspection, and assuming in the alternative that the first defenders [the employer] failed to discover that one of the planks remained and was inadvertently used, it does not follow that that was negligence or that it broke the chain of causation and was the sole cause of the accident.'[3]

Thus, where an accident is caused to A as a result of a breach of duty by B *and* a breach of duty by C, the mere fact that B's breach of duty arose after C's breach of duty will not necessarily break the chain of causation to exonerate C from delictual liability. In *Grant*

---

1 1957 SLT (Notes) 35.
2 1993 SLT 479, OH.
3 1993 SLT 479 at 482 per Judge D B Robertson QC.

v Sun Shipping Co Ltd,[1] ship repairers working on a ship left hatches uncovered. By doing so, they were in breach of a duty of care owed to dock labourers on the ship. The ship owners also failed to ensure that the hatches were covered and did not provide an adequate system of lighting: this constituted a breach of their duty of care to dock labourers on the ship. The pursuer, a dock labourer, fell through an unlit hatch. The House of Lords held that the shipowner's breach of duty did not constitute a *novus actus interveniens* breaking the chain of causation between the accident and the ship repairers' breach of duty of care towards the pursuer by leaving the hatches uncovered. Instead, both the ship owners and the ship repairers were jointly liable in delict.[2] Where there is joint liability, under s 3 of the Law Reform (Miscellaneous Provisions) (Scotland) Act 1940 the court has the power to apportion the damages between the defenders.[3]

(3) Conclusion

Where A's breach of a duty of care is a *causa sine qua non* of B's injuries, the courts appear unwilling to be persuaded that a subsequent act – even if careless – constitutes a *novus actus interveniens* unless it is so unusual or unexpected that it could not have been reasonably foreseeable, or so hazardous on the part of B, that it would be unreasonable to hold A liable. If the subsequent act is that of a third party, C, and constitutes a breach of duty owed by C to B, A and C will be held jointly liable in delict to B. If the subsequent act is that of B, A remains liable, ie B's act will not break the chain of causation but instead it will lead to a reduction of damages on the grounds of contributory negligence. Although this will be the usual result, there can, of course, still be exceptional cases where the chain of causation is broken and A's breach of duty is not treated as the *causa causans* of B's injuries. So, for example, if A injured B's foot and B suffered an infection in hospital, the chain of causation would not be broken as it is reasonably foreseeable that B might get an infection in hospital. But if the surgeon in the hospital is careless and amputates B's uninjured foot, the chain of causation is broken since the surgeon's conduct is so unusual and unexpected that it is not reasonably foreseeable and therefore it constitutes a

---

1 1948 SC (HL) 73, 1949 SLT 25.
2 See also *Davidson v City of Glasgow District Council* 1993 SLT 479, OH, discussed p 146 above.
3 On joint liability, see p 153 below.

novus actus interveniens. This exonerates A from delictual liability in respect of the amputation, but not, of course, in respect of the original injury to B's foot.

The chain of causation is not broken by an act of a third party where the defender's duty of care was to prevent the third party from causing injury or damage to the pursuer.[1] But as a general rule, A does not owe B a duty of care to prevent B from being injured as a result of the deliberate conduct of a third party, C.[2] Here, of course, it is the absence of a duty of care which prevents A from being liable to B in delict.

C. RELATED MATTERS

(1) *Volenti non fit injuria*

The chain of causation will be broken if the pursuer has voluntarily undertaken the risk of harm created by the defender's breach of duty. This is the doctrine of *volenti non fit injuria.* Because the chain of causation is broken and the defender's breach of duty is no longer the *causa causans* of the pursuer's injuries, the doctrine of *volenti* provides the defender with a complete defence to an action in delict. The theoretical basis of *volenti* is that by knowing acceptance of the risk, the pursuer has absolved the defender of the consequences of the defender's breach of the duty of care owed to the pursuer. In other words, the defender still owes the pursuer a duty of care but the chain of causation is broken by the pursuer voluntarily undertaking the risk.[3]

Before the defender will succeed in the defence of *volenti non fit injuria* the defender must prove that before or at the same time as the negligent act or omission,[4] the pursuer knowingly and willingly undertook the risk of the danger created by the defender's breach

---

1 *Dorset Yacht Co Ltd v Home Office* [1970] AC 1004, [1970] 2 All ER 294, HL, discussed at pp 122 ff above.
2 *Modbury Triangle Shopping Centre v Anzil* (2000) 205 CLR 254. There are, of course, exceptions. See, for example, *Empress Car Co (Abertillery) Ltd v National Rivers Authority* [1998] 1 All ER 481, HL (a person causes a pollutant to enter controlled waters even if a necessary condition of the actual escape of the pollutant is the act of a third party, provided the third party's conduct is an act of normal life, eg vandalism, and not extraordinary).
3 *Winnick v Dick* 1984 SC 48, 1984 SLT 185.
4 *Sabri-Tabrizi v Lothian Health Board* 1998 SC 373, 1998 SLT 607.

of duty. In *Titchener v British Railways Board* [1] the defender failed to maintain a fence made of sleepers which was positioned along a railway track. A 15-year-old girl climbed through the fence and went up the embankment to take a short cut across the railway line to a piece of waste ground where she intended to have a kiss and cuddle with her boyfriend. She was injured by a train when she was crossing the line. As we shall see,[2] the House of Lords held that in the circumstances the defender did not owe the pursuer a duty of care. But the House indicated that even if a duty of care had been owed and there had been a breach of duty, the defender would have had the defence of *volenti* since the pursuer knew and accepted the risk of being injured by a train when she crossed the line.

Because the pursuer must have knowledge of, and be *willing* to accept, the risk, the courts are unlikely to accept a plea of *volenti* in an action between employee and employer. Nevertheless, the defence succeeded in *ICI v Shatwell*.[3] Contrary to their employer's instructions, the plaintiff and his brother, who were experienced shotfirers, agreed to test their detonators without first returning to a safety shelter. There was an explosion; the plaintiff was injured and his brother was killed. It was held that the employer had not been in breach of a duty of care towards the plaintiff.[4] However, the plaintiff sued the employer as vicariously liable for his brother's careless act in testing the detonator.[5] The House of Lords held that since the plaintiff had agreed with his brother to run the risk of injury by testing the detonators without first returning to a place of safety, the employer could successfully plead the defence of *volenti*.

The defence of *volenti* does not apply in the case of a rescuer. By virtue of s 149 of the Road Traffic Act 1988, the defence of *volenti* does not apply to a claim by a passenger against the driver of a vehicle which has compulsory third party insurance. Thus, if a passenger accepts a lift from a drunken driver and the car has compulsory third party insurance, the driver cannot plead *volenti* if the passenger is injured as a result of the driver's breach of duty. The passenger's damages could, of course, be reduced on the ground of contributory negligence.

Where the duty of care is to *prevent* the defender from acting in a particular way, it would make nonsense of the existence of the duty

---

1 1984 SC (HL) 34, 1984 SLT 192. See also *Devlin v Strathclyde Regional Council* 1993 SLT 699, OH.
2 Page 198 below.
3 [1965] AC 656, [1964] 2 All ER 999.
4 Or in breach of any statutory duty.
5 On vicarious liability, see pp 221 ff below.

if *volenti* could be used when the defender does the act the pursuer should have prevented. For example, the police owe a duty of care to prevent prisoners from harming themselves while on remand: if, in breach of their duty, a prisoner is able to injure or kill himself, the defence of *volenti* cannot be used.[1]

It is sometimes argued that the reason why a spectator at a dangerous sport, such as motor racing, cannot sue a participant who injures him by crashing into the crowd at high speed is that the spectator is *volens* of the risk of harm inherent in the sport. However, it is thought that the better way to analyse the situation is to argue that in the circumstances the participant does not owe the spectator a duty of care to avoid the possibility of such an accident. The organiser of the event may owe the spectator a duty of care, if, for example, the circuit was not suitable for racing or the safety precautions were inadequate, and the spectator will not be *volens* of these risks simply by attending the event.[2]

Where a participant in a dangerous sport is injured by another participant, again it is thought the reason an action in delict will not be successful is not that the pursuer was *volens*, but that the defender does not owe a duty of care to the pursuer to protect him from injuries the risk of which are inherent in the sport, for example being bruised when tackled at rugby football.[3] If the injury arises from conduct which is contrary to the rules of the game, the pursuer's remedy lies in assault rather than in a breach of a duty of care.

(2) Contributory negligence

As we have seen, where the defender's breach of duty to the pursuer is a *causa sine qua non* of the pursuer's injuries, the courts are reluctant to accept that the pursuer's subsequent conduct is a *novus actus interveniens* or amounts to *volenti* so that the defender is exonerated from delictual liability. This is particularly the case where the pursuer has acted in the 'agony of the moment' ie reacts carelessly in a situation caused by the defender's breach of duty, for example jumps out of a window to escape a fire caused by the defender's negligence. Instead, the court will hold that the pursuer's conduct

---

1 *Reeves v Metropolitan Commissioner* [2001] 1 AC 360.
2 See *Wooldridge v Sumner* [1963] 2 QB 43, [1962] 2 All ER 978, CA; *Lewis v Buckpool Golf Club* 1993 SLT (Sh Ct) 43.
3 However, a referee owes a duty of care to the players. When the referee has been negligent, an injured player is not *volens* merely by participating in the game: *Smoldon v Whitworth* [1997] PIQR P133, (1996) Times, 18 December, CA.

was a contributory cause of the injury. The effect of a finding of contributory negligence is to reduce the damages which would otherwise have been awarded to the pursuer, to reflect the pursuer's responsibility for the damage or injury sustained. Section 1(1) of the Law Reform (Contributory Negligence) Act 1945 provides:

'Where any person suffers *damage as the result partly of his own fault* and *partly due to the fault of any other person or persons,* a claim in respect of that damage shall not be defeated by reason of the fault of the person suffering the damage, but the *damages recoverable* in respect thereof *shall be reduced* to such an extent as the *court thinks just and equitable* having regard to the *claimant's share in the responsibility* for the damage.' [emphasis added]

Before the 1945 Act applies, the pursuer must have suffered damage partly as a result of his own *fault*.[1] Fault covers the pursuer's deliberate as well as negligent actions.[2] In relation to the latter, the pursuer's act must fall below the standard of the reasonable person in the pursuer's position. The onus rests on the defender to prove that the pursuer was at fault. Although, for example, a passenger injured in a motor accident will usually be at fault if he or she fails to wear a seat belt, in *Mackay v Borthwick*[3] the pursuer was held not to be contributorily negligent for failing to wear a seat belt since it was uncomfortable for her to wear it because she was suffering from a hiatus hernia. In *Pace v Culley*[4] the pursuer, who was a taxi driver, failed to wear a seat belt because he had been advised by the police not to do so in the event that he might be attacked by his passengers. Although he accepted that failure to wear a seat belt could amount to contributory negligence, the Lord Ordinary (Weir) thought that the driver's conduct in this case was a misjudgment rather than a failure to take care for his own safety.[5] In *Blackhall v MacInnes*,[6] the pursuer was injured while she was changing the offside wheel of her motor car. She was held to be 20 per cent contributorily negligent because – contrary to the Highway Code – she had made no attempt to get the vehicle off the road although it was practicable to drive on the verge.

---

1 'Fault' is defined in s 5(a) of the Law Reform (Contributory Negligence) Act 1945 as: 'wrongful act, breach of statutory duty or negligent act or omission which gives rise to liability in damages ... '.
2 *Reeves v Metropolitan Commissioner* [2000] 1 AC 360 (prisoner killed himself: family's damages reduced by 50 per cent as a result of his suicide).
3 1982 SLT 265, OH.
4 1992 SLT 1073, OH.
5 The contributory negligence, if any, would have been *de minimis* in respect of the total claim and could therefore be ignored.
6 1997 SLT 649, OH.

The defender must also prove that the pursuer's fault contributed to the harm sustained, ie 'but for' the pursuer's fault, the injuries or damage suffered would not have been as bad as actually occurred. In other words, the defender must establish that the pursuer's fault was a factual cause, a *causa sine qua non*, of the harm sustained. Thus, contributory negligence was established when the defender proved, on the balance of probabilities, that the pursuer would have suffered less severe neck injuries if she had worn a seat belt.[1]

When contributory negligence is established, the proportion to be deducted from the damages is a matter for the discretion of the judge, ie what the judge considers just and equitable having regard to the pursuer's share in the responsibility for the damage. This can vary from as little as five per cent in 'agony of the moment' cases to as much as 80 per cent.[2] It is submitted that 100 per cent deduction is not possible under the Law Reform (Contributory Negligence) Act 1945 since in those circumstances the pursuer would be solely responsible and not 'share in the responsibility for the damage'.[3] A drunken pedestrian run down by a careless driver has had his damages reduced by 50 per cent as a result of contributory negligence.[4] Similarly, a guest injured at a party has had his damages reduced by 50 per cent because he had been drinking heavily.[5]

Damages for pure economic loss can be reduced on the grounds of the pursuer's contributory negligence.[6] However, in a case of

1 *Hanlon v Cuthbertson* 1981 SLT (Notes) 57, OH. Cf *Neil v Docherty and Akram* (23 May 1996, unreported), HC, where the plaintiff's injuries were sustained on initial impact, ie before she was ejected from the taxi because she was not wearing a seat belt.
2 *Uddin v Associated Portland Cement Manufacturers Ltd* [1965] 2 QB 582, [1965] 2 All ER 213, CA.
3 If the pursuer is solely responsible, the defender will escape liability because either his breach of duty is not the *causa causans* or the pursuer is *volens*: see *ICI v Shatwell* [1965] AC 656.
4 *Malcolm v Fair* 1993 SLT 342, OH. See also *Kemp v Secretary of State for Scotland* 2000 SLT 471 (pursuer's damages reduced by one-third because he was drunk at the time of the accident). In *Gilfillan v Barbour* 2003 SL 1127 in cross actions arising from a collision, both parties had their damages reduced by 50 per cent as both had been careless.
5 *Brannan v Airtours* (18 January 1999, unreported), CA. Although there is no duty to prevent an adult from becoming drunk, there may be a duty to look after the drunk person if she becomes incapable of looking after herself. When there is such a duty and it is broken, the plaintiff's damages can be reduced on the grounds that she got inebriated: *Barrett v Ministry of Defence* [1995] 3 All ER 87, CA (two-thirds contributorily negligent).
6 *Platform Home Loans Ltd v Oyston Shipways Ltd* [1999] 1 All ER 833, HL. For further discussion, see beyond p 291.

fraudulent – as opposed to negligent – misrepresentation, the defender cannot seek to have the pursuer's damages reduced on the ground of the pursuer's contributory negligence.[1]

As a matter of public policy, if the pursuer is participating in a criminal activity at the time he is injured, he may be barred from obtaining reparation: for example if A and B steal a car and A is injured as a result of B's careless driving or a thief is shot by the owner of a house in the course of a burglary.[2] However, the bar is not automatic and depends on the circumstances. In *Weir v Wyper*[3] the pursuer was not barred when she was injured in a car crash even though she knew that the driver had only a provisional licence. When the action is not barred, the pursuer's damages could, of course, be reduced on the ground of contributory negligence.[4]

(3) Joint fault

Joint fault arises where harm is caused to the pursuer as a result of the conduct of more than one defender. This is known as joint liability if the harm has been caused as a result of a breach by each defender of a duty of care owed to the pursuer; in the case of other delicts, it is known as joint wrongdoing. Before there can be joint liability, each breach of duty must have materially contributed to, or materially increased the risk of, the *same* delict to the pursuer. Thus, for example, in *Anderson v St Andrew's Ambulance Association*[5] a passenger in a bus was injured in a collision between the bus and an ambulance. The bus driver had failed to observe a 'slow' sign; the ambulance driver had failed to observe a 'halt' sign. The court held that this was a case of joint liability, for both drivers were responsible for the same wrong suffered by the pursuer. Conversely, in *Fleming v McGillivray*[6] the court held that it was not a case of joint liability where an injured pursuer sued a van driver for careless driving and the owner of the van for failing to have compulsory third party insurance: the driver was being sued for

---

1 *Standard Chartered Bank v Pakistan National Shipping Corpn* [2003] 1 All ER 173, HL.
2 *Duncan v Ross Harper & Murphy* 1993 SLT 105n, OH.
3 1992 SCLR 483, 1992 SLT 579, OH.
4 *Taylor v Leslie* 1998 SLT 1248, 1998 Rep LR 110, OH (defender drove car while unlicensed, uninsured and underaged. Passenger killed. Conduct not regarded as reprehensible by the community of Shapinsay, a remote island. The deceased had encouraged the defender to speed. Damages reduced by 50 per cent).
5 1943 SC 248, 1943 SLT 258.
6 1946 SC 1, 1945 SLT 301.

breach of his duty of care (delict 1), while the owner was being sued for breach of statutory duty in not having insurance (delict 2). Since they were not responsible for the same delict, this was not a case of joint liability or joint wrongdoing.

If A and B are jointly liable, the pursuer may sue A or B or both. If the pursuer sues only A and obtains a decree, if A pays the damages the pursuer cannot then sue B; but if A does not pay the damages, the pursuer can sue B. If the pursuer successfully sues both A and B, he will be awarded a joint and several decree. This entitles the pursuer to obtain *all* the damages from either A or B. Where A has paid all the damages, the court can apportion the damages between A and B; and if B was not sued in the original action, A can, nevertheless, recover from B the proportion of the damages which the court deems attributable to B's conduct.[1] Where the pursuer is contributorily negligent, the total damages to be paid by A or B will be reduced to reflect the pursuer's responsibility for the injury or harm suffered.

---

1 Law Reform (Miscellaneous Provisions) (Scotland) Act 1940, s 3. The proportions *inter se* the defenders are what the court, or jury, considers just in the circumstances: see, for example, *BOC v Groves* 1993 SLT 360, OH (75 per cent and 25 per cent).

Part III

DELICTUAL LIABILITY IN SPECIFIC SOCIAL AND ECONOMIC CONTEXTS

Chapter 7.   Professional liability   157

Chapter 8.   Product liability   165

Chapter 9.   Delictual liability for animals   177

Chapter 10.   Delictual liability arising from ownership or occupation of property   185

Chapter 11.   Breach of statutory duty and public law issues   201

Chapter 12.   Employers' liability and vicarious liability   215

Chapter 13.   Delict and the family   237

Chapter 14.   Delict and road traffic   251

Chapter 15.   Defamation and verbal injury   259

Introduction

Having discussed the general principles of delictual liability, it is now proposed to examine the law of delict as it operates in certain specific social and economic contexts. As we shall see, the general principle of delictual liability for harm caused to the pursuer as a result of the defender's *culpa* is often supplemented by other common law principles, for example, nuisance and vicarious liability. More importantly, perhaps, in certain areas common law delictual liability has been supplemented or supplanted by statutory liability. It is thought that these developments are better understood if discussed in the context of the particular social and economic relationships in which they occur.

CHAPTER 7

Professional liability

The general principles of the law of delict apply where a person causes harm to another in the course of his trade, business or profession. Often, of course, the person harmed will be a client or a customer of the defender; if this is so, the pursuer's primary remedy will be to sue the defender in contract. Almost inevitably, the defender will have assumed responsibility for the interests of the client or customer and the customer or client will have relied on the defender's expertise. Accordingly, unless the terms of their contract negative delictual liability, the defender will also owe the pursuer a *Henderson v Merrett*[1] duty of care to prevent economic loss arising from the defender's negligence. Put another way, where the client and professional are directly linked by contract, concurrent liability in contract and delict can arise. If there is no direct contractual relationship between the parties, liability can lie only in delict.

Where the pursuer suffers physical harm or damage to his property, the defender will be liable in delict if the damage or harm was caused intentionally or as a result of a breach of a duty of care owed by the defender to the pursuer. The existence of such a duty of care will be determined by the *Donoghue v Stevenson* neighbourhood principle.[2] Where the pursuer has suffered pure economic loss, liability will lie in delict if the defender intended to harm the pursuer or if a *Henderson v Merrett* duty of care exists. A duty of care could also arise if, for example, the *Caparo* tripartite test is satisfied,[3] or *Junior Books* liability exists.[4]

In determining whether or not there has been a breach of a duty of care, the defender's conduct is judged by the standard of care expected in his or her profession. Put another way, in order to establish that the defender was negligent the pursuer must prove

---

1 See *Henderson v Merrett Syndicates Ltd* [1995] 2 AC 145, [1994] 3 All ER 506, HL, discussed at pp 90 ff above.
2 See *Donoghue v Stevenson* 1932 SC (HL) 31, 1932 SLT 317.
3 *Caparo Industries plc v Dickman* [1990] 2 AC 605, [1990] 1 All ER 568, HL. See, for example, *Weir v National Westminster Bank plc* 1993 SC 515, 1994 SLT 1251.
4 *Junior Books Ltd v Veitchi Co Ltd* 1982 SC (HL) 244, 1982 SLT 492.

that the defender's conduct fell below that of the reasonable accountant, architect, lawyer, medical practitioner or surveyor etc. While ultimately a question of law,[1] the usual practice of persons in the same trade, business or profession as the defender will be a significant factor in determining whether or not the defender was negligent.

It can be particularly difficult to establish negligence where the defender's conduct involves an exercise of professional judgment. Often there will be several courses of action open to the defender. In these circumstances, the defender will *not* be negligent if she adopted a course of action which resulted in harm to the pursuer unless no reasonable professional person in her position would have chosen that option. Nor does it matter that the course of action chosen was *not* the normal practice in the profession. In the leading case of *Hunter v Hanley*[2] the pursuer alleged that the defender, a doctor, was negligent in using a needle which was unsuitable for treating the patient. In discussing the standard of care appropriate to a doctor, the Lord President (Clyde) observed:[3]

' ... in regard to deviation from ordinary professional practice ... such deviation is not necessarily evidence of negligence. Indeed it would be disastrous if this were so, for all inducement to progress in medical science would then be destroyed. Even a substantial deviation from normal practice may be warranted by the particular circumstances. To establish liability by a doctor where deviation from normal practice is alleged, three facts require to be established. First of all it must be proved that there is a normal practice; secondly it must be proved that the defender has not adopted that practice; and thirdly (and this is of crucial importance) it must be established that the course which the doctor adopted is one which no professional man of ordinary skill would have taken if he had been acting with ordinary care.'

Thus it is not enough that the defender's conduct deviated from normal practice: it must be demonstrated that no professional man of ordinary skill would have followed the course taken by the defender. Even if the pursuer can establish that a responsible body of medical opinion regards the defender's decision or conduct as wrong, the defender will not be regarded as having been negligent if there is also a responsible body of medical opinion which regards

---

1 *Bolitho v City and Hackney Health Authority* [1998] AC 232, [1997] 4 All ER 771, HL.
2 1955 SC 200, 1955 SLT 213.
3 1955 SC 200 at 206. Lord Clyde's approach was approved by McNair J in the leading English case, *Bolam v Friern Hospital Management Committee* [1957] 2 All ER 118, [1957] 1 WLR 582.

the defender's decision or conduct as reasonable in the circumstances.[1] This test applies not only to medical treatment[2] but also to diagnosis[3] and advice.[4]

Gordon v Wilson[5] provides an illustration of the formidable difficulties facing a pursuer in an action of medical negligence. In that case, the pursuer argued that a doctor was negligent in delaying to refer a patient to a specialist.[6] Although the pursuer established that there was a responsible body of medical opinion which took the view that a reasonable doctor would have referred the patient to a specialist at an earlier stage, the court held that the defender was not negligent because the defender could show that there was also a responsible body of medical opinion to the effect that a reasonable doctor would not have referred the patient to a specialist until the defender had done so. Accordingly, the pursuer's action failed. Professional negligence cannot be established by preferring one body of professional opinion to another; instead the pursuer must prove that no reasonable doctor exercising his ordinary clinical skills would have taken the defender's course of action in the circumstances of the particular case.[7]

1 *Maynard v West Midlands Regional Health Authority* [1985] 1 All ER 635, [1984] 1 WLR 634, HL. The number of specialist doctors who accept the defender's practices need not be substantial provided they are responsible: *Defreitas v O'Brien* [1995] 6 Med LR 108. If there is no recognised standard practice, the court must determine whether or not the defender took reasonable care in all the circumstances: *AB v Tameside and Glossop Health Authority* [1997] 8 Med LR 91, CA (defendant sent a secret letter to patients informing them that a health worker who had treated them was HIV positive: defendant not negligent simply because they sent a standard letter rather than organising face-to-face disclosure of the tiny risk of infection).
2 *Whitehouse v Jordan* [1981] 1 All ER 267, [1981] 1 WLR 246, HL.
3 *Maynard v West Midlands Regional Health Authority* [1985] 1 All ER 635, [1984] 1 WLR 634, HL.
4 *Gold v Haringey Health Authority* [1987] QB 481, [1987] 2 All ER 888, CA. The same criteria apply to the duty to inform a patient of risks inherent in a medical procedure even if it is carried out properly: *Sidaway v Bethlem Royal Hospital Board of Governors* [1985] AC 871, [1985] 1 All ER 643, HL.
5 1992 SLT 849 n, [1992] 3 Med LR 401, OH.
6 It should also be remembered that in order to establish causation the pursuer must prove that 'but for' the doctor's omission the treatment would have had more than a 50 per cent chance of success: *Kenyon v Bell* 1953 SC 125; *Hotson v East Berkshire Area Health Authority* [1987] 2 All ER 909, HL; *Gregg v Scott* [2002] EWCA Civ 1471.
7 In *Bolitho v City and Hackney Health Authority* [1998] AC 232, [1997] 4 All ER 771, HL, it was stressed by the House of Lords that the body of medical opinion must be reasonable and responsible. In other words, there must be a logical basis for the opinion the experts support. Although this is ultimately a question of law, it would only be in rare cases that the court would reject the medical experts' views as unreasonable.

These cases were concerned with the medical profession. But as indicated above, the test for establishing the requisite standard of care is applicable in relation to other professions where an exercise of professional judgment is involved.[1]

The position of the legal professions requires further treatment. Where a solicitor takes instructions from her client, liability can arise in contract and delict. The contract may stipulate a higher standard of care than that required by the law of negligence ie strict liability rather than a failure to take reasonable care.[2] As a general rule, the solicitor owes a duty of care to her client: she does not owe a duty of care to a third party, for example a person who would benefit from an *inter vivos* transaction.[3] However, where a solicitor gives advice or information to a person who is not a client, ie who does not have a contractual relationship with the solicitor, the solicitor may be liable in delict provided the *Henderson v Merrett* criteria for a duty of care exist.[4] In other words, there must be voluntary assumption of responsibility by the solicitor and concomitant reliance on the third party's part.

Where such a duty exists, the pursuer will only succeed if it can be established that the solicitor was negligent in giving the advice, ie that a reasonable solicitor would not have given that advice in the circumstances.[5]

What of the situation where a solicitor acts on the instructions of a client but as a result of the solicitor's carelessness does not give effect to the client's instructions with the result that a third party suffers loss? Normally, no duty of care is owed to the third party.[6]

1 See, for example, *Gaughan v Bedfordshire Health Authority* [1997] 8 Med LR 182, QBD (midwives); *Henderson v Merrett Syndicates Ltd (No 2)* [1997] LRLR 265, QBD (Comm Ct) (underwriting agents); *Sneesby v Goldings* [1995] 2 EGLR 102, CA (surveyors); *Scott v Lothian Regional Council* 1999 Rep LR 15 (guidance teachers); *Leeds & Holbeck Building Society v Alex Morison & Co (No 2)* 2001 SCLR 41 (lawyers); *Gilfillan v Barbour* 2003 SLT 1127 (police).
2 *Mortgage Corporation Ltd v Mitchells Roberton* 1997 SLT 1305, OH.
3 *Tait v Brown & McRae* 1997 SLT (Sh Ct) 63.
4 *Newcastle Building Society v Paterson Robertson and Graham* 2001 SC 734 (pursuer lent money to borrower. It was a condition of the loan that the defenders, the borrower's solicitors, confirm certain matters in a report. The report was inaccurate. Held that the defenders owed a duty of care to the pursuer since the loan would not have gone ahead if the report had been accurate).
5 When the client is an experienced businessman and a transaction does not involve any hidden legal pitfalls, a solicitor is not obliged to investigate matters outwith his instructions or warn the client of the commercial risks in the transaction: *Pickergill v Riley* (2004), Times 2nd March.
6 *Bristol and West Building Society v Aitken Nairn* 1999 SLT 43, OH. There are very rare cases where a duty can arise because of exceptional degrees of proximity between the parties: *Mortgage Corporation Ltd v Mitchells Roberton* 1997 SLT 1305, OH.

An important exception exists, however, when the third party is a 'disappointed legatee'. Consider the following problem.

A instructs a solicitor to draw up a will under which B is the principal beneficiary. As a result of the solicitor's carelessness the will is invalid and B does not obtain the legacy. There is no contractual relationship between B and the solicitor. Therefore B's remedy, if any, lies in delict against the solicitor. B has suffered pure economic loss and before there is delictual liability the solicitor must owe B a duty of care to prevent B suffering such loss. Unlike the advice and information situations, B has not relied on the solicitor's expertise: B will probably *not* know the solicitor's identity. Even if the solicitor can be said to have assumed responsibility for B's interests, the *Henderson v Merrett* duty of care will not normally arise because of the absence of concomitant reliance on B's part. We have therefore a situation where the courts must be prepared on policy grounds to impose a duty of care before the solicitor can be liable in delict.[1]

For many years, the Scottish courts refused to recognise such a duty of care.[2] However, in England the issue was fully explored by the House of Lords in *White v Jones*.[3] After a family quarrel, a father struck his daughters out of his will. Later he relented. In spite of the family's attempts to encourage their father's solicitor to fulfil the old man's instructions, the father died before the will was altered in favour of the daughters. By a majority,[4] the House of Lords held that the solicitor owed a duty of care to the disappointed legatees. For Lords Goff and Browne-Wilkinson it was enough that the solicitor had assumed responsibility for the potential beneficiaries: this was implicit when accepting their father's instructions. Concomitant reliance was not necessary to impose a duty of care in the case of disappointed legatees. Lord Nolan found actual reliance since the defender had acted as a solicitor for the family, not merely the father. Lord Mustill dissented owing to the absence of concomitant reliance which he felt was constitutive of a *Henderson v Merrett* duty of care.

It is quite clear that the majority in *White v Jones* felt that a negligent solicitor *should* be liable in this situation. But, although we may be sympathetic to the policy, the reasoning is less than happy.

1 Ie the duty of care is being used as a threshold device: see Chapter 4 above.
2 *Robertson v Fleming* (1861) 23 D (HL) 8, (1861) 4 Macq 167 per Lord Campbell LC at 177; *Weir v J M Hodge & Son* 1990 SLT 266 per the Lord Ordinary (Weir) at 270; *MacDougall v MacDougall's Executors* 1994 SLT 1178.
3 [1995] 2 AC 207, [1995] 1 All ER 691, HL.
4 Lord Goff of Chieveley, Lord Browne-Wilkinson and Lord Nolan; Lords Mustill and Keith of Kinkel dissented.

In particular, the absence of the need for reliance makes it impossible to fit *White v Jones* within the *Henderson v Merrett* general duty of care to prevent economic loss. In spite of its difficulties, *White v Jones* has been transplanted into Scots law.[1] Given that the potential pursuer falls into a restricted class, ie the 'legatee' named in the instructions and therefore known to the solicitor, it is thought that a duty of care can be justified in these circumstances.[2]

Where there has been a breach of a duty of care by a solicitor, there may be difficulties in quantifying the pursuer's loss. In *Kyle v P & J Stormonth Darling WS*[3] the defender failed to lodge the pursuer's appeal in time, with the result that the pursuer lost the opportunity to do so. In rejecting the defender's argument that the pursuer was entitled to damages only if it could be established on the balance of probabilities that the appeal would have been successful, the Lord Ordinary (Prosser) said:[4]

'where there has been deprivation of a legal right, that will in itself constitute a completed wrong, and one will be entitled, as a matter of valuation, to take into consideration all reasonable prospects of success, if they exceed nuisance value, even if they fall short of probability.'

In *Arthur J S Hall & Co v Simons*,[5] the House of Lords held that under English law barristers no longer have immunity from being sued for professional negligence in their conduct of civil or criminal cases. In his dissenting speech on the latter point, Lord Hope, a Scottish Lord of Appeal in Ordinary, considered that there should still be immunity in respect of the conduct of criminal proceedings. In *Trevor Rush McCafferty Wright v Paton Farrell*[6] Temporary Judge Coutts held that advocates and solicitors continued to have immunity under Scots law, at least in respect of criminal cases. The position in relation to the conduct of civil proceedings remains unclear.[7] It has been suggested that the same immunity extends to

---

1 *Robertson v Watt & Co* (4 July 1995, unreported), a decision of the Second Division; *Holmes v Bank of Scotland* 2002 SLT 544.
2 A better solution, perhaps, would be to allow the court to rectify the will so that it would correspond to the testator's final intentions, evidence of which would have to be very convincing!
3 1993 SC 57, 1994 SLT 191, affirming 1992 SLT 264, OH.
4 1992 SLT 264 at 268. Contrast the position with medical negligence cases, discussed p 159 above.
5 [2002] 1 AC 615.
6 2002 SCLR 1039.
7 The difficulty is that the House of Lords in *Hall* did not overrule *Rondel v Worsley* [1969] 1 AC 191 which had given barristers immunity in respect of both civil and criminal proceedings. *Rondel* has been followed in Scotland. *Hall* is technically not binding on the Scottish courts.

solicitors in respect of court work.[1] Where a solicitor has acted on counsel's advice, it has been argued that the solicitor should enjoy immunity if counsel would have been immune.[2] It has always been accepted that an advocate can be liable for giving negligent advice, for example an opinion on a point of law.[3]

1 *Murray v Reilly* 1963 SLT (Notes) 49, OH.
2 *Reid v Edinburgh Acoustics Ltd (No 2)* 1995 SCLR 791n, 1995 SLT 982, OH.
3 *Saif Ali v Sydney Mitchell & Co* [1980] AC 198.

CHAPTER 8

Product liability

A. INTRODUCTION

The basis of product liability in Scots law was, of course, laid down in *Donoghue v Stevenson*.[1] There it was held that the manufacturer of a product owes a duty of care to the ultimate consumer when a product is manufactured which is intended to reach the ultimate consumer in the form in which it left the manufacturer without the possibility of intermediate examination. If the product was manufactured carelessly with the result that the ultimate consumer suffered injury or harm to his property, the manufacturer is liable in delict. However, the onus lies on the pursuer to prove that there was a breach of duty by the manufacturer ie that the manufacturer was negligent.[2] If negligence cannot be established, the action fails.

Apart from the difficulty of establishing negligence, other factors could operate to prevent the pursuer from succeeding. Where, for example, a manufacturer has provided an adequate warning that a product is potentially dangerous and this is ignored by the ultimate consumer, then there will be no liability because the pursuer's failure to heed the warning will constitute a *novus actus interveniens* which breaks the chain of causation.[3] Where the product is a complex structure made up of components manufactured by various persons, an action may fail if the pursuer is unable to identify the person who was responsible for the defect in the product. For example, in *Evans v Triplex Safety Glass Co Ltd*,[4] the plaintiff was injured when the windscreen of his motor car disintegrated. The

---

1 1932 SC (HL) 31, 1932 SLT 317. Discussed at pp 60 ff above.
2 If it is established that a product has failed because of a specified defect in the manufacturing process, it is open to a judge to hold that on the balance of probabilities this was due to the manufacturer's negligence: *Carroll v Fearon* [1998] PIQR P416, CA.
3 *Kubach v Hollands* [1937] 3 All ER 907, KB. On causation generally, see Chapter 6 above.
4 [1936] 1 All ER 283.

manufacturer of the car fitted a windscreen made by the defendant. Evans failed to establish whether the accident was the result of the windscreen being fitted carelessly by the manufacturer of the car or whether it was due to a defect in the windscreen caused by the negligence of the defendant. In these circumstances, his action was dismissed. Finally, there is no liability under *Donoghue v Stevenson* if the only loss suffered by the pursuer arises from the fact that the product itself is defective, ie the cost of repair or the difference in value between a defective and a non-defective product. This is pure economic loss and is prima facie not recoverable in delict.[1]

B. STATUTORY REGULATION

Because of these difficulties, but particularly the fact that the onus of proof of negligence lies on the ultimate consumer, the law has now imposed a statutory regime of strict liability in respect of product liability. What this means is that provided the case falls within the statutory provisions, the defender is liable in delict to compensate the pursuer without the pursuer having to prove that the defender was negligent. The strict liability regime for defective products is to be found in Part I of the Consumer Protection Act 1987. This statute implements EC Directive No 85/374/EEC and it is expressly enacted that it should be interpreted to comply with the Directive.[2] The general idea of the Act is simple: it is to place the primary responsibility for personal injury or damage to property caused by a defective product on the producer and to enable the consumer who has been injured by the defective product or whose property has been damaged by the defective product to obtain compensation from the producer without having to prove fault. However, as we shall see, the provisions of the statute are hideously complex. Before considering them, it should be noted that where the statutory regime is not applicable, common law liability remains[3] and the pursuer may bring an action based on a breach of the *Donoghue v Stevenson* duty of care but will, of course, have to prove negligence if he is to be successful.

---

1 For full discussion, see pp 81 ff above.
2 Consumer Protection Act 1987, s 1(1). The Act came into force on 1 March 1988. It is not retrospective. References in this section are to CPA 1987 unless otherwise stated.
3 CPA 1987, s 2(6).

The Consumer Protection Act 1987 imposes strict liability on the producer of a product 'where any damage is caused wholly or partly by a defect in a product'.[1] Damage is defined as 'death or personal injury or any loss of or damage to property (including land)'.[2] Thus, if a person is killed or injured by a defective product, or his land or other property is damaged by a defective product, the producer of the product is liable to pay compensation without proof of fault. In other words, the producer is strictly liable.

(1) Exceptions to strict liability

Damage to certain types of property is excluded from the statutory regime:

(a) loss or damage to the defective product itself.[3] Thus, the cost of repair or the difference in value between a defective and a non-defective product is not recoverable under the Consumer Protection Act 1987. Nor is it recoverable in delict at common law since it is pure economic loss. Where the product is a complex structure, loss or damage to the whole or part of the product caused by a defective component is also excluded. Thus, for example, if a motor car (complex product) is damaged as a result of a defective wheel (component), the damage to the car is excluded but not, of course, injury to the driver or damage to other property;

(b) property damaged or lost as a result of a defective product where the property *damaged or lost* is not for private use.[4] Property is not for private use if it is not of a description of property ordinarily intended for private use, occupation or consumption *and* it is not intended by the person suffering the loss or damage mainly for his own private use, occupation or consumption. What this means is that before the Act applies and there is strict liability, the property damaged must be 'consumer' property ie of a kind ordinarily intended for private use which the person suffering the loss or damage intended to be used for private use. For example, if A produces a defective vacuum cleaner, the Act will apply if it damages the carpet in

---

1 CPA 1987, s 2(1).
2 CPA 1987, s 5(1). 'Personal injury' includes any disease and any other impairment of a person's physical or mental condition: CPA 1987, s 45(1).
3 CPA 1987, s 5(2).
4 CPA 1987, s 5(3).

B's home but not if it damages the carpet in B's office or factory. It is important to note that it is the property which is damaged which must be 'consumer' as opposed to 'business' property. If A produces a defective lorry which is used in B's business, the Act *will* apply if the defective lorry damages C's family motor car, but the Act will not apply if the defective lorry damages C's van which he uses for his business. When the Act is excluded because the property damaged is not 'consumer' property, resort will have to be made to delictual liability at common law when negligence will have to be established;

(c) property damaged or lost as a result of a defective product, where the loss or damage does not exceed £275.[1] Where such loss or damage occurs, resort must again be made to delictual liability at common law when negligence will have to be established.[2] It should be noted that this exception only applies to damage to property. If, for example, A cuts his finger as a result of B's defective product, the Act still applies and B is strictly liable even if A's damages are less than £275.

(2) Definition of 'product'

Strict liability applies where damage is caused wholly or partly by a defect in a product. A 'product' is defined[3] as any goods or electricity. It includes – and this is important – components and raw materials which are parts of a complex product. So, if there is a complex product such as a motor car and a component of the car, for example a windscreen, is defective, that component, as well as the motor car, is regarded as a product for the purpose of the Consumer Protection Act 1987. Thus the problem which arose in *Evans v Triplex Safety Glass Co Ltd*[4] will not arise under the Act. 'Goods' also include 'substances, growing crops and things comprised in land by virtue of being attached to it and any ship, aircraft or vehicle'.[5] 'Substance' means any natural or artificial substance, whether in solid, liquid or gaseous form or in the form of vapour and includes substances which are comprised in or mixed with other goods, for example a cylinder of gas. Things comprised in

1 Consumer Protection Act 1987, s 5(4). This includes interest.
2 Such an action would be brought under the small claims procedure.
3 CPA 1987, s 1(2).
4 [1936] 1 All ER 283, discussed at pp 165 ff above.
5 CPA 1987, s 45(1).

land by virtue of being attached to it include, for example, the window frames of a house, a garden shed or a swing. 'Ship' includes any boat or vessel used for navigation; aircraft includes gliders, balloons and hovercraft; 'vehicle' is not defined. Game or agricultural produce now constitute products for the purpose of the Act.[1] Blood used for transfusions has been held to be a product for the purposes of the Act.[2]

(3) Parties liable

As mentioned above, prima facie strict liability is imposed on the producer of the product. A 'producer' is defined as the person who manufactured the product[3] or who won or abstracted the substance.[4] Where a product is not manufactured, won or abstracted but its essential characteristics are attributable to an industrial or other process, the producer is the person who carried out the process: for example, where the product is pasteurised milk, the producer is the person who carried out the pasteurisation process.[5] A person who merely packages goods is not a producer. Any person who puts his own name on a product, or uses a trade mark on a product, is liable under the Consumer Protection Act 1987 if by so doing he holds himself out to be the producer.[6] This provision brings 'own branders' within the strict liability regime. Similarly, any person who imports products from abroad with a view to distributing them within the EU is liable under the Act.[7] This clearly is to protect ultimate consumers in EU member states from having to sue a producer outwith the EU. The importer may, of course, have a remedy, for example in contract, against the non-EU producer. The producer of a component or of raw materials used in a complex product is prima facie jointly and severally liable with the producer of the complex product if it is defective.

Although strict liability falls on the producer, own brander or importer of a defective product, as a fall back position a supplier of the product may also be liable. Thus all parties in the distribution

---

1 The exclusion of game and agricultural produce was removed by the Consumer Protection Act 1987 (Product Liability) (Modification) (Scotland) Order 2001, SSI 2001/265 in response to the CJD crisis.
2 *A v National Blood Authority (No 1)* [2001] 3 All ER 289.
3 CPA 1987, s 1(2)(a).
4 CPA 1987, s 1(2)(b).
5 CPA 1987, s 1(2)(c).
6 CPA 1987, s 1(2)(b).
7 CPA 1987, s 1(2)(c).

chain from the producer to the own brander or importer are potentially liable under the Act:

Producer ———— Wholesaler ———— Retailer ———— Purchaser

In this example, the wholesaler and retailer are suppliers within the meaning of the Act. However, a supplier will be liable only if the person who suffered the damage asked the supplier within a reasonable time of the damage being sustained to identify the producer or a supplier further up the chain of distribution and the supplier failed to provide the information within a reasonable time, provided it was not reasonably practicable for the person suffering the damage to identify the producer. Thus, in order to escape potential strict liability under the Act, the supplier must keep records of his suppliers or producers.[1]

A supplier will not be strictly liable if the defective goods were not supplied in the course of business.[2] Thus, A will not be strictly liable if A sells his washing machine to his neighbour B in a private transaction or if A gives B the washing machine as a birthday present. Of course, A may be liable for breach of contract or in delict at common law if the washing machine is defective and injures B or damages B's property. Where we are dealing with a producer, own brander or importer, they will escape strict liability under the Act only if the goods were supplied otherwise than with a view to profit.[3] Thus if A makes lemon curd which is *donated* to the local church sale of work, A is not liable, although he is a producer, because the goods were not supplied with a view to A's profit. But if A *sells* the lemon curd to the sale of work, A will remain liable under the Act. In both cases, the church will not be liable under the Act, since the only potential liability is as a supplier and the lemon curd was not sold in the course of a business. The church could, of course, be liable at common law.[4]

1 CPA 1987, s 2(3).
2 CPA 1987, s 4(1)(c)(i). Where a product was supplied and used for a specific medical service which was financed entirely from public funds, the ECJ held that it was nevertheless supplied for an economic or business purpose and the producer remained strictly liable: *Veedfald v Arhus Amtskommune* [2003] 1 CMLR 41.
3 CPA 1987, s 4(1)(c)(ii).
4 If A supplies a 'free gift' when selling another product, A will be strictly liable under the Act if the gift is given away in the course of A's business.

(4) Meaning of 'defective product'

In order to attract strict liability the damage must be caused 'wholly or partly' by a *defect* in the product.[1] What then is a defective product? A product is defective 'if the safety of the product is not such as persons are entitled to expect'.[2] For these purposes, 'safety shall include safety in the context of risks of damage to property as well as in the context of risks of death or personal injury'.[3] It will be noted that the test is what the *consumer* is entitled to expect in terms of the safety of the product: if it falls below the *consumer's* expectations then the product is defective. This is in marked contrast to the concept of negligence at common law which is tested by the standards of the hypothetical reasonable person in the position of the manufacturer.[4] In *Abouzaid v Mothercare (UK) Ltd*,[5] for example, as he was seeking to assist with fastening an elasticated strap to a pushchair, the plaintiff lost the sight in one of his eyes when the strap recoiled. The Court of Appeal held that the test of defectiveness hinged upon the expectations of the public at large as to the safety of the product and the fact that the manufacturer had not appreciated that there was any risk of injury arising from the strap was irrelevant. In *A v National Blood Authority (No 1)*,[6] the producer knew that some of his blood products might be infected but at the time there were no practical precautions that could be taken. The court held that the blood product was defective because the public did not know of the risk and were entitled to expect that blood transfused to them would be free from infection. On the other hand, when the public know there is a risk that a product might fail in its purpose, then the product will not be defective if the risk transpires.[7] Where the risk is obvious, for example that coffee served in a polystyrene cup will be hot to hold, the product is not defective.[8]

---

1 Consumer Protection Act 1987, s 2(1). The onus rests on the pursuer to prove that the product was defective: *Foster v Biosil* (2001) 59 BMLR 178.
2 CPA 1987, s 3(1).
3 CPA 1987, s 3(1).
4 For discussion, see pp 123 ff above.
5 [2001] TLR 136.
6 [2001] 3 All ER 289.
7 *Richardson v LRC Products* [2000] PIQR 164 (condom failed but public knew that no form of contraception is 100 per cent effective and the manufacturer never claimed that the product was).
8 *B (a child) v McDonald's Restaurant Ltd* [2002] EWHC 490 (QB).

Moreover, although the Consumer Protection Act 1987 is concerned with products which are dangerous because badly manufactured or incompetently designed, it also applies to products which are superbly designed and excellently manufactured but which are inherently dangerous if not used carefully, for example drugs.[1] Such products will be defective if there are inadequate warnings, instructions as to use, etc.

In determining what the consumer is entitled to expect, the court must consider all the circumstances of the case.[2] These include:

(a) the purposes for which the product was marketed, its 'get up', any mark in relation to the product and any instructions or warnings.[3] Instructions or warnings are of particular importance where the product is inherently dangerous. Obviously, if no warning is given, the product will be defective. But if there is an adequate warning, for example in respect of drug dosage, will that satisfy the consumer's expectation of safety or must the container of the drug be, for example, child proof?;

(b) what might reasonably be expected to be done with or in relation to the product.[4] Theoretically, this should be what the *consumer* might *reasonably* expect to be done with the product rather than what the producer expects it to be used for. Ultimately, however, it will be the court's view of reasonable expectation which will prevail. The test is clearly objective. So, for example, it is unlikely that a freezer which cannot be opened from within would be held to be defective even though a child climbed into the freezer and could not get out: freezers cannot reasonably be expected to be hiding places for toddlers!;

(c) the time when the product was supplied by its producer to another.[5] The relevant time for assessing the standard of safety of a product is the time at which it was supplied by the producer: the fact that products which are put on the market after that date have more safety features does not per se mean that the earlier product was defective at the time it was supplied.

---

1 *X v Schering Health Care Ltd* [2002] EWHC 1420 (third-generation combined oral contraceptives did not increase the level of risk of thrombosis and not defective).

2 CPA 1987, s 3(2).

3 CPA 1987, s 3(2)(a). *Worsley v Tambrands Ltd* [2000] PIQR 95 (the manufacturer's warnings of the risk of toxic shock syndrome from the use of tampons were sufficient and the product was not defective).

4 CPA 1987, s 3(2)(b).

5 CPA 1987, s 3(2)(c).

Before there is strict liability under the Act, the pursuer has to show that the damage was '*caused* wholly or partly by a defect in a product'.[1] Therefore, as in the case of delictual liability at common law, the claim may fail unless there is a sufficient causative link between the damage and the defective product.[2] However, provided there are no causation problems, the pursuer who has suffered damage is entitled to compensation from the producer, own brander, importer or supplier without having to establish negligence. In other words, there is strict liability.

(5) Defences to claim of strict liability

The Consumer Protection Act 1987 provides the defender with the following defences to a claim based on *strict* liability:

(a) the defect in the product is attributable to the defender's compliance with statutory or EU obligations;[3]
(b) the defender did not at any time supply the product to another, for example the product was stolen;[4]
(c) the defect did not exist in the product at the relevant times.[5] In the case of a producer, own brander or importer this will be the time he first supplied the product to another; in the case of a supplier, when the product was last supplied by a producer, an own brander or an importer into the EU. So in the case of the producer etc, he will escape strict liability if the product was not defective when it entered circulation, but subsequently becomes defective.[6] There can, of course, still be delictual liability at common law. The supplier will escape strict liability if the product was not defective when it was last supplied by a producer etc even though the defect was subsequently caused by the supplier himself. For example, if a butcher keeps meat

---

1 Consumer Protection Act 1987, s 2(1) (emphasis added); *Foster v Biosil* (2001) 59 BMLR 178.
2 Although CPA 1987 applies when a defective product causes psychiatric illness, it will probably not apply to secondary victims since their illnesses are caused by their reactions to the injuries of primary victims rather than by the defective product which injured the primary victim concerned. On delictual liability for nervous shock, see pp 72 ff above.
3 CPA 1987, s 4(1)(a).
4 CPA 1987, s 4(1)(b). *Veedfald v Arhus Amtskommune* [2003] 1 CMLR 41 (kidney flushing fluid supplied when it was used to prepare a kidney for transplantation).
5 CPA 1987, s 4(1)(d).
6 *Richardson v LRC Products Ltd* [2000] PIQR 164 (condom became damaged by ozone after it left the factory!).

which was edible when he obtained it from the producer but sells it when it has gone off, the retailer will not be liable. This is, to say the least, an odd result but, of course, the retailer will be liable in contract to the purchaser and at common law in delict to the ultimate consumer, when negligence will readily be inferred;

(d) the state of scientific and technical knowledge at the relevant time[1] was not such that a producer of products of the same description as the product in question might be expected to have discovered the defect if it had existed in his products while they were under his control.[2] This is known as the 'state of the art' defence. It is controversial in that a producer can escape *strict* liability if the defect in his product would not have been known by manufacturers of a similar product, given the state of scientific and technical knowledge at the time. It is important to stress that the defence is not what the producer actually knew but what he would have known if he had consulted those who might be expected to know the state of research and all the available literature etc.[3] It has been held that the defence is not available if the producer knows that his product might have harmful consequences.[4]

This defence is, of course, similar to the common law principle that a defender cannot be liable in delict if, as a result of the scientific knowledge available to the hypothetical reasonable person at the time, injury to the pursuer was not a reasonable and probable consequence of the defender's conduct.[5] Moreover, the defence expressly refers to the awareness of producers of similar products. This is similar to the important role that the practice of persons in the same trade, business or profession of the defender plays in establishing a breach of a duty of care at common law.[6] Thus, the 'state of the art' defence re-introduces negligence into the regime of strict liability laid down in the Consumer Protection Act 1987.

---

1 See discussion immediately above.
2 Consumer Protection Act 1987, s 4(1)(e).
3 *Richardson v LRC Products* [2000] PIQR 164. In *Abouzaid v Mothercare (UK) Ltd* [2001] TLR 136 the Court of Appeal doubted whether accident reports constituted 'technical knowledge'.
4 *A v National Blood Authority* [2001] 3 All ER 289. This case provides a very full discussion of when a product is defective and the nature of the 'state of the art' defence: see in particular pp 334–342.
5 *Roe v Minister of Health* [1954] 2 QB 66, [1954] 2 All ER 131, CA, discussed at p 119 above.
6 See pp 129 ff above.

In many cases, the defence will not be available to the producer simply because, given the state of scientific and technical knowledge at the time, he[1] should have known the product was defective. Where the defence could be used is in the production of drugs whose side effects could not have been discovered given the state of scientific knowledge which existed at the time they were produced; it may take years before the side effects of certain drugs become apparent in patients. In these circumstances, the defence could be used by the defender. It is somewhat ironic that one of the reasons for the move towards a strict liability regime for defective products was to avoid the shortcomings of the law of negligence which became apparent in the thalidomide tragedy. The European Court of Justice has held that the scope of the Consumer Protection Act 1987, s 4(1)(e) is not in conflict with EU law;[2]

(e) if the defective product is a complex product, the producer of a component or of any raw materials contained in the complex product has a defence if the defect in the complex product is wholly attributable to the design of the complex product or to the fact that he complied with the instructions of the producer of the complex product;[3] otherwise, of course, both the producer of the complex product and the producer of the component or raw materials are jointly and severally liable;[4]

(f) contributory negligence.[5] Liability under the Consumer Protection Act 1987 cannot be excluded by an exemption clause.[6]

This discussion of product liability is important because it illustrates how the common law of delictual liability based on the defender's *culpa* was thought to be inadequate to protect the interests of consumers who might be injured or whose property might be damaged by defective products. Accordingly, a regime of strict liability was introduced by statute so that the ultimate consumer would no longer have to prove fault before obtaining compensation. However, as we have seen, the Consumer Protection Act 1987 is not comprehensive and it will still be necessary on occasion for a pursuer to resort to delictual liability at common law, when, of course, negligence will have to be established.

1 Or, technically, producers of similar products.
2 *Commission of the European Communities v United Kingdom* (C300/95) [1997] All ER (BC) 481, ECJ (Fifth Chamber).
3 Consumer Protection Act 1987, s 2(4)(f).
4 See p 169 above.
5 CPA 1987, s 6(4).
6 CPA 1987, s 7.

CHAPTER 9

Delictual liability for animals

A. DELICTUAL LIABILITY AT COMMON LAW

Where the defender owes the pursuer a duty of care, the defender can be liable where the pursuer's injuries or damage to property is caused by an animal. In *Henderson v John Stuart (Farms) Ltd*[1] an employee was killed by a bull when cleaning out its box. The employer was held to be negligent in failing to fit the box with baffles or escape gaps. In other words, the employer had broken the duty of care he owed to his employee by failing to provide a safe working environment.[2] Similarly, in *Hill v Lovett*[3] an employee of the defenders, who were veterinary surgeons, was bitten by one of their West Highland terriers when she went into the garden to clean the windows of the surgery. As a result, the unfortunate pursuer eventually had to have her leg amputated. The Lord Ordinary (Weir) held that the defenders had broken the duty of care they owed to the pursuer both as employers and occupiers of the garden,[4] in failing to take reasonable care to ensure that the pugnacious dogs were not in the garden when the pursuer was there.

An unusual case is *Cameron v Hamilton's Auction Marts Ltd.*[5] The defenders were driving cattle along the highway. A cow escaped, climbed the stairway of a property adjoining the road, turned on a tap and fell through the floor into the pursuer's shop, causing flooding and damage. Clearly the defender owed a *Donoghue v Stevenson* duty of care[6] to the pursuer as the owner of property adjacent to the highway. In these circumstances, the sheriff held

---

1 1963 SC 245, 1963 SLT 22, OH.
2 On employers' liability, see Chapter 12 below.
3 1992 SLT 994, OH.
4 On occupiers' liability, see pp 194 ff below.
5 1955 SLT (Sh Ct) 74, 71 Sh Ct Rep 285.
6 See *Donoghue v Stevenson* 1932 SC (HL) 31, 1932 SLT 317.

that the defenders would be liable for breach of their duty of care if the cow had escaped because of their negligence.[1]

These cases, then, are examples of breach of an existing duty of care as a result of the defender's carelessness: the fact that the injuries and damage were caused by an animal is largely irrelevant. They are simply examples of common law delictual liability for negligence.

However, at common law, certain animals were regarded as *ferae naturae*, ie as having vicious propensities. These included, for example, lions, tigers and elephants. If such an animal caused injury or damage to a person, the person in charge of the animal was strictly liable, ie there was no need to prove fault. Strict liability applied even though the animal had not shown any vicious propensities before.[2] On the other hand, certain animals were regarded as *domitae naturae*, ie as having no vicious propensities. These included, for example, dogs, cats and cattle, including bulls! If such an animal had *in fact* shown vicious propensities before the pursuer suffered injury or damage, then strict liability would attach to the defender. But as in *Henderson v John Stuart (Farms) Ltd*[3] and *Hill v Lovett*,[4] where the bull and the dog had not hitherto shown vicious tendencies so that strict liability could not be imposed, the defenders were nevertheless successfully sued in negligence for breach of their duty of care.[5]

B. LIABILITY UNDER THE ANIMALS (SCOTLAND) ACT 1987

(1) Introduction

The common law on *strict* liability for injuries or damage caused by animals was regarded as unsatisfactory. For injury or damage caused by an animal after 10 June 1987, the common law on *strict*

---

1 See also *Swan v Andrew Minto & Son* 1998 Rep LR 42; *Wormald v Walker* 2004 GWD 55 (farmer could owe a duty of care to a motorist to prevent a road accident caused by a cow escaping from a field through a hole in a hedge).
2 See the English case of *Behrens v Bertram Mills Circus Ltd* [1957] 2 QB 1, [1957] 1 All ER 583, where the defendants were held strictly liable for the injuries caused to a midget by an elephant which had hitherto appeared docile.
3 1963 SC 245, 1963 SLT 22.
4 1992 SLT 994, OH.
5 Special rules applied to dogs under the Dogs Acts 1906–28; damage done by straying cattle was governed by the Winter Herding Act 1686.

liability has been replaced by the provisions of the Animals (Scotland) Act 1987.[1] However, common law liability for injury or damage caused by an animal as a result of the defender's *negligence* has *not* been replaced by the provisions of the 1987 Act[2] and a pursuer is therefore able to sue on the general principles of *culpa* if his case does not fall within the strict liability regime imposed by the 1987 Act.

Where the Animals (Scotland) Act 1987 applies, the defender's liability is strict, ie the defender is liable without the pursuer having to prove that the defender was negligent. The person who is liable is the *keeper* of the *animal* 'at the time of the injury or damage complained of'.[3] The keeper of an animal for the purposes of the Act is defined as follows:[4]

(a) the owner of the animal: remains the owner, even if the animal has been abandoned or has escaped, until someone else becomes the owner;[5]

(b) the person with possession of the animal:[6] remains in possession, even if the animal has been abandoned or has escaped, until someone else obtains possession.[7] However, a person is not a keeper of an animal by virtue of possession if he is detaining the animal to prevent it from causing injury or damage on his land[8] or is 'temporarily detaining it for the purpose of protecting it or any other person or other animal or restoring it as soon as is reasonably practicable to its owner or a possessor of it';[9]

(c) a person with 'actual care and control of a child under the age of 16' who is the owner or has possession of the animal.[10] Thus, for example, a parent of a child under the age of 16 is regarded as the keeper of any animal owned by the child provided the parent has actual care and control of the child.

Where an animal is owned by A but in the possession of B, A and B can be jointly and severally liable under the Act.

1 Animals (Scotland) Act 1987, s 1(8). References in this section are to the Animals (Scotland) Act 1987 unless otherwise stated.
2 See the Animals (Scotland) Act 1987, s 1(8).
3 A(S)A 1987, s 1(1).
4 A(S)A 1987, s 5(1)(a).
5 A(S)A 1987, s 5(2)(b). The Crown does not become the owner if an animal is abandoned: A(S)A 1987, s 5(2)(c).
6 A(S)A 1987, s 5(1)(a).
7 A(S)A 1987, s 5(2)(b).
8 A(S)A 1987, s 3.
9 A(S)A 1987, s 5(2)(a).
10 A(S)A 1987, s 5(1)(b).

(2) Meaning of 'animal'

What animals fall within the Animals (Scotland) Act 1987? For strict liability to apply, the animal must be of 'a species whose members generally are by virtue of their physical attributes or habits likely (unless controlled or restrained) to injure severely or kill persons or animals, or damage property to a material extent'.[1] Read literally, this definition is potentially very wide indeed. Although bulls can clearly fall within the definition,[2] it could, for example, include a domestic cat, since a cat by virtue of its physical attributes or habits is likely to injure severely or kill animals like birds or mice! It will ultimately be for the court to decide whether or not a certain species falls within the statutory criteria.

For the purpose of s 1(1)(b) of the Animals (Scotland) Act 1987, certain animals are deemed by s 1(3) to be likely (unless controlled or restrained) to injure severely or kill persons or animals by biting or otherwise savaging, attacking or harrying. These are dogs and dangerous wild animals within the meaning of s 7(4) of the Dangerous Wild Animals Act 1976.[3] Therefore all types of dogs are regarded as animals for the purpose of the 1987 Act so that strict liability is imposed on their keepers even if the dog concerned has never shown any vicious tendencies in the past. Before strict liability arises, the dog must have caused the injuries or damage by 'biting or otherwise savaging, attacking or harrying'. Thus there was no strict liability when a woman was 'knocked down' by an overly affectionate labrador.[4]

Where an animal is a dangerous wild animal within the meaning of the 1976 Act, it is regarded as an animal for the purpose of strict liability under the 1987 Act. Dangerous wild animals include wild dogs, wolves, jackals, coyotes, foxes (but not the common red fox), cassowaries, Old World monkeys, crocodiles and alligators, emus, poisonous snakes, lions and tigers, cheetahs and panthers, Gila monsters and Mexican bearded lizards, gibbons, orangutans, gorillas and chimpanzees, ostriches and bears.[5] Again, strict liability

---

1 Animals (Scotland) Act 1987, s 1(1)(b).
2 *Foskett v McClymont* 1998 SC 96, 1998 SLT 892, OH. It is a question of fact whether the particular animal fulfils the statutory criteria.
3 A(S)A 1987, s 1(3)(a).
4 *Fairlie v Carruthers* 1996 SLT (Sh Ct) 56. The court, of course, cannot look into a dog's mind to determine *mens rea*! The test is objective after considering what actually happened. There was also no liability for negligence in this case since the defender had no grounds to believe that the dog would knock the pursuer over.
5 Dangerous Wild Animals Act 1976, s 7(4) and Sch 3.

only arises when the dangerous wild animal has caused the injuries or damage by 'biting or otherwise savaging, attacking or harrying'. In addition, cattle, horses, asses, mules, hinnies, sheep, pigs, goats and deer *in the course of foraging* are deemed to be likely (unless controlled or restrained) to damage to a material extent land or the produce of land for the purpose of s 1(1)(b) of the 1987 Act.[1]

As a result of these provisions a wide range of species are deemed to be animals for the purpose of the Animals (Scotland) Act 1987. But if an animal is not deemed by s 1(3) to fall within the definition in s 1(1)(b), it is, of course, possible to argue that it is nevertheless of a species which by virtue of the physical attributes or habits of its members is likely to injure severely or kill persons or other animals, or damage property to a material extent. In assessing whether this is so, the age and sex of the animal is relevant.[2] Thus, a non-foraging cow is unlikely to fall within the definition in s 1(1)(b), while a non-foraging bull could.[3] The 1987 Act expressly *excludes* from the definition of 'animal' viruses, bacteria, algae, fungi and protozoa.[4]

Where the animal falls within the definition in s 1(1)(b) or is deemed to do so by virtue of s 1(3)(a) or (b), its keeper is strictly liable, ie liable without establishing *culpa*, for any damage or injury suffered by the pursuer which is directly referable to the animal's dangerous attributes or habits.[5] In other words, the damage or injury sustained must arise from the particular attributes or habits of the species which bring the animal within the definition in s 1(1)(b). So, for example, the keeper of a red setter dog is strictly liable under the 1987 Act if the dog bites the pursuer since the injury is directly referable to a dog's attribute or habit to bite.[6] But if the pursuer's injury is sustained as a result of falling over the red setter dog, the keeper is not strictly liable under the 1987 Act although the keeper could be liable if he owed a duty of care to the pursuer and negligence could be established.

---

1 Animals (Scotland) Act 1987, s 1(3)(b). In *Foskett v McClymont* 1998 SC 96, 1998 SLT 892, OH, the bull was not automatically deemed to be an animal for the purpose of the Act since the damage did not occur in the course of foraging and personal injury as opposed to property damage was involved.
2 A(S)A 1987, s 1(2)(a).
3 *Foskett v McClymont* 1998 SC 96, 1998 SLT 892, OH (insufficient averments to allow the pursuer to lead evidence that the bull in question fell within s 1(1)(b)).
4 A(S)A 1987, s 7.
5 A(S)A 1987, s 1(1)(c).
6 So if a domestic cat was a dangerous animal, its keeper would only be liable if, for example, it killed the pursuer's pet bird. In other words, the injury must be referable to the attributes or habits of a domestic cat which bring the cat under the statutory definition.

Strict liability does not apply to injury or damage caused by the *mere* fact that the animal in question was present on a road or in any other place.[1] Thus, if a motorist was injured while trying to avoid running over a dog, the keeper is not strictly liable under the Animals (Scotland) Act 1987, but may, of course, be liable at common law if a breach of a duty of care towards the pursuer can be established. The 1987 Act does not apply if the injury caused by the animal consists of a disease which was transmitted by means which were unlikely to cause severe injury other than disease.[2] So, for example, if A is savaged by a rabid dog and contracts rabies, the keeper is strictly liable under the 1987 Act, because the disease was transmitted by means which were likely to cause severe injury, ie the dog's bites. But if the animal had merely licked the pursuer thereby transmitting the disease, the keeper is not strictly liable under the 1987 Act, since the means, ie the licking, was unlikely to cause severe injury other than the disease. In the latter situation, of course, the keeper could still be liable at common law provided there was a breach of a duty of care owed to the pursuer ie if negligence can be established.

(3) Defences to liability under the Animals (Scotland) Act 1987

Even where the Animals (Scotland) Act 1987 applies and the keeper is prima facie strictly liable, there are several possible defences:

(a) if the injury or damage was due wholly to the fault of the person sustaining it or, in the case of an injury sustained to another animal, the keeper of that animal.[3] This will cover the situation where, for example, the pursuer has goaded a docile animal which attacks the pursuer in defence;
(b) if the person sustaining the injury or damage, or a keeper of the animal sustaining the injury, willingly accepted the risk of it as his.[4] The classic example is a person who willingly puts his head in a lion's mouth. This defence is, of course, a statutory form of *volens non fit injuria;*[5]

---

1 Animals (Scotland) Act 1987, s 1(5).
2 A(S)A 1987, s 1(4).
3 A(S)A 1987, s 2(1)(a).
4 A(S)A 1987, s 2(1)(b).
5 For discussion of the *volens* doctrine, see pp 148 ff above.

(c) if the person who was injured or suffered damage was a trespasser ie was not authorised to be on the keeper's property.[1] The effect of this provision is only to remove strict liability from the keeper. As we shall see,[2] the keeper of the animal as occupier of property owes a duty of care to any person who enters onto the property, including a trespasser. Thus, although the keeper is not *strictly* liable under the 1987 Act to the trespasser who has been injured by an animal, the keeper may be liable as occupier of the property if negligence can be established. Strict liability in relation to a trespasser is not removed by s 2(1)(c) if the animal which caused the injury or damage was there for the purpose of protecting persons or property. But the keeper will get the benefit of s 2(1)(c) if it is shown that it was reasonable to keep such an animal there and that the use made of the animal was reasonable.[3] Consider the following example:

(i) If A, a trespasser, is injured by B's goose,[4] prima facie s 2(1)(c) of the Animals (Scotland) Act 1987 applies and B is not strictly liable. But if the goose was on the land to protect B's warehouse, then s 2(1)(c) is disapplied and B is strictly liable. But if B can show it is reasonable to have a goose as a 'guardbird', s 2(1)(c) is reapplied and B is not strictly liable. It is thought that B would succeed in this case since it is reasonable to have a goose as opposed to a tiger as a 'watch animal'.[5]

Where the animal concerned is a guard dog, the keeper remains strictly liable to a trespasser ie s 2(1)(c) of the 1987 Act is disapplied unless the keeper can show that he has complied with the provisions of s 1 of the Guard Dogs Act 1975.[6] Under this section, *either* the dog's handler must be present and have the dog under his control, *or* the dog must be secured so that it is not at liberty to go freely about the premises. In addition, notices of the dog's presence must be displayed at every entrance to the property.

---

1 Animals (Scotland) Act 1987, s 2(1)(c). In the case of injury to another animal, if the keeper of that animal was not entitled to have the animal on the land.
2 On occupiers' liability, see pp 194 ff below.
3 A(S)A 1987, s 2(2).
4 Assuming, of course, that a goose is an animal for the purpose of A(S)A 1987, s 1(2)(b).
5 A(S)A 1987, s 2(2). In Scotland, geese are traditionally used to guard bonded warehouses!
6 A(S)A 1987, s 2(2).

Consider the following example:
(ii) If A, a trespasser, is injured by B's guard dog, prima facie
    s 2(1)(c) of the Animals (Scotland) Act 1987 does not
    apply and B remains strictly liable. But if B can show that
    he complied with the provisions of s 1 of the Guard Dogs
    Act 1975, then s 2(1)(c) of the 1987 Act is reapplied and B
    is not strictly liable.

In both examples (i) and (ii), B would be liable to A if he was in
breach of the duty of care he owes to A as occupier of the property.
To be successful, A would have to prove that B did not take reasonable care to protect him from the danger arising from having the
animal on the land[1] ie that B was negligent.

Where the Animals (Scotland) Act 1987 applies, there is no
defence on the ground of *damnum fatale* or, for example, of intervention by a third party which caused the animal to escape. This is
because liability is strict. However, the pursuer's damages may be
reduced on the grounds of contributory negligence.[2]

In this chapter we have seen how the general principles of delictual liability for negligence apply where damage or injury has been
caused by an animal. Even at common law it was thought to be in
the interests of society that the owner of a dangerous animal should
be liable without proof of fault. These rules were, however, unclear
and, in so far as strict liability is concerned, they have been replaced
by the regime imposed by the 1987 Act. But where a case does not
fall within the statutory regime of strict liability, the keeper may still
be liable if he was in breach of a duty of care which he owed to the
pursuer, but in these circumstances the onus rests on the pursuer
to prove that the keeper was negligent.

---

1 On occupiers' liability, see pp 194 ff below.
2 The keeper's statutory liability is treated as fault for the purposes of the Law
  Reform (Contributory Negligence) Act 1945: Animals (Scotland) Act 1987,
  s 1(6). On contributory negligence, see pp 150 ff above.

CHAPTER 10

Delictual liability arising from ownership or occupation of property

A. DELICTUAL LIABILITY AT COMMON LAW

The owner or occupier of property may be liable under general principles of *culpa* if a person is injured or if property is damaged as a result of the state of the defender's property. In a case of unintentional acts or omissions, it will be necessary for the pursuer to show that the owner or occupier owed him a *Donoghue v Stevenson* duty of care[1] and that the defender was in breach of that duty.[2] In order to establish a breach of duty, it will, of course, be necessary to show that the defender was negligent. So, for example, if a slate falls off the defender's roof and injures a pedestrian who is using the highway or damages a motor car, the defender may be liable for breach of a duty of care owed to the pedestrian or the owner of the car[3] if the pursuer can establish negligence.[4]

Although it is clear that the owner of property does not act at his peril, ie is not strictly liable,[5] the court will readily infer negligence if the defender has built a structure on his land which if unsafe would cause serious damage. In *Kerr v Earl of Orkney*,[6] the defender built a dam on his land across a stream on which the pursuer had a mill about half a mile lower down. Four months later, after several days of heavy rain, the dam burst and the pursuer's house and his mill were swept away. The court held that the

---

1 See *Donoghue v Stevenson* 1932 SC (HL) 31, 1932 SLT 317, and Chapter 3 above.
2 See Chapter 5 above.
3 It is thought that as a general principle the owner or occupier of property adjoining the highway would owe a duty of care to a pedestrian or motorist.
4 *MacColl v Hoo* 1983 SLT (Sh Ct) 23.
5 *McLaughlan v Craig* 1948 SC 599, 1948 SLT 483.
6 (1857) 20 D 298, 30 SJ 158.

defender was liable unless he could show that the dam had collapsed as a result of a *damnum fatale,* for example an earthquake as
opposed to several days of heavy rain. The fact that the dam had
burst shortly after it had been built implied that the defender was
at fault. Liability arises either because the *opus manufactum* could
not be constructed so as to avoid harm to the neighbouring property, in which case there was fault in building the structure at all, or
the work was built negligently.[1] While achieving a similar result in
cases such as *Kerr,* Scots law does not accept the English doctrine
laid down in *Rylands v Fletcher* [2] that the owner of land is strictly
liable for damage caused by the escape of dangerous things brought
on to his property as a consequence of the defendant's non-natural
use of his land.[3] In *RHM Bakeries (Scotland) Ltd v Strathclyde
Regional Council,*[4] Lord Fraser of Tullybelton was adamant that
Rylands v Fletcher 'has no place in Scots law, and the suggestion
that it has, is a heresy which ought to be extirpated'.[5]

Although reasonable foreseeability of harm to the pursuer or
damage to his property is the usual criterion for the imposition of a
duty of care on the owner or occupier of property, in one situation
at least the duty of care has been used as a threshold device to
restrict the potential delictual liability of proprietors.[6] The question
is whether the owner or occupier of property owes a duty of care to
owners or occupiers of adjacent property to prevent damage to
their property as a result of the acts of third parties. For example,
does the owner of derelict property owe a duty of care to adjacent
proprietors to prevent vandals from entering the derelict property
and starting a fire which spreads and damages the adjacent properties? Or does the owner of a flat owe a duty of care to the owner of
the shop below the flat, to prevent a thief from entering the flat in
order to gain access and steal from the shop?

These difficult issues were explored by the House of Lords in
Maloco v Littlewoods Organisation Ltd.[7] It was accepted by the court

---

1 *GA Estates Ltd v Caviapen Trustees Ltd (No 1)* 1993 SLT 1037, OH, at 1041 per
the Lord Ordinary (Coulsfield).
2 (1868) LR 3 HL 330. The scope of *Rylands v Fletcher* liability was re-examined
by the House of Lords in *Cambridge Water Co v Eastern Counties Leather plc*
[1994] 2 AC 264, [1994] 1 All ER 53, HL.
3 In Scots law liability does not arise simply because a dangerous thing escapes but
from the construction of the *opus manufactum:* see *GA Estates Ltd v Caviapen
Trustees Ltd (No 1)* 1993 SLT 1037, OH.
4 1985 SC (HL) 17, 1985 SLT 214, HL.
5 1985 SLT 214 at 217.
6 On the duty of care as a threshold device, see Chapter 5 above.
7 1987 SC (HL) 37, 1987 SCLR 489, 1987 SLT 425; for facts, see discussion at p
122 above.

that the owner or occupier of property owed a duty to proprietors of adjacent property to take reasonable care of his property so that it did not cause them physical harm or damage to their property. But there was no general duty to take reasonable care of property to prevent a *third party* from using the premises to cause physical injury or damage to neighbouring proprietors. Using the duty of care as a threshold device, the House of Lords held that no such duty arose even if it was reasonably foreseeable that a third party could enter the defender's property and cause harm to the adjacent proprietor. Thus, while it is reasonably foreseeable that if a person leaves his flat unlocked a thief may enter the premises and gain access to an adjacent flat or shop, the owner of the flat does not owe a duty to take reasonable care to prevent this occurrence. In these circumstances, the owner of the adjacent flat or shop must seek redress against the thief, ie against the third party.

However, Lord Mackay was prepared to accept that a duty of care could be imposed on the owner or occupier of property if in the circumstances it was highly probable – as opposed to reasonably foreseeable – that a third party would cause harm to an adjacent proprietor.[1] Lord Goff took the view that this could arise if the owner 'negligently causes or permits a source of danger to be created on his land, and can reasonably foresee that third parties may trespass on his land and, if interfering with the source of danger, may spark it off, thereby causing damage to the person or property'.[2] For example, a duty of care would arise if A kept explosives in his house, told persons that the explosives were there, but took no precautions to prevent trespassers from having access to the premises. Similarly, a duty of care would arise if the owner had allowed his property to become a fire hazard, knew persons had been trespassing on the premises and had already started fires, but did not take reasonable precautions to prevent access.[3] As we have seen,[4] no duty arose in the *Littlewoods* case since the defenders did not know that the derelict cinema had, in fact, become a fire hazard: derelict buildings are not, per se, fire hazards.

Lord Goff doubted[5] whether the owner or occupier of property ever owes a duty of care to adjacent proprietors to prevent a thief from gaining access to their premises:

1 *Maloco v Littlewoods Organisation Ltd* 1987 SLT 425 at 429.
2 1987 SLT 425 at 439.
3 *Thomas Graham & Co Ltd v Church of Scotland General Trustees* 1982 SLT (Sh Ct) 26.
4 Page 122 above.
5 *Maloco v Littlewoods Organisation Ltd* 1987 SLT 425 at 441.

' ... I do not think that liability can be imposed on an occupier of property in negligence simply because it can be said that it is reasonably foreseeable, or even (having regard, for example, to some particular temptation to thieves in adjacent premises) that it is highly likely that, if he fails to keep his property lockfast, a thief may gain access to his property and thence to the adjacent premises. So to hold must presuppose that the occupier of property is under a general duty to prevent thieves from entering his property to gain access to neighbouring property, where there is a sufficient degree of foresight that this may occur. But there is no general duty to prevent third parties from causing damage to others, even though there is a high degree of foresight that they may do so. The practical effect is that everybody has to take such steps as he thinks fit to protect his own property, whether house or flat or shop, against thieves.'

Although obiter, this dictum is a remarkable example of the duty of care being used as a threshold device to deny delictual liability for reasons of policy.[1] As a result, the decision of the Inner House in *Squires v Perth and Kinross District Council* [2] must be regarded as unsound. There the pursuers who were jewellers successfully sued building contractors who were working on a flat above their shop for not adequately securing the flat against entry by a thief who gained access to their shop and stole jewellery. In the light of Lord Goff's dictum, the case should have been dismissed *in limine* because of the absence of a duty of care.[3]

The occupier of property owes the owner a duty of care to prevent damage to the premises. Since there is usually a contract between them, this duty is usually contractual. Nevertheless, it was held in *Fry's Metals Ltd v Durastic Ltd* [4] that the defenders were liable in *delict* for failing to maintain an alarm system after their lease with the pursuer had expired. Their duty of care arose because they had retained the keys and were the only persons who had access to the building to operate the alarm. Moreover, they were liable for the damage caused by vandals who had broken into the premises because, in the circumstances, it was highly probable that this would occur if the alarm system was not working.

---

1 For full discussion, see Chapter 5 above.
2 1986 SLT 30.
3 Even if there was a duty of care it is doubtful whether the defender should have been liable. In his evidence, the thief claimed that although he got the idea of gaining access to the shop via the flat when he saw the defender's scaffolding and the open windows, he in fact entered the flat from the back by going up a drain pipe and entering an open door. The chain of causation between the defender's carelessness and the theft is therefore very fragile – provided, of course, we believe the thief.
4 1991 SLT 689n, OH.

B. THE *ACTIO DE EFFUSIS VEL DEJECTIS* AND THE *ACTIO DE POSITIS VEL SUSPENSIS*

The owner or occupier of property may be liable in delict on general principles of *culpa* for physical injury or damage caused by the defective state of the property: to be successful the pursuer must establish fault on the part of the defender. In Roman law, however, in two situations actions were available in which an owner or occupier was strictly liable ie where there was no need to establish *culpa*. These were the *actio de effusis vel dejectis* where something was poured or thrown out of a building, causing harm to the victim, and the *actio de positis vel suspensis* where something placed on or suspended from a building fell, causing harm to the victim. Under these *actiones* the owner or occupier was strictly liable for personal injuries or damage to property. Given its civilian background, it has been argued that these *actiones* are part of Scots law.[1] In *McDyer v The Celtic Football and Athletic Club*,[2] however, the First Division held that liability for objects falling from buildings required *culpa* in Scots law.[3]

C. *AEMULATIO VICINI*

If the proprietor uses his land in such a way as to interfere with his neighbour's use or enjoyment of his property then the conduct may be actionable *in aemulationem vicini*. Before there is liability, it must be shown that the defender's use of his property was done with the intention of interfering with the neighbour's use or enjoyment of his land. A single incident is sufficient to establish liability. This delict has been fully discussed in the context of the intentional delicts.[4]

---

1 See, for example, D M Walker, *The Law of Delict in Scotland* (2nd edn, 1981, W Green) p 284.
2 2000 SLT 736.
3 Cf *Gray v Dunlop* 1954 SLT (Sh Ct) 75; *MacColl v Hoo* 1983 SLT (Sh Ct) 23. In both cases the argument for liability under the *actiones* was rejected on the ground of absence of fault. In *McDyer* the Lord President (Rodger) pointed out that in his opinion the *actiones* were only concerned with liability for physical harm to the persons who were *outside* the premises: in Scotland liability to persons who were on the premises is now governed by the Occupiers' Liability (Scotland) Act 1960. On the 1960 Act, see beyond.
4 See p 21 above.

D. NUISANCE

The owner of property[1] must not use his land in such a way as to disturb his neighbour's enjoyment of his property or cause damage to his neighbour's land.[2] If a person does so, he may be liable in nuisance. Nuisance is usually a continuing wrong ie there is more than one act. But delictual liability for nuisance arises even if the defender did not intend to cause inconvenience to the pursuer's enjoyment of his land or damage to the pursuer's property. The delict can be summarised in the brocard *sic utere tuo ut alienum non laedas,* namely use your own property in such a way that you do not do harm to others.

Common examples of nuisance are noise, smells, the emission of fumes and burst pipes. The existence of a building per se does not constitute a nuisance even if it interferes with another person's enjoyment of her land, for example by causing interference with her television signal.[3] The essence of the delict is that as a result of the defender's actions on his property, the pursuer has suffered more than he could reasonably be expected to tolerate: *plus quam tolerabile.* Whether this has been established is a matter of fact and degree in the particular circumstances of the case. For instance, the smell of dung may be acceptable in the countryside but not in the confines of a city tenement. Regularly to play CDs of Wagner at full blast may be acceptable in a large detached house but not in a two-bedroomed semi-detached. Even if the defender is a professional musician who has to practise 12 hours a day, if the noise disturbs his neighbour more than the neighbour can be expected to tolerate, it is a nuisance and the fact that it is a normal and familiar use of a musician's home is no defence. Nor can it be argued that the pursuer came to the nuisance. So if in our example the musician's previous neighbour enjoyed hearing him practise, this is no defence to an action of nuisance brought by the new proprietor of the neighbour's house, if the continual practising is driving the pursuer mad!

Noise caused by normal domestic use of a family home does not amount to nuisance provided it would not seriously disturb or substantially inconvenience an average reasonable person living in the

---

1 This can include the owner of a servitude right. Persistent use of a servitude right which involves a serious risk of damage to the servient tenement can constitute a nuisance: *Cloy v Adams & Sons* 1999 GWD 19-908.
2 *Watt v Jamieson* 1954 SC 56 at 58 per the Lord President (Cooper).
3 *Hunter v Canary Wharf Ltd* [1997] AC 655, [1997] 2 All ER 426, HL. The building must, of course, satisfy planning controls.

locality.[1] To constitute a nuisance, the defender's use must amount to offensive conduct, the effects of which are *intolerable:* it is not enough that they merely cause discomfort to the pursuer.[2]

Where the use of the defender's property is in the public interest, this is no defence if it would otherwise constitute a nuisance. In *Webster v Lord Advocate*[3] the pursuer had bought a flat in Edinburgh near the Castle. As the Edinburgh Festival approached, the enjoyment of her flat was disturbed by the noise of workmen erecting the grandstand for the military tattoo. The court held that this was a prima facie case of nuisance: it was irrelevant that the noise could be reduced if the pursuer closed her windows or installed double glazing. While accepting that the tattoo was a valuable and profitable part of the Festival, the court decided that this 'greater good' argument was not sufficient to prevent it from ordering that the nuisance should cease. Accordingly, the court granted declarator that a nuisance was established and that the defender should take steps to ensure that the grandstand was constructed by using less noisy techniques. It is a defence, however, to an action that the conduct constituting the nuisance was carried out with statutory authority.[4]

Because nuisance usually involves *continuing* acts or omissions, the primary remedy is interdict ie an order that the defender's act or omission should cease. In determining whether or not to grant interdict, the court is concerned with the position of the pursuer ie whether the pursuer should have to continue to suffer the nuisance. Whether or not the nuisance was caused by conduct which

---

1 *Davidson v Kerr* 1997 Hous LR 11, 1996 GWD 40-2296, Sh Ct. In *Murdoch v Glacier Metal Co Ltd* [1998] Env LR 732, [1998] EHLR 198, CA, the noise from the defendant's factory did not constitute a nuisance even though it exceeded the maximum level recommended by the World Health Organisation.

2 *Anderson v Dundee City Council* 1999 GWD 1-52.

3 1985 SC 173, 1985 SLT 361. Cf *Dennis v Ministry of Defence* [2003] EWHC 793 (noise of aircraft flying from a military base was a nuisance but the plaintiff's private property rights should be subjugated to the public interest. *Sed quaere?* However, as the nuisance was an interference with the plaintiff's right to respect for his home under article 8(1), he was awarded the equivalent of common law damages under the Human Rights Act 1998. This decision must be doubtful given that the environmental pollution of the noise of night flights from Heathrow has been held not to involve an interference with the article 8(1) rights of property owners around the airport: *Hatton v UK* [2003] All ER (D) 122, approved by the House of Lords in *Marcic v Thames Water* [2004] 1 All ER 135).

4 A planning authority has no jurisdiction to authorise a nuisance unless it has a statutory power to permit a change in the character of the neighbourhood and the nuisance was an inevitable consequence of the change: *Wheeler v J J Saunders Ltd* [1995] 2 All ER 697, [1995] 3 WLR 466, CA.

amounted to *culpa* on the part of the defender is largely irrelevant. Thus, in the context of granting interdict, the defender's liability for nuisance is strict ie there is no need to aver or prove fault.

However, where the nuisance has caused damage to the pursuer's property, no claim for damages will be successful unless the pursuer avers and proves that the nuisance arose as a result of the defender's *culpa*. This was settled by the House of Lords in *RHM Bakeries (Scotland) Ltd v Strathclyde Regional Council.*[1] The pursuer's premises were flooded as a result of the collapse of a sewer, the maintenance of which was the responsibility of the defender. Food and packing materials stored in the bakery were damaged. Even if the failure to maintain the sewer adequately amounted to nuisance, the House of Lords held that the pursuer's action in damages failed because they had not averred, let alone proved, that the collapse of the sewer was due to the negligence of the defender. Thus, before the pursuer can obtain damages for harm caused by nuisance, *culpa* on the part of the defender must be established.

But what constitutes *culpa* in this context? This issue was explored in *Kennedy v Glenbelle Ltd.*[2] The pursuer sought damages for harm sustained to his property as a result of the removal of a wall within the defender's premises. The Lord President (Hope) held[3] that *culpa* would arise if:

(1) the defender deliberately intended to damage the pursuer's property (malice); or
(2) the defender knew that her act or omission would damage the pursuer's property; or
(3) the defender was reckless, ie she had no regard to the question whether or not her conduct might be likely to damage the pursuer's property; or
(4) the defender's conduct had such potentially hazardous consequences for the pursuer's property that knowledge that her conduct would damage the pursuer's property is presumed; or
(5) the defender's acts or omissions were carried out carelessly, ie negligence.

In cases (1) to (4), *culpa* arises because the defender knows (or is deemed to know) that the conduct which constitutes the nuisance will damage the pursuer's property, ie it is intentionally caused harm. It is quite irrelevant that the defender's actions were carried

1   1985 SC (HL) 17, 1985 SLT 214.
2   1996 SC 95.
3   1996 SC 95 at 100 ff.

out carefully. The fault lies in the fact that the defender knows (or is deemed to know) that her conduct will harm the pursuer's property. Given that the defender's conduct must satisfy the *plus quam tolerabile* test before it will constitute a nuisance, it is thought that in case (5) damages will lie if the pursuer can show that the defender's conduct fell below the standard of reasonable care: it is not necessary that the defender owed the pursuer a pre-existing duty of care.

Because of the difficulty of proving *culpa*, in *RHM Bakeries* Lord Fraser expressed the view that the court would readily infer *culpa* from the fact that the sewer had collapsed causing serious damage.[1] Although this may be the case where the defender has built a dangerous *opus manufactum* on his property, it is doubtful that negligence will be inferred from the mere fact that the pursuer has sustained harm. In *Argyll and Clyde Health Board v Strathclyde Regional Council*[2] the Lord Ordinary (McCluskey) held that in an action for damages it was not sufficient for the pursuers simply to aver that a pipe running below their field had burst causing damage. Instead, the pursuers had to have specific averments showing why the defenders were at fault: for example that they were negligent in failing to inspect the pipe and carry out regular maintenance. The fact that the pipe had burst causing damage to the pursuers did not have the effect that the onus automatically shifted to the defenders to show that they were not negligent in maintaining the pipe.[3]

Therefore it is now clear that if a nuisance is established an interdict can be granted without proof of fault, whereas damages are awarded only on proof of *culpa*. The question arises whether

1 *RHM Bakeries (Scotland) Ltd v Strathclyde Regional Council* 1985 SC (HL) 17 at 45.
2 1988 SCLR 120, 1988 SLT 381, OH.
3 In the *RHM Bakeries* case the House of Lords did not overrule its earlier decision in *Caledonian Rly Co v Greenock Corpn* 1917 SC (HL) 56, 1917 2 SLT 67. In that case, Greenock Corporation had altered the channel of a burn to make a paddling pool. After heavy rainfall, the pursuer's property was flooded. The House of Lords awarded the pursuer damages without the need to prove fault ie the defender was held to be strictly liable. This decision was distinguished in *RHM Bakeries* on the ground that it was concerned with the alteration of the natural direction of a stream, not with damage caused by 'unnatural' use of property. It is submitted that the distinction is tenuous and that, at the very least, the decision in the *Caledonian Rly* case rests uneasily with the ratio in *RHM Bakeries* where it was held that when a nuisance has damaged property, compensation is available only if *culpa* on the part of the defender can be established. The exception in relation to altering the natural flow of a stream was accepted by the Lord Ordinary (Coulsfield) in *GA Estates Ltd v Caviapen Trustees Ltd (No 1)* 1993 SLT 1037 at 1041.

this distinction is sensible. Where, for example, the nuisance is fumes emanating from the defender's factory, the effect of an interdict may mean that the defender has to close the factory while extensive – and expensive – repairs are carried out; yet, in theory at least, the defender may not have been negligent. But given that nuisance is often a continuing wrong the defender still remains obliged to ensure that the nuisance stops ie the defender could be interdicted if it were to continue. It is therefore submitted that where the nuisance has caused damage the defender should not have to meet the *additional* obligation of compensating the pursuer unless *culpa* is established: *culpa* is, after all, the basic tenet of the obligation to make reparation in Scots law.

Finally, the function of the law of nuisance is to protect the pursuer's interest in his land. Therefore only a person with a recognised interest in heritable property has title to sue.[1] Moreover, damages are awarded only to compensate the pursuer for any diminution in the value of her *property* caused by a nuisance. In *Glove (Aberdeen) v North of Scotland Water*[2] an Extra Division held that the owner of a pub could seek damages in nuisance for loss of profits which arose because patrons were deterred from coming to the bar as a consequence of the defender's repairs to a sewer which had taken nine months rather than six weeks! Although the pursuer sought reparation for pure economic loss, it is thought that the loss of profits was a legitimate way of assessing the diminution of the value of the property during that period. Where *personal injuries* are involved, the pursuer, even if she is the owner of the land, must sue either for intentional wrongdoing or in negligence, where the defender will not be liable unless he has breached a pre-existing duty of care which he owed to the pursuer.[3]

E. OCCUPIERS' LIABILITY

We have been considering cases where, as a result of acts or omissions on his property, the owner/occupier of property causes harm

---

1 *Harvie v Robertson* (1903) 5 F 338, 10 SLT 581; *Hunter v Canary Wharf Ltd* [1997] AC 655, [1997] 2 All ER 426, HL. See also *Dundee (City of) District Council v Cook* 1995 SCLR 559.
2 2000 SLT 674.
3 For an authoritative statement of the law of nuisance, see 14 *Stair Memorial Encyclopaedia* paras 2001–2168.

to persons who are not on his property, for example adjacent proprietors, neighbouring proprietors, pedestrians or motorists on the highway who pass the defender's property. In this section, we shall consider the delictual liability of the occupier of property towards persons who *enter* upon the property.

Scots common law was strongly influenced by English law. As a result of the decision of the House of Lords in *Dumbreck v Robert Addie & Sons*,[1] the duty of care towards a person entering on to property depended on the status of the person who was injured, ie whether he was a licensee, for example a lodger or member of the occupier's family; an invitee, for example a guest; or a trespasser. In the case of a trespasser, liability was restricted to intentional, as opposed to negligently caused, harm. However, as a matter of law, these classifications were swept away by the Occupiers' Liability (Scotland) Act 1960.[2]

The general thrust of the Act is that occupiers of property owe a duty to take such care in respect of persons entering their land or premises as is reasonable in all the circumstances of the case. The statutory obligation rests on the person 'occupying or having control of land or other premises' who is referred to in the Act as the 'occupier of premises'.[3] Where the owner of the property is also the occupier of the premises, the statutory obligation lies with him. If the owner is not the occupier, he will not be liable under the 1960 Act but may incur liability under the general duty of care incumbent on owners of property provided *culpa* is established.[4] A person occupies the land or other premises if he is in possession of the property, for example he is a tenant. But he will also be treated as the occupier if he has control of the land or other premises. A person has 'control' if he is entitled to take the steps in relation to the land or property which the statute requires in order to fulfil the duty of taking reasonable care of the premises. So, for example, the owner of derelict property who is not *in fact* in possession is nevertheless the occupier because he has control of the premises. The determination whether a defender has sufficient possession or

---

1 1929 SC (HL) 51, 1929 SLT 242. See T B Smith 'Full Circle: The Law of Occupiers' Liability in Scotland' in *Studies Critical and Comparative* (1962, W Green) p 154.

2 In this section, references are to the Occupiers' Liability (Scotland) Act 1960 unless otherwise stated.

3 OL(S)A 1960, s 1(1). The common law rules for determining whether or not a person is an occupier for these purposes is expressly reserved in the Act: s 1(2).

4 See pp 185 ff above.

control to be an occupier is one of fact and degree in the light of the circumstances of the particular case.[1]

While 'land' is self-explanatory, 'premises' are not defined in the 1960 Act. They would include houses, flats, sheds, garages, shops etc; land would include gardens. Moreover, the statutory obligation to take such care as is reasonable in all the circumstances expressly applies to occupiers of 'any fixed or moveable structure, including any vessel, vehicle or aircraft'.[2] Thus, the 1960 Act applies to a wide range of property: for example ships, barges, oil rigs, buses, caravans, cars, tractors, helicopters, planes and hovercraft. It is *not* therefore restricted to heritable property.

Section 2(1) of the Occupiers' Liability (Scotland) Act 1960 lays down the nature and extent of the statutory duty:

'The care which an occupier of premises is required, by reason of his occupation or control of the premises, to show towards a person entering thereon in respect of dangers which are due to the state of the premises or to anything done or omitted to be done on them and for which the occupier is in law responsible shall ... be such care as in all the circumstances of the case is reasonable to see that that person will not suffer injury or damage by reason of any such danger.'

It will be noted that the 1960 Act imposes a positive duty on the occupier to take such care as is reasonable in all the circumstances to ensure that a person entering the premises will not suffer injury or damage by reason of any danger on the premises. Nevertheless, the onus lies on the pursuer to show that the occupier did not take the care that was reasonable in the circumstances: it is not enough simply to aver that there was a danger and that the pursuer suffered injury or damage as a result.[3] In *McGuffie v Forth Valley Health Board*,[4] for example, the pursuer slipped on snow on the defender's premises which had not been removed by the defender. The pursuer's action failed because she had not specified the period in which it would have been reasonable for the defender to have removed the snow or instructed its employees to do so. On the other hand, in *Porter v Strathclyde Regional Council*,[5] the pursuer

---

1 *Feely v Co-operative Wholesale Society* 1990 SCLR 356, 1990 SLT 547, OH. On the difficulties of determining who is the relevant occupier when the property is in multi-occupation, see *Gallacher v Kleinwort Benson (Trustee) Ltd* 2003 SCLR 384.

2 Occupiers' Liability (Scotland) Act 1960, s 1(3)(a).

3 *Wallace v City of Glasgow District Council* 1985 SLT 23. However, the pursuer may be able to rely on the *res ipsa loquitur* principle: *McDyer v Celtic Football and Athletic Co Ltd* 2000 SLT 736.

4 1991 SLT 231.

5 1991 SLT 446.

slipped on food which had been spilled on the floor of a nursery under the control of the defender. She was able to establish that the defender did not have a system of working whereby an employee would mop up the mess soon after it was spilled. The failure to have such a system was held to be a breach of the occupier's statutory duty to take reasonable care to prevent the pursuer from slipping on the floor as it was probable that the accident would not have occurred if such a system had been in operation.[1]

The Occupiers' Liability (Scotland) Act 1960 applies where the injury or damage arose from dangers 'which are due to the state of the premises *or* to anything done or omitted to be done on them'.[2] Dangers 'due to the state of the premises' clearly covers dangers such as dry rot arising from dilapidated buildings. It would also include uneven roads,[3] slippery floors and unsafe furniture or plenishings. In *Taylor v Glasgow Corpn*,[4] where a child died as a result of eating poisonous berries which were growing in the Glasgow Botanic Gardens, the poisonous berries constituted a danger due to the state of the premises. But the statutory duty also applies to dangers which are due to anything done or omitted to be done on the premises. Thus the 1960 Act would apply to dangers caused by the occupier's failure to provide adequate lighting or to secure a fence, as well as by his positively creating a hazard. As we have seen, the failure to ensure that a pursuer would not enter a garden to clean windows while pugnacious West Highland terriers were also there has been held to be a breach of the 1960 Act.[5] But it is submitted that in the usual case there will be no breach of the 1960 Act where the pursuer sustains physical harm as a consequence of the criminal acts of a third party carried out on the defender's property.[6]

It is important to appreciate that the occupier's statutory obligation is only to take such care as is reasonable in all the circumstances to prevent injury or damage from such dangers: it is not to eliminate the risk that an accident might happen.

---

1 However, the pursuer's damages were reduced by 50 per cent as a result of her contributory negligence.
2 Occupiers' Liability (Scotland) Act 1960, s 2(1) (italics added).
3 *Beggs v Motherwell Bridge Fabricators Ltd* 1998 SLT 1215, 1997 SCLR 1019, OH.
4 1922 SC (HL) 1, 1921 2 SLT 254. This was, of course, a case before the 1960 Act.
5 *Hill v Lovett* 1992 SLT 994, OH, discussed in the context of liability for animals, p 177 above.
6 This is for the same policy reasons discussed pp 186 ff above. See *Modbury Triangle v Anzil* (2000) 205 CLR 254 (no breach of duty where plaintiff assaulted by a third party in an unlit car park owned by the defendant).

Accordingly, in determining whether or not the occupier has taken reasonable care, the calculus of risk is relevant. The court will consider such factors as the nature of the danger, the occupier's knowledge of the danger,[1] the extent of the injury or harm, the probability of the injury or harm arising, the age of the person injured, whether or not the pursuer was permitted on to the premises and the cost of eliminating the danger. Thus, in *McGlone v British Railways Board*,[2] the defender was held to have taken reasonable care in respect of the danger of a 12-year-old child being burnt by a transformer. The defender had put up warnings and surrounded the transformer with a barbed wire fence which had proved not to be impenetrable. Nevertheless, the House of Lords held that to provide an impenetrable and unclimbable fence went beyond what was reasonable in the circumstances, given that a 12-year-old child should have realised the danger he would incur if he climbed through the barbed wire. In the circumstances, the defender had discharged its duty of reasonable care by erecting an obstacle which a 12-year-old would take some trouble to overcome before he would be in danger. If the fence could have been penetrated by a 3-year-old, then there might well have been a breach of the duty to take reasonable care in respect of a child of that age. The fact that the pursuer was a trespasser was also held to be a relevant factor in assessing whether or not reasonable care had been taken.[3]

A similar approach can be discerned in *Titchener v British Railways Board*.[4] A young man was killed by a train and his 15-year-old girlfriend was seriously injured. The couple had taken a short cut over the line to have a 'kiss and a cuddle' in a derelict brickworks. The defender had provided a fence made of sleepers but

---

1 It would appear that the defender must know of the danger: *Keane v Walker Contracts (Scotland) Ltd* 1999 GWD 9-410. *Sed quaere*? It is surely enough that the defender ought reasonably to have known of the danger. In *Duff v East Dunbartonshire Council* 2002 Rep LR 98, the First Division held that the owner of land will be presumed to know any physical features which might constitute a danger and should be fenced (drop of six feet from embankment to rocks by river bed: need for fence or at least warning notices).

2 1966 SC (HL) 1, 1966 SLT 2.

3 In *Platt v Liverpool City Council* CCRTF 97/0072/C, CA the court described as 'absurd' the contention that the defendant had not taken reasonable care to prevent children from entering dangerous premises, when it had put an eight-foot-high corrugated metal fence around the property.

4 1984 SC (HL) 34, 1984 SLT 192. See also *Devlin v Strathclyde Regional Council* 1993 SLT 699, OH (no breach of duty in respect of injuries to a 14-year-old child deliberately jumping on a skylight cover on a roof: the child was also a trespasser).

there were gaps in the fence through which it was possible for persons to reach the railway line. It was argued that the Board had been in breach of its duty of reasonable care in failing to maintain the fence and thus ensure that there were no gaps providing access to the railway. The House of Lords held that the statutory duty was owed to the particular pursuer, ie a 15-year-old girl who knew the danger involved in crossing a railway line. Accordingly, in determining whether or not the defender had taken reasonable care, the pursuer's age and knowledge were relevant factors. In these circumstances, the fence – even with gaps – gave adequate warning to a girl of 15 who knew the danger of crossing the line. Indeed, Lord Fraser thought[1] that the defender would have taken reasonable care in respect of the pursuer if there had been no fence at all! It would therefore appear that the more obvious and greater the danger, the *less* by way of warning is required for the average person; conversely, *more* is required if the pursuer is, for example, a young child.

It has been held that any duty on occupiers to fence off dangers does not apply to dangers inherent in the ordinary and familiar features of the landscape whether natural or man made, for example a loch or reservoir.[2] This was recognised a century ago:

'in a town, as well as in the country, there are physical features which may be productive of injury to careless persons or to young children against which it is impossible to guard by protective measures. The situation of a town on the banks of a river is a familiar feature; and whether the stream be sluggish like the Clyde at Glasgow, or swift and variable like the Ness at Inverness, or the Tay at Perth, there is always danger to the individual who may be so unfortunate as to fall into the stream. But in none of these places has it been found necessary to fence the river to prevent children or careless persons from falling into the water'.[3]

In *Tomlinson v Congleton BC*[4] the House of Lords reaffirmed the principle 'that it is contrary to common sense, and therefore not sound law, to expect [the occupier] to provide protection against an obvious danger on his land arising from a natural feature such as a lake or a cliff and to impose a duty on him to do so'.[5] Moreover, it was thought that it would be extremely rare for an occupier to be under a duty to prevent people taking risks inherent in the activities

1 1984 SLT 192 at 195.
2 *Graham v East of Scotland Water Authority* 2002 SCLR 340.
3 *Stevenson v Corpn of Glasgow* 1908 SC 1034 per Lord McLaren at 1039.
4 [2004] 1 AC 46 (boy broke his neck when diving in a lake where swimming was prohibited).
5 [2004] 1 AC 46 per Lord Hutton at 89.

they chose to undertake on the occupier's land, for example swimming or mountaineering.[1] It was not the policy of the law 'to require the protection of the foolhardy or reckless few to deprive, or interfere with, the enjoyment by the remainder of society of the liberties and amenities to which they are rightly entitled'.[2] In other words, an individual should be allowed to engage in dangerous but otherwise harmless pastimes at her own risk, enabling the rest of society fully to enjoy the pleasures of the countryside and saving the occupier considerable expense.

The defence of *volenti non fit injuria* can be used by the defender.[3] Thus, if there had been a breach of duty in *Titchener,* the House of Lords indicated that *volenti* would have been a defence.[4] Damages may be reduced on the ground of contributory negligence. The parties are free to vary the statutory duty by *agreement.*[5] This enables the occupier to undertake a more onerous or less onerous obligation. Where the premises are used for business, any exemption clause excluding or limiting the occupier's liability for death or personal injuries is void and any clause restricting liability for other kinds of damage is unenforceable unless it satisfies the requirement of reasonableness.[6]

By s 3 of the Occupiers' Liability (Scotland) Act 1960, a landlord who is responsible for the maintenance or repair of premises which have been let owes a similar obligation to persons who enter the premises in respect of dangers arising from the landlord's failure to maintain or repair the property. The statutory obligation extends to anyone lawfully on the premises, such as the tenant's child.[7] The landlord is not obliged to *improve* the premises.[8]

---

1 [2004] 1 AC 46 per Lord Hoffmann at 84.
2 [2004] 1 AC 46 per Lord Hobhouse at 96.
3 Occupiers' Liability (Scotland) Act 1960, s 2(1).
4 *Volenti* would also have been a defence in *Devlin v Strathclyde Regional Council* 1993 SLT 699, OH.
5 OL(S)A 1960, s 2(1). A non-contractual notice is therefore ineffective.
6 Unfair Contract Terms Act 1977, s 16.
7 *Guy v Strathkelvin District Council* 1997 SCLR 405, OH.
8 *Scott v Glasgow City Council* 1997 Hous LR 107, Sh Ct.

CHAPTER 11

Breach of statutory duty and public law issues

A. BREACH OF STATUTORY DUTY

The common law principles of delictual liability may be supplemented or supplanted by delictual liability for breach of a statutory duty. Provided the pursuer can establish that he was harmed or suffered damage to his property as a result of the defender's breach of statutory duty, the pursuer will obtain reparation: it is not necessary for the pursuer to establish delictual liability at common law. The statutory duty may be similar to the common law standard of reasonable care as, for example, in the case of the Occupiers' Liability (Scotland) Act 1960.[1] More often, however, the statute may impose a standard which is higher than that expected of the reasonable person at common law, ie the statute imposes strict liability on the defender. We have seen examples of this in Part I of the Consumer Protection Act 1987[2] and in the Animals (Scotland) Act 1987.[3] These statutes expressly stipulate that breach of the statutory duty gives rise to a civil remedy in delict for reparation. Conversely, some statutes expressly stipulate that a breach of statutory duty does not give rise to a civil remedy for reparation even if a person sustains harm as a result.[4]

But there are many statutes which are silent on whether or not a person is entitled to seek reparation in a civil action if he or she suffers personal injury or damage as a result of a breach of statutory duty. Yet it has long been recognised that even where a statute is silent on the matter, a person who has suffered loss may still be able to seek reparation in a delictual action for breach of statutory duty. Thus, for example, where an employee was injured at work and the

1 Discussed in Chapter 10 above.
2 Discussed in Chapter 8 above.
3 Discussed in Chapter 9 above.
4 For example the Health and Safety at Work etc Act 1974, s 47.

injury arose as a result of a breach of the employer's statutory duty to maintain machinery, the court held that the employer was liable to compensate the employee for breach of statutory duty even though the statute provided criminal sanctions for breach.[1]

What criteria are used by the courts to determine whether or not a breach of statutory duty gives rise to a civil action in delict where the statute is silent on the matter? The answer appears to be that it is a question of construction of the particular statute to discover whether Parliament intended to confer on the pursuer the right to obtain reparation for breach of statutory duty. This gives the courts considerable discretion albeit within the confines of the language of the statute. And, like the use of the duty of care as a threshold device,[2] the decision whether or not to allow the pursuer an action for breach of statutory duty will ultimately turn on policy considerations ie whether or not such an action makes social or economic sense. That said, there are certain presumptions which are used by the courts when construing a statute in order to determine whether a civil remedy lies for breach of statutory duty and these will now be briefly considered.

As a general principle, where a statute provides a specific mode of enforcement of the statutory duties, the presumption is that Parliament did not intend that a civil action for damages in delict was necessary as an *additional* sanction if the statutory obligation is breached. Conversely, if the statute does not provide a specific mode of enforcement of the statutory duties, then there is a presumption that Parliament did intend that a civil action for damages would lie. So, for example, in *Dawson v Bingley Urban District Council*,[3] the defendant's breach of statutory duty in failing to provide a notice indicating the position of a fire plug, with the result that there was a delay in putting out a fire at the plaintiff's premises, was held to be actionable by the plaintiff in a civil action. The statute did not provide a penalty or other remedy for breach of the statutory obligations.

Where the pursuer already has a private law remedy against the defender if the statute was broken, for example for breach of contract, it is presumed that Parliament did not intend that the pursuer should have the additional remedy of suing in delict for breach of statutory duty. Although the position is not clear, it is submitted that the existence of a right to seek judicial review should not be

---

1 *Groves v Lord Wimborne* [1898] 2 QB 402, CA.
2 For further discussion, see Chapter 4 above.
3 [1941] 2 KB 149, CA.

presumed to exclude the possibility of a civil remedy for breach of statutory duty: judicial review is simply a procedure and damages are available only if the pursuer has a private law remedy. Accordingly, the right to seek judicial review, while a factor to be taken into consideration by the courts, should not be conclusive in deciding whether or not Parliament intended that the pursuer should also have the private law remedy of suing in delict for breach of statutory duty.[1]

Where a statute provides a penalty for breach of statutory duty, the general presumption is that Parliament did not intend that there should be the additional sanction of delictual liability for breach of statutory duty. There are two exceptions to this rule.[2]

First, if it is apparent that the statutory obligations were passed for the protection of a particular class of individuals, then a delictual action for breach of statutory duty may lie if the pursuer belongs to that class and has suffered injury or loss. This explains how employees were able to sue for breach, for example, of the Factories Acts, even though this legislation imposed criminal penalties on employers who were in breach.[3] Similarly, performers whose work was recorded by record companies without their permission, in breach of the Dramatic and Musical Performers' Protection Act 1958, were held to have been intended by Parliament to be able to pursue private law remedies for breach of statutory duty in spite of the fact that the statute also provided criminal sanctions.[4] But it must be clear that the pursuer falls within the class. So, for example, in *RCA Corpn v Pollard*[5] it was held that companies who had exclusive recording contracts with performers could not sue for breach of statutory duty under the 1958 Act.

If the statute is not designed to protect a particular class and provides penalties for breach, no action for breach of statutory duty will lie. But it may be difficult to determine whether or not the legislation was designed to protect a particular class. In *Cutler v*

---

1 *Hague v Deputy Governor of Parkhurst Prison* [1992] 1 AC 58, [1991] 3 All ER 733, HL, at 752 per Lord Jauncey.
2 *Lonrho Ltd v Shell Petroleum Co Ltd (No 2)* [1981] 2 All ER 456 at 461 per Lord Diplock.
3 See also *Littlejohn v Wood & Davidson Ltd* 1997 SLT 1353, OH (Merchant Shipping Act 1988, s 31(1) intended to protect a particular class of persons ie persons on board ships: civil claims for damages allowed in spite of existence of criminal sanctions).
4 *Ex parte Island Records Ltd* [1978] Ch 122, [1978] 3 All ER 824, CA.
5 [1983] Ch 135, [1982] 3 All ER 771, CA.

Wandsworth Stadium Ltd (in liquidation),[1] for example, the appellant brought proceedings against a licensed dog track to compel it to allow him space at the track to carry on his profession as a bookmaker. Statute provided that the occupier of a licensed track 'shall take such steps as are necessary to secure that ... there is available for the bookmakers space on the track where they can conveniently carry on bookmaking in connection with dog races run on the track'. The House of Lords held that the purpose of the legislation was to protect those members of the public who wished to place bets by ensuring that there was a choice of bookmakers at the track: it was not to give bookmakers the right of a place at the track. Accordingly, the appellant was not entitled to a remedy for breach of statutory duty. But it could equally be argued that it was Parliament's intention to protect the rights of bookmakers to earn their living. The decision in *Cutler* was ultimately a matter of policy. It is interesting to note that the courts are more prepared to construe statutes as giving a delictual remedy for breach of statutory duty where the pursuer has been physically injured[2] than, as in *Cutler*, where the pursuer has suffered only pure economic loss as a result of the breach of the statutory obligations.

Nevertheless, in the leading Scottish case of *Pullar v Window Clean Ltd*,[3] the Inner House of the Court of Session refused to accept that planning legislation which inter alia provided that window sashes should be so constructed to enable the window to be cleaned from the inside, was intended to protect window cleaners. There was therefore no breach of statutory duty when a window cleaner fell from the outside sill because the sashes had not been constructed in accordance with the legislation: 'The solution in each case must depend upon what the intention of Parliament was in enacting the obligation in question, and what persons consequently have a right to enforce it or to found upon it as a basis for a claim in damages'.[4]

Even when the legislation is designed to protect a particular class, there may be other factors which deny an action for breach of statutory duty, albeit that the statute does *not* provide criminal sanctions for its breach. In *X (minors) v Bedfordshire County Council*,[5] children sued a local authority (i) for personal injuries

---

1 [1949] AC 398, [1949] 1 All ER 544, HL.
2 As in the case of the Factories Acts.
3 1956 SC 13, 1956 SLT 17.
4 1956 SC 13 at 20 per the Lord President (Clyde).
5 [1995] 2 AC 633, [1995] 3 All ER 353, HL.

sustained by being removed from their parents in care proceedings, and (ii) for personal injuries sustained by not being removed from their parents in care proceedings. Although the children were clearly within the class of persons the care legislation was designed to protect, the House of Lords held that Parliament did not intend that the children should have a private law right to sue for breach of the statute. This was because the legislation involved an administrative system designed to promote the social welfare of the community and the local authority's duties were expressed in broad language. Moreover, Parliament could not possibly have intended that a local authority should be liable *without proof of fault* merely because a court subsequently decided that children should not have been taken into care and vice versa.[1] In short, given the discretion inevitably involved in child care legislation, bona fide mistakes would arise and such mistakes were not to be compensated in the absence of fault.[2]

In *Lonrho Ltd v Shell Petroleum Co Ltd (No 2)*[3] Lord Diplock maintained that there was a second exception where a private law remedy could arise for breach of statutory duty even though the statute provided criminal penalties for its breach:

'The second exception is where the statute creates a public right (ie a right to be enjoyed by all those of Her Majesty's subjects who wish to avail themselves of it) and a particular member of the public suffers ... "particular, direct and substantial" damage other and different from that which was common to all the rest of the public.'[4]

The extent of this exception has not been developed and need not be discussed further.

Once it has been decided as a matter of construction that Parliament intended that a delictual action should lie for breach of statutory duty, a person who has suffered harm must show that the statute was intended to protect a person in his position ie that the pursuer falls within the class to be protected and that the damage sustained is of the kind that the statute was designed to prevent. In

---

1 On potential liability at common law for negligence see beyond pp 207 ff. In *Thames Trains Ltd v Health and Safety Executive* [2003] EWCA Civ 720, the Court of Appeal held that the HSE did not owe a statutory duty giving rise to a private action by passengers who had sustained personal injuries in a train crash caused by faulty signals: but its failure to exercise its powers carefully could give rise to a claim in negligence of *strict* liability for breach of statutory duty.

2 See also, for example, *O'Rourke v Camden London Borough Council* [1998] AC 188, [1997] 3 All ER 23, HL.

3 [1982] AC 173, [1981] 2 All ER 456, HL.

4 [1981] 2 All ER 456 at 461.

Gorris v Scott,[1] for example, statutory regulations required that sheep or cattle being shipped from a foreign country to the United Kingdom had to be put in pens. The defendant failed to provide the pens and as a result the plaintiff's sheep were washed overboard in a storm. The plaintiff's action for breach of statutory duty failed because the court held that the purpose of the pens was to prevent animals from being infected by contagious diseases, not to prevent them from being swept overboard. If the sheep had died as a result of a contagious disease, a delictual claim for breach of statutory duty would have been successful.

The defender must, of course, have broken the statutory duty which was incumbent upon him. Whether or not the defender's conduct constitutes a breach will depend on the interpretation of the particular provision. Statutes may impose absolute liability, strict liability, or reasonable practicability. If a breach of the statutory duty is established ie the defender has broken the duty,[2] there is no need for the pursuer to prove fault. But the pursuer must establish that the breach of statutory duty caused the harm.[3] Unless, as in the case of the Occupiers' Liability (Scotland) Act 1960,[4] the defence is expressly stated to be available, *volenti non fit injuria* cannot be pleaded.[5] This is because a person cannot agree to take a risk of harm which Parliament has legislated to prevent arising. However, the pursuer's damages may be substantially reduced as a result of contributory negligence.

B. PUBLIC LAW ISSUES[6]

Ministers of the Crown, local authorities and other governmental agencies are often given statutory powers to implement policy. This will often involve the exercise of discretion. Consider the following examples:

---

1 (1874) LR 9 Exch 125.
2 For examples see discussion of Part I of the Consumer Protection Act 1987, the Animals (Scotland) Act 1987 and the Occupiers' Liability (Scotland) Act 1960, above.
3 On causation generally, see Chapter 6 above.
4 Occupiers' Liability (Scotland) Act 1960, s 2(3).
5 See, for example, *Wheeler v New Merton Board Mills Ltd* [1933] 2 KB 669, CA.
6 I am grateful to W Green for allowing me to quote extensively in this section from my article 'Delictual Liability of State Agencies – Further Confusion' 1999 SLT (News) 245.

(1) A minister is given the power to send some criminals to an open prison: if such a criminal should escape, steal and damage a person's motor car, is the minister liable in delict?[1]

(2) A local authority is given the power to inspect and approve the plans of buildings: if the local authority approves the plans for the foundations of a house, is the local authority liable to the owner of the house if the foundations were unsuitable and have to be repaired?

(3) A minister is empowered to give information to the public on the risks of HIV infection: is the minister liable to a person who contracts HIV through injecting heroin if the information only disclosed the risk of infection from sexual contact and omitted the danger of infection from drug abuse?

In *X (minors) v Bedfordshire County Council*,[2] the House of Lords recognised that if a state agency exercised its statutory powers carelessly, there could be liability at common law in negligence. But before there can be liability in negligence, the careless exercise of the statutory powers must amount to a breach of a pre-existing duty of care owed by the agency to the pursuer. Traditionally, the courts have been reluctant to impose on a state agency a duty of care to exercise its powers carefully unless three hurdles were overcome.

(1) If the agency's statutory discretion involves broad issues of policy, the issue is non-justiciable. The paradigm is when an authority has to allocate scarce resources. If, for example, a local authority chose to spend resources on library provision rather than on increasing the number of fire engines, a person who suffered burns in a fire which could not be contained because of the absence of the fire brigade would be unable to sue because the issue of whether more resources should have been spent on fire engines as opposed to books is non-justiciable. In *Kent v Griffiths*[3] Lord Woolf MR recognised that the allocation of resources in respect of the provision of sufficient ambulances and enough staff to man them were matters which were probably not justiciable.

(2) Where the statutory discretion operates at an operational as opposed to a broad policy level, a duty of care cannot be imposed unless the purported exercise of the power is beyond

---

1 Of course, the criminal will be liable in delict.
2 [1995] 2 AC 633, [1995] 3 All ER 353, HL.
3 [2001] QB 36 at 53.

the ambit of the statutory discretion. In determining this issue, the courts have adopted – while occasionally denying they are doing so – quasi-administrative law principles. In particular, this hurdle is said only to be overcome if the exercise of the discretion was such that no reasonable state agency would have acted in this way. In other words, where the mistake, albeit careless, was one which a reasonable state agency or local authority could have made in the bona fide exercise of its powers, a duty of care will not be imposed, and accordingly liability at common law for negligence cannot lie. So, for example, if a fire authority prioritised calls, provided the prioritisation was not unreasonable, the decision would fall within the ambit of the statutory discretion and no liability would arise even if, with hindsight, the prioritisation was mistaken. However, in the light of developments discussed in (3) below, it is doubtful whether this hurdle will be as difficult to satisfy in the future.[1]

(3) Even if the 'public law' hurdle in (2) is satisfied, the *Caparo* criteria for a duty of care have to exist, namely reasonable foreseeability of harm to the pursuer, proximity between the pursuer and defender, and that it is fair, just and reasonable to impose the duty.[2] Until recently, the courts tended to decline to impose the duty of care either because of the absence of proximity or on the broader 'fair, just and reasonable' criteria. Thus, for example, in *Hill v Chief Constable of West Yorkshire*,[3] the House of Lords held that the chief constable did not owe a duty of care to the mother of the last victim of the Yorkshire Ripper. Not only was there no proximity but Lord Templeman also considered that it would not be fair, just and reasonable to impose a duty of care on the chief constable in relation to his function of investigating crime. Similarly, in *X (minors) v Bedfordshire County Council*[4] it was not thought fair, just and reasonable to impose a duty of care on a local authority or its social workers when exercising their discretion whether or not to take potentially

---

1   In *Larmer v Solihull MBC* [2001] RTR 32 the Court of Appeal held that while the statutory duty on local authorities under the Road Traffic Act 1988, s 39 to take action to prevent road accidents gave them a considerable degree of discretion, this did not mean that a common law duty of care did not exist. If the discretion was exercised unreasonably, the authority could be liable in negligence. However, this decision has been disapproved by the House of Lords in *Gorringe v Calderdale MBC* [2004] UKHL 15, discussed at p 213 below.

2   See *Caparo Industries plc v Dickman* [1990] 2 AC 605, [1990] 1 All ER 568, HL.

3   [1989] AC 53, [1988] 2 All ER 238, HL.

4   [1995] 2 AC 633, [1995] 3 All ER 353, HL.

abused children into care. In doing so, the courts were in effect granting to state agencies blanket immunity from liability in negligence when exercising their discretionary powers.[1]

However, the courts can no longer grant blanket immunity as a matter of course. First, in *Osman v United Kingdom*[2] the European Court of Human Rights held that to strike out a claim on the ground that the police enjoyed blanket immunity was a breach of the claimant's right under article 6 of the European Convention on Human Rights which provides that 'In the determination of his civil rights and obligations ... everyone is entitled to a fair and public hearing'. After a period of consternation on the scope of *Osman*,[3] the European Court of Human Rights then took the view that there was no breach of article 6 merely because an action was dismissed due to the absence of a duty of care, provided that the claimant had had the opportunity to argue that in the circumstances of her case it was fair, just and reasonable to impose a duty and that it would be disproportionate to the harm sustained not to do so.[4] Second, the European Court of Human Rights considered[5] that where a local authority failed to take steps to protect a child who was the subject of abuse, there could be a breach of the *child's* right under article 3 of the Convention which provides that 'No one shall be subjected to torture or to inhuman or degrading treatment or punishment'. Similarly, failure to have and follow fair procedures when taking a child into care was held by the Court to constitute a breach of the *parent's* right under article 8 of the Convention 'to respect for his private and family life'.[6] In these

---

1 See also *Forbes v City of Dundee District Council* 1997 SLT 1330, 1997 SCLR 682, OH (not fair, just and reasonable to impose a duty of care on a local authority to ensure that steps were built in accordance with building regulations: the pursuer could, of course, sue the owner/occupier of the building); *Onifade v Secretary of State for Social Security* 1999 GWD 17-819 (no duty of care to prevent pursuer from suffering economic loss as a consequence of an erroneous decision by an adjudication officer refusing the pursuer income support).
2 [1999] 1 FLR 193.
3 See, for example, *Barrett v Enfield Borough Council* [2001] 2AC 550 per Lord Browne-Wilkinson at 559–560; *Kent v Griffiths* [2001] QB 36 per Lord Woolf MR at 50.
4 *Z v United Kingdom* [2001] 2 FLR 612.
5 *Z v United Kingdom* [2001] 2 FLR 612 ('appeal' from *X (minors) v Bedfordshire County Council* [1995] 2 AC 633); *E v United Kingdom* [2003] 1 FLR 348 (action against Scottish local authority for failure to protect children from sex abuse by their stepfather).
6 *TP and KM v United Kingdom* [2001] 2 FLR 549.

cases the claimants obtained substantial damages for breach of their Convention rights in circumstances where damages were not available in delict because of the judges' refusal to impose a duty of care.

As a result of these developments, the courts are now more ready to impose a duty of care on a local authority. In *JP v East Berkshire Community NHS Trust*,[1] the Court of Appeal held that a local authority did owe a duty of care to a *child* in relation to the investigation of suspected abuse and the initiation and pursuit of care proceedings.[2] But the court was not prepared to hold that a local authority owed a duty to the *parents* of a child in such proceedings, while accepting that in certain circumstances a failure to follow fair procedures could result in an infringement of the parent's right under article 8: in the court's view the welfare of the child in care proceedings was the paramount consideration. Earlier, in *Barrett v Enfield London Borough Council*,[3] the House of Lords had distinguished *X (minors) v Bedfordshire Council Council* and held that once a child had been taken into care, a local authority could owe the child a common law duty to prevent him suffering mental harm caused by the authority's failure to provide suitable support: it was irrelevant that the local authority's decisions involved the exercise of discretion on the part of professional social workers.

Of course, the pursuer may still have difficulty in satisfying the *Caparo* tripartite criteria. In cases where a pursuer alleges that the police or local authority were under a duty to prevent her suffering harm as a result of a third party's criminal activities, it may be impossible to establish a sufficient degree of proximity. There is unlikely to be sufficient proximity unless the pursuer knew that she was in danger from a particular person and had made her fears known to the relevant authority:[4] geographical proximity is not enough.[5] Moreover, the courts have become more ready to accept

---

1 [2003] EWCA Civ 1151.
2 To that extent, the Court held that *X (minors) v Bedfordshire County Council* should not be followed, as being inconsistent with the European Convention on Human Rights.
3 [2001] 2 AC 550. See also *S v Gloucester County Council* [2000] 3 All ER 346 (local authority owed a duty of care to a child not to be sexually abused by a foster parent).
4 As happened in *Osman v UK* [1999] 1 FLR 193.
5 *Hill v Chief Constable of West Yorkshire* [1989] AC 53; *Palmer v Tees Health Authority* (2000) 2 LGLR 69 (mental hospital not liable to victim of a discharged patient); *Surrey County Council v M (A child))* [2001] EWCA Civ 691 (local authority not liable for sexual assault on a child by a boy whose family lived in the same neighbourhood as the victim).

that an employee of a state agency may owe a direct duty of care to the claimant for which the local authority is vicariously liable if the employee is negligent. In *Phelps v Hillingdon London Borough Council*,[1] the House of Lords held that while, in the performance of their duties under the Education Acts, education authorities owed no relevant duty of care to school children, nevertheless individual employees of the authorities might be in such a relationship with a particular child as to owe a common law duty of care, breach of which would render the local authority vicariously liable: consequently, the local authority could be vicariously liable for an educational psychologist's failure to assess and provide appropriate assistance for a pupil with special needs.[2]

Once a duty of care is established, the pursuer must prove that there was a breach of duty. As we have seen,[3] it can be very difficult to establish professional negligence. But since the courts can no longer provide blanket immunity, a local authority's major defence is that the authority and its employees were not negligent. In *Bradford-Smart v West Sussex County Council*,[4] for example, a girl was bullied on a bus going to and from school. The Court of Appeal held that the school would not be in breach of duty if it failed to take steps which were unlikely to do much good. A reasonable body of opinion would have taken the view that the school had done enough to protect her from bullying and accordingly her claim failed as she could not prove that the school had been negligent.

The pursuer must also prove that the defender's negligence was the cause of the harm he sustained. He must show that he was worse off as a result of the carelessly delivered service than if the service had not been provided at all. In *Gibson v Orr*,[5] a bridge carrying a public road collapsed. The police assumed control of the hazard. They coned off the north side and positioned a police vehicle on the bridge as a warning to drivers on the south side. After an hour, they left without having received confirmation that any barrier or warning was in place on the south side. The pursuer was injured when the car in which he was a passenger was driven onto the bridge from the south side and fell into the river. In a fully reasoned speech, the Lord Ordinary (Hamilton) held that the police

1 [2001] 2 AC 619.
2 See also *A v Essex County Council* [2003] 1 FLR 615 (local authority vicariously liable for social workers' failure to inform potential adoptive parents that the child to be adopted was seriously disturbed).
3 On professional liability, see Chapter 7 above.
4 [2002] EWCA Civ 7.
5 1999 SC 420. Cf *Alexandrou v Oxford* [1993] 4 All ER 328 (no duty of care to owner of property which police had inspected in response to a burglar alarm).

212 Breach of statutory duty and public law issues

authority owed the pursuer a duty of care. By purporting to take control of the hazard, the police constables entered into proximate relationships with those road users likely to be immediately and directly affected by that hazard. Moreover, unlike the case of the investigation of crime, there were no policy reasons why it would not be fair, just and reasonable to impose the duty. The difficulty is that the accident would have happened in exactly the same way, even if the service had not been provided at all. However, the whole point of the defender's duty was to prevent an accident occurring after the officers had taken control. If the duty of care had been performed, the accident in which the pursuer was injured would not have happened.

This is quite different from the situation where, owing to its operational carelessness, a fire brigade increases the risk of damage to the pursuer's life or property ie when the pursuer's position is worse off as a consequence of the careless delivery of the service. In *Duff v Highland and Islands Fire Board*,[1] it was held that a fire brigade owed a duty of care not to be careless when engaged in fire fighting. The defender had attended to a fire in the pursuer's chimney which restarted after the brigade had left, causing the destruction of the pursuer's house![2]

We have been considering potential liability in negligence for the careless exercise of statutory powers. A similar approach has been taken when a local authority or state agency has failed to use a statutory power which it was not obliged to exercise under the legislation. In *Stovin v Wise and Norfolk County Council*,[3] a local authority had a statutory power to direct a landowner to remove a wall which was a danger to users of the highway. Before the plaintiff was injured in a road accident, the local authority had known

---

1 1995 SLT 1362.
2 In *Capital and Counties plc v Hampshire County Council* [1997] QB 1004, [1997] 2 All ER 865, CA, the Court of Appeal held that a fire brigade did not owe a duty of care to a member of the public to answer calls for help because there was no proximity at that stage. Once the brigade had turned up and begun fighting the fire, a duty of care arose not to increase the risk of injury or damage caused by the original fire as a result of carelessness in carrying out the operations. In *Duff v Highland and Islands Fire Board* 1995 SLT 1362, it was not thought to be necessary that the damage sustained should be worse as a result of the defender's negligence: *sed quaere?* In *OLL v Secretary of State for the Home Dept* [1997] 3 All ER 897, following *Capital and Counties plc*, Moy J held that the coastguard service was under no enforceable private law duty to respond to an emergency call: if it did, it was only liable in negligence for positive acts which directly caused greater injury than would have occurred if it had not intervened at all.
3 [1996] AC 923, [1996] 3 All ER 801, HL.

the wall was a hazard but had not exercised the power to have the danger removed. The House of Lords held that the local authority had a public law duty to consider whether or not to exercise the power, but this did not automatically confer a common law right on an individual to obtain damages if injured as a consequence of the authority's decision not to exercise its powers. A common law duty of care would only arise from such an omission if (i) the local authority's failure to exercise the power was irrational (the 'public law' hurdle), and (ii) the legislation did not exclude the right of a person to seek damages if harm was sustained because the power was not exercised. However, in *Gorringe v Calderdale MBC*[1] Lord Hoffman held that it was 'difficult to imagine a case in which a common law duty can be founded simply upon the failure (however irrational) to provide some benefit which a public authority has power (or a public duty) to provide'[2]. Here the local authority had not provided a warning on a stretch of road of the danger of driving too fast. This omission could not in itself generate a common law duty of care when the authority's failure to exercise its powers under s 39 of the Road Traffic Act 1988 to promote road safety did not give rise to a private law remedy for breach of statutory duty. Accordingly the possibility raised in *Stovin v Wise* of deriving a common law duty of care merely from a failure to exercise a statutory power would appear to be closed.[3]

It is important to appreciate that in this section we have been concerned with the possibility of delictual liability arising from the exercise of a discretionary power by a minister of the Crown, a local authority or another governmental agency. Where there is no degree of discretion involved, then the 'public law' hurdle withers away. In *Kent v Griffiths*,[4] the plaintiff suffered brain damage because an ambulance which she had summoned failed to arrive

---

1 [2004] UKHL 15.
2 [2004] UKHL 15 at para 32.
3 In *McKnight v Clydesdale Buses Ltd* 1999 SLT 1167, the Lord Ordinary (Lady Cosgrove) allowed a proof before answer when the pursuer alleged that an accident occurred as a result of a local roads authority's failure to provide warning signs in respect of a low bridge. The authority had a duty to remedy a situation of foreseeable danger and it was not certain in the absence of evidence that this was simply a case of mere omission to exercise a statutory power: *Stovin* was distinguished. In *Bennett v J Lamont & Sons* 2000 SLT 17 the court refused to impose a duty on a roads authority to take reasonable care to prevent cattle roaming on the highway: there might, of course, be a duty on the owner of the cattle to do so. Cf *Kemp v Secretary of State for Scotland* 2000 SLT 471.
4 [2001] QB 36.

within a reasonable time of her call. No explanation was given for the delay: indeed, the crew had falsified the time records. The Court of Appeal held that since there was an ambulance available and there had been no alternative demands on the crew, they owed the plaintiff a duty of care to arrive within a reasonable time of her call which they had accepted. This was not a case which involved policy or resource issues but consisted of a routine task which had been carried out carelessly, to the plaintiff's cost. Similarly, the driver of a ministerial motor car or a local authority bus, for example, owes the same *Donoghue v Stevenson* duty of care[1] to a fellow road user as an ordinary driver and will be liable in delict if the duty of care is breached. In other words, the defender owes the pursuer a duty of care independent of her status as an employee of a state agency. In these circumstances, the state agency will be vicariously liable for the delict of its employee provided, of course, the employee was acting within the scope of her employment at the time the accident occurred.[2]

1   See *Donoghue v Stevenson* 1932 SC (HL) 31, 1932 SLT 317.
2   On vicarious liability, see Chapter 12 below.

CHAPTER 12

Employers' liability and vicarious liability

A. EMPLOYERS' LIABILITY

It is an implied term of the contract of employment that an employer will take reasonable care for the safety of his employees. If an employer does not take reasonable care, he will be in material breach of contract. In these circumstances, an employee may withdraw his labour and sue for damages. An employer may be in breach of his contractual obligations even if the employee has not suffered any harm. In addition to his contractual obligations, an employer owes a *Donoghue v Stevenson* duty of care[1] to his employees to prevent them from suffering physical or psychiatric harm as a result of the employer's negligent conduct. Accordingly, an employee who is injured may sue his employer in delict as well as for breach of contract; but the employee cannot be compensated twice for the same loss.

The obligation to take reasonable care for the safety of his employees is personal to the employer ie it cannot be delegated by the employer to senior employees or a third party.[2] However, in a modern industrial context, in order to *fulfil* the obligation of reasonable care, an employer may have to appoint a safety officer and/or safety committee. The scope of the duty incumbent on an employer includes taking reasonable care to supply the employee with proper plant and equipment to select competent fellow workers and to provide a safe system of working; but it is a *general* duty to take reasonable care. Thus, for example, an employer can be liable for failure to *devise* a safe system of working: *McGregor v AAH*

---

1 See *Donoghue v Stevenson* 1932 SC (HL) 31, 1932 SLT 317, and Chapter 3 above. The existence of a contract between the employer and employee is an important factor in establishing the 'foreseeability of harm' criterion.

2 *Hislop v Durham* (1842) 4 D 1168. In *MacIver v J & A Gardner Ltd* 2001 SLT 585, it was held that an employer owed a duty of care to a ship's master who was the safety officer in charge of the ship.

Pharmaceuticals Ltd.[1] Where an employer fails to instruct an employee to use protective devices or clothes, or fails to provide adequate training, a breach of the duty to take reasonable care can arise: *Pickford v ICI plc.*[2] An employer may also have to train employees to protect themselves from violent third parties they may meet in the course of their employment, for example school children![3]

Moreover, it cannot be overemphasised that at common law the employer is only expected to maintain the standards of the reasonable person in his position ie it is only to take reasonable care. An employer is not expected to ensure that an employee is never harmed. In assessing whether or not a particular employer has taken reasonable care, the calculus of risk will be relevant.[4] The court will therefore consider such factors as the nature of the danger, the employer's knowledge of the danger, the extent of the harm, the probability of the harm arising and the cost of eliminating the risk.[5]

In *Davie v New Merton Board Mills Ltd*,[6] for example, an employee was injured when a piece of a chisel he was using broke and a splinter entered into his eye. The defect in the chisel was latent and arose as a result of the metal used for the chisel not having been tempered properly by the manufacturer. The employer had bought the chisel from a reputable retailer who had in turn bought it from a reputable wholesaler who had purchased it from the manufacturer. In these circumstances, the House of Lords held that the employer had taken reasonable care and the employee's action against the *employer* failed. The employee could, of course, have sued the manufacturer in delict for breach of the manufacturer's *Donoghue v Stevenson* duty of care which he owed to the ultimate consumer of the product.[7] However, the view was taken that this was placing too heavy an onus on an employee. Accordingly, under the Employers' Liability (Defective Equipment) Act 1969,[8] if an employee suffers physical harm as a

---

1 1996 SLT 1161, OH.
2 [1996] ICR 566, [1996] IRLR 622, CA.
3 *McLeod v Aberdeen City Council* 1999 GWD 23-1115.
4 *Brisco v Secretary of State for Scotland* 1997 SC 14; *McErlean v J & B Scotland Ltd* 1997 SLT 1326, 1997 GWD 6-253, OH. On the calculus of risk generally, see pp 123 ff above.
5 *Latimer v AEC Ltd* [1953] AC 643, [1953] 2 All ER 449, HL; *Hatton v Sutherland* [2002] 2 All ER 1; *Barber v Somerset County Council* [2004] UKHL 13.
6 [1959] AC 604.
7 See *Donoghue v Stevenson* 1932 SC (HL) 31, 1932 SLT 317. On product liability generally, see Chapter 8 above.
8 Employers' Liability (Defective Equipment) Act 1969, s 1(1).

result of a defect in equipment[1] provided by the employer and the defect is attributable wholly or partly to the fault of a third party,[2] for example the manufacturer, then the defect is deemed to be also attributable to negligence on the part of the employer. In other words, the employee can sue the employer without the need to prove that the employer was negligent. The *employer* will then seek redress against the third party either in contract or, theoretically at least, in delict.

The employer has to take reasonable care in selecting competent workers who will not cause harm to the other employees. If the employer fails to do so and an employee is injured as a result, the employee can sue the employee for breach of the duty of care.[3] Again it must be emphasised that the employer is only expected to take reasonable care. Before the employer can be negligent, he must know that the employee he has appointed could be a danger to fellow workers.[4] The contract of employment is not a contract *uberrimae fidei*; the employer must therefore make reasonable enquiries to determine whether or not an aspirant employee would be a source of danger to fellow employees if he were to be engaged. For example, the employer should ask whether or not an applicant for a job as a van driver has a clean driving licence and whether or not he has been convicted of careless or reckless driving.[5]

---

1 The courts have taken a wide view of the meaning of 'equipment' in order to protect employees: see, for example, *Knowles v Liverpool City Council* [1993] 4 All ER 321, [1993] 1 WLR 1428, HL (council employee injured by a defective flagstone: flagstone held to constitute equipment).

2 The pursuer is not obliged to identify the third party who was at fault: *Edwards v Butlins Ltd* 1998 SLT 500, 1997 GWD 21-1052.

3 The duty extends to providing adequate supervision of employees whose behaviour at work might injure a fellow worker: *Gibson v British Rail Maintenance* 1995 SC 7, 1995 SLT 953 (pursuer injured by a ball which was being used in a game played by two other employees: employer liable because foreman was absent when the game was being played); *Ward v Scotrail Railways Ltd* 1999 SC 255 (pursuer suffered a psychiatric disorder as a result of a fellow employee's sexual molestation: employer would be in breach of the duty if he failed to stop the harassment); *Waters v Commissioner of Police of the Metropolis* [2000] 4 All ER 934 (plaintiff claimed to have been raped and buggered by a fellow officer in her police residential accommodation: defendant did not investigate her complaint and she suffered victimisation and harassment from the other officers for bringing a complaint. The House of Lords held that the defendant was in breach of duty in their failure to prevent her fellow officers from taking retaliatory steps against the plaintiff).

4 See, for example, *Hudson v Ridge Manufacturing Co Ltd* [1957] 2 QB 348, [1957] 2 All ER 348.

5 Subject to the offences being spent under the Rehabilitation of Offenders Act 1974.

The duty to provide a safe system of working is owed to the particular employee. Thus, for example, if an employer knows that an employee is an epileptic or has only one eye, the standards required to constitute reasonable care may be greater in respect of that employee than the other workers. Accordingly, the employer may be negligent vis-à-vis that employee even if his conduct would not amount to negligence if the employee were not epileptic or had two eyes.[1]

The employer's general duty includes taking reasonable steps to prevent the employee suffering *psychiatric*[2] as well as physical harm.[3] In *Hatton v Sutherland*[4] the Court of Appeal held that where an employee has sustained psychiatric harm there are no special control mechanisms and the ordinary principles of employers' liability apply. Accordingly, the employee must show that the employer was in breach of the duty of care. As we have seen,[5] there will be no breach unless it can be shown that the harm sustained by the pursuer was a reasonably foreseeable consequence of the employer's conduct. But by its nature psychiatric harm is less foreseeable than physical harm. Moreover, in *Hatton* the court took the view that an employer is usually entitled to assume that an employee can withstand the normal pressures of work unless the employer knows that the employee is particularly vulnerable. This could arise, for example, where the employer was aware that the employee had had a nervous breakdown before[6] or the employee's doctor had informed him that the working conditions were causing the employee to suffer depression[7] or there have been unexplained and uncharacteristic absences from work. But even if psychiatric harm was reasonably foreseeable, there is no liability unless the employee can show that there were reasonable steps which the employer should have taken to prevent him suffering mental harm. The economic costs to the business of reducing the risk and fairness to other employees will be important factors in determining

1 *Paris v Stepney Borough Council* [1951] AC 367, [1951] 1 All ER 42, HL.
2 Stress in itself does not per se constitute psychiatric harm though it may lead to a psychiatric disorder if allowed to continue unabated.
3 *Fraser v State Hospitals Board for Scotland* 2001 SLT 1051; *Cross v Highland and Islands Enterprise* 2001 SLT 1060; *Green v Argyll & Bute Council* 2002 GWD-295. The view that a pursuer had to establish a particular duty to prevent psychiatric harm is no longer followed; cf *Rorrison v West Lothian Council* 2000 SCLR 245.
4 [2002] 2 All ER 1 approved by the House of Lords in *Barber v Somerset County Council* [2004] UKHL 13.
5 Pages 116 ff above.
6 *Walker v Northumberland CC* [1995] 1 All ER 737.
7 *Stevenson v East Dunbartonshire Council* 2003 SLT 97; *Barber v Somerset County Council* [2004] UKHL 13.

whether or not the employer had taken reasonable care. If the only way to prevent the employee suffering was to dismiss him from the job, an employer is not in breach if the employee chooses to continue working.[1] In short, while an employer's general duty of care to protect his employees includes psychiatric as well as physical harm, it will be very difficult to establish a breach of duty in respect of psychiatric harm caused by stressful work unless the employer knew that the employee was particularly vulnerable and there were reasonable – as opposed to difficult or expensive – steps to reduce the pressure on the employee.

Where an employee suffers psychiatric harm from witnessing the physical – or mental – injuries of a third person, for example a fellow employee,[2] the employer does not owe a duty of care unless the employee was within the area of risk of potential physical harm[3] or the *Alcock* criteria for liability in respect to psychiatric injury to secondary victims are satisfied.[4] In *Keen v Tayside Contracts*,[5] for example, a worker was instructed by his employer to assist the emergency services at the scene of a road accident. There he saw the crushed and burned bodies of the victims. The pursuer's supervisor refused him permission to leave the scene of the accident even though he asked to do so. The pursuer claimed that the employer was negligent in (a) failing to instruct supervisors to let employees leave the scene of an accident where there were dead and mutilated bodies and (b) failing to provide post-incident support for employees who had been disturbed by seeing the victims. The Lord Ordinary (Paton) dismissed the action. Although acting in the course of his employment, the pursuer was a secondary victim

---

1 *Walker v Northumberland CC* [1995] 1 All ER 737.
2 See, for instance, *Robertson v Forth Road Bridge Joint Board* 1995 SC 364; *Hunter v British Coal Corporation* [1999] QB 140.
3 In which case the employee is a primary victim and is protected by the employer's general duty to take reasonable care of his employees. It can be difficult to determine whether or not an employee has sufficient proximity to the accident which caused the harm to the third party to be regarded as a participant and therefore a primary victim. See *Robertson v Forth Road Bridge Joint Board* 1995 SC 364; *Campbell v North Lanarkshire Council* 2000 SCLR 245; *Young v Charles Church (Southern) Ltd* 2000 SCLR 373; *Salter v UB Frozen & Chilled Foods Ltd* 2003 SLT 1011.
4 Namely that there was a relationship of love and affection between the employee and the person who was injured, proximity to the accident or its immediate aftermath and direct visual observation of the accident or its aftermath. For discussion of *Alcock v Chief Constable of South Yorkshire Police* [1992] 1 AC 310 and the difficult question of liability for psychiatric harm caused to secondary victims, see pp 74 ff above.
5 2003 SLT 500.

since the psychiatric harm was caused by witnessing the victims of the road accident: the *Alcock* criteria could not be satisfied as there was no relationship of love and affection between the victims and the pursuer.[1]

The employer must provide a safe environment in which his employee works. Where an employee works at a place which is not under the control of his employer, the employer can still be liable for failing to inspect the premises to ensure that the employee is not exposed to unnecessary risks.[2] It has been held that there can be a breach of the duty if the employer has not taken reasonable steps to protect an employee from the risk of illness arising from passive smoking.[3]

At common law the onus lay on the employee to prove that the harm sustained was a breach of the employer's duty of care ie that the employer was negligent. Since the nineteenth century, safety at work has been the subject of statutory regulations. These provide detailed safety requirements for machinery, particular processes and operations. Although earlier statutes provided criminal sanctions in cases of breach, the courts allowed an employee who was injured as a result to sue the employer in delict for breach of statutory duty. Moreover, as the statutes often imposed strict liability, an employee who sued for breach of statutory duty did not have to establish negligence. But, of course, the employee had to show that the employer was in breach of the statutory obligations.[4]

The Health and Safety at Work etc Act 1974 lays down the minimum standards required of employers for safety at the workplace. It is, however, a criminal statute and it is expressly enacted that its breach does not give rise to a private law remedy for breach of statutory duty. Confusingly, the morass of safety legislation, in particular the Factories Act 1961, continued in force for a while and breach of these provisions did give rise to an action for breach of statutory duty. But now much of this legislation has been repealed

---

1 This is consistent with the decision of the House of Lords in *White v Chief Constable of South Yorkshire Police* [1999] AC 455 where the injuries to the third parties witnessed by the plaintiffs were also caused by their employer. For discussion, see pp 77 ff above. It could be argued that in *Keen* the pursuer was only a secondary victim vis-à-vis the wrongdoer who had caused the accident and that the claim against the employer was for breach of his general duty of care towards his employees. *Sed quaere?*

2 *Crombie v McDermott Scotland Ltd* 1996 SLT 1238, 1996 Rep LR 122, OH.

3 *Rae v Strathclyde Joint Police Board* 1999 GWD 12-571.

4 See, for example, *Thomson v Kvaerner Govan Ltd* 2004 SLT 24, HL.

and replaced by statutory regulations implementing EU directives.[1] Breach of these detailed regulations will, in general, continue to give rise to delictual liability. Discussion of these regulations is outside the compass of this current work.[2] Nevertheless, where an employee is injured as a result of a breach of these regulations, it is important to remember that he will still be able to sue for breach of statutory duty and plead the employer's negligence at common law in the alternative. As in all cases of breach of statutory duty, *volens* is not a defence unless expressly allowed in the statutory regulations, but the employee's damages may be reduced on the grounds of contributory negligence.[3]

An employer may owe the employee a duty of care under the Occupiers' Liability (Scotland) Act 1960[4] as well as the general duty of care owed to employees at common law.[5]

B. VICARIOUS LIABILITY

(1) Introduction

In certain circumstances a person may be liable for the delicts committed by another. This is known as vicarious liability. Although the doctrine arises out of several relationships,[6] the most common by far is that of employer and employee. An employer is vicariously liable for the delicts committed by the employee in the

---

1 See, for example, the Provision and Use of Work Equipment Regulations 1992, SI 1992/2932 implementing Council Directive (EEC) 655/89, and the Manual Handling Operations Regulations 1992, SI 1992/2793 implementing Council Directive (EEC) 269/90. On the Provision and Use of Work Equipment Regulations 1992, see *English v North Lanarkshire Council* 1999 SCLR 310 when the Lord Ordinary (Reed) observed at 319 that 'The interpretation of the regulations has to be approached in that [EU] context and, therefore, in the light of the general guidance given by the European Court of Justice ... and by national courts, both in the United Kingdom ... and in other jurisdictions within the European Union'. On the Manual Handling Operations Regulations 1992, see *Cullen v North Lanarkshire Council* 1998 SC 451; *Taylor v Glasgow City Council* 2002 SLT 689; *Davidson v Lothian and Borders Fire Board* 2003 SLT 939. The Regulations should not be interpreted restrictively.
2 For an excellent account of the law, see Craig and Miller *The Law of Health and Safety at Work in Scotland* (2nd edn, 2000).
3 On contributory negligence, see pp 150 ff above.
4 On occupiers' liability, see pp 194 ff above.
5 *Hill v Lovett* 1992 SLT 994, OH.
6 See pp 233 ff below.

course of his employment. This arises when the employee concerned injures or harms a third party or another employee, provided the delict was committed in the course of employment. Although the employer and employee are jointly and severally liable,[1] in practice the pursuer will sue the employer who is more likely to have funds or be insured. Where it is an employee who has been injured, the employer is obliged by statute to have insurance so that funds are available if he is found to be vicariously liable.[2] Where an employee has been negligent, if the employer is found vicariously liable, the employer can, in theory at least, recover the damages he has paid from the employee, since the employee's delictual conduct constitutes a breach by the employee of the contract of employment.[3] In practice, an employer – or his insurers – do not exercise this right to sue the employee for breach of contract.

(2) Delicts of an employee

The first issue is to determine whether the relationship of employer and employee exists between the person who committed the delict and the person alleged to be vicariously liable: whether the person who committed the delict is working under a contract of employment (*locatio operarum*) or is an independent contractor working under a contract for services (*locatio operis faciendi*). The traditional test for distinguishing between a contract of employment and a contract for services is that of 'control':[4] an employer has the power to control not only what the employee should do but also *how* he should do it. If A has a cleaner who regularly cleans A's house, there is a contract of employment since A can tell the cleaner not only what to do but the manner in which the work is to be done. On the other hand, if A wishes to have a suit dry cleaned, while he may tell the cleaners what to do, A does not have the power to tell them how

---

1 On joint and several liability, see pp 153 ff above.
2 Employers' Liability (Compulsory Insurance) Act 1969. In Scotland, it has been held that failure to insure can result in the directors of a company being personally liable in a claim for damages for breach of statutory duty: *Quinn v McGinty* 1999 SLT (Sh Ct) 27. In England, it bas been held by the Court of Appeal that no civil liability lies for breach of the Employers' Liability (Compulsory Insurance) Act 1969: see *Richardson v Pitt-Stanley* [1995] QB 123, [1995] 1 All ER 460, CA.
3 *Lister v Romford Ice and Cold Storage Co Ltd* [1957] AC 555, [1957] 1 All ER 125, HL.
4 *Yewans v Nokes* (1880) 6 QBD 530.

to carry out the dry-cleaning process: here A is simply entering into a contract for the services of the dry cleaner and not a contract of employment.

The 'control' test remains a useful criterion where the work involved is relatively unskilled. But it is of less value where the alleged employer is a company or large organisation and the work involved is specialist and sophisticated. The courts have therefore had to develop other criteria. Where a person works as an integral part of an organisation, he is likely to be working under a contract of employment, particularly if there is some element of control.[1] Although the parties' expressed intention in their contract is an important factor, the 'label' they have used to describe their relationship is not decisive. As Lord Denning MR observed in *Massey v Crown Life Insurance Co*:[2]

'If the true relationship of the parties is that of master and servant under a contract of service [a contract of employment], the parties cannot alter the truth of that relationship by putting a different label upon it'.

On the other hand, if the relationship between the parties is ambiguous, the 'label' in the contract may be a crucial factor in determining the true relationship between them.[3] An important consideration is the economic reality of the situation. If, for example, the worker supplies his own equipment and materials and takes the 'economic risk' inherent in the enterprise, it is more likely that he is an independent contractor than an employee.[4] On the other hand, where the worker purchases equipment using money lent to him by the other party to the contract who has an option to purchase the equipment for a nominal sum at the end of the contract, then the court would be likely to hold that this is a contract of employment, although technically the worker owns the equipment. Other important factors include the payment of National Insurance contributions, the pension position, the payment of Schedule D or Schedule E taxation, whether or not the worker is paid a fee or a sum on a regular basis and the arrangements for termination of the contract.

---

1 *Stevenson, Jordan and Harrison Ltd v MacDonald and Evans* (1952) 69 RPC 10, [1952] 1 TLR 101, CA.
2 [1978] ICR 590 at 594, [1978] 2 All ER 576 at 579, CA.
3 *Massey v Crown Life Insurance Co* [1978] ICR 590 at 594, [1978] 2 All ER 576 at 579, CA.
4 See, for example, *Ready Mixed Concrete (South East) Ltd v Minister of Pensions and National Insurance* [1968] 2 QB 497, [1968] 1 All ER 433.

The courts can therefore consider a wide range of factors. This has long been recognised as the proper approach in Scots law.[1] It should be emphasised that in the vast majority of cases it will be clear whether the contract between the parties is one of employment or for services. However, in hard cases ie where the nature of the contract is ambiguous, the multiple tests approach gives the courts considerable discretion in determining whether or not a contract of employment exists. Where the issue is whether a worker is an employee for the purpose of the doctrine of vicarious liability, it is thought that the courts would be reluctant to find that a worker was not an employee if this would mean that the pursuer would not obtain reparation because the defender was without requisite funds or insurance.

Having established that a contract of employment exists between the parties, the employer will be vicariously liable for the delicts committed by the employee 'in the course of the employment'.[2] In other words, before an employer is vicariously liable, the employee's acts or omissions which constitute the delict must fall within the scope of his employment. In short, the delict must be a mode or method – albeit wrongful – of the kind of work the employee is engaged to do. The classic exposition of the doctrine in Scots law is to be found in the judgment of the Lord President (Clyde) in *Kirby v National Coal Board*:[3]

'But, in the decisions, four different types of situation have been envisaged as guides to the solution of this problem. In the first place, if the master actually authorised the particular act, he is clearly [vicariously] liable for it. Secondly, where the workman does some work which he is appointed to do, but does it in a way which his master has not authorised and would not have authorised had he known of it, the master is nevertheless still responsible, for the servant's act is still within the scope of his employment. On the other hand, in the third place, if the servant is employed only to do a

---

1 See, for example, *Short v J & W Henderson Ltd* 1946 SC (HL) 24, 1946 SLT 230; *United Wholesale Grocers Ltd v Sher* 1993 SLT 284, OH.
2 An employer is not vicariously liable unless all the aspects of the employee's conduct which constitute the delict have occurred in the course of employment. Thus, if A and B commit a delict, the employer of A is only vicariously liable if the combined conduct of both A and B amounts to a delict in the course of A's employment: *Credit Lyonnais Bank Nederland NV (now known as Generale Bank Nederland NV) v Export Credits Guarantee Department* [2000] 1 AC 486. Thus, if A's conduct per se does not constitute a delict, A's employer is not vicariously liable if B's conduct would be outwith the scope of A's employment if A had carried out B's acts or omissions. See also *Royal Bank of Scotland v Bannerman Johnstone Maclay* 2003 SC 125.
3 1958 SC 514 at 532–533, 1959 SLT 7.

particular work or a particular class of work, and he does something outside the scope of that work, the master is not responsible for any mischief the servant may do to a third party. Lastly, if the servant uses his master's time or his master's tools for his own purposes, the master is not responsible.'

Taking these four situations in turn:

(1) If an employer has expressly or impliedly authorised the delictual conduct, the employee is acting within the scope of the employment and the employer is vicariously liable for the delict. In *Neville v C & A Modes Ltd*[1] for example, the pursuer was suspected of shoplifting by employees of the defender. She was forcibly taken from the street back into the shop and there accused of theft. She argued that the defender was vicariously liable for defamation of her character. The Inner House held that the defender's employees had a duty under their contracts of employment to protect the defender's property and take action to prevent theft. The employees' action had therefore been authorised by the defender, ie was within the scope of their employment, albeit that it may have been defamatory in the circumstances of this case.[2]

(2) If the employee does work which he was authorised to do, but does it in a way which the employer has not authorised and would not have authorised, nevertheless the employer is vicariously liable because the employee's act is still within the scope of his employment. In other words, the delictual act or omission is a mode – albeit a wrongful mode – of carrying out the work the employee was authorised to do. An example will illustrate the point. A is employed by B as a van driver. A drives the van carelessly or over the speed limit. As a result of his negligent driving, A injures C. In an action for reparation, B is vicariously liable for A's negligent driving. The careless driving is a mode – albeit a wrongful mode – of carrying out the work A was authorised to do. B would still be vicariously liable even if he instructed A not to drive carelessly or over the speed limit.

An employee's act or omission does not cease to be within the scope of his employment merely because the conduct is fraudulent. In *Taylor v Glasgow District Council*,[3] for example, a building control officer had been given actual authority to issue building warrants and completion certificates. He issued false documents as part of a

---

1 1945 SC 175, 1945 SLT 189.
2 On defamation, see Chapter 15 below.
3 1997 SC 183, 1997 SLT 537.

fraudulent scheme with a development company. The company sold the property to Taylor who sustained economic loss. It was held that the defender could be vicariously liable for the fraudulent conduct of its employee because he had been given actual authority to issue the documents. The fact that the defender did not benefit from the fraud was irrelevant: the only question was whether the employee's conduct was an improper mode of doing what he was authorised to do. Although the courts were prepared to treat fraudulent misconduct as an improper mode of doing what the employee was authorised to do, they were reluctant to include other intentional delicts. Thus in *Trotman v North Yorkshire County Council* [1] the Court of Appeal held that sexual misconduct on the part of a teacher was not an unauthorised mode of carrying out his teaching duties; consequently, the local authority was not vicariously liable for the assault. However, in *Lister v Hesley Hall* [2] the House of Lords held that an employee's unauthorised actions could still be within the scope of his employment if the delictual behaviour was so closely connected with his employment that it would be fair and just to hold the employer vicariously liable. In *Lister* the warden of a school boarding house sexually abused boys who were in his care. He had been employed to look after the children and this would involve physical proximity between them if the warden was to fulfil his responsibilities. There was therefore a very close connection between the nature of the warden's employment and the sexual assault, the risks of which were inherent in that position. In these circumstances it was fair and just to hold the employer vicariously liable for the assaults. [3]

Throughout their opinions, their Lordships stressed that vicarious liability should not be imposed merely because the employer's job gave him an opportunity to commit the delict. For example, E employs a plumber. The plumber is sent to fix a leak at A's house. While he is there the plumber steals money from A. E is not vicariously liable for the theft. Stealing is not a wrongful mode of carrying out plumbing duties. Nor is theft closely connected with the risks inherent in plumbing. On the other hand, if the plumber decided that he wanted to damage A's house, E could be vicariously liable if the plumber deliberately flooded the kitchen where

---

1 [1999] LGR 584, CA.
2 [2002] 1 AC 315.
3 Accordingly, *Trotman* was overruled.

the leak was located: there may be a sufficiently close connection between the plumber's act and the risk of flooding inherent in plumbing.[1] But it is difficult to be certain what risks are inherent in a particular job and until these are known it is impossible to determine whether the employee's wrongdoing is sufficiently closely connected to them to justify vicarious liability being imposed on the employer.

It has been suggested[2] that *Lister* was a case where the employer had assumed responsibility for the welfare of the children and should therefore be liable for the conduct of the persons to whom the children's care had been delegated. Put another way, the local authority had undertaken a direct responsibility to the children (and their parents) which had been breached when they entrusted their care to an employee who was a potential danger to them. Analysed in this way, the local authority would have been in breach of a direct or personal duty of care owed to the children, analogous to the personal duty owed by an employer to his emplyoyees[3] and non-delegable in the same way.[4] However, this was not the approach adopted by their Lordships in *Lister* where the case proceeded as one of vicarious – rather than direct or personal – liability.

Lister v Hesley Hall[5] is a case where the House of Lords was prepared to abandon well-settled rules for the imposition of vicarious liability in order to avoid a result that their Lordships considered unjust in the circumstances, namely that the local authority would not be vicariously liable for the sexual assaults perpetrated by their employee on children in their care. Purporting to proceed on the basis of principled but practical justice, the House found the local authority to be vicariously liable for their employee's delicts because his wrongful conduct was closely connected to the risks inherent in the acts he was authorised to do. The scope of this

---

1 But A would not be vicariously liable if the plumber deliberately set the house on fire as the risk of fire does not appear to be inherent in plumbing.

2 M Loubser and E Reid 'Vicarious Liability of Intentional Wrongdoing' 2003 JR 143.

3 Discussed at pp 215 ff above.

4 In *Gorrie v Marist Brothers* 2002 SCLR 436, the pursuer was the victim of sexual abuse by one of his teachers. He claimed that the defender was in breach of a primary duty owed to the pursuer to take reasonable care to appoint fit and proper persons as teachers.

5 [2001] 1 AC 215.

development is uncertain. The traditional rules remain and are probably adequate to deal with the situation where the employee's wrongful conduct is unintentional, for example negligence. The close connection criterion may well be restricted to cases of an employee's intentional wrongdoing which does not amount to an improper mode of doing what he was employed to do.[1]

(3) If the employee is employed to do a particular task or a particular class of work, and does something outside the scope of his work, then the employer is not vicariously liable since the employee was not acting within the scope of his employment. For example, A is employed by B to pack goods at B's warehouse. A decides to deliver goods to a customer and drives B's van. If A injures C as a result of A's careless driving, prima facie B is not vicariously liable because A was not employed as a driver and was therefore not authorised to drive B's van. A's driving of the van is outside the scope of his employment and B is therefore not vicariously liable.

It may be difficult to determine what is the scope of a worker's employment. Obviously the terms of the contract are important, but the courts are not prepared to accept that for the purpose of vicarious liability the scope of employment is limited to the employee's express contractual duties. In the example above, if, to B's knowledge, A had delivered goods to a customer in the van on previous occasions, driving the van could well fall within A's employment, even though A's job description in his contract is that of a packer. Moreover, given that the pursuer has *ex hypothesi* been injured or suffered harm, courts will be reluctant to allow an employer to escape vicarious liability by arguing that the employee's failure to follow the employer's detailed instructions resulted in the employee acting outside the scope of employment (no vicarious liability) as opposed to engaging in a wrongful mode of carrying out the work the employee was authorised to do (vicarious liability).

Thus, in *Rose v Plenty*,[2] a milkman was expressly instructed by his employer not to use boys to help him deliver milk or to give boys lifts in his milk float. In breach of this order, he continued to use a 13-year-old boy to help him. The lad was injured as a result of the

---

1 The test has been applied in the context of fraud: *Dubai Aluminium Co Ltd v Salaam* [2003] 1 All ER 97. Cf *Royal Bank of Scotland v Bannerman Johnstone Maclay* 2003 SC 125 where the employee's false journal entries and tampering with vouchers only incidentally facilitated a fraudulent scheme carried out by the customer to whom the defender provided accountancy services. In these circumstances, the defender was held not to be vicariously liable. *Sed quaere?*

2 [1975] ICR 430, [1976] 1 All ER 97, CA.

milkman's negligent driving of the float. The employers argued that they were not vicariously liable because the employee was acting outside the scope of his employment. In other words, his particular work was delivering milk without the help of young boys and therefore he was acting outside the scope of his employment when he delivered milk with the help of a 13-year-old lad. However, the Court of Appeal held[1] that the express prohibition did not change the scope of the milkman's employment. As Lord Denning MR explained:[2]

'In considering whether a prohibited act was within the course of the employment it depends very much on the purpose for which it is done. If it is done for his employer's business, it is usually done in the course of his employment, even though it is a prohibited act ... But if it is done for some purpose other than his master's business, as, for instance, giving a lift to a hitchhiker, such an act, if prohibited, may not be in the course of his employment ... In the present case it seems to me that the course of Mr Plenty's [the milkman's] employment was to distribute the milk, collect the money and to bring back the bottles to the van. He got, or allowed this young boy, Leslie Rose, to do part of that business which was the employer's business. It seems to me that although prohibited, it was conduct which was within the course of employment ... I agree it is a nice point in these cases on which side of the line the case falls.'

In certain situations it will be a question of degree whether the employee's conduct is or is not within the scope of his employment. In *Williams v Hemphill (A & W) Ltd*,[3] members of the Boys' Brigade were at a camp at Benderloch. A company of Girl Guildry was also at the camp. The girls were to return to Dollar by train. A lorry driver was instructed by his employer to take the boys back to Glasgow. He was persuaded by some of the boys to return to Glasgow via Connell, Stirling and Dollar railway stations, so that the boys could catch a glimpse of the girls. The shortest route back to Glasgow was via Loch Lomond. There was an accident and one of the boys, who had not instigated the change of route, was injured. The employers would not have authorised the route the driver had taken. The question was whether, by deviating from the authorised route, the driver was no longer acting within the scope of his employment with the result that the employer would not have been vicariously liable. The House of Lords held that it was ultimately a question of degree whether, as a result of the deviation,

---

1 Lord Denning MR and Scarman LJ; Lawton LJ dissented.
2 *Rose v Plenty* [1976] 1 All ER 97 at 100–101.
3 1966 SC (HL) 31, 1966 SLT 33.

230 *Employers' liability and vicarious liability*

the employee was no longer engaged on the employer's business. In this case, the dominant purpose of the journey was to transport the boys to Glasgow and the driver was still engaged on that task when the accident occurred in spite of not having taken the most direct route. As Lord Pearce explained:[1]

'In weighing up, therefore, the question of degree whether the admittedly substantial deviation of the vehicle with its passengers and baggage was such as to make the lorry's progress a frolic of the servant unconnected with or in substitution for the master's business, the presence of the passengers is a decisive factor against regarding it as a mere frolic of the servant. In the present case the defenders remained liable, in spite of the deviation, for their driver's negligence.'[2]

(4) If an employee uses his master's time or his master's equipment for the employee's own purpose, the employer is not vicariously liable because the employee is no longer acting within the scope of his employment. As Lord Pearce indicated, in these circumstances the employee is acting on a 'frolic' of his own. So, for example, if, during the time he is supposed to be working, an employee goes shopping, the employer will not be vicariously liable for any delict the employee may commit since shopping is clearly outside the scope of the employment. Similarly, if a van driver, without authorisation, uses his employer's van to help a friend move house, the employer is not vicariously liable if an accident occurs during the move because that is outside the scope of the employment.

Difficulties may arise if the employee's delictual act or omission occurs at the workplace. In *Kirby v National Coal Board*,[3] a miner during a temporary break went to a prohibited place in order to smoke. When he struck a match, there was an explosion and the pursuer was injured. The court held that by going to the prohibited area in order to smoke, he was no longer acting within the scope of his employment – mining – and consequently the defender was not vicariously liable. On the other hand, in *Century Insurance Co Ltd v Northern Ireland Road Transport Board*,[4] an explosion took place when an employee lit a cigarette while transferring petrol. The House of Lords held that this was an unauthorised mode of doing his job which was to transfer petrol and that the employer therefore remained vicariously liable.

---

1 1966 SC (HL) 31 at 46.
2 Lord Pearce did indicate, however, that there must be limits set by common sense: for example, if the deviation involved going to Glasgow via Inverness!
3 1958 SC 514, 1959 SLT 7.
4 [1942] AC 509, [1942] 1 All ER 491, HL.

Where a person is injured at work as a result of horseplay by other employees, the employer may escape vicarious liability if the horseplay constitutes 'a frolic of their own'. In *Smith v Crossley Bros Ltd*,[1] an apprentice was injured by fellow employees during initiation rites.[2] It was held that the employer was not in breach of the general duty of care to provide competent fellow workers.[3] Nor was the defendant vicariously liable because the actings constituted a frolic and were outside the scope of the workers' employment. On the other hand, in *Harrison v Michelin Tyre Co Ltd*[4] the employer was held to be vicariously liable when an employee who was standing on a duckboard was injured as a result of a fellow employee jumping on the other end of the duckboard for a lark. The court took the view that a reasonable person would consider that, even though the act was unauthorised, it was nevertheless 'part and parcel' of the job and accordingly not outside the scope of employment.[5]

It is generally accepted that travel to and from work is outside the scope of employment and that the employer is not vicariously liable for an employee's delicts at that time. However, where the employer retains an element of control, vicarious liability may continue before or after work. Thus in *Bell v Blackwood, Morton & Sons Ltd*,[6] an employer was held to be vicariously liable when the pursuer was injured by a fellow employee when leaving work. The employers had attempted to prevent employees from rushing downstairs to catch their buses and had supervised the descent of the stairway from time to time. In these circumstances, the employees were still within the scope of their employment when on the stairway where the accident occurred. Where an employee works at two places, it has been held that he is within the scope of his employment when travelling between them.[7]

---

1 (1971) 95 So Jo 655, CA.
2 The unfortunate lad had a compressed-air pipe placed in close proximity to his rectum.
3 See pp 215 ff above.
4 [1985] 1 All ER 918, [1985] ICR 696. It is doubtful if the same result would be reached on the *Lister* 'close connection' criterion.
5 An owner of a night club has been held to be vicariously liable for assaults carried out by 'bouncers' on a customer who had kicked in the door of the premises: the bouncers were not on a frolic of their own but had been attempting to preserve the integrity of the club, albeit in a *very* unauthorised way! See *Vasey v Surrey Free Inns plc* [1996] PIQR P373 CA. Post-*Lister*, it has been accepted that such assaults are sufficiently closely connected with the risk of physical harm inherent in the nature of a bouncer's job for vicarious liability to be imposed: *Mattis v Pollock (t/a Flamingo's Nightclub)* [2003] 1 WLR 2158, CA.
6 1960 SC 11, 1959 SLT (Notes) 54, OH.
7 *Thomson v British Steel Corpn* 1977 SLT 26, OH.

In certain situations, an employee may be hired out to work under the instructions of another employer. For example A, a general contractor, may hire equipment from B to be operated by an employee of B but under A's instruction. If the 'borrowed' employee is negligent and injures one of A's employees or a third party, who is vicariously liable, A or B? The general rule is that the employer with whom the borrowed employee has a contract of employment remains vicariously liable even though the employee works under the general instructions of another. Thus, in our example, B remains vicariously liable. B will only escape vicarious liability if he has delegated to A not only the power to control what B's employee does but also *how* the employee should do the job. The onus rests on B to establish that the full plethora of control has passed from B to A. This will be almost impossible to establish where B's employee operates sophisticated equipment.

This principle was settled by the House of Lords in the leading case of *Mersey Docks and Harbour Board v Coggins and Griffith (Liverpool) Ltd.*[1] The plaintiff hired a mobile crane to the defendant which was to be operated by an employee of the plaintiff. It was agreed in the contract of hire that the operator of the crane was to be treated as an employee of Coggins. The craneman injured a worker while operating the crane negligently. The question arose whether the plaintiff or the defendant should be vicariously liable. The House of Lords held that *in a question with the injured third party,* vicarious liability could not be determined by the contractual arrangements made between the plaintiff and defendant to which the injured person had not been a party. Prima facie the plaintiff was the employer and was vicariously liable unless it could be established that full control of the craneman had passed to Coggins. While Coggins could tell the craneman what to do, since he was a highly skilled worker they could *not* tell him *how* to do his job. Accordingly, Mersey Docks had failed to discharge the onus which lay upon them to prove that their employee had been transferred *pro hac vice* to Coggins. Therefore, as far as the injured person was concerned, he could sue Mersey Docks as vicariously liable for the negligence of their employee, the craneman. But because of the terms of their contract of hire with Coggins, Mersey Docks could recover the damages from Coggins since they had agreed to treat the crane man as their employee.[2]

1 [1947] AC 1, [1946] 2 All ER 345, HL.
2 This principle has been accepted as part of Scots law: see *Park v Tractor Shovels Ltd* 1980 SLT 94, OH; *Royal Bank of Scotland v Bannerman Johnstone Maclay* 2003 SC 125 (employee transferred *pro hac vice* to act as financial controller for customer of the defenders).

(3) Vicarious liability for independent contractors

As a general rule, a person is not vicariously liable for the delicts of an independent contractor whom he hires to undertake a particular job, for example a taxi driver, a plumber, a builder etc. If, for example, A, a general contractor, hires the services of B, an independent contractor, and through his negligence B causes injury to C, an employee of A, A is not vicariously liable for B's delicts. If C is injured by the negligence of an employee of B, B will, of course, be vicariously liable to C. However, A may be liable in delict to his employee, C, if A's act in hiring B is a breach of A's general duty to take reasonable care for the safety of his employees.[1] But this is a breach of A's personal duty of care towards his employees – it is not *vicarious* liability for B's delictual act. To succeed against A, C must show that A did not take reasonable care in hiring B's services, for example if A knows that B is incompetent or unqualified. The duty is analogous with that of taking reasonable care to provide an employee with competent fellow workers. However, in *Marshall v William Sharp & Sons Ltd*,[2] the defender hired the services of a worker who was paid an hourly rate for work done. The defender had full control over the actings of the worker concerned. The pursuer, an employee of the defender, was injured as a result of the worker's negligence. The Inner House held that the defender was *not* in breach of his personal duty to the pursuer to provide a competent independent contractor to work with him. Nevertheless, the court found that the defender was vicariously liable in spite of the fact that the person who had injured the pursuer was an independent contractor. It is submitted that this decision can be supported on the ground that the defender had the power to control not only what the independent contractor could do but how he should do it. This is not usually the case when a person hires an independent contractor, for example a taxi driver or a plumber. Thus, unless the hirer has the full plethora of control over an independent contractor, he will not be vicariously liable for the delicts of an independent contractor in carrying out a job.

In building contracts, an employer is liable to third parties for loss sustained as a result of an independent contractor carrying out hazardous operations on the site:

Employer —— Main Contractor —— Sub-contractor —— Sub-sub-contractor

---

1 On an employer's duty to take reasonable care, see pp 215 ff above.
2 1992 SCLR 104, 1991 SLT 114.

But the main contractor is *not* liable for the delicts of the sub-
or sub-sub-contractors; nor is the sub-contractor liable for the
delicts of the sub-sub-contractor. Thus a main contractor cannot
sue a sub-contractor for damage to property owned by the
main contractor as a consequence of a sub-sub-contractor's negligence.[1]

(4) Principal and agent

A principal can be vicariously liable for the delicts of his agent.
This will arise if (i) the acts of the agent were expressly authorised by the principal; or (ii) the principal ratified the agent's acts
after they were done; or (iii) the delict is within the actual or
ostensible authority of the agent. For vicarious liability to arise it
is not enough that X permits Y to do a particular act, for example
drive X's car: instead, X must have delegated a task or duty to Y.[2]
The principle is important in the context of employment where
an employer prima facie escapes vicarious liability because the
employee is working outside the scope of his employment: the
employer may still be vicariously liable as principal if in the circumstances the employee is acting within his actual or ostensible
authority as the employer's agent at the time of the delictual act.[3]
A partnership can be vicariously liable for the delicts of its
agents, the partners, provided the wrongful conduct can fairly
and properly be regarded as done by the partner while acting in
the ordinary course of the firm's business: such conduct can
include fraud.[4]

C. CONCLUSION

The discussion of vicarious liability is important because it illustrates how the common law developed an exception to the principle
that a person is not obliged to make reparation unless he has
caused injury or harm as a result of his own *culpa* or fault. As a
result of industrialisation, it became apparent that those who were

---

1 *MTM Construction Ltd v William Reid Engineering Ltd* 1998 SLT 778, 1997
  SCLR 778, OH.
2 *Morgans v Launchbury* [1973] AC 127, [1972] 2 All ER 606, HL.
3 *Taylor v Glasgow District Council* 1997 SC 183, 1997 SLT 537.
4 See, generally, *Dubai Aluminium Co Ltd v Salaam* [2003] 2 AC 366, [2003] 1 All
  ER 97.

injured by the delicts of workers would, in practice, have little likelihood of obtaining compensation from the worker himself. Accordingly, the doctrine of vicarious liability arose to enable the pursuer to sue the employer, in addition to the employee, since the employer was more likely to have funds or be insured.

CHAPTER 13

Delict and the family

It is now proposed to consider delictual liability in the context of family relationships. We will be concerned with delictual liability *between* members of the family and the rights of members of the family to seek reparation if a relative is injured or killed.

A. TITLE TO SUE

At common law, spouses could not sue each other in delict. Thus, if a woman was injured as a result of her husband's negligent driving, she could not obtain reparation. This rule was clearly anachronistic, especially as the loss would ultimately fall on her husband's insurance company. The position was changed by s 2(1) of the Law Reform (Husband and Wife) Act 1962, which provides that each of the spouses has 'the like rights' to bring proceedings against the other in respect of a delict 'as if they were not married'. Where the action is brought during the subsistence of the marriage, the court has a discretion to dismiss the proceedings if it appears that no substantial benefit would accrue to either party if the action continued.[1] The court's discretion is unlikely to be invoked because the action will proceed if any benefit accrues to the pursuer, even though the couple, as a family unit, will be no better off. Since the discretion in s 2(2) is both anomalous and unnecessary, the Scottish Law Commission has proposed that it should be repealed.[2]

A spouse is not liable for the delicts of the other spouse unless liability is established on a basis other than marriage itself. So, for example, a wife could be vicariously liable for a delict committed by her husband if she were his employer and the delict arose in the course of his employment.

---

1 Law Reform (Husband and Wife) Act 1962, s 2(2).
2 Report on Family Law (Scot Law Com No 135) rec 54.

As a general rule, a child or young person under the age of 16 has no active legal capacity.[1] However, a child under 16 can instruct a solicitor in connection with any civil matter, provided she has a general understanding of what it means to do so. A child of 12 or more is presumed to be of sufficient age and maturity to have such understanding, although a child under 12 may instruct a solicitor if she in fact has such an understanding.[2] If the child has the capacity to instruct a solicitor, she has capacity to pursue or defend a civil action.[3] Thus a child with sufficient capacity can pursue an action in delict. If the child does not have such capacity, the action must be brought by the child's legal representative, who will usually be the child's parents.[4]

The Age of Legal Capacity (Scotland) Act 1991 does not affect the delictual responsibility of children and young persons under the age of 16.[5] Thus a child under the age of 16 can, theoretically at least, be sued if the child has committed a delict. Parents are not vicariously liable for the delicts committed by their children. But where a child causes injury or damage as a result of a parent's negligence, the parent may be liable for a breach of a duty of care which the parent owed to the pursuer. For example, if a child runs in front of a car and the driver is injured trying to avoid the child, the mother may be liable in delict if she has not taken reasonable care to ensure that the child was not on the road.[6] Because the 1991 Act does not affect the age of delictual responsibility, a child who has been injured may have any damages awarded reduced on the ground of contributory negligence.[7] In *McKinnell v White*,[8] for example, a child of five was held to be 50 per cent contributorily negligent because he ran in front of a speeding motorist. The Lord Ordinary (Fraser) took the view that by the age of five a child brought up in an urban environment should have been aware of the

---

1 Age of Legal Capacity (Scotland) Act 1991, s 1(1)(a).
2 ALC(S)A 1991, s 2(4A).
3 ALC(S)A 1991, s 2(5A).
4 Children (Scotland) Act 1995, s 1(1)(d). If the parent is the defender, for example if the child was injured as a result of her mother's careless driving, a curator ad litem will be appointed to represent the child.
5 ALC(S)A 1991, s 1(3)(c).
6 *Hardie v Sneddon* 1917 SC 1, 1916 2 SLT 197.
7 On contributory negligence, see pp 150 ff above.
8 1971 SLT (Notes) 61, OH. See also *McCluskey v Wallace* 1998 SC 711 (four-year-old child, 20 per cent contributory negligence). There is no general rule to determine the degree of a child's contributory negligence. The danger to which the child is exposed and the child's capacity to appreciate that risk are important: *Galbraith's Curator ad Litem v Stewart (No 2)* 1998 SLT 1305, OH (eight-year-old child, no contributory negligence).

danger of road traffic. It has always been competent for a child to sue his or her parent in delict.[1]

Where a foetus sustains injury *in utero,* the unborn baby has no right to sue in delict unless and until it has been born alive. Only on birth does a child obtain legal personality. However, provided the defender owed a duty of care towards the foetus, if the baby is born alive, an action in delict can be brought on the child's behalf in respect of the harm sustained *in utero.* This is sometimes said to be a consequence of the civil law principle *nasciturus pro iam nato habetur quotiens de eius agitur,* namely that in a matter affecting its interests, an unborn child *in utero* should be deemed to be born (the *nasciturus* doctrine).[2] It is submitted that there is no need to rely on the *nasciturus* doctrine to achieve this result. Given that the defender owes a *Donoghue v Stevenson* duty of care[3] to the foetus, based on reasonable foreseeability of injury *in utero,* then if there is a breach of the duty which causes harm to the foetus, a delict will be committed when the baby is born. It is at that stage, ie when the baby is born alive, that the delict is completed because, while the breach of duty took place during the pregnancy, harm for the purpose of delictual liability is not sustained by the child until the child is born.[4] It is only then that *damage* arises as a result of the breach of the duty of care: *damnum injuria datum.*

Because it is competent for a child to sue a parent, a mother who injures her foetus during the pregnancy could be sued by her child in delict, provided the child is born alive. A mother clearly owes a duty of care to the foetus. If during her pregnancy she fails to take reasonable care, for example if she abuses drugs or falls down the stair when drunk, then she can be liable in delict if her breach of duty of care results in damage to the child when born alive. It would therefore appear that a mother carries a potential litigant in her womb for nine months! Similarly, a father who injures his wife's foetus through, for example, negligent driving may be liable in delict if the child is born alive suffering from harm as a result of the injuries sustained *in utero.*

In practice, it is likely that where a foetus is injured *in utero* the mother will also have sustained physical or psychiatric harm. If the defender owed her a duty of care which has been broken, the mother may sue for the harm she has suffered. Where the mother

---

1 *Young v Rankin* 1934 SC 499, 1934 SLT 445.
2 *Cohen v Shaw* 1992 SCLR 182n, 1992 SLT 1022, OH.
3 See *Donoghue v Stevenson* 1932 SC (HL) 31, 1932 SLT 317.
4 *Hamilton v Fife Health Board* 1993 SC 369, 1993 SLT 624.

miscarries as a result of the defender's breach of duty, she may obtain damages for the loss of her baby. Of course, in these circumstances, the unborn child has no title to sue because the child has not been born alive.

B. PERSONAL INJURIES TO A RELATIVE

In *Robertson v Turnbull*,[1] it was held that where a person was injured, the defender did not owe a threshold duty of care to the victim's spouse or relatives who had suffered economic loss as a result of the injuries sustained. So, for example, members of the injured person's family could not sue in delict for loss of support.[2] The victim can, of course, sue for loss of future earnings as derivative economic loss.[3] Moreover, at common law, a pursuer who was injured could not recover damages for the economic loss suffered by a relative as a result of the pursuer's injuries, for example where a spouse had given up work in order to nurse her injured husband.[4]

The common law on this point has now been superseded by s 8 of the Administration of Justice Act 1982.[5] This provides that where a person has sustained personal injuries, the injured person can recover damages which amount to reasonable remuneration for necessary services rendered to the pursuer by a relative.[6] The services rendered by the relative must be physical services, such as

---

1 1982 SC (HL) 1, 1982 SLT 96.
2 This is an example of non-recoverability of secondary economic loss. Similarly, a child cannot sue for economic loss incurred as a result of serious injuries suffered by his mother (she was in a persistent vegetative state): *Buckley v Farrow* [1997] PIQR Q78, CA.
3 On loss of future earnings, see pp 294 ff below.
4 *Edgar v Lord Advocate* 1965 SC 67, 1965 SLT 158.
5 As amended by the Law Reform (Miscellaneous Provisions) (Scotland) Act 1990, s 69.
6 'Relative' includes the injured person's spouse or divorced spouse, heterosexual cohabitee, any ascendant or descendant, any brother, sister, uncle or aunt or their issue and any person accepted by the injured party as a child of the family: illegitimacy is irrelevant: Administration of Justice Act 1982, s 13. Since opposite-sex cohabitants are regarded as relatives, the 1982 Act should be amended to include same-sex cohabitants if a violation of article 8 read with article 14 of the European Convention on Human Rights is to be avoided (discrimination on the grounds of sexual orientation).

nursing.[1] Thus it has been held that s 8 of the 1982 Act did not apply when a relative had donated bone marrow to the pursuer who would otherwise have died.[2] The damages can be reduced to take into account the injured persons contributory negligence.[3]

The pursuer, ie the injured person, then accounts to the relative for any damages recovered under this provision.[4] Originally, damages could only be awarded in respect of services rendered up to the date of the action;[5] but now damages can be awarded for services likely to be rendered by a relative to the injured person in the future.[6] Damages are not available under s 8 of the 1982 Act if the relative expressly agreed that no payment should be made in respect of the services rendered or to be rendered.[7] Where the injured person has died before the action is concluded, the deceased's executor may recover damages for necessary services rendered by a relative before the victim died.[8]

Where a person who was not in employment was injured, at common law he had no right to sue for loss of earnings since *ex hypothesi* he was not earning. This was particularly unfair to wives who had given up their jobs to look after the home or children. Section 9(1) of the Administration of Justice Act 1982 gives an injured person who has been providing unpaid personal services to a relative[9] the right to sue for damages if the pursuer is unable to

1 BNA nursing and home help rates can be useful but are by no means conclusive of what reasonable remuneration should be in a particular case. See, for example, *Kennedy v Lees of Scotland* 1997 SLT 510 (use of agency rates rejected as unsuitable where victim had not received substantial nursing, but only short visits from relatives).

2 *Duffy v Lanarkshire Health Board* 1998 SCLR 1142, 1998 Rep LR 119, OH. In *Sturgeon v Gallacher* 2003 SLT 67, the pursuer ran a farm in partnership with his wife. After he had been injured in an accident, his son laboured on the farm for £50 a week. The Lord Ordinary (Emslie) held that the son's work did not constitute necessary services for the purpose of Administration of Justice Act 1982, s 8 as they were rendered to the partnership, not the pursuer. The pursuer could, however, include the extra outlay (the son's wages) in his claim for loss of earnings.

3 *Yale v Forbes* 2004 SLT (Sh Ct) 13.

4 Administration of Justice Act 1982, s 8(2). But where the relative is the defender, it has been held that a claim under s 8 is incompetent: *Kozikowska v Kozikowski* 1996 SLT 386. It was thought contrary to public policy that the pursuer should remunerate the person she blamed for her injuries – *sed quaere?*

5 *Forsyth's Curator Bonis v Govan Shipbuilders* 1989 SCLR 78, 1989 SLT 91.

6 Administration of Justice Act 1982, s 8(3), added by s 69 of the Law Reform (Miscellaneous Provisions) (Scotland) Act 1990.

7 Administration of Justice Act 1982, s 8(1) and (3). See *Denheen v British Railways Board* 1988 SLT 320n, 1986 SLT 249, OH.

8 See, for example, *McManus' Executrix v Babcock Energy Ltd* 1999 SC 569 *Murray's Executrix v Greenock Dockyard Co Ltd* 2004 SLT 346.

9 For the definition of 'relative', see the Administration of Justice Act 1982, s 13, discussed at p 240, note 6 above.

continue to do so as a result of the injuries sustained. The personal services must be services which (a) were or might have been expected to have been rendered by the pursuer before the injuries; (b) were of a kind which when rendered by a person other than a relative would ordinarily have been obtainable on payment; and (c) the injured person but for the injuries in question might have been expected to render gratuitously to a relative.[1]

In *Ingham v John G Russell (Transport) Ltd*[2] the Inner House refused to restrict the concept of personal services to services which were rendered to the person of the relative, such as nursing, as opposed to the relative's property, such as cleaning the relative's house. It was enough that the services had been rendered *in person* by the injured person and therefore included maintenance or DIY services rendered by the injured person to his spouse. It is therefore clear that an injured woman, for example, can recover damages if she is unable to provide unpaid housekeeping and child-rearing services for her spouse, cohabitee or children. Because the personal services must have been rendered gratuitously before s 9 applies, the Administration of Justice Act 1982 recognises the fact that work in the home is still prima facie unpaid but that its economic value is such that justice demands that the injured person should receive compensation for the inability to continue to provide it, even though technically the pursuer has not suffered any patrimonial loss ie loss of earnings.

Where the injured person has died, a relative may claim as a head of loss a reasonable sum in respect of the loss of gratuitous personal services rendered to the relative by the deceased.[3] Before he can do so, the pursuer must be a relative who has the right to claim damages for loss of support by the deceased under the Damages (Scotland) Act 1976. Accordingly, it is to the provisions of the 1976 Act that we shall now turn.

1   Administration of Justice Act 1982, s 9(3).
2   1991 SC 201, 1991 SLT 739.
3   Administration of Justice Act 1982, s 9(2); *Ingham v John G Russell (Transport) Ltd* 1991 SC 201, 1991 SLT 379. It can be difficult to quantify the value of such services, particularly when the deceased was simply 'a normal, average married man living in family who did the correspondingly normal, average things which a father and husband does around the house, the garden and the family car': *Beggs v Motherwell Bridge Fabricators Ltd* 1997 SCLR 1019, 1998 SLT 1215 at 1223 per the Lord Ordinary (Eassie). See also *Ferrelly v Yarrow Shipbuilders Ltd* 1994 SCLR 407, 1994 SLT 1349n, OH; *McManus' Executrix v Babcock Energy Ltd* 1999 SC 569. *Murray's Executrix v Greenock Dockyard Co Ltd* 2004 SLT 346 (£2,100 awarded as deceased only occassionally helped out).

C. DEATH OF A RELATIVE

If a person dies as a result of another's delict, two potential claims arise. First, the deceased's own claim which can transmit to the deceased's executor who can pursue the action for the benefit of the deceased's estate. Second, a dependent claim by the deceased's relatives.

(1) The deceased's claim

Where a person is killed outright as a result of the defender's delict, the deceased's executor cannot raise an action in delict in respect of the death.[1] In these circumstances, the only claims are those of the deceased's relatives. However, if a person is injured and subsequently dies as a result of the injuries, the deceased's right to sue in delict in respect of personal injuries transmits to the executor who can sue on behalf of the deceased's estate. This complex area of the law is now regulated by the Damages (Scotland) Act 1976.[2]

Where a person dies on or after 16 July 1992, the rights which vested in the deceased immediately before his death to sue for damages in respect of personal injuries transmit to the executor.[3] As a result, the executor can raise an action or, if an action has been raised by the deceased before he died, continue the action on behalf of the deceased's estate.[4] The executor may sue in respect of patrimonial loss, for example loss of earnings sustained by the deceased, but only up to the date of death.[5] In other words, patrimonial loss attributable to any period after the deceased's death, for example loss of future earnings, is non-transmissible to the executor. This is necessary to prevent double compensation given that the defender

---

1 Where death is caused by a fatal accident, the courts, in England at least, will not award the deceased's executor damages for the deceased's fear of impending death: *Hicks v Chief Constable of South Yorkshire Police* [1992] 2 All ER 65, HL. In Scotland, the deceased's immediate family may have such a claim: see p 248 below.

2 This Act has been amended by inter alia the Administration of Justice Act 1982, the Law Reform (Parent and Child) (Scotland) Act 1986, the Consumer Protection Act 1987 the Damages (Scotland) Act 1993 and the Protection from Harassment Act 1997; it now bears little resemblance to the original Act. References in this chapter are to the Damages (Scotland) Act 1976 as amended unless otherwise stated.

3 Damages (Scotland) Act 1976, s 2(1).

4 D(S)A 1976, s 2A.

5 D(S)A 1976, s 2(2).

may have to meet claims for loss of support brought by the deceased's relatives.

The deceased's right to damages by way of solatium is also transmissible to the executor,[1] but again in assessing damages for solatium the court is to have regard only to the period ending immediately before the deceased's death.[2] Solatium is damages for pain and suffering arising from the personal injuries. In assessing damages for solatium, the court is entitled to have regard to the extent to which the deceased suffered because he was aware that his expectation of life had been reduced as a result of the injuries.[3]

The effect of these provisions can be illustrated by the following example. A is seriously injured as a result of the negligent driving of B. A dies two years after the accident.[4] If A had begun an action against B, A's executor can continue the action provided it has not been concluded.[5] If A had not begun proceedings, A's executor can bring an action against B.[6] However, the executor's claims for patrimonial loss and solatium are restricted to losses incurred by the deceased at the date of death: any patrimonial loss referable to a period after the date of death cannot be recovered by the executor. If the action is successful,[7] the damages awarded become part of the deceased's estate. This means that they will be distributed to the deceased's legatees if there is a will or to a surviving spouse and the deceased's heirs according to the rules of intestate succession where the deceased died without a will. If A has relatives, they may have a claim against B if A's death *was* as a result of the personal injuries A has sustained. It is to the relative's dependent claim that we now turn.

---

1 Damages (Scotland) Act 1976, s 2(1). See, for example, *McManus' Executrix v Babcock Energy Ltd* 1999 SC 569 This case was distinguished in *Murray's Executrix v Greenock Dockyard Co Ltd* 2004 SLT 346 on the ground that the deceased while dying of an insidious disease had suffered less than McManus.
2 D(S)A 1976, s 2(3).
3 D(S)A 1976, s 9A(l). In an action in respect of personal injuries, damages can also be awarded in respect of patrimonial loss arising from the fact that the injured person's expectation of life has been reduced: ss 9(1) and 9(2). Where the action is brought by the executor, however, only patrimonial loss arising before the date of death can be recovered: s 2(2).
4 It is irrelevant whether or not the death was a result of A's injuries.
5 Damages (Scotland) Act 1976, s 2A(1)(b). An action is not concluded while any appeal is competent or before any appeal taken has been disposed of: s 2A(2).
6 D(S)A 1976, s 2A(1)(a).
7 Any defences, for example *volens*, which B could use in an action by A are good against an action brought by A's executor. Similarly, damages can be reduced as a result of A's contributory negligence.

(2) The dependent claims

Where a person dies in consequence of personal injuries sustained by him as a result of the defender's conduct, then if the defender would have been liable to pay damages to the deceased if he had lived, she is also liable to pay damages to a certain class of the deceased's relatives.[1] It will be seen that a relative's right to sue is *dependent* on the defender being liable to pay damages if an action had been brought by the deceased in respect of the personal injuries sustained. Accordingly, the relative's claim can be defeated if the deceased would not have succeeded against the defender, for example if the defender did not owe a duty of care to the deceased or had not broken the duty or the deceased was *volens*. The relative's damages can also be reduced on the grounds of the deceased's contributory negligence.[2]

Before a relative's claim is triggered, the deceased must have died 'in consequence of *personal injuries* sustained by *him*'.[3] The Scottish courts have experienced difficulties where a child dies shortly after birth as a result of injuries sustained while *in utero*. In *Hamilton v Fife Health Board*,[4] the Lord Ordinary (Prosser) held that parents of a child had no title to sue on the ground that before s 1(1) of the Damages (Scotland) Act 1976 was applicable the death had to have been as a result of personal injuries sustained when the deceased had legal personality. Accordingly, since their baby had died shortly after birth as a result of injuries suffered while *in utero*, s 1(1) of the 1976 Act was not triggered because a foetus has no legal personality until born alive. This narrow construction of s 1(1) of the 1976 Act was rejected by the Lord Ordinary (Lord Morton of Shuna) in *McWilliams v Lord Advocate*[5] decided seven months later.

The conflict was resolved as a result of the decision of the Inner House in an appeal from Lord Prosser's decision in the *Hamilton* case.[6] There the court held that, although the injuries were sustained by the foetus while *in utero*, the delict was completed only when the baby was born alive and suffered harm as a result of the defender's breach of a duty of care: *damnum injuria datum*. At that stage, ie when born alive, the child could have sued the defender for

---

1 D(S)A 1976, s 1(1).
2 See, for example, *Beggs v Motherwell Bridge Fabricators Ltd* 1998 SLT 1215, 1997 SCLR 1019, OH (deceased 20 per cent contributorily negligent).
3 D(S)A 1976, s 1(1) (italics added).
4 1992 SCLR 288, 1992 SLT 1026, OH.
5 1992 SCLR 954, 1992 SLT 1045, OH.
6 *Hamilton v Fife Health Board* 1993 SC 369, 1993 SCLR 408.

damages for personal injuries. Consequently, when the child died as a result of these injuries, the parents' dependent action in respect of the death arose ie s 1(1) of the Damages (Scotland) Act 1976 was triggered.

It should be noted that if the baby is not born alive, the parents do not have a dependent claim under s 1(1) of the Damages (Scotland) Act 1976. The reason is that the defender is not under any obligation to pay damages to the child because the delict was never completed since the child never had legal personality. In this situation, the mother may well have her own individual right of action if the defender's acts which injured the foetus *in utero* amounted to a breach of a duty of care which was owed to the mother herself.

The nature of the dependent claim turns on whether the pursuer is a member of the deceased's immediate family or a wider class of relatives specified in the Damages (Scotland) Act 1976.

(a) The immediate family

The deceased's immediate family consists of the following relatives:[1]

(1) the deceased's spouse;
(2) the deceased's cohabitee ie any person not being the spouse of the deceased who immediately before the death was living with the deceased as husband or wife: it will be noted that this is restricted to heterosexual cohabitation;[2]
(3) the deceased's children: this includes step-children and children accepted by the deceased as children of the family. Relationships by affinity are covered ie the deceased's daughter-in-law or son-in-law.[3] Illegitimacy is irrelevant. In *Cohen v Shaw*,[4] the Lord Ordinary (Cullen) held that a child *in utero* at the time of his father's death had title to sue as a child provided the child was born alive ie a posthumous child is included;

---

1 Damages (Scotland) Act 1976, s 10(2) and Sch 1.
2 It would appear that the 1976 Act should be amended to include same-sex cohabitants if a violation of article 8 read with article 14 of the European Convention on Human Rights is to be avoided (discrimination on the grounds of sexual orientation). The Scottish Law Commission has recommended that same-sex cohabitants should be included: *Title to Sue for Non-Patrimonial Loss* (Scot Law Com No 187) rec 10.
3 *McAllister v Imperial Chemical Industries plc* 1997 SLT 351, 1996 Rep LR 136, OH.
4 1992 SCLR 182n, 1992 SLT 1022, OH. In this case, Lord Cullen relied on the *nasciturus* principle.

(4) the deceased's parents: it is irrelevant that the deceased was illegitimate. Relationships by affinity are covered and consequently the deceased's mother-in-law or father-in-law are included.[1]

Members of the deceased's immediate family may claim damages for the following:

(1) Damages for loss of the financial support they would have obtained if the deceased had not died as a result of the injuries. This covers both loss of support up until the date of death and loss of support in the future. These claims can be substantial. Where both spouses were earning, the normal practice is to add their incomes together and deduct a percentage to reflect maintenance for the deceased. The net figure so arrived at *minus* the earnings of the surviving spouse forms the loss of dependency.[2] An appropriate multiplier is then obtained by reference to the Ogden tables.[3] Where a woman married her husband knowing that he was dying as a result of personal injuries, her action for loss of support was still relevant.[4] As the Lord Ordinary (Clyde) observed:[5] 'The proposition appeared to be that a widow could claim no loss if the death was one which could have been reasonably expected. I find no precedent or principle to justify such an approach and no warrant for it in the simple wording of the statute'.

No account is taken of a widow's remarriage prospects[6] or her entitlement to a widow's pension.[7] If the deceased had

---

1 *Monteith v Cape Insulation Ltd* 1998 SC 903. In its report *Title to Sue for Non-Patrimonial Loss* (Scot Law Com No 187) the Scottish Law Commission has recommended that relationships by affinity should be excluded. However, persons who had accepted the deceased as a child of the family should have title to sue. It also recommended that title to sue for non-patrimonial loss should be extended to include the deceased's siblings, grandparents and grandchildren.

2 *Wotherspoon v Strathclyde Regional Council* 1992 SCLR 806, 1992 SLT 1090. Where there are no dependent children, the dependency lies between 50 and 60 per cent of the combined incomes: *Phillips v Grampian Health Board* 1991 SCLR 817, 1992 SLT 659. Where there are dependent children, the dependency lies around 70–75 per cent of the combined incomes. This percentage should be proportioned between the children and the surviving spouse: *Campbell v Gillespie* 1996 SLT 503, OH. Damages for a widow's loss of support after the deceased would have retired have been assessed as half the likely pension and an appropriate multiplier: *Beggs v Motherwell Bridge Fabricators Ltd* 1997 SCLR 1019, 1998 SLT 1215.

3 *McManus' Executrix v Babcock Energy Ltd* 1999 SC 569.

4 *Phillips v Grampian Health Board* 1991 SCLR 817, 1992 SLT 659, OH.

5 1992 SLT 659 at 660.

6 Law Reform (Miscellaneous Provisions) Act 1971, s 4.

7 Damages (Scotland) Act 1976, s 1(5). See *Campbell v Gillespie* 1996 SLT 503, OH.

obtained a provisional award of damages before his death, in assessing the relative's loss of support the court takes into account such part of the provisional award as was intended to compensate the deceased for any period beyond the date when he died.[1]

(2) Such sum of damages, if any, as the court thinks just by way of compensation for all or any of the following:

    (a) distress and anxiety endured by the relative in contemplation of the suffering of the deceased before he or she died;[2]

    (b) the grief and sorrow of the relative caused by the deceased's death;[3]

    (c) the loss of such non-patrimonial benefit as the relative might be expected to derive from the deceased's society and guidance if the deceased had not died.

These heads of loss replace the former loss of society award and were introduced by the Damages (Scotland) Act 1993[4] which amended s 1 of the Damages (Scotland) Act 1976. In making such an award, the court is not obliged to ascribe any of the award to any of the heads of damage. It has been judicially recognised that the amendment was intended to clarify the previous law as it had been developed by the courts, not to change the basis of such an award.[5] Accordingly, awards under the pre-1993 law can still be looked at for guidance. It has also been accepted that the amounts awarded under the pre-1993 law had fallen out of step with the general level of awards of damages for personal injuries.[6] Juries, in particular, have reacted by making much more generous awards, for example £30,000–£35,000 to a parent for the death of an adult child.

---

1 D(S)A 1976, s 1(5A).

2 It has been questioned whether Parliament intended the court to carry out 'the difficult – and often distasteful – task of trying to assess the feelings of pain and apprehensions of mortality of someone so abruptly and severely injured as so be in the imminent and real danger of death within a period of minutes': *Beggs v Motherwell Bridge Fabricators Ltd* 1998 SLT 1215 at 1223–1224 per the Lord Ordinary (Eassie). The sum awarded was £250!

3 The pursuer is entitled to establish the gravity of her grief and sorrow by bringing evidence that she sustained a psychiatric disorder as a consequence of the death: *Gillies v Lynch* 2003 SCLR 467. However, damages for psychiatric disorder will only arise if the defender owed an independent duty of care to the pursuer to prevent her sustaining psychiatric harm: for discussion, see above pp 72 ff

4 Damages (Scotland) Act 1993, s 1(1). The heads of loss apply in relation to deaths occurring after 18 April 1993.

5 *McManus' Executrix v Babcock Energy Ltd* 1999 SC 569.

6 *McManus' Executrix v Babcock Energy Ltd* 1999 SC 569 *Murray's Executrix v Greenock Dockyard Co Ltd* 2004 SLT 346.

However, in *Shaher v British Aerospace Flying College Ltd*[1] an Extra Division considered that such awards were excessive and that £20,000 to each parent was a fair and proper award.

(3) Reasonable funeral expenses can also be awarded

(b) Specified relatives

The specified relatives include the deceased's divorced spouse, but not former cohabitee, grandparents, grandchildren, brothers and sisters, uncles and aunts, nephews and nieces and cousins. Such relatives include the appropriate 'in-laws'. Specified relatives are entitled to claim only for loss of the deceased's support and reasonable funeral expenses. The fact that the deceased had no legal obligation to support the specified relative is irrelevant: reparation is made for the loss of *de facto* financial support both before the date of death and in the future.

Transmission

The right of a relative of the deceased to a dependent claim under s 1 of the Damages (Scotland) Act 1976 can transmit to the executor of the relative if the relative dies before an award of damages is made.[2] Thus, for example, if A dies leaving his wife, B, B's right to sue as a member of A's immediate family transmits to her executor if she dies before an award of damages has been made to her. This applies where B, ie the deceased's relative, dies on or after 16 July 1992. In determining the amount of damages payable to the relative's executor, the court can only have regard to the period ending immediately before the relative's death.[3] This proviso, while obviously important in respect of the relative's claim for loss of support, could also affect a claim under s 1(4) of the 1976 Act if the relative died shortly after the deceased person.

By virtue of s 9 of the Administration of Justice Act 1982[4] both the deceased's immediate family and the specified relatives can also

---

1 2003 SLT 791.
2 Damages (Scotland) Act 1976, s 1A.
3 D(S)A 1976, s 1A.
4 *Ingham v John G Russell (Transport) Ltd* 1991 SC 201, 1991 SCLR 596; *McManus' Executrix v Babcock Energy Ltd* 1999 SC 569.

seek compensation for the loss of the deceased's gratuitous personal services to them. Otherwise,[1] no person is entitled by reason
of relationship to damages in respect of the death of another person
except by virtue of the provisions of the Damages (Scotland) Act
1976.[2]

---

1 An exception is also made for claims under s 1 of the International Transport
  Convention Act 1983.
2 D(S)A 1976, s 1(7).

CHAPTER 14

Delict and road traffic

A. INTRODUCTION

In modern society, motor vehicles which are driven carelessly are a major cause of accidents. Accidents involving vehicles are probably the area of the law of delict with which ordinary people are most likely to be involved. Where a person suffers personal injuries or damage to property as a result of a road accident, the general principles of delictual liability apply. Indeed, the paradigm of a duty of care based on reasonable foreseeability of harm[1] is the duty of care which a driver owes to other road users. The pursuer must establish a breach of duty on the part of the defender, causation and damage, as in any other action for reparation.[2] However, because of the frequency of such accidents, the common law has been supplemented by statutory provisions designed to ensure that victims of road accidents receive compensation. Moreover, the practices of insurance companies are of particular importance in this area. The 'peculiarities' of delictual liability for careless driving are discussed in this section.

B. THE STANDARD OF CARE

As stated above, before a driver is liable in delict the pursuer must establish that he was in breach of duty; in other words, that the defender did not reach the standard of care of the reasonable driver in his situation and was therefore negligent. In road traffic cases, considerable assistance in establishing that the defender did not exercise reasonable care is provided by the Highway Code, an HMSO publication. The Road Traffic Act 1988 provides:[3]

---

1 On duty of care generally, see Chapter 3 above.
2 See Chapters 5 and 6 above.
3 Road Traffic Act 1988, s 38(7).

'A failure on the part of a person to observe the provisions of the Highway Code shall not in itself render that person liable to criminal proceedings of any kind but any such failure may in any proceedings (whether civil or criminal ...) be relied upon by any party to the proceedings as tending to establish or negative any liability which is in question in those proceedings.'

Although a breach of the terms of the Highway Code will not per se establish negligence,[1] if the conduct averred is in fact in breach of the Code then this will be highly persuasive in establishing that the defender did not take reasonable care.[2]

Under the Road Traffic Act 1988, it is a criminal offence to cause death by dangerous driving;[3] to drive dangerously;[4] to drive without due care and attention;[5] and to cause death while driving without due care and attention when unfit to drive through drink or drugs.[6] Moreover, statutory regulations designed to protect road users provide offences where vehicles are (1) constructed in such a manner as to create a hazard[7] and (2) used in such a way as causes danger to other road users.[8] Although breach of these statutory provisions and regulations does not give rise to delictual liability for breach of statutory duty,[9] a conviction will be important evidence in establishing negligence on the part of the defender.

---

1 For example, merely because the defender was driving above the speed limit does not in itself establish that he was not taking reasonable care: speed is not per se the cause of an accident. See *Colborne v Wallace* 1993 GWD 17-1121 per the Sheriff Principal (Nicholson).

2 See, for example, *Robertson v J Sidney Smith* 1999 GWD 4-214. Although the Highway Code is within judicial knowledge, its provisions cannot be used in place of evidence: *Cavin v Kinnaird* 1993 SCLR 618, 1994 SLT 111.

3 Road Traffic Act 1988, s 1. For these purposes, dangerous driving means driving which falls below what would be expected of a competent and careful driver when it would be obvious to a competent and careful driver that driving in that way would be dangerous. The 1988 Act was amended by the Road Traffic Act 1991.

4 RTA 1988, s 2.

5 RTA 1988, s 3.

6 RTA 1988, s 3(A). It is enough to be above the prescribed limits for alcohol.

7 For example, it is an offence to drive a vehicle which exceeds the maximum length stipulated in the Road Vehicles (Construction and Use) Regulations 1986, SI 1986/1078.

8 For example, it is an offence to carry an object on a vehicle which overhangs that vehicle in excess of a distance prescribed in the regulations, without the leading edge being suitably marked.

9 On breach of statutory duty, see Chapter 11 above.

C. THE NATURE OF THE LOSSES

Where there has been a road accident, any damages for death or personal injury will be assessed according to the ordinary principles of delict.[1]

Where a motor car is damaged in an accident, the owner is entitled to the value of the car if it is 'a write off' or the cost of repair. In addition, the owner is entitled to loss of use of the damaged car while it is being repaired or replaced. This is calculated as being the reasonable cost of hiring a car while the damaged vehicle is off the road. Car hire companies usually require the motorist to produce an acceptable debit or credit card 'up front' so that they will be paid for the rental which the motorist will eventually recover from the defender's insurer. However, there are accident hire companies or credit hire companies which do not require a debit or credit card 'up front'. Instead, when the motorist seeks a replacement car while his own is off the road, the company assesses the merits of his case. If satisfied that the claim is unanswerable, the company provides a car and then pursues the motorist's claim against the defender's insurer. For these services, the accident or credit hire company charges an additional fee beyond the 'spot rate' for simple car hire.

In *Dimond v Lovell*[2] the House of Lords held that compensation for loss of use of a damaged car was restricted to the spot rate for hiring a car from a company other than an accident or credit hire company, ie the additional fee element charged by an accident or credit hire company was not recoverable. Given the number of claims involved, this was a very important decision for insurance companies who would have to meet only the reasonable cost of hire of the car and not the additional fees charged by an accident or credit hire company. In *Lagden v O'Connor*,[3] however, the motorist was unable to afford the cost of hiring a replacement car from a car hire company: unless he was able to use the services of an accident or credit hire company, he would have been unable to have a replacement car at all. In these circumstances the House held that the motorist's loss could be calculated on the basis of the accident or credit hire company's charges including the additional fee. In reaching this conclusion, the majority of their Lordships held that the impecuniosity of the plaintiff should be taken into account:

1 On death, see Chapter 13 above; on personal injury, see beyond Chapter 16.
2 [2002] 1 AC 384.
3 [2004] 1 All ER 277.

Lord Wright's opinion in *The Liesboch*[1] that a claimant's lack of means should *not* be taken into account when assessing his loss was no longer to be followed. The court realised that there could be difficulties in determining when a motorist was so impecunious that he was entitled to use the services of an accident or credit hire company but thought that the fear this would lead to an increase in litigation and delay in reaching settlements was exaggerated[2]. This remains to be seen.

D. OBTAINING COMPENSATION

It is obvious that cars and other motor vehicles create considerable hazards to road users, whether they be pedestrians, cyclists or other drivers. To ensure that there is a fund available to provide compensation in the event of delictual liability as a result of a road accident, the owner of a vehicle is obliged to take out insurance. A motor vehicle must be insured in respect of 'third party liability' ie it must be insured in respect of delictual liability for a person other than the owner himself. This compulsory third party insurance covers liability for causing death or personal injuries or property damage to the victim. It is a criminal offence to drive a vehicle which does not have a valid third party liability policy of insurance[3] or to allow a vehicle to be driven without such insurance.[4]

Although it is only third party liability insurance which is compulsory, many drivers purchase additional insurance to cover their own losses which are incurred in an accident for which they are wholly or partly responsible. These losses include, for example, the cost of repair of the insured's own vehicle and the cost of hiring an alternative vehicle for a limited period while the insured's vehicle is being repaired. These are known as insured losses. Where a driver purchases additional insurance as well as third party liability insurance, this is known as a comprehensive policy of insurance. Comprehensive insurance does not usually cover death or personal injuries sustained by the driver as a result of his own negligence. It

1 [1933] AC 449.
2 For example, there are persons who are quite well off but do not have credit or debit cards or persons who are unable to hire a car without using an agreed overdraft facility. Why should the latter not recover the cost of borrowing to hire the replacement car?
3 Road Traffic Act 1988, s 143(a).
4 RTA 1988, s 143(b).

is common practice for the insurer to require the holder of a comprehensive policy to meet the first part of a claim made under that policy. This is typically between the first £50 and £300 of the claim. This sum of money is known as uninsured loss. Any loss not covered by the comprehensive policy, such as a claim in respect of death or personal injury of the driver, is an uninsured loss.

To summarise the position. If, as a result of negligent driving, A causes physical harm or property damage to B, B can sue A in delict and his compensation will be covered by A's compulsory third party insurance. If B has a comprehensive insurance policy, he may elect to claim for his insured losses under the policy but he is not obliged to do so; he must, of course, sue A for any uninsured losses. If the accident was not the result of A's negligence, B cannot sue A; but if B has a comprehensive policy of insurance, he can claim under the policy for insured losses even if the accident was the result of B's negligence.

Where a person suffers property damage as a result of another driver's negligence, if he elects to claim for insured losses under his comprehensive policy of insurance then the principles of subrogation apply. This means that the insurer 'steps into the shoes' of the insured and is entitled to sue the negligent driver to recover the monies paid out under the comprehensive policy of insurance. In these circumstances, the action is raised in the name of the insured rather than in the name of the insurance company. The defender is cited personally but, again under principles of subrogation, the defender's compulsory third party insurance company will in effect take over the defence if the action has been intimated to them.

In practice, insurers may have inter-office agreements whereby actions do not have to be raised even if delictual liability is disputed. In order to reduce their overall expenses, the insurers accept that they will meet their own outlays under the appropriate insurance policies without attempting to recover these from each other in defended civil proceedings. However, such agreements, often known as 'knock for knock' agreements, are becoming less common because insurers are battling to minimise losses. Insurers who previously would have 'confirmed' a 'knock for knock' agreement with the third party insurers are resorting to litigation to recover their outlays under their comprehensive insurance policy in full.

It should be emphasised that whether or not a comprehensive insurer confirms a 'knock for knock' agreement with a negligent driver's third party insurer, this does not affect the insured driver's right to sue the negligent driver personally in delict to recover his uninsured losses. If he is successful, he is entitled to look to the defender's compulsory third party insurer for any sums not recovered from the defender which are due under the decree provided appropriate intimation of the action has been made to the insurance company.

An insurance company may be entitled under general principles of contract to refuse to indemnify the insured losses. This could arise, for example, if the insured was in material breach of the terms of the policy of insurance by not paying the premiums or if the policy could be rescinded by the insurance company on the ground of misrepresentation. However, where a pursuer successfully obtains decree against a negligent driver and seeks to recover his compensation from the defender's compulsory third party insurer, under the Road Traffic Act 1988 the insurance company cannot refuse payment on the ground that under general principles of contract it is not bound to indemnify the insured defender unless the insurance company takes steps to obtain a declarator from the court that it is entitled to avoid the policy.

Similarly, should a driver cancel a compulsory third party liability policy of insurance, the insurer remains liable for any losses suffered by a third party in a subsequent accident caused by the negligence of the driver provided the contract has not been rescinded. The insurance company can then recover its outlays from the 'former' insured driver. In these circumstances, the insurer is known as a 'Road Traffic Act insurer'. The Road Traffic Act insurer will escape liability if the company does not retain an insurable interest in the vehicle. This would occur, for example, if the 'former' insured driver sold the car with the actual policy document in the glove compartment!

Motor Insurers' Bureau

The legislation requiring owners of vehicles to have third party liability insurance was clearly designed to protect third parties. Such protection is not afforded where an individual flouts the law and drives a vehicle without appropriate insurance cover, although, of course, it is possible in these circumstances that the defender will have sufficient assets to meet a successful action for reparation.

In order to protect third parties in this situation, a body called the Motor Insurers' Bureau (MIB) entered into an agreement with the Ministry of Transport on 17 June 1946 to provide from 1 July 1946 compensation for victims of road accidents where the injured parties were unable to obtain compensation due to the defender's lack of appropriate third party insurance. There have been various revised agreements since then, but the present text covering accidents on or after 31 December 1988 provides compensation for victims of those accidents in respect of death, personal injury and property damage. The December 1988 Agreement followed an EEC Directive[1] on motor insurance requiring member states to extend third party insurance to include property damage.

Clause 2 of the agreement provides that the MIB will 'pay or satisfy or cause to be satisfied to or to the satisfaction of the person or persons in whose favour the judgment was given' any sum due under the decree or judgment which remains unsatisfied for a period of seven days from the time at which the decree or judgment should have been in force. The MIB's liability includes any element of interest or expenses included in the decree.

This obligation is subject to certain conditions, the most important being that notification of the commencement of the proceedings must be given to the MIB before, or within seven days after, the commencement of the proceedings. The claimant must take all reasonable steps to obtain judgment or decree against all those liable for the death, personal injury or property damage, and against any principal where such a person is a servant or agent. Additionally, the MIB will have no liability where the claim is in respect of damage to a motor vehicle where the claimant knew or ought to have reasonably known that at the time of the use of the vehicle it was not properly insured in terms of the Road Traffic Act 1988.

Similarly, where the claim is in respect of personal injury, the MIB has no liability where the claimant was a passenger in or on a vehicle which he knew or should reasonably have known was not insured in terms of the Road Traffic Act 1988, although this exception applies only where the decree the MIB is being asked to satisfy is obtained against the owner or person using the vehicle in which the claimant was a passenger. The MIB has no liability if the accident does not take place on a road or highway to which the public has access.[2]

The MIB's liability in respect of property claims is limited by the fact that there is currently a £175 excess payable, ie the first £175 is not paid. The Bureau's maximum liability is £250,000. The MIB is only required to compensate for damage which is required to be insured against by law, ie under compulsory third party insurance.

---

1 Second Council Directive 84/5, OJ L8 11.1.84 p 17. This Directive has been held not to be directly effective: *Evans v Motor Insurers' Bureau* [1999] Lloyd's Rep JR 30.
2 *Clarke v Kato* [1998] 4 All ER 417, [1998] 1 WLR 1697, HL (MIB not liable where accident took place in car park).

Where an offending driver cannot be traced, this agreement is of no effect. However, a sister agreement, referred to as 'the MIB untraced drivers' agreement' then comes into play. Amongst other variations, it should be noted that this scheme differs from the foregoing by excluding claims for property damage. Moreover, it covers only claims for death or personal injury as a result of accidents in or after May 1969.[1] There have been a number of revised agreements: the fourth agreement, operates in respect of accidents on or after 1 July 1996.

For accidents on or after 1 October 1999, the relevant agreement is that of 13 August 1999. Under clause 5 the MIB undertakes to pay any sum due under a decree which remains unsatisfied for a period of seven days after it could have been enforced. Notice must be given to the MIB within 14 days of commencement of proceedings: commencement of proceedings is the date of service. At least 35 days' notice requires to be given if an application is made to the court for decree.

In cases of personal injury the MIB has no liability where the claimant was a passenger in a vehicle which he knew or ought to have known was stolen or was being used in the course of a crime or was being used to escape from lawful apprehension. In respect of property damage there is now an excess of £300.

Owing to the expenses involved in pursuing a claim against an uninsured driver, the MIB has now arranged free legal expenses cover for which the pursuer can apply when a claim is being brought against such a driver. The scheme, MIBLES, is available in respect of claims made on or after 13th November 2003.

Untraced Drivers Agreement

For accidents on or after 14 February 2003, the relevant agreement is that of 7 February 2003. It covers property damage as well as personal injury. Application must be made within three years of the injury being sustained or within 9 months if there is a claim for property damage.

---

1 Second Council Directive 84/5 does not cover the circumstances where the driver cannot be traced.

CHAPTER 15

Defamation and verbal injury

A. INTRODUCTION

The law has long recognised a person's interest in her honour and reputation. Accordingly, where A makes a false statement about B with the intention of harming B's honour or reputation then B has a delictual action against A. In Roman law, there was a specific remedy, the *actio injuriarum*, which provided compensation (solatium) for insult *(contumelia)*. In order to succeed, it had to be established that a false statement was made with the intention of insulting the victim. It followed, therefore, that the action lay even if the statement had only been made to the victim herself, ie where the statement had not been made to a third party. If the statement had been published to a third party and, as a result, the victim suffered economic (patrimonial) loss, in the later Roman Empire such loss could, in theory at least, be recovered under general principles of *culpa: damnum injuria datum*. Accordingly, where intention to insult could not be established, but the statement was made carelessly to a third party, the only damages that could be obtained were for patrimonial loss: but, if intention to insult could be established, solatium would also be available under the *actio injuriarum*. Given the influence of Roman law, Scots law could have developed a simple set of principles:

(1) if A makes an untrue statement about B to B, with the intention of insulting B, then B can sue A for solatium even if the statement is not published to a third party, provided intention to insult can be proved;

(2) if A makes an untrue statement about B to C, then B could recover damages for patrimonial loss on the basis of *culpa* but only obtain solatium if intention to insult could also be established.

But since *culpa* covers both intentional and unintentional, but careless, conduct, the fact that the remedies were originally based on two separate, if related, principles, ie *culpa* and the *actio injuriarum*, was overlooked.[1] Moreover, the law in this area was influenced by the English law of libel and slander with its emphasis on the defendant's malice. As a result, the Scots law of defamation and verbal injury is complex and contentious, and it is difficult to reconcile all the authorities.

The modern law appears to proceed on two major delicts: defamation and verbal injury. These will be considered in turn.

B. DEFAMATION

Defamation is the delict which is committed when a person makes an injurious and false imputation against the character or reputation of another person. The victim is usually a natural person but could be a trading company,[2] partnership or voluntary association. However, since legal persons such as companies have no feelings, they can only recover for patrimonial loss and not solatium. Because, by statute, it does not have corporate status, a trade union cannot sue.[3] A local authority also cannot sue,[4] but if individuals, for example councillors, are defamed by attacks on a council, they can sue in their own right. Where a person has died, the executor can continue any action raised by the deceased before his death and recover both solatium and patrimonial loss. If no action has been raised by the deceased, the executor can raise an action but can only recover any patrimonial loss to the estate incurred before the death.[5] These rules are not affected by the Damages (Scotland) Act 1976.[6]

---

1 For discussion of the confusion, see T B Smith *A Short Commentary on the Law of Scotland* (W Green, 1962) pp 724–732.
2 *Incorporation of Fleshers of Dumfries v Rankine* Dec 10 1816 FC. If the individual board members are also defamed, they can sue in their own right. If the defamation is actually of the individuals, the company cannot sue.
3 Trade Union and Labour Relations (Consolidation) Act 1992, s 10(1); *Electrical, Electronic, Telecommunication and Plumbing Union v Times Newspapers Ltd* [1980] QB 585, [1980] 1 All ER 1097.
4 *Derbyshire County Council v Times Newspapers Ltd* [1993] AC 534, [1993] 1 All ER 1011, HL. Similarly, the government cannot sue *qua* government; cf individual ministers. This principle has been extended to political parties: *Goldsmith v Bhoyrul* [1998] QB 459, [1997] 4 All ER 268, QBD.
5 Ie the executor cannot recover solatium. See generally *Neilson v Rodger* (1853) 16 D 325; *Auld v Shairp* (1874) 2 R 191; *Smith v Duncan Stewart & Co Ltd (No 2)* 1961 SC 91, 1961 SLT 67.
6 Damages (Scotland) Act 1976, s 2(4), as substituted by the Damages (Scotland) Act 1993, s 3. On the 1976 Act generally, see pp 243 ff above.

For an action to be successful, it must be shown that the defender made a false statement which was defamatory of the pursuer with the intention to harm the pursuer's character or reputation. However, and this is very important, if the pursuer proves that the statement concerned the pursuer (a question of fact) and is defamatory (a question of law), then the court presumes that the statement is false and was made with the intention to harm him. The onus thereafter lies on the *defender* to prove either that the statement was true (*veritas*) or that it was made without the intention to harm the pursuer. The onus on the defender to justify the 'essence or sting' of any attack on an individual's reputation has been held not to be a disproportionate interference with the right to freedom of expression under article 10 of the European Convention on Human Rights.[1] Moreover, the law will also presume that a person will be upset if defamed and it is therefore not necessary for the pursuer to prove loss in respect of insult (solatium); but if patrimonial loss is also claimed, such loss has to be established by the pursuer.

(1) The false statement

The pursuer must establish that the defender made a statement about the pursuer: this is a question of fact. The statement will usually take the form of words, written or spoken. Scots law does not make a distinction between oral and written communication for the purpose of the law of defamation.[2] However, any form of communication can amount to a statement so that it could consist of a television or radio broadcast, a picture, cartoon or effigy.[3] In Scots law the statement does not have to be communicated to a third party: it is enough if it is communicated only to the victim himself.[4] In these circumstances, however, only damages for insult (solatium) can be awarded. Before damages for patrimonial loss can be awarded, the statement must have been published to third parties.[5] If a defamatory statement is repeated, every person who

1 *Berezovsky v Forbes Inc (No 2)* [2001] EMLR 48, CA.
2 In English law such a distinction is made: oral communication constitutes slander; written communication constitutes libel.
3 In *Monson v Tussauds Ltd* [1894] 1 QB 671, CA, placing a waxworks effigy of the plaintiff who had been acquitted of murder in the Chamber of Horrors along with convicted murderers constituted a slanderous statement.
4 *Ramsay v Mackay* (1890) 18 R 130.
5 If the pursuer published the statement to a third party, he is personally barred from claiming patrimonial loss: *Will v Sneddon, Campbell and Munro* 1931 SC 164, 1931 SLT 125.

repeats the statement commits a separate delict. So, for example, if A makes a defamatory statement about B to a newspaper reporter who repeats it to his editor who publishes it in his newspaper, then the editor and the reporter, as well as A, are liable to B in delict.[1]

It should be emphasised that once the pursuer has established that a defamatory statement was made by the defender, the law *presumes* that the statement is false. The onus then lies on the defender to show that the facts in the statement were true (*veritas*). But before the pursuer has the benefit of this presumption, the statement must be defamatory. It is to that concept that we now turn.

(2) Defamatory nature of the statement

A defamatory statement is one which 'tends to lower [the pursuer] in the estimation of right thinking members of society generally'.[2] Although it is settled that some types of statement are clearly defamatory, the categories of defamation – like the categories of negligence[3] – are never closed. The question whether or not a statement is defamatory is one of law, to be decided by the court.[4] The test is objective, ie whether the reasonable person would decide that this type of statement was defamatory. The statement must be read in the context of the publication as a whole.[5]

The meaning of the material is that which an ordinary, reasonable, fair-minded reader would infer from the language, not what the author intended the statement to mean.[6] It is the general view of society as a whole which is important, not the views of the section of society in which the pursuer moves. As the mores of society change, what might once have been regarded as derogatory by right-thinking members of society in the past, may not be so

---

1 See, for example, *Carroll v British Broadcasting Corpn* 1997 SLT (Sh Ct) 23.
2 *Sim v Stretch* [1936] 2 All ER 1237, HL, at 1240 per Lord Atkin.
3 *Donoghue v Stevenson* 1932 SC (HL) 31 at 70 per Lord MacMillan.
4 Accordingly, the defence can make a plea to the relevancy of the issue.
5 *Charleston v News Group Newspapers Ltd* [1995] 2 AC 65, [1995] 2 All ER 313, HL (defendant published pornographic photograph superimposing the plaintiffs' heads on the bodies: accompanying article explained that the plaintiffs had been victims of an illicit computer game. The meaning of the material had to be determined on the basis that the reasonable person would have read the article and not simply looked at the photograph and headlines). See also *Norman v Future Publishing Ltd* [1999] EMLR 325; *McCann v Scottish Media Newspapers Ltd* 1999 GWD 10-473.
6 *Charleston v News Group Newspapers Ltd* [1995] 2 AC 65, [1995] 2 All ER 313, HL; *McCann v Scottish Media Newspapers Ltd* 1999 GWD 10-473.

regarded by them today. Thus, for example, in 1934 it was thought to be defamatory falsely to state that a woman had been the victim of rape.[1] That might not be regarded as defamatory today when victims of rape are treated with sympathy rather than shunned.

The following are examples of defamatory statements but it must always be remembered that these are only examples and that other types of defamatory statements may arise.

(a) Imputations on moral character

It is defamatory to undermine a person's moral character. Thus it is defamatory to call a woman a prostitute or an adulteress or even to suggest that she lacks 'proper womanly delicacy'.[2] At one time it was clearly defamatory to state that a person was homosexual.[3] But with the increasing tolerance of homosexuality, it has been observed judicially that an allegation of homosexuality should no longer be regarded as defamatory per se.[4] Nevertheless, allegations that a nun was dishonest, unchaste and a lesbian have been held to be capable of amounting to defamation.[5]

Defamatory statements are not restricted to imputations on sexual morality. Thus it is defamatory to call a person a hypocrite.[6] It appears no longer to be defamatory merely to call a person a liar or a 'stranger to the truth':[7] but to call a person a thief and a liar has been held to be defamatory.[8] To state that a woman whose child had died was a heartless and uncaring mother is defamatory.[9]

(b) Imputations of criminality

It is defamatory to accuse a person of a serious crime which ordinary people do not commit or condone, such as murder[10] or theft.[11]

---

1 *Youssoupoff v Metro–Goldwyn–Mayer Pictures Ltd* (1934) 50 TLR 581, CA.
2 *Cuthbert v Linklater* 1935 SLT 94. But would this be regarded as defamatory today?
3 *AB v XY* 1917 SC 15, 1916 2 SLT 210; *Kerr v Kennedy* [1942] 1 KB 409, [1942] 1 All ER 412.
4 *Quilty v Windsor* 1999 SLT 346.
5 *Prophit v British Broadcasting Corpn* 1997 SLT 745, OH.
6 *Stein v Beaverbrook Newspapers Ltd* 1968 SC 272, 1968 SLT 401.
7 *Carroll v British Broadcasting Corpn* 1997 SLT (Sh Ct) 23. Cf *Watson v Duncan* (1890) 17 R 404.
8 *Gilbert v Yorston* 1996 SCLR 1122, 1997 SLT 879, OH.
9 *McCabe v News Group Newspapers Ltd* 1992 SLT 707, OH.
10 *Waddell v British Broadcasting Corpn* 1973 SLT 246; *Berezovsky v Forbes Inc (No 2)* [2001] EMLR 45, CA.
11 *Sutherland v British Telecommunications plc* 1989 SLT 531.

It would not perhaps be defamatory to accuse a person of careless driving (or tax evasion?). If the defender pleads *veritas*, he can rely on the fact that the pursuer committed such a crime even if the offence is 'spent' under the Rehabilitation of Offenders Act 1974.[1] Similarly, it is defamatory to say that a person should be in jail since this implies that he is guilty of a crime.

(c) Imputations against competence or conduct

Statements which disparage a person's professional competence or conduct are defamatory, for example, to accuse a doctor of gross professional negligence[2] or a professor of his inability to teach[3] (or write textbooks on delict?). Allegations of conduct which is unprofessional in the circumstances are also defamatory, for example, to accuse a solicitor of conducting a case for his own – as opposed to his client's – interests,[4] or to allege that a prison warden had sexual relations with a prisoner.[5]

(d) Imputations of financial unsoundness

It is defamatory falsely to allege that a person is insolvent[6] or is unwilling[7] or unable to pay his debts.[8]

(e) Disparaging public character

Persons who enter public life are expected to be able to withstand a degree of criticism[9] – or even ridicule[10] – in respect of the way in which they carry out their public duties. However, although the test may be stricter, allegations of, for example, dishonesty in carrying out a public office would, it is thought, constitute defamation. Statements undermining a public figure's sexual morality, ie

1 Rehabilitation of Offenders Act 1974, s 4.
2 *Simmers v Morton* (1900) 8 SLT 285, OH.
3 *Auld v Shairp* (1875) 2 R 940.
4 *McRostie v Ironside* (1849) 12 D 74.
5 *Winter v News Scotland Ltd* 1991 SLT 828.
6 *AB v CD* (1904) 7 F 72.
7 *Outram v Reid* (1852) 14 D 577.
8 *Mazure v Stubbs Ltd* 1919 SC (HL) 112, 1919 2 SLT 160.
9 *Mutch v Robertson* 1981 SLT 217.
10 *McLaughlan v Orr Pollock & Co* (1894) 22 R 38 at 42 per Lord McLaren; *Brooks v Lind* 1997 Rep LR 83, 1997 GWD 13-570 (pursuer was said to be part of the council 'mafia' and a joint venture he was involved in was described as 'sheer lunacy and gross administration': held not to be defamatory).

concerned with his private as opposed to public life, are, of course, defamatory. In England, it has been held to be potentially defamatory to call a famous actor 'hideously ugly': this could lead an ordinary person to infer that he was repulsive and consequently lower him in the public's estimation and make him an object of ridicule.[1]

(f) Imputations on health

It is defamatory falsely to allege that a person is insane or has obnoxious physical defects or is suffering from certain illnesses, such as venereal disease or AIDS.

A statement or action may appear to be harmless, yet when taken in the context of the facts and circumstances in which it was made, a defamatory meaning may be inferred. For example, it is not prima facie defamatory to display a wax effigy of a person in a waxworks: but to put it in the Chamber of Horrors along with those of convicted murderers implies that the person concerned is also a murderer.[2] Similarly, to announce the birth of twins to a married couple in a newspaper appears innocuous until it is appreciated that they married only a month before, thus implying pre-marital sexual intercourse.[3] In this situation, Scots law allows a pursuer to plead the facts and circumstances from which the defamatory meaning of the statement or act can be drawn. This is known as 'the doctrine of innuendo'.

The onus rests on the pursuer to state the meaning of the acts or statement in the light of the relevant facts and circumstances. Thus, in *Cuthbert v Linklater*[4] the pursuer argued that the defender, an author, had defamed her when a female character in his novel took a Union Jack from Edinburgh Castle and placed it in a men's public urinal. An ardent Scottish nationalist, the pursuer had in fact taken a Union Jack from Stirling Castle and had tossed it at a guard. Consequently, by innuendo, a reasonable reader would assume that the character in the novel was meant to be her and that she was capable of acting indelicately. The court accepted the argument.[5]

---

1 *Berkoff v Burchill* [1996] 4 All ER 1008, [1997] EMLR 139, CA.
2 *Monson v Tussauds Ltd* [1894] 1 QB 671, CA.
3 *Morrison v Ritchie & Co* (1902) 4 F 645.
4 1935 SLT 94.
5 See also *Wragg v D C Thomson & Co Ltd* 1909 2 SLT 315, where a newspaper published an article that a certain George Reeves had shot his wife twice and then killed himself. The paper omitted to mention that the incident took place in the USA. At the time it was published, George Reeves, a famous music hall artiste, was appearing in Glasgow. The court held that there was an innuendo that the incident referred to him.

The test on whether an innuendo can be inferred is that of the ordinary reasonable person,[1] ie whether a reasonable person would regard the words as offensive if placed in the same position as the pursuer. The question whether the statement or act plus the innuendo placed upon them by the reasonable person amounts to defamation is a matter of law to be decided by the court. It is a question of fact whether the statement or act was taken as having a defamatory meaning by those to whom it was actually communicated.

(3) Intention to harm the pursuer

Once it has been established that a statement is defamatory, not only is it presumed to be false but it is also presumed that the statement was made with the intention of harming the particular pursuer (malice). A defender can rebut the presumption of falsehood by pleading *veritas,* ie that the statement was in fact true.[2] The question then arises whether or not the defender can rebut the presumption of malice by proving that he did not intend to harm the particular pursuer.

Authority suggests that the presumption of intention to harm cannot be rebutted. In *Hutton (E) & Co v Jones,*[3] a newspaper published an article about an apparently fictitious character, Artemus Jones. This article contained material which would have been defamatory if Artemus Jones was an actual person. However, there was a 'real' Artemus Jones who sued the newspaper. The defence was that since the newspaper did not know of the existence of the plaintiff, it could not have intended to defame him. The House of Lords rejected this defence.

Although *Hutton v Jones* was an English case, Scots law appears to be similar. In *Outram v Reid,*[4] a newspaper published a list of bankruptcies including 'John Reid, wine and spirit merchant, Glasgow'. There were two John Reids who were wine and spirit merchants in Glasgow, one of whom was indeed bankrupt, while the other was solvent. The latter successfully sued in defamation even though the defender was not aware of his existence. Similarly, the unfortunate couple, the birth of whose twins was prematurely

---

1 *Duncan v Associated Scottish Newspapers Ltd* 1929 SC 14 at 21 per Lord Anderson.
2 On *veritas,* see pp 268 ff below.
3 [1910] AC 20.
4 (1852) 14 D 577.

announced, sued successfully in spite of the fact that the defender did not know of their existence nor had intended any harm.[1] And Mr Reeves was also able to sue even though the story concerned another Mr Reeves who lived in America.[2]

Although the issue appears to be settled, it is the present writer's view that the solution adopted by the courts is unprincipled. Instead, the courts should have accepted that the defender did not have the intention to insult the pursuers in these cases and accordingly no damages should have been awarded for solatium. However, as is clear from the Scottish decisions, there was an element of fault on the part of the defenders in publishing the statements. In *Outram v Reid*,[3] for example, the defender omitted the address of the bankrupt Mr Reid which had been published in the Official Gazette: if it had been published in the newspaper, the confusion would have been avoided. Again, in *Morrison v Ritchie & Co*,[4] the defender was criticised by the court for failing to check that the facts in the announcement were accurate. Given that it is (at least) arguable that the defenders were at fault in these cases, the pursuers were entitled to damages for patrimonial loss on general principles of *culpa* but not solatium. They would also have had to establish patrimonial loss which would have been difficult in *Morrison*. But until the issue is reconsidered by the Inner House, it must be accepted that the presumption of intention to insult is now irrebuttable and solatium, as well as patrimonial loss, can be recovered in these circumstances.

It is unlikely that the matter will be litigated. The Defamation Act 1996[5] provides a statutory defence. The publisher can make an offer of amends. An offer of amends can be made even if the statement was not made innocently.[6] The offer must contain a correction and an apology which can then be published: it should also provide for compensation.[7] Once the offer is accepted, the aggrieved party can no longer sue for defamation but can enforce the offer by proceedings in court.[8] The court can award compensation if this has not been agreed by the parties.[9]

1 *Morrison v Ritchie & Co* (1902) 4 F 645.
2 *Wragg v D C Thomson & Co Ltd* 1909 2 SLT 315.
3 (1852) 14 D 577.
4 (1902) 4 F 645.
5 Defamation Act 1996, ss 2–4.
6 Ie even if the publisher intended to refer to the pursuer or did not take reasonable care in relation to the publication.
7 DeA 1996, s 2(4).
8 DeA 1996, s 3(2) and (3).
9 DeA 1996, s 3(5).

If an offer of amends is made but not accepted by the aggrieved party, this is a defence in any subsequent action for defamation.[1] But this defence is not available if the defender knew or had reason to believe that the statement referred to the aggrieved party *and* was false and defamatory of the pursuer: but it is presumed until the contrary is shown that the defender did not know and had no reason to believe that was so.[2]

(4) Defences

(a) Veritas

As we have seen, if a statement is defamatory, the law presumes that it is false. This presumption can be rebutted. The onus lies on the defender to prove that the statement was true.[3] If truth (*veritas*) is established, this is a complete defence. What is necessary to establish *veritas* will depend on the nature of the defamatory statement. To allege that someone is a murderer can be justified by proof of one act of murder; but to say someone is a thief implies that he is currently dishonest and *veritas* is not established simply by showing he was twice convicted of petty theft 23 years before.[4] A similar approach is taken in respect of immorality: to allege that a 50-year—old man is homosexual would not be justified by establishing that he engaged in homosexual acts with the captain of the First XV when he was a schoolboy.[5]

If more than one fact is alleged, *veritas* will operate only if all the facts which are defamatory are proved true.[6] Conversely, if some non-defamatory facts are admitted to be false, then the defence will still succeed if the defamatory facts can, nevertheless, be shown to be true.[7] By s 5 of the Defamation Act 1952 it is provided that:

---

1 Defamation Act 1996, s 4(2).
2 DeA 1996, s 4(3). In *Milne v Express Newspapers* [2003] 1 All ER 482, it was held that the defence will not be lost unless the publisher was in bad faith, ie 'reason to believe' that a statement was false meant choosing to ignore or shutting the mind to information which should have led to a belief, not merely a suspicion, that the allegation was false.
3 *Baigent v British Broadcasting Corpn* 1999 GWD 10-474.
4 *Fletcher v Wilsons* (1885) 12 R 683.
5 Assuming, of course, that it is still defamatory to allege that a person is homosexual. On allegations of immorality, see *Brownlie v Thomson* (1859) 21 D 480 at 483 per Lord Murray.
6 *Fairbairn v Scottish National Party* 1979 SC 393, 1980 SLT 149.
7 *Sutherland v Stopes* [1925] AC 47, HL.

'in an action for defamation in respect of words containing two or more distinct charges against a pursuer, a defence of *veritas* shall not fail by reason only that the truth of every charge is not proved if the words not proved to be true do not materially injure the pursuer's reputation having regard to the truth of the remaining charges.'[1]

If, however, the allegations are not separable but are part and parcel of a single defamatory allegation, the section does not apply.

(b) In rixa

Statements made *in rixa*, ie during a quarrel, an argument or a brawl, do not give rise to an action in defamation unless the pursuer can prove that they were made with intent to injure.[2] The defence is more likely to succeed if the defender has apologised. It is *not* a defence that the statement was made as a joke.[3]

(c) Vulgar abuse

If the words used amount to mere vulgar abuse, then no action in defamation lies. To call someone a 'bitch' or a 'dickhead' is not actionable, since it is not meant to be taken seriously.

(d) Fair retort

If A makes a statement about B, B is entitled to the opportunity to reply. If B's retort is defamatory, it is not actionable unless A can prove that it was said with intent to injure.[4]

(e) Fair comment

Where a defamatory remark takes the form of an opinion, for example that a novel is badly written or an actor gave a bad performance, the defender can plead the defence of fair comment. In

---

1 Section 5 does not have to be construed so as to bring lesser meanings of the words complained of within the adjective 'distinct': *Berezovsky v Forbes Inc (No 2)* [2001] EMLR 45, CA.
2 *Christie v Robertson* (1899) 1 F 1155; *Carroll v British Broadcasting Corpn* 1997 SLT (Sh Ct) 23.
3 *Prophit v British Broadcasting Corpn* 1997 SLT 745.
4 *Gray v Scottish Society for the Prevention of Cruelty to Animals* (1890) 17 R 1185; *Carroll v British Broadcasting Corpn* 1997 SLT (Sh Ct) 23.

order to succeed, the defender must prove: (1) that the statement is a comment on a fact or facts; (2) that the facts upon which the comment is made are true;[1] and (3) that the facts concern some matter of public interest. If this can be proved, the onus shifts to the pursuer to show that the comment was made with the intention of harming the pursuer. The comment must be honestly made and relevant to the facts upon which it was based. Thus, a theatre critic who criticises a play must honestly hold the opinion that the play is bad[2] and must restrict his comments to the play rather than the playwright.[3]

(f) Privilege

A person who makes a defamatory statement may have the defence of privilege. In certain situations, public policy demands that a person should be free to speak without fear of litigation on the grounds of defamation. There are two forms of privilege: absolute privilege and qualified privilege.

(i) Absolute privilege   Where a statement is protected by absolute privilege, it cannot form the basis of an action for defamation or verbal injury.[4] It does not matter that the statement is defamatory or was made with the intention to harm the victim (malice). The following situations are covered by absolute privilege:

(a) Statements made in the Westminster Parliament. Any statement made in the Westminster Parliament has the protection of absolute privilege. This includes statements made in parliamentary committees. The statement does not have to be relevant to the proceedings. It is not restricted to statements made by members of either House: it would include, for example, a statement made by a witness giving evidence to a Select Committee. It does not extend to statements made by members of Parliament outside the Houses. Where the conduct of a person in or in relation to proceedings in the Westminster Parliament is in issue in defamation proceedings, that person

---

1 Where the statement contains facts and opinion, the defence of fair comment is not lost if the facts upon which the opinion is based are true even if other facts are false: Defamation Act 1952, s 6.
2 *Turner v Metro–Goldwyn–Mayer Pictures Ltd* [1950] 1 All ER 449, [1950] WN 83, HL; *Telnikoff v Matusevitch* [1992] 2 AC 343, [1991] 4 All ER 817, HL.
3 *Merivale v Carson* (1887) 20 QBD 275, CA.
4 On verbal injury, see pp 276 ff below.

can waive, for the purpose of the defamation action, the privilege that prevents proceedings in Parliament from being impeached or questioned in court.[1] This is to enable an MP, for example, to rely on his own conduct in Parliament in order to pursue an action of defamation while, of course, retaining the defence of absolute privilege for statements he has made in Parliament!

(b) Statements made in judicial proceedings. A statement made by a judge in the course of judicial proceedings is protected by absolute privilege even if it was made maliciously.[2] However, the statement must be made while the judge is acting judicially ie it must be relevant to the case which is subject to the proceedings.[3] Advocates or solicitors pleading the case also enjoy absolute privilege,[4] provided the statement is relevant to the case. Witnesses giving evidence have absolute privilege as long as the evidence is pertinent to the case.[5] Any findings of fact by a jury are subject to absolute privilege. But parties to a civil action do not enjoy absolute privilege – only qualified privilege.[6] Absolute privilege extends in like way to the participants in quasi-judicial proceedings or tribunals, for example, courts martial, public inquiries, arbitrations, children's hearings, employment tribunals and disciplinary tribunals.[7]

(c) Reports authorised by the Westminster Parliament. Reports of proceedings and papers etc published by or under the authority of either House of Parliament attract absolute privilege.[8] Fair and accurate reports of proceedings before a court are absolutely privileged provided they are published contemporaneously with the proceedings.[9]

---

1 Defamation Act 1996, s 13; *Hamilton v Al Fayed* [2001] 1 AC 395.
2 *Haggart's Trustees v Lord President Hope* (1824) 2 Sh App 125, HL; *Primrose v Waterston* (1902) 4 F 783, 10 SLT 37.
3 *Watt v Thomson* (1870) 8 M (HL) 77.
4 *Rome v Watson* (1898) 25 R 733, 5 SLT 377. The privilege extends to written pleadings.
5 *Watson v McEwan* (1905) 7 F (HL) 109. This privilege extends to statements made in precognitions: *B v Burns* 1994 SLT 250.
6 See p 274 below.
7 *Thomson v Ross* 2002 SLT 807 (Scottish Solicitors Discipline Tribunal).
8 Parliamentary Papers Act 1840.
9 Defamation Act 1996, s 14. Courts include any court in the United Kingdom, the European Court of Justice, the European Court of Human Rights and United Nations' international criminal tribunals.

(d) Any statement made in proceedings of the Scottish Parliament and any publication of any such statement authorised by the Scottish Parliament are absolutely privileged.[1]

(e) Miscellaneous. The Lord Advocate is absolutely privileged in respect of what he does in relation to prosecutions on indictment. This protection extends to procurators fiscal and Advocates Depute acting on the Lord Advocate's instructions. Ministers of the Crown are also protected provided the statement is made in the proper exercise of their functions. Reports of the various ombudsmen are also absolutely privileged.

(ii) Qualified privilege   When a statement is protected by qualified privilege, the defender is assumed to have acted in good faith and an action of defamation or verbal injury[2] will not succeed unless the pursuer can show that the statement was made with the intention of harming the pursuer (ie with malice). Qualified privilege arises in the following circumstances:

(a) Duty or interest to speak. Where a person has a legal duty to speak, the statement is protected by qualified privilege. The protection extends to situations where there is a moral or social duty to speak, for example, to report a crime or inform a reporter to a children's hearing of child abuse. Complaints to the chief constable about the conduct of police officers attracts protection if an action of defamation is brought against the complainer by the officer who was the subject of the complaint.[3] Similarly, a letter to the deputy chief executive of the prison service about the unfitness of an employee to serve as an officer has been held to attract qualified privilege.[4] A person who gives a reference enjoys qualified privilege.[5] Whether a situation involves a duty to speak which attracts qualified privilege is a question of law to be determined by a court. Qualified privilege also arises where a person has an interest to speak, for example, replying to criticism.[6] In these situations, the

---

1 Scotland Act 1998, s 41.
2 On verbal injury, see pp 276 ff below.
3 *Fraser v Mirza* 1993 SC (HL) 27, 1993 SLT 527.
4 *Quilty v Windsor* 1999 SLT 346. In *Pearson v Educational Institute of Scotland* 1997 SC 245, 1998 SLT 189, a report on the competency of the pursuer to be head of a college, which the union had sent on to a government department, was held to attract qualified privilege.
5 *Farquhar v Neish* (1890) 17 R 716. However, even if not made maliciously, the writer of the reference may be liable in negligence: *Spring v Guardian Assurance plc* [1995] 2 AC 296, [1994] 3 All ER 129, HL, discussed at p 92 above.
6 *Campbell v Cochrane* (1905) 8 F 205; *Carroll v British Broadcasting Corpn* 1997 SLT (Sh Ct) 23.

person who receives the statement must have a reciprocal interest in the information. So, for example, a complaint about the conduct of a police officer is protected by qualified privilege if made to the relevant chief constable but not if made to a newspaper editor.

In *Reynolds v Times Newspapers*[1] the House of Lords held that qualified privilege would protect the publication of material which the writer was under a moral or social duty to publish and the intended recipients had an interest in receiving[2]. In determining whether the defence was appropriate the court should consider all the circumstances of the case including the nature, status and source of the material. This is known as the 'duty–interest' test or 'right to know' test. The public has an interest in the maintenance of free expression through the promotion of a free press:[3] on the other hand, publishers, editors and journalists have a duty to act responsibly. Responsible journalism for this purpose is not determined by whether the published material was in fact true or false: the question is whether the public has an interest in its publication irrespective of its truth and whether there was some evidence to support the allegations.[4] In *GKR Karate v Yorkshire Post Newspapers Ltd (No 2)*[5] qualified privilege applied to an article in a local newspaper alleging malpractice by a karate instructor who gave classes in the area. The journalist had a social and moral duty to write the article and the local inhabitants had a proper interest in knowing about the alleged malpractices as they might attend the classes. In writing the piece, the journalist had acted responsibly on information supplied to her from reliable sources. On the other hand, in *Grobbelaar v News Group Newspapers Ltd*[6] qualified privilege did not attach to a massive and relentless campaign of vilification in which Grobbelaar's guilt was unequivocally asserted, with some of the allegations going far beyond what could be supported by the evidence the newspaper had obtained. A publisher cannot claim that he acted responsibly by relying on information that came to his knowledge after the date of publication of the defamatory material.[7]

1 [2001] 2 AC 127.
2 The House refused to develop a new subject category of qualified privilege in respect of political information.
3 Indeed, the right to free expression is guaranteed by article 10 of the European Convention on Human Rights.
4 *Loutchansky v Times Newspapers Ltd (No 2)* [2002] QB 783.
5 [2000] EMLR 410.
6 [2001] 2 All ER 437, CA.
7 *Loutchansky v Times Newspapers Ltd (No 1)* [2002] QB 321.

(b) Reports of proceedings in Parliament in the press or other media attract only qualified privilege. The position is the same in respect of reports of judicial and other quasi-judicial proceedings.[1]

(c) Parties to a civil action enjoy only qualified privilege in respect of statements made in civil proceedings. If, however, the pursuer can prove that the statement was made with the intention of harming the pursuer (ie maliciously) then an action for defamation or verbal injury may lie.[2] This delict is often called 'judicial slander'.

(d) Under the Defamation Act 1996,[3] the publication of certain types of reports is subject to qualified privilege.

(g) Responsibility of publication

By s 1 of the Defamation Act 1996, a person has a defence to an action of defamation if he can show that: (i) he was not the author, editor or publisher of the defamatory statement; (ii) he took reasonable care in relation to its publication; and (iii) he did not know and had no reason to believe that what he did caused or contributed to the publication of a defamatory statement. The defence is designed to protect persons concerned with printing, processing, producing, distributing or selling newspapers, books, films, CDs, software etc which contain the defamatory material.[4]

As we have seen, where a statement is subject to qualified privilege, it can be the subject of an action of defamation or verbal injury[5] if the pursuer acted maliciously. In the present writer's view, this simply means that the defender intended to harm or insult the pursuer, although it has been contended that it is sufficient to show that the defender was not motivated by duty or interest. But if that were so, at least in the case of duty or interest to speak, qualified privilege would not attach in the first place. However, as the authorities stand,[6] malice can be established if it can be shown that

---

1 *Richardson v Wilson* (1879) 7 R 237, 17 SLR 122; *Cunningham v Scotsman Publications Ltd* 1987 SC 107, 1987 SCLR 314, OH.
2 *Williamson v Umphray and Robertson* (1890) 17 R 905, 27 SLR 742.
3 Defamation Act 1996, s 15 and Sch 1. Detailed treatment is outwith the scope of the present text.
4 See, for example, *Godfrey v Demon Internet Ltd* [2001] QB 201. It should be noted that by para 12 of Sch 1, qualified privilege extends to fair and accurate reporting of a public meeting: this includes a press conference and a press release distributed at such a conference. See *McCortan Turkington Breen (a firm) v Times Newspapers Ltd* [2000] 4 All ER 913; *Thomson v Ross* 2002 SLT 807.
5 See pp 276 ff below.
6 See especially *Fraser v Mirza* 1993 SC (HL) 27, 1993 SLT 527 at 531 per Lord Keith of Kinkel.

the defender abused the privileged occasion – as well as proving that he intended to injure the pursuer. Nevertheless, proof of malice is difficult.[1] It may be inferred from extreme language, a previous personal vendetta between the parties or the fact that the defender did not believe that the statement was true.[2] It is not enough simply to establish that the statement was defamatory.[3]

(5) Damages

In an action for defamation and verbal injury,[4] the pursuer is entitled to solatium in respect of insult and hurt feelings and compensation for any patrimonial loss. Where the case is one of defamation, insult is presumed but any patrimonial loss must be averred and proved. Although patrimonial loss, if it has been sustained, is relatively easy to assess, solatium is more difficult because it involves no little degree of speculation. In practice, solatium is usually a modest sum in Scots law.[5] Everyone is assumed to be of good character, so solatium is unlikely to be increased if the pursuer is particularly good. But the more eminent the pursuer, the greater the loss of reputation, and, consequently, more will be awarded by way of solatium. In general, the worse the allegation, the greater the sum that will be awarded; in particular, the sum may be increased if the defender has persisted in the defamatory allegations against the pursuer.[6] However, at the end of the day, solatium is intended to compensate loss:[7] a person who brings an action primarily to clear his name will receive only a nominal sum.[8]

An award of solatium can be mitigated as a result of a number of factors. First, if the pursuer's character or reputation is already tainted before the defamatory statement, evidence can be led by the defender to show that the pursuer did not therefore suffer as

---

1 For an example of the difficulties, see *Fraser v Mirza* 1993 SC (HL) 27, 1993 SLT 527.
2 *Horrocks v Lowe* [1975] AC 135, [1974] 1 All ER 662, HL.
3 *Adam v Jackson* [1917] AC 309.
4 On verbal injury, see pp 276 ff below.
5 See, for example, *Gilbert v Yorston* 1996 SCLR 1122, 1997 SLT 879, OH (no evidence that any third party believed the defamatory material: no effect on pursuer's career. Pursuer was awarded £1,500 damages for solatium).
6 *Baigent v British Broadcasting Corpn* 1999 GWD 10-474 (awards of £60,000 and £50,000 were made against the BBC: the attack on the pursuers' personal integrity and professional ability was very vindictive).
7 *Stein v Beaverbrook Newspapers Ltd* 1968 SC 272, 1968 SLT 401.
8 *Gilbert v Yorston* 1996 SCLR 1122, 1997 SLT 879, OH.

much as an ordinary person.[1] An immediate retraction of the statement and an apology will mitigate the loss.[2] This will also be the case if the pursuer provoked the defender into making the defamatory statement.[3] If the statement has been published by more than one person, the defender can mitigate the damages the pursuer should receive if the pursuer has already received damages in respect of the same words, or words to the same effect, from a third party.[4] So, for example, if A and B defame C using the same words, if C sues A, A can plead mitigation if C has already received damages from B.

C. VERBAL INJURY

Where a statement is made which is not defamatory,[5] the law will not presume that it is false, made with intent to injure and caused insult to the victim. It does not follow that where the non-defamatory statement has undermined a person's character or reputation that he is without a remedy. Scots law recognises that non-defamatory statements can amount to civil wrongs which are actionable in delict. These are known as verbal injuries.

The most common situation where an action will lie for verbal injury are cases where a non-defamatory statement is made which holds up the pursuer to public hatred, ridicule and contempt. In *Paterson v Welch*,[6] the defender stated that the pursuer had made the comment that if children from the poorer classes were allowed to attend Madras College, this would 'contaminate the genteel children' currently attending that school. To state that a person holds a controversial opinion is not defamatory ie it does not lower him in the estimation of right-thinking persons. However, the court was prepared to allow the case to proceed as an action for verbal injury provided the pursuer could aver and prove that: (1) the statement was false; (2) the statement was intended to injure the pursuer; and (3) that injury had in fact been sustained by the pursuer.[7] Thus,

1 *C v M* 1923 SC 1,1922 SLT 634.
2 *Morrison v Ritchie & Co* (1902) 4 F 645.
3 *Paul v Jackson* (1884) 11 R460.
4 Defamation Act 1952, s 12.
5 On the categories of defamatory statements, see pp 262 ff above.
6 (1893) 20 R 744.
7 *Paterson v Welch* (1893) 20 R 744 at 749 per the Lord President (Robertson).

unlike a case of defamation, where falsity, intention to injure and injury are presumed, in cases of verbal injury the onus lies on the pursuer to prove these facts.

In *Steele v Scottish Daily Record and Sunday Mail Ltd*[1] the defender made a statement in its newspaper's legal advice and consumer rights page that the pursuer, a car dealer, had acted harshly in refusing to cancel a hire purchase agreement with a customer who had got into financial difficulties. 'Have a heart, that's my message to Motor Dealer, Mr Steele' ran the headline. The statement was not defamatory since it merely suggested that the pursuer was a hard businessman. Nevertheless, the Inner House held that Steele would have an action if he could prove that the statement was false, that it was intended to harm him and had, in fact, caused him harm. The case failed on the basis that the article was not intended to hold Steele up to public hatred, ridicule and contempt, but had been written to persuade him to give his unfortunate customer a better deal. Therefore, before an action can lie for verbal injury on this ground, the effect of the statement, apart from being false, must have been intended to cause the pursuer to be despised or condemned by ordinary members of the public.[2]

An action for verbal injury will also lie if A makes a false statement about the state of B's property, for example that B's house is falling down[3] (slander of property). Similarly, an action will lie if A falsely alleges that B does not own property which he wishes to sell[4] (slander of title) or if A falsely states that B's business is not run well[5] (slander of business). To succeed in these situations, B must prove that the statement was false, intended to harm B economically and actually caused B patrimonial loss.[6] But because there is no intention to injure the pursuer's character or reputation, solatium cannot be awarded.[7]

Finally, an action for verbal injury may lie if A defames B with the intention of harming C. Because C has not been defamed, ie C's reputation has not been directly attacked, C cannot sue A in

---

1 1970 SLT 53.
2 *Steele v Scottish Daily Record and Sunday Mail Ltd* 1970 SLT 53. See also *Burns v Diamond* (1896) 23 R 507, (1896) 3 SLT 274.
3 *Argyllshire Weavers Ltd v A Macaulay (Tweeds) Ltd* 1965 SLT 21, OH.
4 *Philp v Morton* (1816) Hume 865.
5 *Craig v Inveresk Paper Merchant Ltd* 1970 SLT (Notes) 50, OH.
6 *Argyllshire Weavers Ltd v A Macaulay (Tweeds) Ltd* 1965 SLT 21, OH.
7 Unlike the 'public hatred, ridicule and contempt' cases where, as in defamation, both solatium and patrimonial loss are recoverable. Unlike defamation, insult must be proved before solatium can be obtained.

defamation. But if C can prove that A's defamatory statement in respect of B was false, was intended to harm C and did harm C, then in principle C should have an action for verbal injury against A.[1] So, for example, if a person defames a woman by calling her a prostitute, not only can she sue in defamation but her husband could have an action based on verbal injury if he could prove that the statement was false, that it was made to injure him and in fact did so. Unlike his wife's case of defamation where these three requisites are presumed in her favour, in his action for verbal injury the onus lies on the husband to establish these facts.

A defender in an action of verbal injury can rely on the same defences that are available in an action of defamation.[2]

D. *CONVICIUM*

It is an essential requirement of defamation and verbal injury that the statement is false. Some writers have argued that Scots law recognises another form of verbal injury, *convicium*, where *veritas* is no defence.[3] *Convicium* involves holding the pursuer up to public hatred, ridicule and contempt, and in so far as it ever had an independent existence in Scots law, it is thought that it has been overtaken by the genus delict of verbal injury where the statement has to be false before it is actionable.[4]

In the present writer's view, it is too late for the courts to revive this delict, particularly since it could undermine freedom of speech, given that *veritas* is no defence. Instead, the legislature must give consideration to whether it is desirable to introduce a statutory remedy for unwarranted intrusions into an individual person's privacy.[5] The scope of the remedy – where *veritas* would be

1 *North of Scotland Banking Co v Duncan* (1857) 19 D 881 at 887 per Lord Deas. Cf *Broom v Ritchie & Co* (1905) 6 F 942, where the distinction between defamation and verbal injury was not clearly drawn.
2 Discussed at pp 268 ff above.
3 See, in particular, Walker *Delict* (2nd edn, 1981) p 736.
4 See pp 276 ff above.
5 See *Infringement of Privacy* (Lord Chancellor's Dept, Scottish Office, July 1993). There is also potential liability if the defender's conduct amounts to a breach of the pursuer's rights under article 8 of the European Convention on Human Rights (right to respect for his private and family life, his home and his correspondence): see, for example, *Martin v McGuiness* 2003 SCLR 548.

no defence – would be determined after balancing an individual's interest in privacy against the public interest in freedom of speech. This is clearly a task for the Scottish Parliament rather than the judiciary, who would have to develop principles which were, arguably, never part of Scots common law.[1]

1 This chapter is strongly influenced by Dr K McK Norrie's seminal article 'Hurts to Character, Honour and Reputation: a Reappraisal' 1984 JR 163.

Part IV

DAMAGES

Chapter 16.   Damages   283

Introduction

The purpose of this last chapter is to give a short account of the law of damages. It begins with a discussion of the difficulties raised by the question of remoteness of damages. There follows an explanation of how damages are calculated. Finally, there is an outline of the rules on prescription and limitation which are relevant to delictual liability.

CHAPTER 16

Damages

A. REMOTENESS OF DAMAGES

It will be remembered that Scottish courts once took the view that delictual liability would not be imposed upon a defender if the pursuer's injury was too remote.[1] However, in the present writer's view, these cases should now be analysed as situations where the court was unwilling to impose a duty of care on the defender, ie the duty of care was being used as a threshold device to deny delictual liability. But even where there has been a breach of a duty of care and the defender is liable to make reparation to the pursuer in respect of the pursuer's personal injuries or damage to property, it does not follow that the defender must compensate the pursuer for every loss arising from the delict. Some losses are 'too remote'. Consider the following example:

As a result of his careless driving, A knocks down a pedestrian, B. B will recover damages for pain and suffering (solatium)[2] and derivative economic loss. The latter will include loss of wages between the date of the accident and the date of the action; future loss of earnings from the date of the action, if B is unable to work or can work only at a lower-paid job;[3] the cost of medical treatment and nursing up to the date of the action and the cost of such care in the future. However, if as a result of the accident, B was unable to give instructions to his stockbroker to purchase shares which he had intended to buy, or if B was unable to post his football coupon, the profits B would have made on the shares or the dividend he would have won if the coupon had been posted are not recoverable even though they arise from the fact that B was incapacitated as a result of the accident. These losses are too remote and cannot therefore be recovered.

What criteria do the courts use to determine whether or not losses are too remote? The classic statement of the rule on remote-

1 See pp 131 ff above.
2 For the calculation of solatium, see pp 292 ff below.
3 For the calculation of loss of future earnings, see pp 294 ff below.

ness of damages in Scots law was articulated by the Lord Ordinary (Kinloch) in *Allan v Barclay*:[1]

'The grand rule on the subject of damages is, that none can be claimed except such as naturally and directly arise out of the wrong done; and such, therefore, as may reasonably be supposed to have been in the contemplation of the wrongdoer.'

However, there is a potential contradiction inherent in this statement. While many losses which are reasonably foreseeable also directly arise from the wrong done, it is possible to envisage situations where a loss directly arises from the delict but is not reasonably foreseeable and vice versa, ie a loss which is reasonably foreseeable but does not arise directly from the delict.

This problem has been a matter of particular concern in England. In *Re Polemis and Furness, Withy & Co Ltd*,[2] the Court of Appeal held that the question whether particular damages are recoverable depends only on whether they were the direct consequence of the delictual act; provided some damage was reasonably foreseeable so that there was a breach of a duty of care, the defendant is liable to compensate for all the damage directly resulting from the breach of duty even if those losses were unforeseeable.

In this case, stevedores carelessly allowed a plank to fall into the hold of a ship. The falling plank caused a spark which in its turn ignited petrol vapour in the hold. The vapour caused a fire which destroyed the vessel. The court held that while the fire was not a reasonably foreseeable consequence of allowing the plank to fall, some damage to the vessel was. In the light of these findings, the court was prepared to hold that since it was reasonably foreseeable that some form of damage would result from the negligent act, damages in respect of the fire, albeit not reasonably foreseeable, were nevertheless recoverable as a direct consequence of the foreseeable harm. Although this case is often cited as authority for the proposition that reasonable foreseeability plays no part in determining the extent of recoverable damages, such a conclusion may not be entirely justified. If it had been held that it was not foreseeable that the plank would cause any damage at all, the court might well have held that the consequences of the fire were too remote.

---

1 (1864) 2 M 873. The case was concerned with whether an employer could recover damages for the loss of his injured employee's services. In other words, it was concerned with the defender's liability rather than remoteness of damages. Today it would be analysed as an example of non-recoverability of secondary economic loss: see pp 105 ff above. However, the passage has always been regarded as an authoritative statement of remoteness of damages. The grand rule has been analysed by the House of Lords in *Simmons v British Steel plc* [2004] UKHL 20.

2 [1921] 3 KB 560, CA.

However, it may appear illogical to insist that some damage to
the pursuer must be foreseen as a reasonable and probable consequence of the defender's act or omission before there is a breach of
a duty of care, ie delictual liability, yet allow the pursuer to recover
losses directly arising from that breach which were not reasonably
foreseeable. In *Overseas Tankship (UK) Ltd v Morts Dock and
Engineering Co, The Wagon Mound*,[1] the Privy Council declined to
follow *Re Polemis*.[2] In this case, a ship was being bunkered when
some oil being loaded on board spilt into the harbour as a result of
the carelessness of the appellant's employees. Morts' employees
were welding nearby when the spillage happened. Molten metal
from their operations fell onto some debris which caught fire; this
in turn set the oil alight, causing substantial fire damage to the
wharf owned by Morts.

It was found as a fact that it was not reasonably foreseeable that
the oil could have been ignited in such a way. Although it was reasonably foreseeable that the oil spillage would cause some harm to
the respondent's dock, ie by fouling the dock, nevertheless the
court held that the appellants were not liable for the damage caused
by the unforeseeable fire. If *Re Polemis*[3] had been applied, it is
arguable that the appellants would have been liable for the damage
caused by the fire, because some damage, ie the fouling of the dock,
was foreseeable and the fire could be regarded as a *direct* result of
the breach of duty[4] – albeit that the fire was unforeseeable.
However, since damage by fire was not reasonably foreseeable as a
probable consequence of the spillage, it is submitted that in this
case there was no breach of duty of care, ie there was no delictual
liability, and therefore it is not a remoteness of damages case at all.[5]

The Scottish courts have not given authoritative guidance on the
matter; instead, reliance is simply placed on Lord Kinloch's 'grand
rule'. In *Kelvin Shipping Co, The Baron Vernon v Canadian Pacific
Railway Co, The Metagama*,[6] Viscount Haldane LC opined[7] that
when

---

1 [1961] AC 388, [1961] 1 All ER 404, PC.
2 *Re Polemis and Furness, Withy & Co Ltd* [1921] 3 KB 560, CA.
3 *Re Polemis and Furness, Withy & Co Ltd* [1921] 3 KB 560, CA.
4 Although in this case it is equally arguable that the fire was *indirectly* caused as a
  result of the molten metal falling on the oil.
5 Cf *Hughes v Lord Advocate* 1963 SC (HL) 31, 1963 SLT 150, where injury by fire
  was reasonably foreseeable: only the extent of the injuries was not. For full discussion, see pp 120 ff above.
6 1928 SC (HL) 21, 1928 SLT 117.
7 1928 SC (HL) 21 at 25.

'a collision takes place by the fault of the defendant's ship, the damage is recoverable, in an action for damages if it is the natural and reasonable result of the negligent act, and it will assume that character if it can be shown to be such a consequence as in the ordinary course of things would flow from the situation which the offending ship created.'[1]

Although there are obiter dicta that *Re Polemis*[2] does not reflect the law of Scotland,[3] in *Campbell v F and F Moffat (Transport) Ltd*[4] the Lord Ordinary (Lord Cameron of Lochbroom) held that the test was not whether the loss was reasonably foreseeable but whether it arose naturally and directly out of the wrong. In that case, the pursuer was injured in a road accident and, as a result, his employment was terminated in 1989. Two years later, his former employer closed the mill where the pursuer had worked and gave the employees working at that date *ex gratia* redundancy payments. In his action for damages, the pursuer sought compensation for the loss of the redundancy payment he would have received if his employment had not been terminated two years earlier as a result of the accident. Lord Cameron took the view that this loss was not so utterly speculative that it could not amount to a natural and direct consequence of the accident.

It is submitted that in Scots law it is too simplistic to see the question of remoteness of damages in terms of reasonable foreseeability on the one hand and direct consequences on the other. The courts use a combination of both tests in assessing whether the loss is a natural consequence of the delictual act. It is only if the loss is utterly speculative[5] that the loss will be too remote and not recoverable in an award of damages.

What is clear, however, is that in a case of personal injuries, the defender takes her victim as she finds him. If, for example, A, as a result of her carelessness, burns B, if B has a predisposition to cancer which is triggered by the burn, with the result that B dies, A is liable for B's death even if that was not reasonably foreseeable as a consequence of the burn. In this situation, reasonable foreseeability of death is treated as irrelevant or, alternatively, the defender is

---

1 However, this case was clearly concerned with the existence of liability rather than remoteness of damages.
2 *Re Polemis and Furness, Withy & Co Ltd* [1921] 3 KB 560, CA.
3 See, for example, *Cowan v National Coal Board* 1958 SLT (Notes) 19, OH, per the Lord Ordinary (Cameron).
4 1992 SCLR 551, 1992 SLT 962, OH.
5 As it is submitted is the case in the examples of the loss of profits on the shares and the loss of a football pools' dividend: see p 283 above.

deemed to have reasonably foreseen that the pursuer could have been an ill, as opposed to healthy, person.[1] Moreover, as we have seen, where the pursuer is a primary victim, the defender is liable for causing mental or psychiatric illness, even though such illness was not reasonably foreseeable: a case of an eggshell personality rather than an eggshell skull![2]

We have been considering the question of remoteness of damages in the context of delictual liability for unintentional, but careless, conduct. Where the intentional delicts are concerned, the defender is liable to make reparation for all losses suffered by the pursuer which directly arise from the delict – whether or not these losses are reasonably foreseeable. The intention to injure the pursuer, which is an essential requisite of these delicts, disposes of any question of remoteness of damages.[3]

B. CALCULATION OF DAMAGES

(1) Introduction

The purpose of an award of damages is to compensate the pursuer for those losses which arose as a result of the delict. It is intended, so far as money can, to place the pursuer in the financial position he would have been if the delict had not occurred.[4] Where the claim is in respect of damage to property, damages are relatively simple to assess, ie the cost of repair or replacement of the property.[5] If after repair the property is worth less than before it was damaged the pursuer can recover the diminution in value.[6] It is now settled that if the cost of repair is greater than would reasonably be expected because of the owner's impecuniosity at the time the property was damaged, the pursuer can recover for the increased costs of repair.[1]

---

1 *McKillen v Barclay Curle & Co Ltd* 1967 SLT 41. This is known as 'the eggshell-skull rule'.

2 *Page v Smith* [1996] AC 155, [1995] 2 All ER 736, HL: discussed at p 73 above.

3 *Smith New Court Securities Ltd v Scrimgeour Vickers (Asset Management) Ltd* [1997] AC 254, [1996] 4 All ER 769, HL; *Barry v Sutherland* 2002 SLT 413.

4 See, for example, *O'Brien's Curator Bonis v British Steel plc* 1991 SC 315, 1991 SCLR 831, 1991 SLT 477 at 480 per the Lord President (Hope); *Cantwell v Criminal Injuries Compensation Board* 2002 SC (HL) 1.

5 The pursuer still incurs a reparable loss even though he could have pursued a contractual claim against a third party to repair the property: *Ford Motor Co Ltd v HLM Design Ltd* 1997 SLT 837, OH.

6 *Hunter v National Specialist Steeplejacks* 2004 GWD 49.

Greater difficulties arise in calculating damages in wrongful conception and wrongful birth, pure economic loss and personal injury cases and these deserve fuller treatment.

(2) Wrongful conception and wrongful birth

As we have seen,[2] the infringement of a parent's right not to have a child is a reparable interest in Scots law. Applying the remoteness of damages rule, the parents should be entitled to receive compensation for the losses which are reasonably foreseeable as a direct consequence of the wrongful conception. These would include the mother's pain and suffering during the pregnancy and birth of the child (solatium); any loss of the mother's earnings during the pregnancy; and the cost of rearing the child. However, in *McFarlane v Tayside Health Board* [3] the House of Lords held that parents could not recover as damages the cost of bringing up a healthy and normal child conceived as a result of medical negligence. Their Lordships did so on grounds of legal policy. Departing from the principle that the function of the law of delict is corrective justice ie to compensate the pursuer for the losses arising from a wrong, the House held that as a matter of distributive justice compensation for the cost of alimenting a healthy and normal child could not be condoned. To do so would be (i) disproportionate to the defender's fault; (ii) a further inroad to the principle that pure economic loss is prima facie not recoverable in delict (albeit that the economic loss in such cases is derivative, ie *derives* from the wrongful conception); (iii) to regard the a child as a financial liability and nothing else; (iv) to necessitate an attempt to balance the cost of a child's upbringing against the unquantifiable rewards of parenthood; and (v) a potential drain on the limited resources of the NHS which would affect the community's sense of how such resources should be allocated.

The 'principle' in *McFarlane* that the cost of rearing a healthy and normal child could not be recovered in wrongful conception cases was reaffirmed by the House of Lords in *Rees v Darlington Memorial Hospital NHS Trust*.[4] In this case, the child was normal and healthy but the mother was blind. A majority of their

---

1 *Alcoa Minerals of Jamaica v Herbert Broderick* [2002] 1 AC 371; *Lagden v O'Connor* [2004] 1 All ER 277. In these circumstances, the pursuer is not in breach of his duty to mitigate the loss by waiting until he could afford the repairs.
2 Pages 80 ff above.
3 2000 SC (HL) 1.
4 [2004] 1 AC 309, [2003] 4 All ER 987.

Lordships[1] held that the mother's disability was not a ground for distinguishing *McFarlane*. However, they took the view that an award of solatium did not adequately recognise the wrongful infringement of the mother's freedom to limit the size of her family.[2] Accordingly, she should receive a conventional – non-compensatory – award of £15,000 to afford some measure of recognition of the wrong she had suffered.[3]

McFarlane involved the wrongful[4] conception of a healthy and normal child. What of the situation where a handicapped child is born but the mother lost the opportunity to terminate the pregnancy as a result of the defender's failure to carry out the appropriate pre-natal tests? In *McLellan v Glasgow Health Board*[5] an Extra Division held that in wrongful birth cases the principle in *McFarlane* also applied to exclude the cost of the child's basic maintenance: however, any increased costs attributable to the child's special needs could be recovered. In England, the Court of Appeal reached a similar conclusion in *Parkinson v St James and Seacroft University Hospital Trust*.[6] Accordingly, it would appear that while the basic costs of alimenting a handicapped child cannot be recovered, any extra expenditure involved in attempting to make the child's upbringing as normal as possible can

These decisions illustrate once against the readiness of the House of Lords to depart from the application of recognised rules of delictual liability to avoid a result which is not consonant with their Lordships' view of what is desirable in terms of social and economic policy.

(3) Pure economic loss claims

In some situations when delictual liability for pure economic loss has been recognised, it is relatively simple to calculate the loss. For example, in the case of a disappointed legatee, the loss is the value of the lost legacy.[1] Where a surveyor has been negligent and failed

---

1 Lords Bingham, Nicholls, Millet and Scott; Lords Steyn, Hope and Hutton dissenting.
2 *Quaere* whether this also applies to a father's freedom to do so.
3 There can be few more blatant examples of judicial 'legislation'.
4 Ie a conception arising from a failed sterilisation as a result of medical negligence.
5 2002 SLT 446. It should be noted that the father as well as the mother received solatium in respect of the birth of the handicapped child.
6 [2002] QB 266. This decision was approved by Lords Steyn, Hope and Hutton in *Rees*.

to discover defects, the loss to the purchaser is either the cost of repair or the diminution in the value of the property.[2] But difficulties have arisen in quantifying loss when the pursuer has been induced to enter into a transaction as a result of the defender's misrepresentation.

(a) Fraudulent misrepresentation

It is well settled that when A has entered into a transaction as a result of B's fraudulent misrepresentation, B is liable for all A's losses arising directly from the transaction, even though some of them might not be reasonably foreseeable.[3] This would include losses which A incurs as a result of a general fall in the market value of the assets involved in the transaction.

(b) Negligent misrepresentation

What is the position if A has entered into a transaction as a result of B's negligent misrepresentation? When the misrepresentation takes the form of *advice*, ie B advises A to enter into a particular transaction, then B is liable for all the losses incurred by A as a consequence of entering into the transaction, provided such losses are reasonably foreseeable.[4] Again, this could include losses which A incurs as a result of a general fall in the market value of the assets involved in the transaction.

However, when the misrepresentation takes the form of B providing *information* which A uses to decide whether or not to enter a particular transaction, the House of Lords[5] has imposed a cap on B's potential liability. In other words, B is only liable for that part of

---

1 *White v Jones* [1995] 2 AC 207, [1995] 1 All ER 691, HL; *Holmes v Bank of Scotland* 2002 SLT 544.

2 *Patel v Hooper & Jackson* [1999] 1 All ER 992, CA.

3 *Smith New Court Securities Ltd v Scrimgeour Vickers (Asset Management) Ltd* [1997] AC 254, [1996] 4 All ER 769, HL; *Barry v Sutherland* 2002 SLT 413.

4 *Bristol and West Building Society v Rollo Steven and Bond* 1998 SLT 9, OH; *Hamilton v Allied Domecq plc* 2004 SLT 191, OH. The pursuer's transaction must be within the nature and scope of the defender's duty of care: *Newcastle Building Society v Paterson Robertson and Graham* 2001 SC 734. Where, as a consequence of negligent advice, the pursuer loses an interest in land, the potential development value of the land can be recovered: *Paul v Ogilvy* 2002 SLT 171. The time spent by the pursuer in dealing with the problems resulting from the defender's negligence is a recoverable head of loss but not the time spent in preparation for the litigation: *Lomond Assured Properties v McGrigor Donald* 2000 SLT 797.

5 *South Australia Asset Management Corpn v York Montague Ltd* [1997] AC 191, [1996] 3 All ER 365, HL.

A's loss which was a reasonably foreseeable consequence of the information being wrong. Consider the following examples:

(i) B *advises* A to lend £10 million to C, using C's property as security. C defaults. Owing to a general fall in the market value of property, C's property is now worth only £5 million. A can recover from B all foreseeable losses arising from his entering into the transaction with C, ie £10 million – £5 million = £5 million.

(ii) B tells A that C's property is worth £15 million. In fact, it is worth only £12 million. A decides to lend C £10 million, using C's property as security. C defaults. Owing to a general fall in the market value of property, C's property is now worth only £5 million. A's loss is £10 million – £5 million = £5 million. However, B is only liable to the extent that his information was wrong, ie the difference between the negligent valuation and the actual value at the time the information was given: £15 million – £12 million = £3 million.

There are difficulties in defending the judicial reasoning for applying a cap in negligent information cases.[1] Nevertheless, it appears to be settled law. Moreover, where the pursuer has been contributorily negligent in entering into the transaction (which is often the case), the House of Lords has held that the deduction should be made from the pursuer's total loss, not the loss recoverable after the cap has been fixed.[2] So if, in example (ii), A was 20 per cent contributorily negligent, A's damages would be £5 million – £1 million = £4 million: and A would still recover £3 million from B.

It should also be remembered that in cases of fraudulent as well as negligent misrepresentation, the pursuer must take reasonable steps to mitigate his loss.[3]

(4) Personal injury claims

Where a party suffers personal injuries as a result of the delictual conduct of the defender, he is entitled to obtain reparation in respect of the physical injury and for any derivative economic loss which he has sustained as a result. Again, 'the objective' is, so far as

---

1 See eg Joe Thomson 'Damages for Misrepresentation' 1997 SLT (News) 301.
2 *Platform Home Loans Ltd v Oyston Shipways Ltd* [2002] 2 AC 190, [1999] 1 All ER 833, HL.
3 *Standard Chartered Bank v Pakistan National Shipping Corpn* [1995] 2 Lloyd's Rep 365.

money can, to compensate the injured party for the consequences of the wrongful act.¹ The pursuer can claim in respect of loss, injury and damage suffered. It is now the practice to divide the claim into various heads of damages. Although it is sensible and convenient to do so, it is always important to remember that these are not several discrete claims but a *single* claim which can be regarded as falling into several parts for the purposes of quantification.² Compensation for the pain and suffering as a result of physical injury is known as solatium; compensation in respect of derivative economic loss is known as patrimonial loss.

(a) Solatium

It is, of course, clear that no money sum can in effect compensate for physical injury. In *Wright v British Railways Board*³ Lord Diplock said of the English equivalent of solatium that

'such loss is not susceptible of *measurement* in money. Any figure at which the assessor of damages arrives cannot be other than artificial and, if the aim is that justice meted out to all litigants should be even handed instead of depending on idiosyncrasies of the assessor, whether jury or judge, the figure must be "basically a conventional figure derived from an experience of awards in comparable cases".'⁴

In *McMillan v McDowall* the judge opined that 'While the assessment of solatium is not a precise science and has frequently been called a jury question, the view of (a Lord Ordinary] in a similar case must be treated with respect'.⁵

The court therefore approaches the question of solatium on the basis of comparing one case with another and making a determination taking into account the severity and nature of the injuries sustained by the pursuer. The court assesses solatium as at the date of the proof and does not attempt to assess solatium as it would have been at the date of the injury itself.

In making an award for solatium the court takes into account not only the extent of the injury but also the pursuer's awareness of pain.⁶ No award can be made under this head therefore if, as a

---

1 *Admiralty Comrs v SS Susquehanna (Owners)* [1926] AC 655, HL.
2 *Irving v Hiddleston* 1998 SCLR 350, 1998 SLT 912, OH.
3 [1983] 2 AC 733, [1983] 2 All ER 698, HL.
4 [1983] 2 All ER 698 at 699 (Lord Diplock's emphasis). It is submitted that the position is the same in Scots law.
5 *McMillan v McDowall* 1993 SLT 311, OH, at 312 per T G Coutts QC.
6 *Lim Poh Choo v Camden and Islington Area Health Authority* [1980] AC 174, [1979] 2 All ER 910, HL.

result of his injuries, the pursuer has been rendered permanently unconscious. Such awards are made not only in respect of physical injury. A person who, for example, suffers from an identifiable psychological condition can be awarded damages where the condition arises as a consequence of a delict.[1] In *Maclean v Lothian and Borders Fire Brigade*,[2] an award of solatium took into account the pursuer's loss of congenial employment.

In making its assessment of solatium, the court takes into account not only the pain and suffering which has been experienced by the pursuer but also the pain and suffering which he is likely to have in the future. A global award is made. The award also takes into account the pursuer's loss of amenity. Everything which reduces the pursuer's enjoyment of life, which has been sustained as a result of the accident, will be reflected in a claim for solatium. It has been held in England that the important element in such a claim is the fact of deprivation of amenity and not whether the injured person is aware of such deprivation.[3] Also included in an award of solatium is the pain and suffering occasioned when the pursuer is, was, or at any time will be, likely to become aware that his expectancy of life has been shortened by his injuries.[4]

(b) Patrimonial loss

Having assessed damages in respect of solatium the court must then turn to the question of patrimonial loss. The court first of all assesses damages in respect of past loss, that is loss incurred between the date of the accident and the date of the proof. It then attempts to assess the pursuer's future loss.

(i) Damages for patrimonial loss to the date of proof If the pursuer has been out of work since the date of his accident, he will

1 *Clark v Scottish Power plc* 1994 SCLR 202, 1994 SLT 924; *Lawson v Scotdem Ltd* 1999 GWD 8-393. Distress has, on occasion, been the subject of an award of solatium even in the absence of physical injury or mental illness: *Fraser v D M Hall & Son* 1997 SLT 808; *McLelland v Greater Glasgow Health Board* 2002 SLT 446 (distress to a parent caused by the wrongful birth of a handicapped child).
2 1998 SCLR 1004, OH.
3 *Lim Poh Choo v Camden and Islington Area Health Authority* [1980] AC 174, [1979] 2 All ER 910, HL. Of course, if the person has been rendered unconscious, he will not obtain compensation for pain and suffering.
4 Damages (Scotland) Act 1976, s 9A, as added by the Damages (Scotland) Act 1993, s 5. However, the deceased's fear of impending death in a fatal accident is not included in any award of solatium: *Hicks v Chief Constable of South Yorkshire Police* [1992] 2 All ER 65, HL.

be entitled to be compensated for his loss of income. This loss can take various forms such as loss of wages or salary, a reduction in a share of partnership profits or loss of a dividend in a single-employee company.[1] In addition, the pursuer will frequently have a claim for expenses. The general rule is that reasonable expenses are recoverable. Consequently, reasonable medical expenses can be recovered even if it is shown at a later stage that they are unnecessary.[2] Expenses need not be confined to medical or nursing services. By s 8 of the Administration of Justice Act 1982,[3] when a person has sustained personal injuries or has died in consequence of the personal injuries he has sustained, the defender is liable to pay damages in respect of necessary services which have been, or will be, rendered to the injured person by a relative in consequence of the injuries in question. Section 9 of the Administration of Justice Act 1982[4] also imposes an obligation upon the wrongdoer to pay to the injured person a reasonable sum by way of damages when he is unable, as a result of the accident, to render gratuitous personal services to his family.

In calculating loss of earnings, the pursuer's income tax must be taken into account and his liability to pay National Insurance contributions.[5] Accordingly, in so far as past patrimonial loss is concerned, the wages which form the basis of the calculation are the pursuer's net earnings.

(ii) Damages for future patrimonial loss This head of claim is by far the most important in assessing damages in respect of personal injury. The first stage is to assess damages in respect of future loss of earnings. This is done by taking the loss of the pursuer's net earnings at the date of proof and calculating that on an annual basis. The courts do not attempt to speculate on future rates of taxes and National Insurance contributions, but base their calculation on the rates current at the date of proof.[6] No allowance is made for possible increases in the pursuer's earnings if he had not been injured. The figure produced is known as the 'multiplicand'.

---

1 *Anthony v Brabbs* 1998 SLT 1137.
2 *Clippens Oil Co Ltd v Edinburgh and District Water Trustees* 1907 SC (HL) 9, 15 SLT 92; *Rubins v Walker* 1946 SC 215.
3 Discussed at pp 240 ff above.
4 Discussed at pp 241 ff above.
5 *British Transport Commission v Gourlay* [1956] AC 185, [1955] 3 All ER 796, HL; *Cooper v Firth Brown* [1963] 2 All ER 31, [1963] 1 WLR 148.
6 *British Transport Commission v Gourlay* [1956] AC 185.

The second stage is to find a 'multiplier'. The Ogden tables provide actuarial calculations of lump sums which are required to provide incomes for different persons at different ages. In *Wells v Wells*,[1] the House of Lords laid down that the rate of return on the investment of the damages should be 3 per cent, and that the Ogden tables should be used as the *starting–point* for finding the appropriate multiplier. The traditional Scottish approach was to use the Ogden tables as a check on the multiplier which was found by less scientific methods. Nevertheless, the guidelines laid down by the House of Lords in *Wells*[2] have been followed by the Scottish courts.[3] After taking the appropriate multiplier for the tables, there will usually be a deduction to take into account contingencies relating to the pursuer other than death, for example early retirement or redundancy.

The third stage is for the court to multiply the multiplicand by the multiplier to give a lump sum. So, for example, if the multiplicand is £20,000 and the multiplier is 10, then the total sum awarded is £200,000. The court can also take into account lost wages which the pursuer would have earned if his life expectancy had not been reduced as a result of the accident.[4] The pursuer is expected to live off the income and capital, the theory being that the lump sum will have been consumed by the date the pursuer dies!

Where a pursuer is severely injured, damages can be awarded for the cost of her maintenance, nursing and medical care in the future. Again, the multiplicand/multiplier method is adopted. The court assesses the cost of maintenance and care on an annual basis and then applies a multiplier based on the Ogden tables.[5] It should be noted that in a personal injuries case, the multiplier is applied at the date of proof: if, however, the pursuer died of his injuries

---

1 [1999] 1 AC 345. The House of Lords felt empowered to lay down a 3 per cent return because the pursuer would be assumed to invest the damages in index-linked government stock rather than in equities which might give a higher return but which, of course, are a less safe investment. Under s 1 of the Damages Act 1996, the Lord Chancellor and the Secretary of State for Scotland have the power to prescribe the rate of return. This has now been reduced to 2.5 per cent: Damages (Personal Injury) (Scotland) Order 2002 (SI 2002 No 46), art 3.

2 *Wells v Wells* [1999] 1 AC 345.

3 *McNulty v Marshalls Food Group Ltd* 1999 SC 195; *McManus' Executrix v Babcock Energy Ltd* 1999 SC 569.

4 Damages (Scotland) Act 1976, s 9(1) and (2).

5 For the courts' approach before *Wells v Wells* [1998] 3 All ER 481, [1998] 3 WLR 329, HL, see *O'Brien's Curator Bonis v British Steel plc* 1991 SC 315, 1991 SCLR 831, 1991 SLT 477.

between the date of the accident and the proof, the multiplier is applied at the date of death.[1]

Loss of pension rights can also be taken into account in assessing future patrimonial loss,[2] as can the pursuer's general loss of value in the labour market. In *Hill v Wilson*,[3] damages were awarded for impairment to earning capacity as opposed to loss of future wages. It is particularly difficult to assess damages when the injured person is a child. In such a case, 'it has never been suggested that damages should be assessed on such a basis, namely on a basis which provides not only reasonable compensation but in effect a guarantee of future financial security'.[4] In some cases, the court will abandon the multiplicand/multiplier method of calculating future patrimonial loss. This would happen where, for example, the pursuer has been able to continue working albeit on light work at a reduced wage, or there is evidence that the pursuer will be able to resume employment in the very near future, even though the job may be lower paid than previously.[5]

In the last few years, many personal injury cases have been tried by jury. Juries tend to award higher damages than judges, particularly in relation to solatium. Although a court can order a new trial if the sum awarded is excessive, it will not do so unless the damages awarded are beyond what a reasonable jury would award and there is serious injustice: the fact that a judge would have awarded considerably less is not sufficient.[6]

(5) Interest

Having assessed the quantity of damages, the court is obliged to consider the question of interest. Interest is payable under the Interest on Damages (Scotland) Act 1958, as amended by the Interest on Damages (Scotland) Act 1971.

Although solatium is awarded as a lump sum, it is important for the purpose of awards of interest to distinguish past and future solatium. Interest is only awarded on past solatium[7]. Past solatium

1 On death from personal injuries, see pp 243 ff above.
2 *Mitchell v Glenrothes Development Corpn* 1991 SLT 284, OH (conventional multiplicand/multiplier method used); *Cantwell v Criminal Injuries Compensation Board* 2002 SC (HL) 1.
3 1998 SC 81, 1998 SLT 69, OH.
4 *O'Connor v Matthews* 1996 SLT 408 at 412, per the Lord Ordinary (Marnoch).
5 *Stevenson v British Coal Corpn* 1989 SLT 136.
6 *Girvan v Inverness Farmers Dairy (No 2)* 1998 SC (HL) 1, 1998 SCLR 72, 1998 SLT 21.
7 *Smith v Middleton* 1972 SC 30.

is a sum awarded for the pursuer's pain and suffering until the date of proof. But if the pursuer is experiencing pain and suffering and loss of amenities at the date of the proof, the court will estimate damages to compensate the pursuer for the fact that these may continue in the future. So, for example, a court might award a total sum of £10,000 by way of solatium, made up of £6,000 for past solatium and £4,000 for future solatium. Interest on past solatium is paid at the average court rate for the period between the date of the accident and when the 'pain' diminished: this could, of course, have occurred before the date of the proof. If the pursuer is still suffering pain at the date of proof, interest will be awarded on past solatium at half the average court rate.[1]

Subject to the court's discretion, interest on patrimonial loss runs from the date of the accident.[2] Again, although a global sum is awarded, damages are divided between past and future loss. In the case of past losses, interest is awarded at one half of the average court rate from the date of the accident to the date of proof. There is no interest payable on awards in respect of future patrimonial loss.[3] The rules applicable to interest in respect of personal injuries operate without prejudice to the general rule which awards interest at the court rate from the date of decree until the date of payment by the defender.

(6) Deductions from awards

Deductions may have to be made from an award of damages for patrimonial loss. Section 10 of the Administration of Justice Act 1982 prohibits the taking into account for the purposes of reduction of damages any benefit the pursuer received in respect of: (a) any contractual pension or benefit[4] (b) any pension or retirement benefit to which s 2(1) of the Law Reform (Personal Injuries) Act

---

1 *Keicher v National Coal Board* 1988 SLT 318; *Preston v Grampian Health Board* 1988 SLT 435.
2 *Macrae v Reed & Mallik Ltd* 1961 SC 68, 1961 SLT 96.
3 *Hill v Wilson* 1998 SLT 69.
4 *Lewicki v Brown & Root Wimpey Highland Fabricators Ltd* 1996 SC 200, 1996 SCLR 680, 1996 SLT 1283 (payment under employer's long-term disability scheme held to be a contractual benefit and not deducted: cf if it had been treated as earnings or remuneration from employment). Where the pursuer's claim is in respect of loss of earnings and loss of a contractual retirement pension, then s 10(a) applies to the claim for loss of earnings so that his ill-health pension is not deducted but s 10(a) does *not* apply to the claim for loss of a contractual retirement pension so that his ill-health pension has to be brought into account: *Cantwell v Criminal Injuries Compensation Board* 2002 SC (HL) 1.

1948 applied; (c) any benefit payable from public funds in respect
of any period after the date of the award of damages which is
designed to secure to the injured person or any relative of his a minimum level of subsistence; (d) any statutory redundancy payment;[1]
(e) any payment made to the injured person or to any relative of his
by the injured person's employer following upon the injuries in
question where the recipient is under an obligation to reimburse
the employer in the event of damages being recovered in respect of
his injuries; and (f) any payment of a benevolent character made to
the injured person or to any relative by any person following upon
the injuries in question. The section directs, however, that any
remuneration or earnings from employment, any unemployment
benefit payable from public funds payable prior to the date of the
award of damages, or any payment of a benevolent character made
by the person responsible for the accident to the injured person,
shall be taken into account. Any savings to the pursuer as a result of
being maintained in hospital or accommodation provided by a care
home service is deducted.[2]

Prior to the introduction of the Social Security Act 1989, in
assessing damages for patrimonial loss a deduction was made of
only one-half of the value of certain specified benefits, ie sickness,
invalidity or disablement benefit, which the pursuer had received
during a period of five years from the date of the accident; but in
Hodgson v Trapp[3] the House of Lords held that the full value of
other benefits, such as attendance and mobility allowances, was to
be deducted. However, the Social Security Act 1989 made major
changes and the law was consolidated in the Social Security
Administration Act 1992, Part IV (ss 81–404): Part IV has now
been restated, with amendments, in the Social Security (Recovery
of Benefits) Act 1997.

When damages are awarded, heads of loss are relevant for the
purpose of the Social Security (Recovery of Benefits) Act 1997:

(1) compensation[4] for earnings lost during 'the relevant period';
(2) compensation for the cost of care incurred over the relevant
    period; and

---

1 Reversing *Wilson v National Coal Board* 1981 SC (HL) 9, 1981 SLT 67. An *ex
   gratia* non-statutory payment falls to be deducted: *Duncan v Glacier Metal Co Ltd*
   1988 SCLR 320, 1988 SLT 479, OH.
2 Administration of Justice Act 1982, s 11 (a) and (b), (amended and added by the
   Regulation of Care (Scotland) Act 2001 (asp 8), Sch 3, para 9).
3 [1989] AC 807, [1988] 3 All ER 870, HL.
4 Compensation includes interest on an award of damages for loss of earnings:
   Griffiths v British Coal Corpn [2001] 1 WLR 1493.

(3) compensation for loss of mobility during the relevant period.

The following benefits paid over the relevant period are deducted as follows:

From head (1): disability working allowance, disablement pension, incapacity benefit, income support, invalidity pension and allowance, jobseeker's allowance, reduced earnings allowance, severe disablement allowance, sickness benefit, statutory sick pay, unemployability supplement and unemployment benefit;

From head (2): attendance allowance, the care component of disability living allowance and any disablement pension increase;

From head (3): mobility allowance and the mobility component of disability living allowance.[1]

The 'relevant period' is five years from the date of the accident or five years from first claiming benefit as a consequence of a disease. Thus, benefits paid over that five-year period are recoverable from the relevant head of loss. Payments which are paid thereafter are not recoverable. When damages are paid *before* the end of five years, the relevant period ends at the date of payment; therefore, benefits paid after that date but before the five-year period ends are not recoverable.[2] The person paying damages, the compensator, deducts the amount of recoverable benefits from the pursuer's compensation[3] which he then pays to the Secretary of State.[4]

A major effect of the legislation is to abolish the provision that only one-half of the specified benefits should be taken into account in assessing damages. Under the Social Security (Recovery of Benefits) Act 1997, all the specified benefits received by the pursuer during the relevant period are fully to be taken into account. Benefits received after the relevant period are not affected and are not to be taken into account. The position is therefore that both pursuers and defenders are worse off under the new legislation.

---

1 Social Security (Recovery of Benefits) Act 1997, Sch 2.
2 SS(RB)A 1997, s 3. See *Mitchell v Laing* 1998 SC 342. This case provides an excellent example of literal construction of a statute by the Lord President (Rodger).
3 SS(RB)A 1997, s 6. The compensator obtains a certificate specifying the amount of recoverable benefits paid to the pursuer.
4 SS(RB)A 1997, s 7.

As far as the pursuer is concerned, he is worse off by not keeping half the value of any sickness, invalidity or disablement benefit received during the relevant period. He is, however, better off in that after the relevant period, those benefits which would have previously been deducted in full when assessing damages under the rule in *Hodgson v Trapp*,[1] for example attendance and mobility allowances, are no longer taken into account. Most importantly, damages awarded for solatium are no longer subject to deduction of recoverable benefits. The defender is worse off in that (i) he now pays the specified benefits in full during the relevant period, whereas before he paid only half their value to the pursuer as damages, and (ii) he can no longer take advantage of the rule in *Hodgson v Trapp*,[2] ie that the full value of other benefits paid to the pursuer would be deducted when assessing the damages.

When the compensation is less than a prescribed sum, it will be treated as a small payment, and no deduction in respect of benefits paid during the relevant period will be made.[3]

C. PROVISIONAL AND INTERIM DAMAGES

The normal rule in actions of damages for personal injuries is that the damages are assessed once and for all at the date of proof. As a consequence, pursuers used to delay bringing proceedings for a considerable period until they could ascertain the full extent of their loss. Pursuers often suffered hardship during the period between the accident and the date of proof. The situation was particularly unfair if the pursuer's physical condition was likely to deteriorate as a result of the injuries at some time in the future after the date of the proof. In *Stevenson v Pontifex and Wood* [4] the Lord President (Inglis) observed:[5]

'I hold the true rule of practice based on sound principle to be, that though the delict ..., be of such a nature that it will necessarily be followed by injurious consequences in the future, or though it may for this reason be impossible to ascertain with precise accuracy at the date of the action ...

1 [1989] AC 807, [1988] 3 All ER 870, HL.
2 [1989] AC 807, [1988] 3 All ER 870, HL.
3 Social Security (Recovery of Benefits) Act 1997, Sch 1.
4 (1887) 15 R 125.
5 (1887) 15 R 125 at 129.

the amount of loss which will result, yet the whole damage must be recovered in one action.'[1]

A pursuer's position in these circumstances has, to some extent, been alleviated by s 12 of the Administration of Justice Act 1982, which provides that the court is entitled to make an award of provisional damages in respect of personal injuries. Such an award can be made when it is proved, or admitted, that there is a risk that at some definite or indefinite time in the future, the pursuer will, as a result of the act or omission of the defender, which gave rise to the cause of the action, develop some serious disease or some serious deterioration in his physical or mental condition.[2] Provisional damages can only be awarded where the defender was, at the time of the accident giving rise to the cause of action, either a public authority or an insured person.[3] The purpose of this provision is therefore to give the pursuer an opportunity to claim damages in circumstances where his position is likely to worsen but where he cannot assess the full extent of his loss because the condition will take some time to deteriorate.

Before an award of provisional damages can be made, the pursuer must establish that there is a risk[4] that at some time in the future he will develop some serious disease or some serious deterioration in his physical or mental condition. Although assessment of the risk may be difficult,[5] it is clear that the risk must be more than *de minimis*.[6] There must be evidence that there is the possibility of a *serious* deterioration in the pursuer's condition.[7] If, for example, the pursuer's health or disability will become worse incrementally,

---

1 See also *Dunlop v McGowans* 1979 SC 22, 1979 SLT 34 at 39 per the Lord Justice-Clerk (Wheatley).
2 Administration of Justice Act 1982, s 12(1)(a).
3 AJA 1982, s 12(1)(b).
4 Cf the approach of the Lord Ordinary (Dervaird) who suggested (obiter) that if there was no risk but a certainty that there would be a deterioration, this would not be a suitable ease for provisional damages: *Prentice v William Thyne Ltd* 1989 SLT 336n, OH, at 337.
5 *Potter v McCulloch* 1987 SLT 308, OH, at 310 per the Lord Ordinary (Weir).
6 *White v Inveresk Paper Co Ltd* 1987 SC 143, 1988 SLT 2, OH, at 6 per the Lord Ordinary (Murray).
7 *White v Inveresk Paper Co Ltd* 1987 SC 143, 1988 SLT 2, OH, at 5 per the Lord Ordinary (Murray). See also *Potter v McCulloch* 1987 SLT 308, OH, at 310 per the Lord Ordinary (Weir); *Meek v Burton's Gold Medal Biscuits Ltd* 1989 SLT 338n, OH, at 339 per the Lord Ordinary (Prosser). In *Bonar v Trafalgar House Offshore Fabrication Ltd* 1996 SLT 548, OH, the Lord Ordinary (Gill) held that the court must determine what the apprehended deterioration is: contingent liability cannot be imposed on a defender unless the nature and extent of that liability is clear.

there are no grounds for an award of provisional damages because there is no 'clear cut and severable threshold' when the pursuer could apply for damages in the future on the basis that a serious deterioration had in fact taken place.[1] Although the deterioration must be as a consequence of the delictual act or omission of the defender that led to the pursuer's personal injuries in the first place, nevertheless in deciding whether or not the deterioration is serious, account must be taken of the effect of such deterioration upon the pursuer's physical abilities in the context of his ordinary life: '[s]eriousness cannot be assessed in a vacuum'.[2] Damages can only be deferred in respect of the serious deterioration in the pursuer's condition.[3]

Even if the pursuer satisfies the statutory criteria, the court is not obliged to defer the award of damages. The interests of the defender in not being called upon to pay further damages at some indefinite time in the future must also be considered.[4] Accordingly, an application for provisional damages is unlikely to be successful unless the medical evidence establishes that the deterioration is likely to take place in, say, a period of not more than ten years. Moreover, the court has the discretion to stipulate a time limit after which the pursuer is unable to claim further damages for a deterioration in his condition.[5] In *McColl v Barns*,[6] for example, where it was established that there was a risk that post-traumatic epilepsy might occur within seven years of the date of the accident, the pursuer was allowed to apply within that period for a further award of damages if the risk should in fact materialise. In the course of his judgment, the Lord Ordinary (Morison) said:[7]

'In my opinion this is a most appropriate case for such an order to be made. An assessment made to reflect the possibility of the condition occurring would be unrealistic and impracticable. If no assessment were made and the risk were to materialise, the pursuer would be unjustly deprived of compensation for a serious injury which would be a result of the accident.

---

1 See also *Prentice v William Thyne Ltd* 1989 SLT 336n, OH ('clear and sensible threshold'); *Robertson v British Bakeries Ltd* 1991 SLT 434 ('recognisable threshold').
2 *Robertson v British Bakeries Ltd* 1991 SCLR 450n, 1991 SLT 434, OH, at 439 per the Lord Ordinary (Osborne).
3 *Meek v Burton's Gold Medal Biscuits Ltd* 1989 SLT 338n, OH.
4 *Paterson v Costain Mining Ltd* 1988 SCLR 71, 1988 SLT 413, OH.
5 Administration of Justice Act 1982, s 12(2).
6 1992 SCLR 907, 1992 SLT 1188, OH; see also *Lappin v Britannia Airways Ltd* 1989 SLT 181n, OH (five years).
7 *McColl v Barns* 1992 SLT 1188 at 1190.

Since the additional risk becomes negligible after a period of seven years from the date of the accident I shall restrict the order ... to that period ...'.

The court is also entitled to award interim damages. Interim damages are to be distinguished from provisional damages in so far as they do not depend upon a pursuer suffering from a continuing disability, the eventual seriousness of which cannot be ascertained. Interim payments can be made in the Court of Session in terms of Rule of Court 89A(1) and will be awarded if the court is satisfied that the defender or defenders have admitted liability or that if the action proceeded to proof the pursuer would succeed in a question of liability without any substantial finding of contributory negligence on his part.[1] The court must be satisfied that it is 'practically certain' that the pursuer will succeed on the question of liability and that any finding of contributory negligence will not be so large as to have a material effect on the assessment of the amount the pursuer is likely to recover as damages.[2] An interim award is taken into account in making the final award and will not be made against the defender unless that defender is either a person who is insured in respect of the pursuer's claim or is a public authority or 'is a person whose means and resources are such as to enable him to make interim payment'.[3]

D. PRESCRIPTION AND LIMITATION

A pursuer may lose her right to obtain reparation if she does not begin proceedings against the defender within certain prescribed periods. By s 6 of the Prescription and Limitation (Scotland) Act 1973[4] the obligation to make reparation for a delictual act[5] is extinguished after five years. The five-year prescriptive period runs from

---

1 See, for example, *Hutcheson v Ascosmit Co* 1992 SLT 1115
2 *Cowie v Atlantic Drilling Co Ltd* 1995 SC 288, 1995 SCLR 335, 1995 SLT 1151; *Cleland v Campbell* 1998 SLT 642, OH.
3 Rule of Court of Session 89A(1).
4 In this section references are to the Prescription and Limitation (Scotland) Act 1973, as amended, unless otherwise stated.
5 PL(S)A 1973, Sch 1, para (1)(d). Periods during which the pursuer was induced to refrain from bringing the action by reason of the debtor's fraud or error induced by the words or conduct of the debtor are not reckoned as part of the prescriptive period: s 6(4)(a). See *BP Exploration Operating Co Ltd v Chevron Transport (Scotland)* 2002 SC (HL) 19. Any period under which the original creditor was under a legal disability does not count: s 6(4)(b).

the date on which the delict is complete, ie when the pursuer suffers *damnum* (harm).

'The right to raise such an action accrues when *injuria* concurs with *damnum*. Some interval of time may elapse between the two ... and ... in such circumstances time is to run from the date when *damnum* results, not from the earlier date of *injuria*.'[1]

This could cause injustice in cases where the damage suffered is latent and the pursuer does not discover that, for example, his house is unstable as a result of defective foundations until five or more years after the damage was in fact sustained. In such situations, time begins to run only when the pursuer first became or could with reasonable diligence have become aware of the damage.[2] Where the pursuer was the victim of sexual abuse, it has been held that he had sustained injuries, ie the *damnum* had occurred, at the time of the abuse even though he was seeking reparation for a psychiatric disorder which did not present itself until 40 years later: the defender's obligation to make reparation was therefore extinguished by the long negative prescription (20 years).[3]

There are, however, important exceptions to the general rule. First, liability for defective products under Part I of the Consumer Protection Act 1987 is extinguished after 10 years.[4] Liability for defamation prescribes after 20 years.[5] Importantly, delictual liability in respect of personal injuries or death no longer prescribes.[6] However, a claim for damages for personal injuries, death or defamation must be brought within a period of three years. This is known as a limitation period. If the action is not commenced within the three-year period, the pursuer cannot enforce his rights

---

1 *Dunlop v McGowans* 1980 SC (HL) 73, 1980 SLT 129 at 132–133 per Lord Keith of Kinkel; see also *Renfrew Golf Club v Ravenstone Securities Ltd* 1984 SLT 170, OH; *Strathclyde Regional Council v Border Engineering Contractors Ltd* 1997 SCLR 100, 1998 SLT 175, OH; *Osborne & Hunter Ltd v Hardie Caldwell* 1999 SLT 153; *K v Gilmartin's Exrix* 2002 SC 602.

2 Prescription and Limitation (Scotland) Act 1973, s 11(3). However, the long-stop 20 years' prescription begins to run from the date the damage occurred: s 7. In theory, therefore, a claim for reparation for latent damage could prescribe after 20 years without the five-year prescriptive period being triggered.

3 *K v Gilmartin's Exrx* 2002 SC 602. The abolition of the long negative prescription in respect of death and personal injuries by the Prescription and Limitation (Scotland) Act 1984, s 6(1) and Sch 1, para 2 is not retrospective.

4 PL(S)A 1973, s 22A, Sch 1, para 2(ggg). In this case the 10 years run from the date the product is first put on the market, not the date when the *damnum* occurs.

5 PL(S)A 1973, s 7(1) and Sch 1, para 2(gg).

6 PL(S)A 1973, ss 6(2) and 7(2) and Sch 1, para 2(g).

unless the defender waives his right to defend the action on the ground that the limitation period has expired.

In the case of personal injuries or property damage as a result of a defective product, the action is not competent if it is brought after a period of three years from the date when the pursuer knew that it was reasonably practicable for him to be aware that there was a defect in the product, that the injury or damage was caused by the product, that the injury or damage was sufficiently serious to bring an action for reparation and that the defender was liable under s 2 of the Consumer Protection Act 1987.[1] A similar limitation period applies to actions brought in relation to death caused by a defective product.[2] In respect of defamation actions, it is simply stated that the three-year limitation period runs from the date when the right of action accrued.[3]

An action for damages for personal injuries must commence within three years from the date on which the injuries were sustained.[4] However, the three-year period does not begin to run from the date when the injuries were sustained unless it was reasonably practicable for the pursuer to be aware of all the following facts: that the injuries were sufficiently serious to bring an action of damages;[5] that the injuries were caused by an act or omission; and that the defender was responsible for the act or omission.[6] So, for example, where a pursuer sustained personal injury as a result of the defender's delictual conduct but the pursuer did not know that he was injured, as in the case of an insidious disease, the three-year period only begins to run when it was reasonably practicable for him to realise that the illness was attributable to the defender's acts or omissions, ie when he knows he is ill. Similarly, the three-year period will only begin when the pursuer knows that the defender is responsible for the delictual conduct; if this knowledge arises after the date when the injuries were sustained, the three-year period only begins to run from the later date. A similar limitation period

---

1 Prescription and Limitation (Scotland) Act 1973, s 22B.
2 PL(S)A 1973, s 22C.
3 PL(S)A 1973, s 18A(1).
4 PL(S)A 1973, s 17(1) and (2). If the act or omission which caused the injuries was continuing, the three-year period runs from the date when the injuries were sustained or the date when the act or omission ceased, whichever is later: see *Mather v British Telecommunications plc* 2001 SLT 325.
5 *Blake v Lothian Health Board* 1993 SLT 1248, OH.
6 *Kirk Care Housing Association Ltd v Crerar and Partners* 1996 SLT 150, OH. The onus rests on the pursuer to prove when he was actually aware of these facts or did not have constructive knowledge of them: *Agnew v Scott Lithgow Ltd (No 1)* 2001 SC 516.

applies to actions for damages brought in relation to death which has resulted from personal injuries.[1] In all these limitation periods, time does not run against a pursuer who is or was under legal disability by reason of non-age or unsoundness of mind.[2]

However, in the case of the limitation periods in respect of actions for damages in respect of personal injuries or death from personal injuries *and* actions for defamation or verbal injury, the court has a discretion to allow the action to proceed outwith the three-year period if 'it seems equitable to do so'.[3] All the circumstances of the case are taken into consideration, including the length of time in bringing the action, whether the pursuer was responsible for the delay, whether there is an action available against the pursuer's solicitor if the solicitor was responsible for the delay, the inconvenience to the defender etc.[4] The issue is entirely a matter for the discretion of the presiding judge. In practice, the power is used sparingly in claims for personal injuries or death from personal injuries as a result of the knowledge provisions which have to be satisfied before the three-year limitation period begins to run.

1 Prescription and Limitation (Scotland) Act 1973, s 18.
2 PL(S)A 1973, ss 17(3), 18(3), 18A(2), 22B(4) and 22C(3). No causal connection is required between the period of non-age and the delay: *Paton v Loffland Bros North Sea* 1994 SLT 784.
3 PL(S)A 1973, s 19A.
4 For examples, see *McCullough v Norwest Socea Ltd* 1981 SLT 201, OH; *Carson v Howard Doris Ltd* 1981 SC 278, 1981 SLT 273; *Donald v Rutherford* 1983 SLT 253, 1984 SLT 70; *Whyte v Walker* 1983 SLT 441, OH; *Clark v McLean* 1994 SCLR 564, 1995 SLT 235; *Gorrie v Marist Brothers* 2002 SCLR 436.

Index

Actio de effusis vel dejectis, 189
Actio de positivis vel suspensis, 189
Actio injuriarum, 259
Administrative powers. *See* PUBLIC AUTHORITIES
Adultery, damages, 17
Advocates
  immunity, 162–163
  privilege, 271
  professional negligence, 162–163
Aemulatio vicini, 21–22, 189
Age of legal capacity
  delictual liability, 238
  instructing solicitors, 238
  legal proceedings, 238
  medical treatment, 13[n1]
Agency, vicarious liability, 234
Agricultural products, 169
Air space, 20
Aircraft, 20, 168, 169, 196
Animals
  common law liability, 177–178, 179, 184
  damnum fatale, 184
  dangerous wild animals, 180–181
  delictual liability, 177–184
  diseases, 182
  domitae naturae, 178
  ferae naturae, 178
  guard dogs, 183–184
  keepers, 179
  meaning, 180–182
  occupiers' liability, 177, 183
  statutory liability, 178–184
  strict liability defences, 182–184

Animals – *contd*
  third party interventions, 184
  and trespassers, 183
Arbitrations, 271
Assault
  consent, 12–13
  criminal injuries compensation, 16
  defences, 14
  generally, 12–16
  medical treatment, 13
  mental harm, 12
  physical punishment, 14–15
  scope, 12, 72
  self-defence, 14
  violent sports, 13–14
Assignation, delictual rights, 112
Assythment, 3–4
Attendance allowance, 298, 299, 300
Auditors, duty of care, 85–86

Barges, 196
Barristers. *See* ADVOCATES
Blood, 169
Blood feuds, 3
Bone marrow, 241
Boycotts, 49, 50
Breach of arrestment, 3
Breach of duty of care. *See* NEGLIGENCE
Breach of statutory duty
  burden of proof, 205–206
  Caparo criteria, 208, 210
  civil remedies, 201–206
  class protection, 203–205
  court discretion, 202

Breach of statutory duty – *contd*
employment, 203, 220–221
fairness, 208, 212
human rights, 209–210
negligence, 207
penalties, 203
presumptions, 202
proximity, 210
public law. *See* PUBLIC AUTHORITIES
volenti non fit injuria, 206
Building contracts, 233–234
Building regulations, 101
Buildings. *See* DEFECTIVE BUILDINGS
Bullying, 211
Burst pipes, 190
Buses, 196
Business
slander of business, 277
wrongful interference with,
42–44, 51

Caparo **criteria,** 66, 68, 208,
210
Caravans, 196
Carelessness
careless misrepresentation,
83–90, 105, 290–291
and duty of care, 59, 64, 72
Cars, 168, 169, 196, 253–256
Causa causans, 142, 143, 144,
147
Causation
'but for' test, 135–138, 141–142,
147
contributory negligence. *See*
CONTRIBUTORY NEGLIGENCE
factual causation, 135–142
generally, 135–154
joint liability, 153–154
legal causation, 142–148
multiple causes, 138–142, 147
novus actus interveniens, 143,
144, 146–148, 165
and order of events, 146–147
and product liability, 173
public authority negligence,
211
pure economic loss, 138

Causation – *contd*
third party intervention,
foreseeability, 144–146, 147
volenti non fit injuria, 148–150
Caution, lawburrows, 5
Children
abuse, 209, 210, 226, 227
care proceedings, 205, 208–209,
210
contributory negligence, 238–239
damages
death of parents, 246
posthumous children, 246
detention, 17^{n1}
grandchildren, 249
illegitimacy, 246
legal capacity, 13^{n1}, 238
physical punishment, 14–15
title to sue parents, 239
unborn. *See* UNBORN CHILDREN
Childrens' hearings, 271
Circumvention, 3
Closed shops, 48–49
Cohabitees, damages, 246, 249
Companies, defamation, 260
Competition, 2, 37
Complex structures, 103, 167,
168
Computer hacking, 32
Confidential information
delict, 30–35
human rights, 34
national security, 34
nature of obligation, 30–31
public domain, 32
and public interest, 33–34, 35
test, 32
unintentional breach, 33
Consent, medical treatment,
13–14
Conspiracy
boycotts, 49, 50
delict, 47–52
lawful means, 47–49
unlawful means, 49–52
Contract
contractual or delictual liability,
61, 66, 82, 100–101, 157, 215

Contract – *contd*
defective performance, 93–99
disclaimers, 88, 91–92, 98
employment. *See* EMPLOYMENT
    CONTRACTS
fraudulent misrepresentation, 53
inducing/ procuring breach of
    contract, 38–41
Junior Books criteria, 94–99
misrepresentation, 89
product liability, 82
professional negligence, 157
subcontractors, 94–99
unfair contract terms, 88,
    91–92
wrongful interference with
    performance of contracts,
    41–42, 97, 99
Contractors, vicarious liability,
    233–234
Contravention of lawburrows,
    3, 5
Contributory negligence
breach of statutory duty, 206
burden of proof, 151–152
children, 238–239
damages, 143, 145, 151,
    152–153
and fraud, 153
generally, 150–153
legislation, 143, 151
occupiers' liability, 200
product liability, 175
pure economic loss, 152–153
road traffic offences, 149, 151
**Control, and employment
    status,** 222–223
Contumelia, 13, 259
Convicium, 278–279
Corporal punishment, 14–15
Courts martial, 271
Criminal associations, 153
**Criminal injuries
    compensation,** 16
Culpa
carelessness, 59
meaning, 1, 11, 59, 123, 259
nuisance, 192–194

Damages
adultery, 17
breach of confidence, 34
breach of human rights, 35,
    209–210
breach of statutory duty, 202
calculation, 287–300
contributory negligence, 143,
    145, 151, 152–153
death
    deceased's claims, 241,
        243–244
    dependants, 245–249
    discretionary awards, 248
    funeral expenses, 249
    generally, 243–250
    in utero, 246
    loss of gratuitous services,
        242, 250
    loss of society, 248
    loss of support, 240, 244, 247
    patrimonial loss, 243
    prenatal injuries, 245
    provisional awards, 248
    solatium, 244
    transmission, 241, 243, 249
defamation, 261, 267, 275–276
economic loss, 82, 100
ejection, 21
fraud, 53
human rights, breach, 209–210
interest, 296–297
interim damages, 303
joint liability, 154
and jury trials, 296
limitation of actions, 304–306
loss of earnings, 240, 243,
    294–296
miscarriages, 240
miscarriages of justice, 18
nuisance, 192, 194
personal injuries
    deductions, 297–300
    eggshell skull rule, 286–287
    generally, 291–296
    interest, 297
    mental harm, 287
    patrimonial loss, 293–296

Damages – *contd*
personal injuries – *contd*
relatives, 240–242
solatium, 292–293
prescription, 303–304
product liability, 63
property losses, 287
provisional damages, 301–303
pure economic loss. *See* PURE
ECONOMIC LOSS
purpose, 287, 292
relatives
death, 243–250
personal injuries, 240–242
remoteness. *See* REMOTENESS OF
DAMAGES
road traffic accidents
Motor Insurers' Bureau,
256–258
untraced drivers, 258
vehicles, 253–256
services
by relatives to injured,
240–241
loss of services of dead
relatives, 242, 250
loss of unpaid services by
injured relatives, 241–242
medical services, 294
statutory duty, breach, 213
trespass, 19, 20
vicarious liability, 222
wrongful births, 80, 289
wrongful conceptions, 81, 288
Damnum absque injuria, 2
Damnum fatale, 184, 186
Damnum injuria datum, 1
Dangerous driving, 252
Death, damages. *See* DAMAGES
Defamation
burden of proof, 261, 262
damages, 261, 267, 275–276
defamatory nature of statements
criminality, 263–264
disparaging public character,
264–265
generally, 262–266
health allegations, 265

Defamation – *contd*
defamatory nature of statements
– *contd*
homosexuality, 263, 268
immorality, 268
imputations on moral
character, 263
incompetence, 264
innuendo, 265–266
insolvency, 264
misconduct, 263
defences
absolute privilege, 270–272
fair comment, 269–270
fair retort, 269
generally, 268–275
in rixa, 269
no responsibility for
publication, 274–275
qualified privilege, 272–274
veritas, 262, 266, 268–269
vulgar abuse, 269
delict, 260
development, 259–260
false statements, 261–262
and freedom of expression,
34–35, 261, 273
generally, 260–276
intentions, 266–268
limitation of actions, 305, 306
malice, 260, 266–268, 272,
274–275
prescription, 304
presumptions, 261, 262, 266
repeating false statements, 262
requirements, 261
title to sue, 260
transmission of actions, 260
Defective buildings
complex structures, 103
dangerous buildings, 212–213
local authority duties, 101–105,
207, 212–213
pure economic loss, 101–105
Defective products. *See* PRODUCT
LIABILITY
Deforcement, 3
Degrading treatment, 209

Delictual liability
development, 2–7
fairness, 7, 106
judge-made law, 6
limits, 6, 11, 59
requirements, 1
strict liability. *See* STRICT LIABILITY
Depression, 218
Desuetude, 3
Detention, wrongful detention,
17–18
Disability living allowance, 299
Disability working allowance,
299
Disablement benefit, 298, 300
Disablement pensions, 299
Disciplinary tribunals, 271
Disclaimers, 88, 91–92, 98
Diseases
animals, 182
defamation, 265
Dolus, 12
Driving without due care and
attention, 252
Drugs, 172, 174, 239
Drunkenness, 149, 152, 239
Duty of care
auditors, 85–86
breach. *See* NEGLIGENCE
Caparo criteria, 66, 68, 208, 210
concept, 11, 59
Donoghue v Stevenson, 60–69,
82, 100, 214, 215
drivers, 251
dynamics, 64
economic loss, 65–67. *See also*
PURE ECONOMIC LOSS
employers, 215
fairness, 7, 106
foreseeability, 65, 66, 67, 68
latent defects, 62
local authorities, 101–105,
210–211
and mental harm, 72–79
neighbourhood principle, 60–69
and omissions, 71–72
physical harm, 65, 67
producers. *See* PRODUCT LIABILITY

Duty of care – *contd*
public authorities, 101–105,
208, 210–211, 213, 214
special duty, 84
standards. *See* STANDARDS OF CARE
subcontractors, 94–99
surveyors, 86–88, 105
threshold device, 59, 68–69,
71–113, 115, 186–188
to unborn children, 79
tripartite test, 66–68, 157, 208,
210
wrongful birth, 80
wrongful conceptions, 80–81
wrongful life, 79

Earnings. *See* LOSS OF EARNINGS
Economic delicts
anticipatory delicts, 46
conspiracy, 47–52
fraud. *See* FRAUD
generally, 37–52
inducing/ procuring breach of
contract, 38–41
intimidation, 44–46
principles, 37–38
wrongful interference with
business, 42–44, 51
wrongful interference with
performance of contracts,
41–42, 97, 99
Economic loss
damages, 82, 100
derivative loss, 82, 100, 240, 291
and duty of care, 65–67
loss of future earnings, 240
parasitic economic loss, 82
product liability, 63, 65–67
pure economic loss. *See* PURE
ECONOMIC LOSS
relatives, 240–242
reparation, 2
secondary economic loss, 105–112
Ejection, 3, 21
Emergencies, 13^{n2}, 126–127
Employment
breach of statutory duty, 203,
220–221

Employment – *contd*
competent staff, 217, 231
confidential information, 30
contractual or delictual liability,
  215
course of employment, 224–231
defective equipment, 216–217
employers' liability, 215–221
  burden of proof, 220
employment status, 222–224
health and safety, 215–216,
  220–221
insurance, 222
negligence, 218
occupiers' liability, 221
protective equipment, 216
psychiatric problems, 218–219
safe system of working,
  215–216, 218
safe working environment, 177,
  220
secondary economic loss, 105
secondary victims, 219–220
standards of care, 216–219
supervision of employees, 217^{n3}
training, 216
tribunals, 271
vicarious liability. *See* VICARIOUS
  LIABILITY
volenti non fit injuria, 149
Employment contracts
breach, 46, 50
and contracts for services, 222–224
implied duties of employees, 225
inducing breach, 39, 41–42
nature of contract, 217
and vicarious liability, 225, 228
Enticement, 17
Entrapment, 16
Epilepsy, 302
EU law
competition, 37
health and safety at work, 221
motor insurance, 257
product liability, 166, 175
**Executors, transmission of
  damages,** 241, 243, 244,
  249, 260

Extortion, 3

Fairness
duty of care, 7, 106
exercise of statutory powers,
  208, 212
False statements
defamation, 259, 261–262
fraud, 54–55
Ferae naturae, 178
Fire services, 212
Foreseeability
consequences of acts/ omissions,
  116–123
damages, 284–286
Donoghue v Stevenson, 82
and duty of care, 65, 66, 67, 68
exercise of statutory powers, 208
extent of injuries, 120–121
harm to unborn children, 239
injury of rescuers, 119
injury to pursuers, 119–120
intervention of third parties,
  122–123
mental harm, 73, 218–219
and neighbourhood principle, 71
occupiers' liability, 65, 186
probabilities, 124–125
reasonable foreseeability,
  116–123
secondary victims, 120
third party interventions,
  144–146
Forgery, 3
Fraud
and contributory negligence,
  153
damages, 53, 290
delict, 53–56
entrapment, 16
mens rea, 54–55
passing off, 29
vicarious liability, 225–226
Freedom of expression
and confidential information, 34
and *convicium,* 278
and defamation, 34–35, 261,
  273

Fumes, 190, 194
Funeral expenses, 249

Geographical names, 27
Get up, 27, 29, 172
Good Samaritans, 71
Goodwill, 27–30
Grandchildren, 249
Grandparents, 249
Guard dogs, 183–184

Hacking, 32
Harassment, 18–19
Health and safety at work,
  215–216, 220–221
Helicopters, 196
Heritable property
  aemulatio vicini, 21–22, 189
  delictual liability, 101–105
  occupiers. *See* OCCUPIERS'
    LIABILITY
  trespass, 19–21
Highway Code, 251–252
Hire purchase, 24–26
Homosexuality, 263, 268
Horseplay, 231
Hovercraft, 196
Human rights
  and confidential information, 34
  damages, 7, 35, 209–210
  impact of 1998 Act, 7
  inhuman/degrading treatment,
    209
  and physical punishment, 16
  proportionality, 209
  respect for privacy, 2, 34, 35,
    278
  right to fair hearing, 209
  right to family life, 209

Importers, 169, 170, 173
Incapacity benefit, 299
Income support, 299
Industrial espionage, 32
Inhuman or degrading
  treatment, 209
Injuries to liberty, 17–18
Innuendo, 265–266

Institutional writers, 3, 5–6
Insurance
  driving without insurance, 254
  employers, 222
  knock for knock agreements,
    255
  motor insurance, 251, 254–256
  Motor Insurers' Bureau,
    256–258
  and provisional damages, 301
  subrogation, 255
Interdict
  harassment, 19
  nuisance, 191–192, 193
  passing off, 30
  trespass, 19, 20
Interest, damages, 296–297
Interim damages, 303
Intimidation, 44–46
Invalidity allowance, 299
Invalidity benefit, 298, 300
Invalidity pension, 299
Involuntary actions, 116

Judges, immunity, 18
Judicial review, 202–203
Jury trials, 296
Justification defence, 46

Landlords, occupiers' liability,
  200
Landscape features, 199–200
Latent defects, 62, 102–105
Lawburrows, 5
Lawyers
  privilege, 271
  professional negligence,
    160–163
Leases, 110, 187
Legacies, disappointed
  legatees, 161–162, 289
Legal proceedings
  age of legal capacity, 238
  privileged statements, 271, 274
Letters of slam, 3
Lex Aquilia, 6
Liberty, injuries to liberty,
  17–18

Limitation of actions, 304–306
Local authorities
  care proceedings, 205, 208–209
  children in care, 227
  defamation, 260
  and defective buildings, 101–105
  discretionary powers, 206–214
  duty of care, 101–105, 210–211
  failure to act, 212–214
  negligence, 211–213
  resource allocation, 207
  vicarious liability, 211, 227–228
Lord Advocate, 272
Loss of earnings
  calculation, 294
  deductions, 295
  future earnings, 240, 243,
    294–295
  loss of earning capacity, 296
  multiplicands, 294
  multipliers, 295
  Ogden Tables, 295
  recovery by executors, 241, 243
Loss of society, 248
Loss of support, 240, 244, 247

Malice
  aemulatio vicini, 22
  defamation, 260, 266–268, 272,
    274–275
  economic delicts, 37–38
  wrongful imprisonment, 18
Marriage, 16
Medical expenses, 294, 295
Medical negligence
  chances of success, 137
  failure to treat, 137
  and professional opinion, 137
  standards of care, 158–159
  state of scientific knowledge, 119
Medical treatment, 13
Members of Parliament,
    270–271
Mens rea, **fraud,** 54–55
Mental harm
  children in care, 210
  criteria, 77
  damages, 287

Mental harm – *contd*
  and duty of care, 72–79
  employment, 218–219
  foreseeability, 73
  law reform, 79
  nervous shock, 75, 78
  reasonable foreseeability, 120
  secondary victims, 74–77
  sexual abuse, prescription, 304
Miscarriages, 240
Miscarriages of justice, 18
Misrepresentation
  careless misrepresentation,
    83–90, 105, 290–291
  causation, 138
  contractual liability, 89
  damages, 290–291
  fraudulent misrepresentation,
    53, 290
  Hedley Byrne criteria, 83–89
  passing off, 28, 29–30
Mobility allowance, 298, 300
Molestation, 3
Motor Insurers' Bureau,
    256–258
Moveable property
  confidential information, 30–35
  delicts, 22–35
  goodwill, 27–30
  passing off, 27–30
  trespass, 22–23
  wrongful interference with, 23–26

Names, and goodwill, 27
Nasciturus **doctrine,** 239
National insurance, 223, 294
National security, 34
Negligence
  criteria, 115–133
  foreseeability. *See* FORESEEABILITY
  involuntary actions, 116
  public authorities, 211–213
  remoteness of injuries, 131–132
  standards. *See* STANDARDS OF CARE
  voluntary acts/ omissions,
    115–116
Neighbourhood principle. *See*
    PROXIMITY

Nervous shock, 75, 78
Noise, 190–191
Non-harassment orders, 19
Novus actus interveniens, 143,
    144, 146–148, 165
Nuisance
    continuing wrong, 190, 191, 194
    damages, 192, 194
    generally, 190–200
    in public interest, 191
    interdict, 191–192, 193
    negligence, 192–194
    noise, 190–191
    and planning, 191[n4]
    pure economic loss, 194
    title to sue, 194
    under statutory authority, 191
Nursing services, 294, 295

Occupation of land
    actio de effusis vel dejectis, 189
    actio de positivis vel suspensis, 189
    aemulatio vicini, 189
    common law liability, 185–188
    damnum fatale, 186
    duty to adjacent occupiers,
        186–188
    duty to owners, 188
    foreseeability, 65
    generally, 185–200
    negligence, 185–188
    non-natural use of land, 186
    nuisance. *See* NUISANCE
    occupiers' liability. *See*
        OCCUPIERS' LIABILITY
    Rylands v Fletcher, 186
Occupiers' liability
    animals, 177, 183
    categories of property, 196
    common law, 195
    contributory negligence, 200
    employers, 221
    extent of duty, 196–197
    generally, 72, 194–200
    landlords, 200
    landscape features, 199–200
    owners and occupiers, 195
    risk calculation, 198–199

Occupiers' liability – *contd*
    statutory liability, 195–200, 201
    volenti non fit injuria, 200, 206
Ogden Tables, 295
Oil rigs, 196
Omissions, and duty of care,
    71–72
Own branders, 169, 170, 173

Parents
    abuse of unborn children, 239
    children's delicts, 238
    children's title to sue, 239
    damages, death of children, 247
    title to sue, prenatal injuries,
        245–246
Parliamentary privilege,
    270–272, 274
Passing-off, 27–30
Patrimonial loss
    death, 243
    deductions, 294, 297–300
    expenses, 294, 295
    future loss, 294–296
    generally, 293–296
    interest, 297
    and jury trials, 296
    loss of earnings, 294–296
    pension rights, 296
    services, 294, 295
    to date of proof, 293–294
Pensions, 223, 296
Performers' rights, 203
Personal injuries, damages
    eggshell skull rule, 286–287
    generally, 291–296
    limitation of actions, 305–306
    patrimonial loss, 293–296
    prescription, 304
    relatives, 240–242
    solatium, 292–293
Personal names, 27
Physical punishment, 14–15
Planning, 191[n4], 204
Pledges, 110
Police, 150, 211–212, 272–273
Prescription, 303–305
Prison service, 150, 272

Privacy rights, 2, 34, 35, 278
Private prosecutions, 3
Privilege
  absolute privilege, 270–272
  defence to defamation, 270–274
  legal proceedings, 271, 274
  Parliamentary privilege,
      270–272, 274
  qualified privilege, 272–274
  right to know test, 273
Probability. *See* FORESEEABILITY
Procurators fiscal, 272
Product liability
  causation, 173
  complex products, 175
  contractual liability, 82
  contributory negligence, 175
  course of business, 170
  definition of product, 168–169
  Donoghue v Stevenson, 60–69,
      82, 165, 166
  drugs, 172, 174
  generally, 165–175
  importers, 169, 170, 173
  inherently dangerous goods, 172
  instructions, 172
  limitation of actions, 305
  meaning of damage, 167
  meaning of defective product,
      171–173
  non-private use, 167–168
  or employers' liability, 216
  own branders, 169, 170, 173
  parties liable, 169–170
  prescription, 304
  private transactions, 170
  producers, 169–170, 173
  pure economic loss, 100–105,
      166
  and scientific/ technical
      knowledge, 174–175
  small claims, 168
  state of the art defence, 174–175
  statutory regulation, 166–175
  strict liability, 166–175
  strict liability defences, 173–175
  strict liability exceptions,
      167–168

Product liability
  suppliers, 169, 170–171, 173
  warnings, 165, 172
Professional negligence
  barristers, 162–163
  disappointed legatees, 161–162
  generally, 157–163
  medical negligence, 158–159
  professional practice, 129–131,
      157–158
  public authorities, 211–213
  solicitors, 160–163
  standards of care, 129–131,
      157–159
  surveyors, 86–88, 105, 289–290
Property delicts, 19–35
Proportionality, 209
Protective equipment, 216
Provisional damages, 301–303
Proximity
  Donoghue v Stevenson, 60–69,
      111, 157, 177, 185
  and foreseeability, 71
  police, 212
  public authorities, 208, 210,
      212
  requirements, 71–72, 77
  secondary economic loss, 108
  subcontractors, 95–96
Psychiatric disorder. *See* MENTAL
  HARM
Public authorities
  Caparo criteria, 208, 210
  delictual liability, 206–214
  duty of care, 208, 210–211, 213,
      214
  exercise of discretionary powers,
      206–214
  human rights, 209–210
  negligence, 207, 211–213
    burden of proof, 211–212
    causation, 211
    failure to act, 212–214
  provisional damages, 301
  proximity, 208, 210, 212
  right to fair hearing, 209
  vicarious liability, 214
Public inquiries, 271

**Public interest, and
   confidential information,**
   33–34, 35
Public policy
   breach of duty of care, 119
   breach of statutory duty, 202, 204
   competition, 2, 37
   criminal associations, 153
   privilege, 270
   unborn children, 79–80
   wrongful births, 289
Pure economic loss
   auditors' negligence, 85–86
   causation, 138
   contributory negligence,
      152–153
   controversy, 2, 112–113
   damages
      disappointed legatees, 289
      fraudulent misrepresentation,
         290
      generally, 289–291
      negligent misrepresentation,
         290–291
      surveyors, 289–290
   defective buildings, 101–105
   defective performance of
      contracts, 93–99
   defective products, 63, 65–66,
      100–105, 166
   disappointed legatees, 161–162,
      289
   disclaimers, 88
   fraud, 53, 153, 290
   generally, 81–113
   Hedley Byrne criteria, 83–89
   Henderson v Merrett criteria,
      90–93, 101, 104, 107, 108,
      157, 160, 161, 162
   hire purchase goods, 25
   Junior Books criteria, 94–99,
      101, 104, 107, 108, 109,
      111, 157
   negligent misrepresentation,
      83–90, 290–291
   nuisance, 194
   secondary economic loss,
      105–112

Pure economic loss – *contd*
   services, 101
   and subcontractors, 94–99
   surveyors' negligence, 86–88,
      105, 289–290
   wrongful conception, 288

Rape, 16, 263
Redundancy pay, 298
References, 272
Relatives
   damages
      death, 245–250
      funeral expenses, 249
      loss of support, 240, 244
      necessary services to,
         240–241, 294
      personal injuries, 240–242
      unpaid personal services by
         injured relatives,
         241–242, 250
   title to sue, 237–240
Remoteness of damages
   English case law, 284–285
   foreseeability, 284–286
   generally, 283–287
   intentional delicts, 287
   and remoteness of injuries, 132,
      283
   rule, 284
   scenario, 283
   Scottish case law, 285–286
   wrongful conception, 288
Remoteness of injuries,
      131–132, 283
Reparation, 1, 2. *See also* DAMAGES
Rescuers, 119, 149
Right to fair hearing, 209
Right to family life, 209
Right to physical integrity, 2, 13
Right to privacy, 2, 34, 35, 278
Risks
   cost of precautions, 128–129
   employment, 216, 220
   obvious risks, 171
   occupiers' liability, 198
   practicality of precautions,
      127–128

Risks – *contd*
  seriousness of injuries, 125–126
  and social value of activities,
    126–127
  and standards of care, 124–125,
    216–219
  and trade/professional practice,
    129–131
  volenti non fit injuria, 148–150,
    182
Road traffic accidents
  contributory negligence, 151
  damages, 253–254
  drunkenness, 149
  generally, 251–258
  and Highway Code, 251–252
  insurance, 251, 254–256
  Motor Insurers' Bureau,
    256–258
  remoteness of damages, 283
  standard of care, 251–252
  statutory provisions, 251
  untraced drivers, 258
  and *volenti non fit injuria,* 149
Road traffic offences, 252
Roman law, 6, 189, 259

Safe system of working,
    215–216, 218
Scientific knowledge, 174–175
Scottish Parliament, 272
Seat belts, 151
Secondary economic loss
  fairness, 106
  generally, 105–112
  possessory title, 110–111
  proximity, 108–109
  remoteness of injuries, 131
  title to sue, 107, 110
  transferred loss, 109–110
Secondary victims
  employment, 219–220
  mental harm, 74–77
  reasonable foreseeability, 120
Seduction, 16
Self-defence, 14
Services
  contracts for services, 222–224

Services – *contd*
  loss of services by dead relatives,
    242, 250
  medical expenses, 294, 295
  necessary services to injured
    relatives, 240–241, 294
  patrimonial loss, 294, 295
  pure economic loss, 101
  unpaid personal services by
    injured relatives, 241–242
Severe disablement allowance,
    299
Sexual abuse, 304
Sexual misconduct, 226, 263
Shipping law, 66
Ships, 168, 169, 196
Siblings, 249
Sickness benefit, 298, 299, 300
Slander of business, 277
Slander of property, 277
Slander of title, 277
Smells, 190
**Social security benefits, and
    damages,** 298–300
Socii criminis, 153
Solatium
  awareness of pain, 292–293
  deductions, 300
  defamation, 261, 275
  future suffering, 293
  interest, 296–297
  meaning, 2, 244
  personal injuries, 292–293
  product liability, 63
  psychological conditions, 293
  transmission, 244
Solicitors
  disappointed legatees, 161–162,
    289
  privilege, 271
  professional negligence, 160–163
Sports, 13–14, 150
Spouses
  damages, death, 246, 249
  delictual liability, 237
  economic loss, 240
  title to sue, 237
  vicarious liability, 237

Spuilzie, 3, 5, 23
Squatting, 20–21
Stair, Lord, 3, 5–6
Standards of care
  cost of precautions, 128–129
  employment, 216–219
  negligence, 123–131
  potential seriousness of injuries,
    125–126
  practicality of precautions,
    127–128
  probability of injuries, 124–125
  reasonable care, 123–124
  reasonableness, 64
  road drivers, 251–252
  trade/ professional practice,
    129–131, 157–158, 174
  usefulness of activities, 126–127
State of the art defence,
    174–175
Statutory duty. *See* BREACH OF
    STATUTORY DUTY
Statutory sick pay, 299
Step-children, 246
Strict liability
  animals, 178–184
  meaning, 6–7
  nuisance, 192
  product liability, 166–175
Strikes, 37–38, 41, 45–46, 52
Strip searches, 12
Subcontractors, 94–99
Substances, 168
Surveyors
  contractual liability, 105
  damages, 289–290
  duty of care, 86–88, 105

Taxation, 223, 294
Technical knowledge, 174–175
Theft, vicarious liability, 226
Third party interventions
  animals, 184
  and causation, 144–147
  foreseeability, 122–123,
    144–146, 147
Title to sue
  common law, 3

Title to sue
  conspiracy, 50
  defamation, 260
  nuisance, 194
  parents, prenatal injuries,
    245–246
  possessory title, 110–111
  relatives, 237–240
  secondary economic loss, 107,
    110
  spouses, 237
  statutory right, 3
Torture, 209
Trade names, 27
Trade unions
  defamation, 260
  immunity, 52
  strikes, 37–38, 45–46, 52
Transferred loss doctrine,
    109–110
Trespass
  air space, 20
  and animal damage, 183
  damages, 20
  heritable property, 19–21
  interdict, 19, 20
  moveable property, 22–23
  neighbours' duties, 187

Unborn children
  damages, 245–246
  death from pre-natal injuries,
    245–246
  death *in utero,* 246
  duty of care to, 79
  legal personality, 239, 246
  nasciturus doctrine, 239
  parental abuse, 239
  title to sue, 239
  wrongful life, 79
Unemployability supplement,
    299
Unemployment benefit, 299
Unfair contract terms, 88,
    91–92
Unjustified enrichment, 1, 24,
    25

Vehicles, 168, 169, 196, 253–256
Verbal injury
  damages, 275–276
  generally, 276–278
  privilege, 270, 272
  slander of business, 277
  slander of property, 277
  slander of title, 277
Vicarious liability
  actions outside scope of work,
    225, 228–230
  agency, 234
  authorised actions, 224, 225
  borrowed employees, 232
  building contracts, 233–234
  contractors, 233–234
  course of employment, 224–231
  damages, 222
  employees' delicts, 117, 222–232
  employees' frolics, 230–231
  employment status, 222–224
  expressly prohibited conduct,
    228–229
  fraudulent conduct, 225–226
  horseplay, 231
  insurance, 222
  parents, 238
  public authorities, 211, 214

Vicarious liability – *contd*
  sexual misconduct, 226
  spouses, 237
  travelling time, 231
  unauthorised methods of
    working, 224, 225–228
  unauthorised work, 225,
    230–232
Violent profits, 5, 21
Volenti non fit injuria
  animals, 182
  breach of statutory duty, 206
  employment, 149
  generally, 148–150
  occupiers' liability, 200, 206
  rescuers, 149
  road traffic offences, 149
  sports, 150

Warnings, 165, 172
Widow's pension, 247
Wills, disappointed legatees,
    161–162, 289
Wrongful birth, 80, 289
Wrongful conceptions, 80–81,
    288
Wrongful life, 79